WARS OF PLUNDER

PHILIPPE LE BILLON

WARS OF PLUNDER

Conflicts, Profits and the Politics of Resources

OXFORD
UNIVERSITY PRESS

OXFORD
UNIVERSITY PRESS

Oxford University Press, Inc., publishes works that further
Oxford University's objective of excellence
in research, scholarship, and education.

Oxford New York

Auckland   Cape Town   Dar es Salaam   Hong Kong   Karachi
Kuala Lumpur   Madrid   Melbourne   Mexico City   Nairobi
New Delhi   Shanghai   Taipei   Toronto

With offices in

Argentina   Austria   Brazil   Chile   Czech Republic   France   Greece
Guatemala   Hungary   Italy   Japan   Poland   Portugal   Singapore
South Korea   Switzerland   Thailand   Turkey   Ukraine   Vietnam

Copyright © 2013 Philippe Le Billon

Oxford is a registered trade mark of Oxford University Press in the UK
and certain other countries.

Published by Oxford University Press, Inc
198 Madison Avenue, New York, New York 10016

Published in the United Kingdom in 2013 by C. Hurst & Co. (Publishers) Ltd.

www.oup.com

Oxford is a registered trademark of Oxford University Press

Library of Congress Cataloging-in-Publication Data
Le Billon, Philippe.
Wars of Plunder: Conflicts, profits and the politics of resources / Philippe Le Billon.
— First edition.
p. cm.
Includes bibliographical references and index.
ISBN 978-0-19-933346-2 (alk. paper)
1. War—Economic aspects. 2. Natural resources—Political aspects. 3. War—Causes.
4. Conflict management—Developing countries. 5. Natural resources—Government
policy—Developing countries. 6. Developing countries—History, Military—Case studies.
I. Title.
HB195.L37 2013
333.7—dc23
2013017005

1 3 5 7 9 8 6 4 2

Printed in India
on Acid-Free Paper

CONTENTS

PREFACE

I left the business of biomedical research for wartime environmentalism in 1992. Many countries were in turmoil, yet the world was full of hope. While the number of armed conflicts in the world was at its highest since World War Two, the Cold War was over and democracy was flourishing. Environmentalism was *de rigueur*, as highlighted by Rio's Earth Summit that same year.[1] I had left France for Cambodia to assist with the creation of the new Ministry of Environment while the country was under the transitional (and superficial) authority of the largest United Nations peacekeeping mission ever deployed. Establishing national parks in Khmer Rouge areas while the Peace Accords were unraveling was perceived by most as an odd, or even grotesque, priority. Given the rate at which forests were being logged, and that both the Khmer Rouge and corrupt politicians pocketed the profits, I thought that it was in fact a priority. Bypassing one of the two co-Prime Ministers through a Royal Decree, we managed to create protected areas covering close to 19 percent of the country.[2] Yet while this decree officially preempted new logging concessions, these "paper parks" did little to stop logging on the ground, especially in Khmer Rouge areas along the Thai border. A UN Security Council embargo had also largely failed because of UN unwillingness to confront the Khmer Rouge, the complicity of Thai politicians, and the collusion of a Cambodian ruling elite eager to make money however it could. Most amazingly, some international donor agencies seemed content with the situation as long as some revenue flowed into Cambodian state coffers.

Although it was widely known that logging funded the Khmer Rouge, no one had yet done a detailed field investigation, publicly denounced these practices, and successfully lobbied for immediate change. Hearing of this situation, three young environmentalists in London decided in 1995 to challenge the status quo. Patrick Alley, Simon Taylor and Charmian Gooch were the founders of Global Witness, a new London-based Non Governmental Organisation (NGO) that would revolutionise the way in which resource-based war economies were understood and how the international community would intervene to end war profiteering. As veterans of the Environmental Investigation Agency, which made its name tracking ivory smugglers, these environmentalists had decided that people deserved as much attention as elephants, especially in the midst of war. Their first report, "Forest, Famine and War: The Key to Cambodia's Future," collected damning evidence on the links between Thai logging, the Khmer Rouge, and the Royal Government of Cambodia. The report and press briefing in Bangkok proved to be a diplomatic and media hit, which pushed the Thai government to close its border to log shipments from Cambodia.[3] I had the chance to briefly work with Global Witness a year later, when I returned to Cambodia for my doctoral research in 1996, as bankrupted Khmer Rouge units started defecting. The London-based NGO has since tenaciously reported on resources, conflicts and corruption, broadening its investigations to a dozen other countries. Seeking lasting structural change, Global Witness has led international campaigns on conflict diamonds and revenue transparency in extractive sectors, making a major difference in the ways resource sectors are managed for the sake of peace and development. They have been an inspiration ever since.

This study draws on personal fieldwork experiences in Angola, Cambodia, Colombia, the Democratic Republic of the Congo (DRC), the former Yugoslavia, and Sierra Leone. In each of these places, of which I spent years in some and only briefly visited others, I encountered people trying to make the most of very difficult circumstances. Some did so for sheer survival, others in the hope of vast profits or a brighter future: an eight-year-old boy head-carrying bags of gravel down the muddy paths of diamond mining fields for the sake of a meal; an enterprising young Chinese businesswoman casually recounting how her car was partly blown away by an anti-personal mine in Khmer Rouge controlled territory; a well-intentioned Norwegian engineer arguing that it was better to pump oil rather than let it stay underground for the sake of possible future improvement, even if the Angolan war was just restarting. While it may seem straightforward to denounce corruption and war profiteering, ambiguities often arise. In Angola, tens of thousands of artisanal miners from the Congo came to risk their lives to support murderous guerrillas fighting an equally ruthless government. Certainly they were complicit in pillage and indirectly associated with war crimes, but what sense of despair and what options of hope had driven them to become the slaves of war criminals? Such situations put all the more responsibility on the key economic and political actors that drive the trade. So who is plundering? Child soldiers abducted into rebel movements digging for diamonds, corporate tycoons signing mining deals with presidents in the capital city, or consumers buying cheap garden furniture made of looted timber? Levels of responsibility vary greatly along the path linking battlefields to shopping malls. My view is that responsibilities should reflect the profits made, the resulting number of victims, and the level of awareness resulting from due diligence. An oil major signing a contract with a corrupt dictator, who violently represses the population, is arguably no less criminal than a diamond smuggler dealing with a warlord. Beyond understanding and assigning guilt, ending abuses and positively transforming economies remain the priorities. In this respect, the latter part of this book reflects on the many initiatives that have sought to address these problems over the past fifteen years or so.

That part of the study builds mostly on participant observation in many policy initiatives targeting war economies and resource-related conflicts, most of which brought together government, corporate and civil society representatives. These were protracted and at times difficult affairs, bringing quite different worlds together. Because of the engagement of some of the wealthiest companies and countries in the world, and thanks to the support of generous sponsors, meetings were often held in lavish settings, sharply contrasting with the conditions of conflict-affected populations. Commenting on the luxury of some of these conference meetings, many civil society members could rightly ponder about cooptation, neutering, and delaying tactics. At times, provided with a silver platter to deliver their message, some civil society members worried about being "prisoners of a process" of constructive engagement that was not delivering. The silver platter at times turned into a golden cage. The irony of meetings at the Rockefeller Foundation Bellagio Center on the shore of Lake Como in Northern Italy, or at the Ritz-Carlton in Qatar, evaded only the most innocent. At one of the exuberant banquets, a friend and colleague pondered what the best metaphor that could come out of a melting ice sculpture spelling the word "corruption" would be: was it a symbol of corruption melting from the heat of the initiative or a lofty objective vanishing from so much hot air? For a luxury hotel usually hosting well-heeled business meetings, this anti-corruption conference was simply "business as usual." For organisers, fighting corruption, like some grand corruption itself, required some "wining and dining" to build trust and personal relationships.

Some of these meetings provided a platform for ludicrous speeches, such as that on financial transparency and accountability by the Prime Minister of Equatorial Guinea. Policies coming out of these meetings were themselves open to interpretation, as with a corporate representative happily confiding what a "wonderful insurance" diamond certification was for his industry, perhaps rejoicing at the presumed impunity it granted for the trading of hundreds of millions of dollars in pillaged goods. To the cynic, these could be considered a sick and farcical instrumentalisation of well intentioned but naïve initiatives, with everyone being polite and pretending that the world was becoming "better governed." Yet even declarations of good intentions are more worthy than the disdainful look of corporate-sponsored sovereigns: at least one could quote these sovereigns verbatim when contradictions arose. The same applied to companies, among whom the active engagement of some, contrasted with the fig leaf of dubious legality presented by others. Soft law, after all, is made of publicly stated good intentions. At the end of the day, however, the hard law of war crime prosecution for pillage and the sharp end of "humanitarian" interventions present the two most forceful options. Very few leaders and companies have been prosecuted for pillage, wartime corruption, or embezzlement, but judicial processes are slowly gaining ground. As for "humanitarian" interventions, their shocking costs for local populations, and at times dubious motives, warrant an alternative. No doubt lessons will be drawn from the latest such interventions in Iraq and Libya.[4]

Over the past decade or so that led to this book, I have accumulated many debts. My first one is to the directors and staff of Global Witness, who served as a source of both inspiration and information. Field investigations would not have been possible without many great people including: Charmian Gooch, Stephen Jackson, Morlai Kamara, Estelle Levin, Raphael Marques, Gilberto Neto, Cheam Somean, Babar Turay, Gregory Woodsworth, and many others who will remain anonymous. Much of this work draws on a decade of stimulating discussions and workshops with many colleagues, including Tony Addison, Richard Auty, Karen Ballentine, Matthias Basedau, Zobel Behalal, Mats Berdal, Art Blundell, Gilles Carbonnier, Paul Collier, Chris Cramer, Jonathan Goodhand, Don Hubert, Macartan Humphreys, Mary Kaldor, Terry Karl, David Keen, Paivi Lujala, Joanna Macrae, Mike Moore, Mansoob Murshed, Ricardo Soares de Oliveira, Nancy Lee Peluso, Michael Ross, Siri Rustad, Frances Stewart, Mark Taylor, Alex Vines, Koen Vlassenroot, Michael Watts, Jeremy Weinstein, and Elizabeth Wood, among others. I also warmly thank students and colleagues at the University of British Columbia, including Ian Baird, Erin Baines, Alejandro Cervantes, Derek Gregory, Sara Elder, Karl Hosti, Brian Job, Eric Leinberger, Estelle Levin, Eric Nicholls, Simon Springer, James Stewart, Arthur H. Westing, and Marc Zacher, and those at the different institutes I collaborated with, including CERI, IDRC, IISS, ODI, and UNU-WIDER. The manuscript evolved over several stages, and I particularly thank the financial support of the Ford Foundation and the Social Sciences and Humanities Research Council. An IISS Adelphi Paper provided the initial impetus for this book, and it greatly benefited from the insights and suggestions of Matts Berdal and Jonathan Stevenson. Two of the current chapters draw from previously published papers, in the *Annals of the Association of American Geographers* (Chapter 4 on diamonds), and in *International Peacekeeping* (Chapter 6 on conflict termination initiatives). Special thanks to Corin de Freitas and an anonymous reviewer for their critical comments, David Harrison and Jonathan Derrick for initial copy editing, and Daisy Leitch and Michael Dwyer at Hurst for their enthusiasm. My deepest thanks are to my spouse Karen for her support and enduring patience, and to our two children for welcome and cheering distraction.

March 2011, Vancouver

INTRODUCTION

Natural resources have a conspicuous presence in the history of armed conflicts. From violent competition over wild game, to brutal land dispossession and imperialist wars over precious minerals, natural resources have motivated and rewarded many different types of hostilities.[1] The post-Cold War era has been no exception, but distinctive processes have also informed the last two decades. Most conflict-related deaths during this period took place in countries trapped in primary commodity export dependent economies, many of them poor or bankrupt, like the Democratic Republic of the Congo (DRC), Iraq or Rwanda, and others with middle-income revenues but authoritarian rulers, such as Libya.[2] These wars seemed the result of deadly political decisions influenced by resource-specific circumstances. This book seeks to understand if resource sectors do indeed influence the occurrence and course of wars, how they do this, and what can be done about it.

The number of armed conflicts sharply dropped during the 1990s, many of the remaining conflicts were tied to resource sectors. If insurgencies have long fought to change resource redistribution or have used resource sectors as a source of funding, many belligerents came to rely more heavily on commercial sources of support to sustain their military and political activities after the end of the Cold War.[3] As armed groups came to rely more heavily on militarised commerce than on ideological sponsorship, there was a growing concern that wars were being waged for financial motives rather than for a political agenda.[4] This demise of political ideology concerns informed, for example, assumptions that war profiteering was a key dimension of protracted conflicts in Liberia and Sierra Leone.[5]

A second relevant process over the last two decades was the "third wave" of democratisation and the rapid restructuring of the global economy—first around a Western project of liberalisation, and secondly around the rise of Asian economies—which reshaped resource sectors and led to major fluctuations in primary commodity prices.[6] These two events related in part to the "commodity crisis" experienced by resource producers between the mid-1980s and the late 1990s. This period first saw declining terms of trade for most primary commodities, especially oil, that resulted in a widespread economic downturn among producing countries. Not least among these were the Soviet Union, but also Persian Gulf countries such as Iraq, Iran, and even Saudi Arabia.[7] The oil-related growth collapse contributed (even if only modestly) to the fall of the Soviet Union by cutting into government revenue and foreign currency access.[8] Iraq's military invasion of Kuwait in 1990 put the conduct of resource-rich but bankrupted regimes front and center of the new post-Cold War international security agenda. Growing dissent in Saudi Arabia in a context of low oil prices in the 1990s, and fears of nuclear proliferation in a politically defiant Iran, broadened and exacerbated these concerns. This mix of deviance, dissent and defiance coming from oil-rich states—as well as the "hidden energy agenda" of the US in Iraq and Afghanistan—put the resource issues squarely on the post-9/11 "War on Terror" agenda.

The downfall of primary commodity prices and investments in extractive sectors during the 1990s also led to the liberalisation of resource sectors, with negative tax implications for many producing countries when prices rebounded in the following decade. Cheap resources during the 1990s facilitated the rapid growth of industrialising countries, including China, for both export and domestic infrastructure building. The broader context of high public debts, structural adjustments and democratisation challenging authoritarian regimes led some ruling elites to seek survival through privatisation and criminalisation of state institutions, with such "shadow states" personalising control over export-oriented resource sectors.[9] The first decade of the twenty-first century, in contrast, saw massive commodity price increases, particularly as a result of Asian growth, while resource production levels in some conflict-affected countries such as Angola and Sudan soared as a result of investment flows from the late 1990s onwards.[10] The result was a massive tax revenue windfall for those governments able to capture a large proportion of resource revenue.[11]

This would help explain the prolongation of some wars in the 1990s and their termination by the mid-2000s; after the doldrums of the 1990s, the resource boom of the 2000s provided greater financial incentives for peace, and an increased military capacity on the part of governments, which implied a greater ability to negotiate peace or win militarily. The commodity price hike was not all positive, however. Rising prices also meant growing tensions within and between importing countries, most worryingly in the food sector, as well as increased revenue for rebel groups able to tap into resource economies. The challenges of the "resource curse" remained acute for those countries that benefited from both higher oil prices and a transition to peace, including Angola and South Sudan.[12]

The third historical process was the arrival of new resource companies from "emerging countries," chiefly China but also India, Malaysia and Brazil. Motivated by a search for resources with which to fuel their fast-growing economies, and facilitated in part by liberalisation reforms pushed by International Financial Institutions in the 1990s, these companies expanded activities in many conflict-affected countries. The rise of these companies challenged both the established order of collusion between Southern elites and Western companies and the "good governance" agenda with which Western foreign aid and investment were supposed to be tied. The end result, so far, has been a bolstering of incumbent Southern elites and greater competition between resource companies and importing governments. According to some observers, this is a recipe for disaster, as poor governance and growing resource scarcity will lead to further grievances among local populations and a militarisation of resource sectors.[13] According to others, this represents a chance for poor countries to be better rewarded for their resources and to seek alternative paths to development to those imposed by the West, especially through bartering resources for infrastructure and development projects and thus supposedly reducing the risks of corruption.[14]

Focus of the book

This book focuses on so-called "extractive" resources, and more specifically on oil, gems and timber. These three resources, along with narcotics, account for most of the resource-related armed conflicts examined during the period under consideration for this study (see Chapter 6). I only briefly touch upon narcotics, however, as these have received considerable attention and relate to a distinct set of issues given their illegal character.[15] Water is a vital natural resource, but much ink has already flowed about "water wars."[16] Crops and fish are also major primary commodities, and they do deserve more attention. Whereas the agricultural sector was a focus of security studies through "peasant wars" between the 1960s and the early 1980s, this sector has since been largely ignored apart from environmental security debates associating resource scarcity with violent conflicts.[17] There is now renewed interest in the agricultural sector, especially in relation to the geopolitics and local impacts of farmland acquisitions and international agribusiness, as well as growing security concerns over "food riots" and food supply, including the effects of collapse of fisheries, but I leave that to another book.

The argument

My central argument is that resource sectors influence the likelihood and course of armed conflicts. In short, some resources make wars more likely, nasty, and lengthy. This is bad enough in itself, of course, but what is even more troubling is that these conflicts turn assets into liabilities. Popular ideas about resource wars are generally associated with massive resource wealth, but most countries affected by conflicts, including resource-related conflicts, are poor; think Liberia, not Kuwait. These countries can ill afford a war. In many cases, resource revenues are barely sufficient to sustain minimal public services, but they are sufficient to keep an insurgency going and to maintain a corrupt elite in power.

However, all resource sectors influence conflicts in the same way. The characteristics of resource sectors such as relative location, level of economic dependence, mode of production and transport, industry structure, and revenue accessibility matter a great deal. This argument may sound very deterministic, and I must clarify from the onset that I do not believe that resources *cause* conflicts. Geology and biogeography are not destiny. But resources do contribute to shaping social relations and are in turn expressive of social relations. Thus I take seriously the hybrid character of resources as products of joint social and natural processes. This means paying attention to the physical materiality and geography of resources, as well as to their historical conditions of productions and multiple connections with social relations. In contrast to most studies of environment and conflict studies, I also seek to depart from claims that armed conflicts stem exclusively from resource abundance or scarcity.[18] Rather, I want to stress the importance of historically grounded resource dependence and the specificities of the resource sectors involved. I articulate this argument around three claims.

The first claim is that economic dependence upon some resource sectors increases vulnerability to armed conflicts, but resource abundance—or high levels of per capita resource revenue—can mitigate these negative effects.[19] In other words, you had better be rich if you are resource dependent. This is at one level a statement of the obvious, but I seek to counter the idea that resource wealth necessarily brings trouble. In this respect, while I generally agree with the "resource curse" argument, I treat it with caution and stress that it does not apply equally to all resource sectors and societies.

The second claim is that some resource sectors are more prone to conflicts and various forms of violence than others because of the social relations of production associated with these resource sectors, and the value attributed to resources. What I call here the risk of conflict constitutes the most direct relationship between resources and armed conflicts, precisely because the object of the conflict is the resource itself or the conditions of its exploitation. Thus "resource conflicts" are more likely in some sectors and places than in others. This calls for attention to social relations, such as historical inequalities, and material conditions of production, such as pollution linked to resource exploitation.

The third is that opportunities for armed insurgents are closely associated with some of the characteristics of particular resources, especially with what is often referred to as their "lootability," or the ability of insurgents to derive revenue from these sectors. Diamonds, for example, are more accessible to insurgents if located in shallow deposits and located in a remote region, than if located deep in an underground mine close to the capital city.

In turn, these three dimensions—vulnerability, risk, and opportunity—engender various types of violence, three of which I engage with in this book. The first type of violence is that of unrealised potential. Resource sectors can do a lot to improve the lives of populations in producing countries, but they often do not. Failing to harness this potential and "spread the wealth" constitutes a form of "structural violence," one that curtails opportunities, fosters inequalities, and arouses frustrations.[20] Mismanagement, corruption, profit maximisation, racism, and ethnocentrism can all contribute to this type of violence. The fairness, competence and robustness of governing institutions thus matter a great deal for resource sectors to deliver "broad" development.[21] Care should be taken, however, not to present the governance of resource sectors as the single cause of developmental failure or as its sole remedy.

The second type of violence is associated with resource control and exploitation. This "environmental violence" relates to the negative social and environmental impacts of resource extraction, as well as the cycle of resistance and repression associated with the subjugation of the rights of people to control resources and determine the use of their environment.[22] Again, caution is required, particularly in balancing the interests of "local" and "national" populations so that resource sites are neither systematically turned into "local conservation areas," for the supposed benefit of nearby residents, nor pillaged as "national sacrifice zones," putting the often dubious "national interest" ahead of the wellbeing of local populations.

The third type of violence consists of the multiple forms of violence associated with armed conflicts, from killing to forced displacement. Because of its physical basis, this category is the most obvious;[23] thus, it tends to be the focus of much of the literature on resource conflicts. In my analysis, I argue for an expanded conceptualisation of violence, which integrates the three dimensions that I have outlined above.

The approach

This book is largely the result of direct field experience acquired over about a decade of engagement with advocacy and policy initiatives seeking to end resource-related conflicts. Many of the ideas arose when confronted with practical challenges, such as curtailing illegal logging that was benefiting armed groups in border areas, or seeking to improve resource-based livelihoods while reducing environmental impacts and political corruption in "post-conflict" contexts. Much of the empirical material was thus collected on an "ad hoc" basis, reflecting the focus of advocacy groups and policy-making agencies with which I have collaborated.[24] Participation over more than a decade in policy processes, such as the Kimberley Process Certification Scheme for conflict diamonds, provided me with insights into the complexities and compromises involved but also complicated my critique.[25]

This undoubtedly introduced an initial bias to my research, as I focused on what political scientists term "positive" cases—here, conflicts that were related to resources. I have sought to correct this bias by considering a wider set of cases than those targeted by the "war economies" policy community. I was also lucky to benefit from the work of several economists and political scientists who were not suffering from the same aversion to quantitative studies from which my field, political geography, currently suffers.[26] As discussed below, this work has its own limitations, but such large-N studies also provide broad datasets, analytical concision and statistical tools to test some major hypotheses on resource and armed conflict linkages.

To address some of the limitations of econometric approaches, I also read broadly and sought to provide some historical depth and contextual nuances through a relatively narrow range of case studies in countries where I have field experience[27] or access to detailed accounts. History matters a great deal for this topic, in at least three ways. First, memories of past conflicts contribute to identity formation and future conflicts, often through the perceived inequities associated with past hostilities. Second, the quality of institutions prior to resource discovery and exploitation is a crucial determinant of future socio-economic outcomes. In short, a country with poor quality state institutions will attract few investments that concentrate in sectors with few alternative locations. Unsurprisingly, these are extractive sectors, and countries thus become, or remain resource dependent.[28] History also matters because the quality of institutions, in turn, is partly influenced by past resource exploitation. Resource-driven colonialism, in this respect, paved the way for predatory institutions.[29] The third way in which history matters is that geography itself is in large part the result of historical processes (such as the influence of colonial resource "scrambles" in defining the national boundaries and political geography of producing regions). The approach followed in this book reflects these diverse influences and methodologies.

The structure

This book follows a tripartite structure. I start in Part I with a discussion of the main perspectives on resource wars, presenting key concepts and a brief historical overview. Dominated by socio-biological and geopolitical explanations of struggles over resources, most accounts of "resource wars" have focused on resource scarcity in terms of the simplistic material aspects of resources, failing to take their broader material and social dimensions into account. I argue that these approaches—which persist in popular interpretations of contemporary resource wars—posit an over-simplistic view of resource wars, both in terms of human nature (for example, soldiers motivated solely by greed) and geography (for example, regions being inherently conflict-prone because of resource abundance or scarcity). I then introduce my analytical framework in Chapter 2, where I explore debates over the three main concepts used to understand relations between wars and resources: the resource curse, resource conflicts, and conflict resources.

In Part 2, three successive chapters examine three resources in detail: oil, diamonds, and timber. Oil has generated some of the largest profits in history and the oil industry is probably the world's most despised and most essential in a hydrocarbon-based economy. From transport to food and plastics, oil is integrated into nearly every aspect of daily life. The world's largest internationally traded commodity and an essential component of modern economies and military supremacy, oil is associated with spectacular booms and busts and with both extreme wealth and abject poverty. Oil is also the resource most commonly associated with armed conflict, and whereas the number of conflicts declined overall after the Cold War, it actually grew among oil producing countries.[30] Chapter 3 seeks to explain why armed conflicts take place in some oil-producing countries and not others, but also points at the different forms of violence relating to the oil sector. I look in particular at the importance of oil abundance versus dependence, the history of exploitation, and the location of oil fields. In Chapter 4, I turn to diamonds—a resource that captivated the attention of conflict analysts, media outlets, and the broader public because of its funding of rebel movements in Angola and Sierra Leone. I first question the idea of a "diamond curse" and then investigate the risk of conflicts and forms of violence associated with diamond exploitation. Noting that diamonds have been frequently dubbed a "rebel's best friend," I then highlight the political and tactical ambivalence of opportunities presented by diamond exploitation for rebellions. In Chapter 5, I come back to my initial research on logging, rebel financing and corruption in Cambodia, broadening the analysis through other cases such as Liberia.

In Part 3, I discuss avenues to address resource-related conflicts, first by considering the main options used to end hostilities in Chapter 6, and then by looking more broadly at conflict prevention initiatives in Chapter 7. My conclusion sums up the implications of this study, and presents some of the major questions facing resource industries, authorities, and consumers.

1

RESOURCE WARS REFRAMED

Water wars, drug wars, diamond wars, and oil wars have all entered the popular lexicon of international relations and media reports. People fight over resources, but why? Are resources really the issue, or is the problem rather with the context of resource exploitation? These questions became particularly acute at the end of the twentieth century with the apparent proliferation of so-called resource wars: armed conflicts supposedly motivated and fuelled by resources such as oil, minerals, and timber.

The idea that wars are associated with resources is probably as old as war itself. The central question is not whether resources and wars are connected, but how. Embedded in this question is a set of contested definitions and views on the nature of resources and wars.

What is a resource?

The term "resource" is used in this book to stand for natural resources, raw materials, and primary commodities. Etymologically related to the Latin *resurgere*, meaning "to rise again," the term resource conveys a sense of (re)empowerment and opportunity, but also dependence and vulnerability. Without a resource, one may not be able to stand back up after falling. This fear is often reinforced by adjectives attached to resources, such as "critical," "vital," "crucial" or "strategic."

More specifically here, the term refers to natural substances that are produced for satisfying human needs and desires. The notion of production is central to this definition: while nature creates these substances, it is their use by humans that turns them into resources, thus "resources are not; they become."[1] This underscores a distinctive feature of resources: the role of humans in their identification, production and consumption. Becoming a resource "is a property of things—a property that is the result of human capability."[2] Viewed from this perspective, human knowledge and capabilities are the prime resources "defining" all others. This perspective, for example, leads some resource companies to claim that they "create" resources.

If resources are produced as the result of human capabilities, needs and desires, they remain first and foremost materials from nature. The resources that I cover in this book—oil, gems, and timber from mostly old growth forests—are not materially produced from nature, as agricultural crops are. Rather, they are materially extracted from nature. Biodiesel can be produced out of crops and organic residues, but conventional oil can only be extracted. This emphasis on extraction over production implies more hotly contested ownership claims. Again, some resource companies argue that resources belong to those extracting them, rather than those sitting on them,[3] while landlords, on the contrary, argue that primary ownership resides with territorial rights since these resources are "simply" extracted and not produced.

The notion of resource extraction, here, often gives way to that of exploitation—a term that conveys for some the sense of making the best out of an area but for many others the sense of selfish abuse of the land. The terms production, creation, extraction, and exploitation are often politically loaded and should be used with care.

Resources vary in their spatial location, relative abundance, physical characteristics, technologies of extraction and transformation, use, social and environmental impacts, and economic value. Resources (and their relative availability or scarcity) are, in other words, simultaneously material and socially constructed. A simple, well-known example is that of diamonds for which desirability, scarcity and high prices are functions of cultural constructions and corporate control (by companies such as De Beers) as much as of intrinsic biophysical properties. In other words, resources should not be considered as simply raw materials that come out from nature, but as complex objects produced by socio-natural processes.[4]

More controversially, resources are also understood as subjects influencing social relations. From this perspective, resources can "act" and have a "role" in armed conflicts. Such an idea does not mean ascribing a fixed and deterministic sense of agency to resources; oil itself does not declare war. Rather it is about recognising what Arjun Appadurai calls the "social life of things": that resources both reflect and contribute to material cultures.[5] Demand for resources is not simply driven by human needs but by the social practices that resources, as objects, enable.[6] Oil is not in demand simply because people need to move, but because automobility is part of so many social practices—from economic production to car fetishism and individualised mobility.[7] Power relations are deeply embedded into these social practices and their material dimensions, a perspective that is crucial to understanding the broader social dimensions of resources in relation to armed conflicts.

Such an understanding of resources counters the environmental determinism implicit in some accounts of "resource wars" (as I explore below), and if handled appropriately, it also avoids overlooking concrete environmental constraints to which resource extraction is subject. It is also helpful in pointing out that resources are not fixed and finite and that scarcity and availability are relative rather than absolute. Furthermore, many in resource industries hold the view that resources are born out of capacity, with implications for resource ownership. In this perspective, resource ownership comes from the capacity to discover and "produce" a resource (that is, extract it), not from the ownership of surface rights. In contrast, the perspective of some land owners is that resource discovery and extraction is simply a "facilitating" exercise and that customary rights such as "ancestry" decide ownership. As a result, it is unsurprising that definitions of resources are often disputed, and that debates over resource appropriation tend to center on the question of who has the right to define resources and on what terms.

How to define "resource wars"?

The term "war" is similarly subject to dispute. War can take many forms, and multiple definitions exist. One definition adopted for the study of early warfare is that of a "collective armed conflict in which the deaths of other persons are envisioned in advance, and this envisioning is encoded in the purposeful act of taking up lethal weapons."[8] In other words, war under this broad definition is framed as intentional and potentially lethal organised violence. Violence in times of war, however, takes many dimensions and does not simply include acts of physical violence conducted by armed combatants (warriors) within the confines of the objectives of warfare. The two concepts are distinct and should be decoupled.[9] Violence, in this regard, encompasses structural and symbolic as well as physical forms of violence.[10]

Although, as I shall relate, debates over the role of resources in war have a long pedigree, the term "resource wars" is of relatively recent origin. The twentieth century, characterised by a rapid increase in rates of resource extraction, gave rise to a vast literature on conflicts over "raw materials."[11] The term resource wars was popularised in the 1980s as a geopolitical device to both explain and exacerbate renewed tensions between the US and the Soviet Union over the control of fuel and minerals in disputed "peripheries," especially minerals in Southern Africa and oil in the Middle East.[12] The term is also applied to popular struggles against large-scale resource exploitation projects and neoliberal reforms in resources and in public utility sectors.[13] And it is widely used for "trade wars," as in the examples of bananas, tomatoes, or wheat.[14] As detailed in Chapter 3, resource wars—or rather, resource conflicts—are understood as conflicts taking place over a resource for its own sake.

Conventional geopolitical perspectives define resource wars as armed conflicts revolving around the "pursuit or possession of critical materials."[15] To paraphrase the Prussian war thinker Clausewitz, resource wars are, from this perspective, the continuation of resource politics by military means. The concept is mostly used in reference to inter-state conflicts over the supply of "strategic resources," giving way to a narrow and militaristic notion of "resource security" and in particular "energy security." Resource wars are thus in some ways the result of a lack of imagination, knowledge, and capacity to find alternative resources; going to war over resources is testimony of an incapacity to acquire them, or their alternatives, through less costly and risky means.

Conceptual framework

Having defined resources and resource war, I now turn to the task of mapping out my conceptual framework. Two main perspectives dominate contemporary academic debates over resource wars. The first perspective is an econometric approach, characterised by large-N studies of the relationships between specific resources and conflict-related variables. The other approach tends to attract sociologists, geographers and political ecologists, who employ a mix of ethnographic, political economy, and spatial science methods—often through detailed case studies of specific conflicts. These disparate approaches are emblematic of one of the critical cleavages in contemporary social science. But they are also instrumental in developing in this chapter a conceptual framework that will enable a broader understanding of resource-related conflicts, and which I will use in subsequent chapters to examine specific resources, including oil, diamonds, and timber.[16]

The analysis in this chapter, and the next, develops a critique of conventional geopolitical views of resource wars. I argue, first, that resources must be understood as social processes (embodying values, desires, needs, and capacities) as well as material substances. Without this understanding, we risk falling into the trap of environmental determinism, such as the argument that some resources (and some countries, by virtue of their resource endowment) are inevitably conflict-prone. Second, I suggest that conventional views tended to focus on resources through a security lens, but that this overlooked many other dimensions of conflicts and undermined the understandings and relationships necessary to fostering peace. Third, I reason that studies of resource wars would benefit from "thick" historical and geographical contextualisation, as a means of deconstructing the politicised narratives of threat and insecurity often associated with resource wars. These elements will now be explored in greater detail in an analysis of the potential connections between resources, conflicts, and various forms of violence.

There are three important views of the relationship between resources and wars. The first is the "resource curse" argument, which asserts that resource dependence results in economic underperformance and a weakening of governing institutions, rendering a society more vulnerable to armed conflict; vulnerability to war, in other words, is associated with the institutional and economic impacts of resource exploitation. The second is the "resource conflicts" argument, which suggests that grievances, conflicts and violence associated with resource control and exploitation increase the risk of onset of larger-scale armed conflicts. In other words, violence and conflicts, are directly linked to the control and exploitation of resources. The third is the "conflict resources" argument, which focuses on the financial opportunities that sustain armed conflicts, or the instrumentalisation of opportunities related to resources by belligerents.

Each of these dimensions of resource-conflict relationships has something to offer our understanding of the interrelationships between resources and wars. Taken singly (as they often have been), they fail to capture the complexity of the relationship. Taken together, however, they help explain how resource endowments, exploitation practices, social entitlements, and discursive representation contribute to shaping greater vulnerability to, risk of, and opportunities for armed conflicts.

This approach rejects the simplistic association, widespread in the popular literature, that conflicts are most frequently associated with absolute resource scarcity. In other words, it refutes the notion that the likelihood of conflict increases as resources become scarcer (whether through depletion, increased degradation, more uneven capture or allocation, or rising demand). Individual and comparative case studies have generally disproved a simple and direct causal relation between resource scarcity and conflicts. Rather, they have identified indirect linkages with increased poverty, social segmentation, migrations, and institutional disruptions.[17] According to this "resource scarcity" argument, widening the scope of the (international) security agenda to include environmental breakdown and livelihood resource access could help provide a basis for peace,[18] especially through bridging an "ingenuity gap" to address what are mostly widespread, chronic, low-intensity and intra-state conflicts.[19] Some of this work has received potent critiques for its methodological approach,[20] neo-Malthusian assumptions, and essentialising character,[21] as well as for naturalising an environment-insecurity nexus in the South exonerating (Northern-led) modernity and development.[22] Recent geospatial quantitative analyses also stress the importance of political and economic factors (rather than demographic and environmental factors) as key mediators of the link between climate change, environmental degradation, and armed conflicts.[23] In short, the experience of resource scarcity is mediated (and can be usefully interpreted) by social, political, and discursive processes. The analytical challenge, as I shall indicate, is to integrate these processes with a robust understanding of the biophysical, institutional and economic dimensions of resource conflicts that tend to dominate policy debate and popular accounts. It is to this task that I now turn.

Econometric perspectives: Resource dependence, institutions, and opportunities

Departing from the contingencies of detailed historical narratives and geopolitical speculations on future struggles over resources, an increasing number of scholars have deployed econometric approaches to identify and understand broad patterns in resource and conflict relationships. Quantitative approaches initially using a narrow range of (at times inadequate) variables have yielded some statistically powerful but analytically controversial results, with critiques denouncing their reductionism and biased power effects. Perhaps most controversially in this respect have been the findings and arguments of the economists Paul Collier and Anke Hoefler. Their econometric work on the causes of civil wars suggested that primary commodity export dependence constitutes "the strongest single driver of the risk of conflict" and that "the true cause of much civil war is not the loud discourse of grievance but the silent force of greed."[24] In response to the controversy and broad media coverage surrounding this statement, numerous studies have tested its validity and interpretation.

Debates over econometric approaches have focused on the selection of variables (primary commodity exports as a share of gross domestic product, resource production, or resource stock per capita), the conceptualisation of motivations ("greed" versus "grievances") and practices ("looting"), the specificities of the models, and the robustness of findings, as well as the validity of quantitative approaches.[25] Early misinterpretations included, for example, the absence of sub-national location criteria, so that the combination of hostilities in Chechnya and diamond production in Siberia would appear as a "diamond war" in Russia; the conflation of resource dependence and abundance, so that Botswana and Sierra Leone would be identified as comparable "diamond rich" countries while in fact their common diamond dependence hid a thirty-fold difference in per capita diamond wealth; the idea that resource exploitation enticed greed and looting opportunities, but not grievances and social mobilisation. Many of these initial faults were addressed and databases and models got further refined. Yet large-N comparative studies based on a narrow range of variables provided only a limited perspective open to criticisms, leading some researchers to work with a smaller number of cases allowing for a much richer contextualisation.[26]

Overall, the onset of war does not seem to be robustly related to the broad category of "primary commodities"—at least as defined in terms of export dependence. By distinguishing between different types of commodities and types of conflicts, however, some patterns emerge.[27] Oil wealth seems to increase the likelihood of civil war,[28] especially onshore compared to offshore oil.[29] In contrast, "contraband" goods such as gemstones, drugs and narcotics do not increase the likelihood of conflict (with the exception of alluvial diamonds in relation to ethnic conflicts and during the 1990s when many wars were funded by these goods) but do prolong conflicts.[30] Whereas forests offer a frequent hideout for insurgents and timber is a source of finance, quantitative testing does not confirm these two common relationships.[31] Dependence on agricultural commodity exports seems associated with increased conflict likelihood,[32] but this relationship remains under-tested. An examination of conflict severity finds that gemstone, oil and gas exploitation in conflict zones increases the severity of conflicts (but drug cultivation decreases it), oil and gas exploitation outside conflict zones lessens severity, while secessionist conflicts in oil production regions are the most severe.[33] As discussed below, the location and type of resource thus appear to be important.

To explain the potential relationship between resource wealth and armed conflicts, political economy perspectives have framed three main arguments about resources: an institutional weakening effect, increasing vulnerability to conflict; a motivational effect, increasing the risk of armed conflict; and an opportunity or feasibility effect, associated with resources financing belligerents. The mechanisms are summarised in Table 1.1.

The first argument relates to the idea of a "resource curse," according to which resource wealth results in economic and political underperformance, as resource rents distort the economy and states rely on them rather than on broad taxation. Several studies have focused on economic collapse and political instability associated with the resource curse.[35] The case of Rwanda demonstrates the impact of political and economic dependence on resource rents, as the Habyarimana regime in Rwanda switched from buying political loyalty through coffee revenue redistribution, to holding on to power through massive repression following the late 1980s collapse of international coffee prices.[36] The institutional weakening effects of resources are also supported in the case of oil exports, which have little direct influence on conflicts once their effect on state capacity is accounted for; what matters is state capacity—shown by taxation/gross domestic product (GDP) ratio.[37] This finding echoes the argument that the taxability (or "tax handle") of resource sectors can become an important factor of political stability.[38] In this regard, industrial exploitation provides the state with more secure fiscal revenue than artisanal exploitation. The impediment of hard-to-tax resources, however, can be resolved in part through institutions of "joint-exploitation" between the

Table 1.1: Mechanisms Linking Resources and Armed Conflicts[34]

INSTITUTIONAL WEAKENING EFFECT

Resource dependence weakening of states and societal organisation.

Weak state mechanisms

- Poor taxation/representation nexus (as government fiscally autonomous from population).
- Authoritarianism and corruption.
- Weak tax handle (resource sectors hard to tax due to ease of illegal activities and poor bureaucratic control capacity).

Weak socioeconomic linkages

- Low socio-professional diversification, social cohesion, regional integration.

MOTIVATIONAL EFFECT

Resource wealth and exploitation motivating armed conflict.

Grievance mechanisms

- High income inequality.
- High economic vulnerability to growth collapse.
- Grievances over socio-cultural-environmental "externalities."
- Grievances over unfair revenue distribution.

Greedy rebel mechanisms

- "Economic violence" by domestic groups.
- Greater rewards for state capture.
- Greater rewards for secessionism.

Greedy outsider mechanisms

- High (future) profits.
- Strategic leverage on competitors through resource supply control.

OPPORTUNITY EFFECT

Resource revenue financing hostilities

- Higher viability of armed hostilities (resources financing the weaker party, but also covering for war-related budgetary expenditure).

state and private actors, whereby even for illegal resources, such as narcotics, an enforceable agreement can emerge between both parties.[39] Earnings from corruption can be channelled through patronage networks to maintain some degree of political stability.[40] As suggested by the example of diamond-funded clientelism in Sierra Leone, the informal character of these bargains can leave countries vulnerable to armed conflicts when they break down.[41] Departing from a focus on state institutions, the political scientists Pauline Jones Luong and Erika Weinthal suggest that private ownership in resource sectors reduces the risk of "resource curse" and hence potentially the incidence of "resource wars."[42]

The second argument is that resources motivate rebellion because of high potential gains (resource revenue) and low opportunity costs (prevalent poverty and lack of revenue alternative in many low-income and resource-dependent countries). Most prominently, the economist Paul Collier argues that youth in poor countries often fight in the hope of gaining access to resource revenues.[43] Although the prospect of loot has long been used to recruit and motivate fighters, many contemporary armed groups forcibly recruit fighters, especially among children and youth, which brings into question such assumptions about motivation. Furthermore, young people integrated (often by coercion) into rebel movements, such as the Revolutionary United Front (RUF) in Sierra Leone, more frequently report social justice, including economic equity, as a motivational factor rather than individual rewards, with actual "conflict diamonds" being inaccessible to foot soldiers and only petty rewards being provided by the movement on a relatively egalitarian basis.[44] Economically motivated leaders, however, appear to displace those driven by ideology in resource-rich contexts, taking control of armed groups to pursue financial rather than political goals.[45] Although motivation can be focused on long-term objectives, support for the hypothesis of individual financial motivation and "economisation" of armed insurgencies remains tentative. Therefore, studies should be sensitive to the temporality of the conflict, as prolonged conflicts appear to favour economic motivations.

The third argument relates to the escalating and prolonging effects of resources on armed conflicts, and it has received broader empirical support. Access to resource revenue ensures that more arms can be purchased and conflicts may thus escalate. There is little evidence that resource revenue funds rebellions in their initial phase of escalation, at least in most recent civil war cases involving financing by resources, but more evidence exists in terms of conflict prolongation.[46]

Political ecology perspective: Resources, power relations, and forms of violence

Econometric perspectives have provided a high degree of formalisation and statistical "testing" of resource-conflict relationships. But the strength of quantitative approaches is also a straitjacket that can restrict and narrow explanations. A third set of perspectives has therefore been brought to bear in a search for a broader contextualisation, the aim being to identify the multidimensional power relations that exist around resources, and to examine a variety of conflicts and forms of violence not encompassed by either geopolitical, or econometric perspectives.

The first argument to be drawn from the debate among these different perspectives is that resource scarcity, abundance and dependence are geographically and historically contingent. Resolving the puzzle of resource wars consequently requires attention to the uneven distribution of resources, and the unbalanced production and circulation of commodities. War frequently has a direct impact on this unevenness. Foreign investments respond to the risk of political instability and prevalence of hostilities. Oil reserves in Iraq, for example, have been "underexploited" since the 1980s, with the uneven effects of increasing current oil prospecting elsewhere (for example in the Gulf of Guinea) and the stakes of Iraqi oil control in the future (as shown by the 2003 US-led invasion of Iraq). Cambodian forests were either "protected" or "destroyed" between the late 1960s and 1990s according to the various forms taken by the conflicts (for example, internationally unopposed genocide or massive US carpet-bombing). In the early 1990s, ongoing but low-intensity conflict allowed many civilians and "self-demobilised" soldiers to illegally access forest resources.[47] As we shall see, uneven resource entitlements also reflect the antagonising effects of war on social identities, with sectarian violence in particular reshaping conditions of access and control over resources.

Scale also plays a central role in interconnecting various places when we try to make sense of local or global patterns of violence and resource flows.[48] The question is not only at what location a conflict involving resources is taking place, but also on what scale the conflict is occurring.[49] In this respect, much of the case literature supporting the "resource scarcity" argument has been sensitive to scale, at least in terms of the processes involved—arguing, for example, that "environmental scarcity

19

contributes to diffuse, persistent, subnational violence …[i]t rarely, if ever, contributes directly to conflict among states."[50] Econometric studies have also included sub-national level variables allowing for a better specification of models used in large N-studies.[51] Yet, as demonstrated by a study of land conflict in the Eastern Brazilian Amazon, such analyses have to be complemented by detailed and historically grounded case studies, including at the micro-scale.[52] In a study of chronic violence in oil-rich Nigeria, the geographer Michael Watts argues that violence not only relates to the territorial control of oil fields of the Niger Delta, but is more broadly associated with the construction of identities at different scales, with petro-capitalism undermining the project of secular modern governance through the reshaping of incompatible community identities, from the indigenous to the national scale.[53] The interplay of identities and civil war in Sri Lanka on access to common-pool resources, fisheries and water, suggests that the "dynamics of the political economy of war cross different scales and go beyond simple place-based struggles, for they are rooted in broader spatial dynamics of warfare creating place-space tensions in the sense that spatial dynamics of military control impinge changing access regimes upon specific places."[54]

The second key argument is that there is a broader range of violence than that which is accounted for by geopolitical and econometric perspectives. For example, the geographers Nancy Peluso and Michael Watts call not only for understanding of conflicts as contextualised by history, power relations, and material transformation taking place at a diversity of scales, but also for multiple forms of violence to be acknowledged in relation to resources.[55] Beyond the coercive use of physical force to control or access resources, such studies engage with broader understandings of violence, such as the political scientist Johan Galtung's notions of physical, cultural and structural violence or multiscalar forms of social, economic and political violence.[56] As noted earlier, the form of violence recognised by quantitative studies defines the spatiality and temporality of armed conflicts studied (that is, armed conflicts are not accounted for when fewer than twenty-five people die per year directly from battles engaging the state against at least one recognised armed group). This definition can overlook, for example, long histories of one-sided "repressive" violence by the state or high levels of "criminal" violence in the post-conflict period.[57]

Political ecology perspectives have also contributed to theories of resource access and control in relation to conflicts and various forms of violence.[58] Access being defined as "the ability to derive benefits" using all possible means, access to resource benefits is shaped through a "bundle of powers," not only a "bundle of [property] rights."[59] These perspectives distinguish in turn between gaining, controlling, and maintaining access to resources, and the power relations that these entail. Building on this approach, control can be defined as the ability to enforce the rights to benefit from resources using all possible means, including various forms of violence.[60] Historical analysis, in-depth interviews of individual or communal perceptions of violence, anthropological methodological approaches, and gender-sensitive analyses can address these gaps and help to explain what constitutes violence in relation to resources, and how resources in turn relate to violence. Studies of opium production in Afghanistan, for example, demonstrate the dual standard of the US in relation to narcotics production, as well as various dimensions through which opium relates to the financing of war crimes, peasant coping strategies, and legally criminal yet socially accepted "shadow" economies.[61] The case of wildlife conservation and poaching in Africa suggests that war has become "a common model and metaphor for conceptualising and planning biodiversity protection in Africa [shaping] a new moral geography wherein parks and protected areas have become spaces of deadly violence."[62]

These examples of connections between resources and violence imply analyses of violence within processes of commodification (how "things" become resources or how commodities are defined by their exchange value), fetishisation (how imaginative aspects of resource production and consumption affect power relations), and representation (how the places in which these processes unfold are imagined and concepts such as "war" are mobilised to convey meaning). Political ecology perspectives have made use of commodity chain analysis to bridge site-specificity and multiscalar interconnections between resources and wars. At its most basic, this approach follows resources from their point of production to their point of consumption and "disposal." In this process, connections can be seen because actors' motivations and power relations are more easily identified; this allows analysis to highlight all the accountable actors, rather than just blaming the immediate perpetrators of physical violence. Commodity chain analysis can help identify the links between different scales of resource production, transformation, circulation, and consumption.[63] Analyses of everyday commodities, such as coffee, can reveal the structural violence at play in highly unequal power relations.[64] Commodity chain analysis also helps to identify responsibilities, regulatory spaces (and absence thereof), and licit or illicit (socially acceptable or unacceptable) and legal or illegal (legally banned) social practices.[65]

Human rights organisations, such as Global Witness, or UN expert panels investigating sanction busting have successfully taken this approach to publicly expose resource businesses and politicians implicated in financing war crimes. One of the purposes of commodity chain analysis is to bridge or fold scales in order to counter the "localism" present in many narratives of contemporary armed conflicts. By showing the connections between "killing fields" and "shopping malls," commodity chain analysis moves from one scale to the other, broadening understandings of local forms of violence away from the most physically direct consequences, capturing the interest of the media, and recasting the violence within much larger processes of global commodity circulation and consumption. Scale here intervenes as both an analytical concept bridging the local and the global, and an interpretive framework. The different forms of violence relating to resources are better understood through the scales that resources link and (re)produce. For example, scales entail a hierarchical power relation between global demand (and global firms promoting it) and local sites of supply. In turn, these hierarchical relations are matched by different forms of violence, from the structural violence of mass consumption in retail spaces to physical violence on the bodies of workers and ecosystems in production sites. Human rights and environmental advocacy campaigns have stressed the need for fair trade along such lines. In the case of diamonds, multi-scalar analysis demonstrates various forms of violence—structural (for example, inequity), cultural (for example, racism), and physical (for example, amputations)—involved in the diamond sector.[66]

Commodity chain analyses are frequently used to examine commodification and its links with violence. Vertical commodity chain analyses identify actors and processes directly involved in the successive transformation of "nature" into consumed resources. As vertical analyses follow resources from the fields to the dumps, they seek to explain power relations and various forms of violence along the chain, often with ethical purposes in mind, such as pointing to responsibilities hidden by distant or publicly undisclosed connections. Horizontal analyses seek to deepen the understanding of particular links or nodes along the commodity chain by studying their broader context and indirect relations.[67] In this way, individuals involved in mining "conflict diamonds," for example, are not understood simply as "greedy thugs" profiting from war but as individuals and communities making choices in part dictated by prevalent conditions of destitution and repression,[68] as well as historical and spatial contexts.[69]

Defetishisation is a second approach to examining the social construction of resources and their connections to violence. The "conflict diamond" campaign successfully reconnected "violent" spaces of diamond exploitation and "peaceful" spaces of jewellery consumption. By exposing diamond trading practices and deceitful diamond marketing strategies, it demonstrated that many diamonds were "tainted" by hatred and grave human rights abuses. Through the defetishising of diamonds as constructed objects of love and purity, violence captured the attention of the media and forced the diamond industry to accept significant trade reforms through the Kimberley Process Certification Scheme against "conflict diamonds." Mobilising such powerful terms as "war," "blood" or "terror" in consumption politics can in this sense prove highly rewarding for advocacy campaigns and media coverage. Yet it may also be ambivalent in terms of the effects on producers, consumers, and the actual advocacy campaigns. The inclusion of racialised images of Africa in the reporting of "diamond wars," for example, arguably burnished the "reputable" character of Western industrialised mining interests at the expense of their historical accountability while associating terror with artisanal diamond miners in Africa.[70]

The defetishisation of narratives such as that of "conflict diamonds" is often narrow and essentialises the localities and social relations constitutive of these commodities, such as "places of origin."[71] When unveiling the nasty aspects of resource production and consumption for the sake of getting the message across to the public, defetishising narratives may underplay the positive sides of production and consumption, and use images that are themselves tainted by prejudice. Informing consumers of unethical practices in a market full of "smoke and mirrors" is ethically necessary, but such an exercise can occasionally prove counterproductive if it mostly (re)produces prejudiced imaginative geographies and agendas.[72] Arguably, this risk may be increased as advocacy campaigns against conflict resources rely on distant perceptions of problems and people, co-depend on the mass media to build seductive storylines, and outbid each other in caricaturing situations to attract maximum attention and public support.[73]

Finally, representation plays an important role, particularly through the stereotyping of resource exporting countries and the essentialising of places and actors supposedly involved in resource wars. With simplistic representations of "resource geography," the regions at war often become caricatured through the concept of resource war, brushing aside issues of scale and the multiplicity of distinct spaces and places. As each particular region becomes caricatured through its dominant resource sector, other aspects of conflicts get brushed aside. Agrarian issues in "diamond-mining Sierra Leone," for example, are overlooked in resource war narratives.[74] Popular geopolitics conveyed through films contribute to the cultural reproduction of world politics and representations of conflicts.[75] Recent James Bond films reinforce stereotypes of resource exporting countries, such as *The World is Not Enough* (1999), based on the control of Central Asian oil exports, or *Die Another Day* (2002), linking West African conflict diamonds to North Korean weapons of mass destruction. Not all Western mass audience films reinforce these caricatures, however. Some address links between resources and conflicts in relatively more nuanced ways, such as *Syriana* (2005), *Lord of War* (2005), and even *Blood Diamond* (2006). In the case of Iraq, *Three Kings* (1999, with the working title *Spoils of War*) provided a sharp critique of US petro-imperialist motives and betrayal of Iraqi people during the 1991 Gulf War (ironically providing ground for the US-led invasion of Iraq to remove Saddam Hussein in 2003).

Framework: Vulnerability, risk and opportunity

The analytical framework I shall now put forward mobilises three general arguments about the relationship between resources, conflicts, and violence.[76] The first argument (the "resource curse" argument) asserts that resource dependence results in economic underperformance and a weakening of governing institutions which make a society more vulnerable to armed conflict. The second argument (or the "resource conflicts" argument) suggests that grievances, conflicts, and violence associated with resource control and exploitation increase the risk of onset of larger-scale armed conflicts. The third argument (the "conflict resources" argument) focuses on financial opportunities provided by resources, which both motivate belligerents and financially sustain armed conflicts.

Rethinking the resource curse: Conceptualising vulnerability

The resource curse argument suggests that resource dependence creates a context for the emergence of armed conflicts through its negative effects on economic performance and the quality of governing institutions.[77] Rather than simply explaining war through "greed-driven" belligerents motivated by "lootable" resources, this argument emphasises resource dependence as both reflecting and shaping conditions that increase vulnerability to armed conflicts. According to the political economy literature, the characteristics of countries most vulnerable to civil war since 1946 are low per capita income, declining economic growth rate, geographical conditions favouring insurgencies, "weak" state coercive capacity and institutional authority, and political regimes in transition, while the influence of different kinds of inequalities remains debatable.[78]

Empirical evidence for the resource curse argument is strong, although historically and institutionally contingent, with studies suggesting that resource-dependent countries tend to underperform economically, to be more poorly governed, and to present lower social indicators compared to other countries with similar income levels.[79] Economic explanations include exposure to high price fluctuations, declining terms of trade, natural capital depreciation, and a crowding-out of the non-resource sectors through local currency overvaluation and rent-seeking, as well as over-consumption and misguided economic and social policies.[80] Political explanations range from resource rent effects on over-optimistic and short-sighted policies, policy capture by special interests, higher levels of corruption, and state fiscal independence resulting in a lack of democratic bargaining power for the population.[81] There is good statistical evidence to relate the "curse" of oil dependence with increased conflict likelihood, but little consensus for other resource sectors.[82]

Theories of uneven development suggest that resource dependence has spatial dimensions, expressed as selective processes of modernisation and peripheralisation combined with the production of hierarchical scales, predominantly defined by their relationship with the resource sector.[83] Resource dependence is also constitutive of, and constituted by, core-periphery relations between (and within) producing and consuming countries, which, although not fixed in time, entail historical legacies with potent political and economic impacts.[84] Contemporary low income per capita, for example, is strongly correlated with the prevalence of extractive institutions—institutions that came to dominate the political economy of colonies inhospitable to European settlers.[85] In other words, high mortality rates among European settlers were deadly for long-term economic growth, especially because colonial institutions enabled a small cadre of Europeans to extract as much wealth as possible. Quantitative studies of the resource curse have not systematically tracked the historical origins and evolution (rather than the level) of resource dependence as variables in relation to conflicts. As the relative economic and political importance of resource production areas increases, other areas are comparatively peripheralised. Within resource production areas themselves, non-resource aspects often become marginalised—a simple example being the frequent demise of agriculture in the vicinity of booming mining areas, due to labor shortages. The uneven development resulting from such processes of relative centralisation and peripheralisation/marginalisation, in turn, reflects the social construction, spatial distribution, and mode of production of resources.[86] Peripheralisation and uneven development entail tangible spatial effects far beyond the narrow confines of the resource sector, extending into social identities, territorialities, political governance, economic marginalisation, and environmental outcomes of relevance to the study of conflicts.[87]

Resource conflicts and conflict resources: Conceptualising risk and opportunity

Overlapping with "environmental security" studies,[88] the "resource conflicts" arguments associate resources with specific conflicts (over resource access, for example) and occurrences of violence (for example militarisation of resource areas, pollution, or labor abuses). This association has focused on livelihood conflicts pertaining to mostly renewable resources,[89] and on national or military resource security pertaining to mostly nonrenewable resources, such as oil and "strategic" minerals.[90] Although involving distinct case studies and often guided by very different ideological agendas, these approaches share a central assumption: that the diversity of patterns of violence involved in resource control and exploitation can lead to "war," ranging from its discursive deployment to organised physical violence.[91] The spatial dimensions of "resource conflicts" are generally conceived in terms of scarcity (that is, relative distribution of resources) and identity-related endowments (for example, who controls what where).

In contrast, the "conflict resources" argument (the most prominent in the case of "conflict diamonds") associates resources with specific opportunities (mostly understood as financial) afforded to belligerents. From this perspective, some resources are more prone to sustaining and motivating war than others—especially highly valuable resources most easily accessible to the weaker party in a war. A narrow definition of "conflict resources" refers to resources financing rebel groups, as in the case of the official definition of "conflict diamonds" by the UN General Assembly: "rough diamonds used by rebel movements or their allies to finance conflict aimed at undermining legitimate governments."[92] A broader definition is that of the control, exploitation, trade, taxation, or protection of natural resources, which contributes to, or benefits from, the context of armed conflict. Broader definitions widen the range of responsibility from "illegal armed actors" to all those profiteering or maintaining economic relations prolonging hostilities, including companies, governments, and consumers.[93] As I explain in the case of diamonds, "opportunity" is understood to have spatial dimensions reflecting the biophysical aspects and spatiality of this resource and its mining and marketing context—that is, what is accessible, to whom, and in what place.

The concepts of "resource conflicts" and "conflict resources" are not mutually exclusive. Rather, they are complementary in their respective focus on the risks of engendering armed conflict and the economic opportunities made available to combatants. Two distinct conceptions of the spatiality of resource-related conflicts underlie these approaches. The geography of risk, shaping resource conflicts, is understood to revolve largely, but not exclusively, around processes of territorialisation, predicated upon perceptions of resources as spatially fixed but socially constructed "natural" endowments. From this perspective, entitlements are in large part articulated and contested through processes of territorialisation—including a militarisation of regulatory responses to resource conflicts.[94] In contrast, the geography of opportunity, shaping conflict resources, reflects processes of interconnection between actors at local, regional, and international scales. While financing of war can rely on the territorialisation of resource production areas (possibly entailing a resource conflict), it also involves spatial connections enabling the circulation of commodities (resources, money, arms, and labor). Furthermore, belligerents can generate revenue through the control of resource-related flows, such as threats of destruction or obstruction of oil pipelines or the kidnapping and ransoming of resource project staff.[95] The geography of resource wars is not defined only by front lines around the production area, but also by spaces along the commodity chain. Regulatory responses affecting the behavior of commodity chain actors thus work in part through strategies of re-territorialisation, such as the military capture of key resource production areas, and disconnection, such as economic sanctions—as discussed in Chapter 6.

Characterising resources and their implications

Focusing on the spatial characteristics of resources and their mode of control and production, the characteristics of control can define resources as proximate or distant while those of access can distinguish them as point or diffuse.[96] The control of resources results in part from the relative spatial position of a resource towards the center(s) of power. Proximate resources are close to the center of power (that is, firmly under the control of the government, whether through a physical spatial relationship or a socially constructed one) and are less likely to be captured by rebels than those close to a border region inhabited by a group lacking official political representation. Distant resources are located in remote territories along porous borders or within the territory of social groups politically marginalised or in opposition to the extant regime (that is, under tenuous or controversial control of the government). These criteria are thus not only defined by the physical location of resources but also by their broader political geography relating to socially constructed space.[97]

Access to resources results in large part from the spatial spread of resource production areas and the mode of exploitation and control.[98] Resources are more easily accessed by insurgent movements if they are spread over a large area and are produced by a larger number of firms, rather than being spread over a small area and being produced by a very small number of firms that can be more easily defended. Point resources are spatially concentrated in small areas and socio-economically concentrated through technological means or corporate structures. They include mainly resources that can be exploited by capital-intensive extractive industries, such as deep-shaft mining or oil exploitation, which generally employ a small workforce and can be spatially concentrated, as in the case of offshore oil platforms. Diffuse resources are spatially spread over vast areas and access to their revenue is socio-economically dispersed.

They are often exploited by less capital-intensive industries than point resources and include, for example, alluvial gems and minerals, timber, agricultural products, and fish, but also onshore oil wells and facilities. Other resource characteristics have also been examined in relation to conflicts. Important characteristics include legality (for example, narcotics versus legal cash crops), transportability (weight/volume ratio, for example), and "obstructability" (to give one example, surface onshore pipelines are more vulnerable to attacks and obstruction than offshore or deep-buried pipelines and are thus more likely to result in extortion schemes).[99] These, in turn, also inform control and access of resources.

Implications for conflict types

On the basis of the four main categories I have outlined, particular types of resources are more likely to be associated with different types of conflicts (see Table 1.2).[100] The argument is not that oil, for example, should be associated in deterministic fashion with conflicts taking the form of secession if oil is located in politically marginalised areas; chronic civil unrest and warlordism if oil is onshore; or a coup d'état if oil is offshore. My point is rather that the characteristics of resource sectors provide a context for political mobilisation as well as for the motivations, strategies and capabilities of belligerents. Some of these characteristics are influenced by the context in which belligerents operate, so that, for example, initial conditions that would make a resource materially inaccessible to a rebel group are superseded by the complicity of government officials. The balance of opportunities between opposing groups is thus not rigidly fixed by the material conditions of resource production but is rather dynamic, depending on the behavior of different parties.

Table 1.2: Resource Characteristics and Conflict Types

Characteristics	Point	Diffuse
Proximate	Coup d'état	Mass rebellion
Distant	Secession	Warlordism

To take an example, a point resource distant from the center of power should be more likely to be associated with armed secession. Point resources, such as oil, are less likely to generate direct revenue access for local populations than diffuse resources through local participation in resource exploitation. Access to resource revenue thus depends on the "goodwill" of the central government, or the influence that local elites can exert on the central government. In contrast, local populations are more likely to bear the costs of exploitation, such as pollution and restricted land access. Political marginalisation of local populations in production areas effectively makes point resources distant from the center. Those called "sons and daughters of the soil" are thus more likely to be mobilised to challenge the government through a secessionist struggle, rather than through warlordism (resource revenue being harder to access without the control of sovereign rights) or a coup d'état (the central state being able to afford its security through point resource rents). Moreover, point resources tend to have a low local employment rate with little scope to set in motion class-based mass rebellion or "peasant wars." This is not to argue that oil deposits will automatically transform local people into armed secessionists. Yet, when unable, or unwilling, to secure the control of resources through the existing center of power, political movements in resource production areas have an interest in asserting secessionist sovereign claims over the lucrative periphery they claim as theirs. No less than ten secessionist movements were active in regions with large point resource endowments in the 1990s.[101] Most secession or decolonisation attempts have a pre-existing historical basis, yet these movements have often been reinforced by the socioeconomic and political transformations affecting resource rich regions, and by the resource stake, not to mention immediate financial opportunities. I briefly review examples of each type of conflict and their resource dimensions below.

Resources and coups d'état

Because point resources are generally less lootable than diffuse resources, and exploitation and trade often depend on international political recognition for mobilising investors and accessing markets, they are much more accessible to governments than to rebel movements. In the case of high-investment energy and mineral sectors, only when staff or infrastructure is vulnerable to attack, as with pipelines or railways, can rebels effectively practice extortion. In the absence of alternative sources of finance and a political basis for secession, the best option left to an armed opposition movement is to rapidly capture the state through a coup d'état in the capital city.

The conflicts in the Republic of Congo (Brazzaville) in 1993–94 and 1997 between competing politicians—Sassou Nguesso, Lissouba and Kolelas—were a contest for state power, exacerbated by the control of an offshore oil sector representing 85 percent of export earnings. The fact that these conflicts took the shape of coup attempts in the capital city was in this respect predictable, and Lissouba's government should have rapidly won the war through its control of the oil rent and associated military power. However, the war in 1997 dragged on for five months before being brought to a conclusion in favour of former President Nguesso by the military intervention of the Angolan government. That government in turn, as an ally of the former President, was eager to protect Angolan claims over the oil-rich enclave of Cabinda, and prevent the use of Congo as a platform for UNITA diamonds-for-arms deals.

Destroying a large part of the capital and leaving thousands dead, the stalemate in Brazzaville resulted from several factors. First, a large part of the army did not engage in the conflict, while others supported Sassou Nguesso, their former patron and ethnic affiliate. Second, both contenders benefited from access to the oil rent, as Sassou Nguesso was allegedly favoured over Lissouba by the French oil company dominating the sector, and parallel channels helped Sassou's arms purchases.[102] Finally, at street level, the conflict rapidly changed in nature as the different militias supporting politicians benefited from the looting of the capital city. Urban youths on all sides used the political conflict to challenge the legitimacy of a corrupt political elite that had dominated and plundered the country for more than thirty years.[103] Looting became known as "killing the pig" or "taking a share in Nkossa [the new Elf oil field]."[104] This form of justification echoed the devastating plundering of the Liberian capital Monrovia in 1996, when NPFL fighters hijacked their leaders' military offensive, renaming it "Operation Pay Yourself" and seeing it as a form of compensation for years of fighting "without compensation from their leaders."[105]

Resources and warlordism

Diffuse resources are more easily exploited and marketed than point resources by illegal groups, especially if they are distant from the center of power. This is typically the case with alluvial diamonds or forests located along border areas, hence their association with economically viable forms

31

of warlordism. While rebel movements generally attempt to overthrow the incumbent regime, the existence of lootable diffuse resources distant from the center of power, can provide an economically viable fallback position in case of failure. Rebel groups thereby create areas of de facto sovereignty imposed through violence and defined by criminal and commercial opportunities such as mining areas, forests, or smuggling networks.

In Liberia, Charles Taylor's bid for power in 1989 first targeted the capital, Monrovia. Failing to capture the Presidential Palace because of the intervention of international troops, he nevertheless succeeded in establishing his rule over "Greater Liberia," and took control of lucrative sectors such as timber and rubber, as well as key infrastructure such as the port of Buchanan crucial to iron ore exports. Taylor did not limit his resource grab to Liberia, but extended it to neighbouring Sierra Leone, where his support for the Revolutionary United Front (RUF) provided him with access to diamonds. Similarly, the RUF was able to sustain a guerrilla war essentially targeting the civilian population during the 1990s thanks to its control of diamond mining areas, as well as gold and cash crops. In the Philippines, the lucrative taxation of logging sustained many insurgent groups and transformed some from political opposition into self-interested groups.[106]

Resources and secessions

Because opposition groups are often required to assume sovereign rights to access point resources, they are more likely to support secession than warlordism. Unable or unwilling to gain control over the existing center of power, secessionist movements have an interest in asserting sovereign claims over the lucrative peripheral regions they claim as theirs. Although these valuable resources can prove difficult, if not impossible, to access through direct exploitation, theft or extortion, their existence or in some cases their "mythology" is a powerful tool for political justification and mobilisation, and the prospect of future revenues is an additional source of motivation.

Most secession attempts have a historical basis. Yet the economic and social changes associated with the development of the Western Sahara's important phosphate industry, for example, laid "the basis for the rise of a modern nationalist movement, setting its sights on the creation of an independent nation-state."[107] Sahrawis recognised the prospect of an economically viable or even prosperous country, and the simplistic assumption that Morocco aimed to capture their new-found mineral wealth served to mobilise armed resistance. Secessionist armed movements can also emerge around the socio-environmental impact or wealth redistribution associated with the commercial development of resources. Secessionism in Aceh is historically rooted in the independent sultanate that prevailed until the Dutch militarily defeated it in the late nineteenth century. Yet the formation of the Aceh Freedom Movement (GAM) coincided with the exploitation of major gas reserves in the early 1970s, and GAM's Declaration of Independence in 1976 specifically claimed that US$15 billion in annual revenue was exclusively used for the benefit of "Javanese neo-colonialists."[108] Land expropriation and exploitation of other resources, such as timber, by Javanese-dominated businesses, further exacerbated the conflict.

Similarly, the island of Bougainville has a history of separatism based on geographical and identity distinctiveness. Yet local politicians' demands for "special status" in Papua New Guinea, including favourable funding allocations during the period of transition to independence, centered on the economic significance of the island's gold and copper mine in Panguna. The secessionist agenda set in 1989 by Francis Ona was related to the impact of copper mining, compensation and closure of the mine, as well as a "Government of PNG [that] is not run to safeguard our lives but rather to safeguard the few rich leaders and white men."[109] Ona, a former mine surveyor, is a local dweller but not a titleholder of the mining lease area. As such he had little say in the allocation of the new trust fund set up in 1980 by the mine to compensate local communities. Although Ona's agenda "is most reasonably understood as part of his conflict with his own relatives in the kind of land dispute ... characteristic of [local] Nasioi culture," his analysis nevertheless resonated throughout the local Nasioi community, especially after repression by PNG forces started.[110]

In Sudan, a Nuer fighter provided a telling explanation for the renewal of conflict after the first phase of the war for self-determination of southern Sudan between 1955 and 1972: "We fought for seventeen years without even knowing of the true wealth of our lands. Now that we know the oil is there, we will fight much longer, if necessary!"[111] The second phase of the war ended up lasting twenty-three years. Yet while the redrawing of provincial borders by the central government to create a new "Unity" province around the main oil fields contributed to the resurgence of rebellion in the South in 1982, oil development about two decades later ended up providing an incentive for both parties to share oil wealth and carry out a referendum through which South Sudanese obtained their independence, in 2011.[112]

Most recently, the presence of large oil reserves around Kirkuk in northern Iraq (or southern Kurdistan) significantly heightened the stakes around the creation of an autonomous Kurdish state in the region during the invasion of Iraq by US-led forces. It was clear to the Turkish government that large oil revenues falling under Kurdish control would constitute a threat to the territorial and political integrity of Turkey.[113] Because of the current reluctance of the international community to reshape international borders under the United Nations Charter, nationalist claims need to be backed by historical sovereign rights. Turkey has long rejected such formal rights for Iraqi Kurds even though southern Kurdistan has been a quasi-independent country since 1991.[114]

Resources and peasant war

Diffuse resources involving large numbers of producers are more likely to be associated with rioting in nearby centers of power, such as a provincial or national capital, and with support for peasant or mass rebellions involving class or ethno-religious identity issues. The displacement or exclusion of peasants by agribusinesses and poor labor conditions on large plantations has prompted political mobilisation and the expansion of revolutionary struggles in Latin America and Southeast Asia. In Nicaragua, landlessness, neglect by the state and exclusion from, or marginalisation within, local patron-client schemes, provided fertile ground for peasant support for the Sandinista revolution. Yet the creation of state farms by the Sandinista regime, rather than the rapid provision of individual plots, reinforced the bonds between some landed patrons and their client peasants, rapidly increasing their support for and participation in the US-sponsored Contra movement.[115] In the Ivory Coast, the context of democratisation and an economic downturn precipitated by the fall of cocoa prices and the liquidation of the commodity Stabilisation Fund dictated by the International Monetary Fund (IMF) and World Bank, migrant labor issue associated with agriculture was repeatedly used for political gains in the late 1990s. Although the media focused on coup attempts in the capital, migrant workers were also the targets of violence, including forced displacement.

Highly coercive forms of warlordism are less likely to be economically viable than participatory forms of rebellions because of the need to sustain a large volume of labor input, and the difficulty of controlling workers over large areas. Conditions of slavery and control of labor can be imposed through hostage-taking over short periods, but like most predatory economic activities, these cannot be sustained over the long term. Over time, to minimise grassroots challenges, the armed faction is likely to act as a "protector" towards local populations, even if more in the sense of a Mafia group than a welfare state. The Revolutionary Armed Forces of Colombia (FARC) guerrilla units in Colombia, for instance, provide protection to peasants on land holdings and guarantee minimum prices for both coca and agricultural products.[116] While there has recently been a drift towards more criminal activities, FARC's maintenance of a balance of economic incentives and threats to sustain peasant productivity have been key to the viability of the revolutionary movement since its inception in the 1950s. Similarly, the expansion of the New People's Army (NPA) in the Philippines in the 1970–80s largely came from a "symbiotic" relationship with a peasant population whose subsistence agriculture was threatened by agribusinesses, logging companies and hydropower projects.[117] The NPA provided an alternative to the regime of Ferdinand Marcos that had lost all legitimacy and even presence among rural communities. Yet both the FARC and the NPA secured most of their support and funding from taxation and extortion schemes related to drugs trafficking and cattle ranches, and plantations, logging and mining respectively.

Resources and foreign intervention

Foreign interventions occur in all types of armed conflicts detailed above, and often involve indirect control over "strategic resources," such as oil or major mineral deposits, and the protection of major commercial and strategic interests. Although there is as yet no evidence of US support for a short-lived coup by business leaders and military officers against the democratically elected President Chavez of Venezuela on 12 April 2002, the failure of the US administration to condemn it demonstrated US dependence on Venezuelan oil and its distrust of Chavez. Foreign intervention can also reflect vested commercial interests in a regional context, as with the Zimbabwean and Ugandan presence in the DRC, as well as a means of self-financing transborder security operations, which seems to have partly sustained Rwanda's involvement in the DRC.

External actors may also intervene in secessionist attempts by manipulating local political identities into providing access to resources. In the late nineteenth century, the discovery of gold and diamonds in the newly created Boer republics in South Africa led to both stronger resistance to annexation by Britain, and a massive influx of British and other white immigrant prospectors. The refusal of Boer authorities to grant political rights to these *uitlanders* (outlanders) led British entrepreneurs such as de Beers' founder Cecil Rhodes to assist conspiracies among them, and contributed to the Boer Wars.[118] In 1957, the French government saw its resource interests threatened by the war of independence in Algeria, and organised the institutional secession of the resource-rich Sahara in the south, placing it along with parts of Mauritania and French Soudan (Mali) under the direct control of Paris through the Organisation Commune des Régions Sahariennes. In response, the National Liberation Front (FLN) placed the territorial integrity of the country at the top of its ceasefire negotiation agenda with the French, to ensure its control of Saharan resources.[119] Despite its political character, the Biafra secession in Nigeria and its repression by the government were largely motivated by local oil reserves. French oil interests supported the Biafra secession attempt and the Nigerian army started fighting in July 1967 "more than a month after the declaration of independence but only days after Shell … agreed to pay its royalties to Biafra rather than Nigeria."[120] Within the turmoil of the Belgian Congo's independence, US and Belgian commercial interests, eager to secure their hold on copper mines in the province of Katanga, supported a secession led by Moïse Tshombe, leading to military clashes between corporate-funded foreign mercenaries and UN troops supporting the unity of the country.[121] The de facto secession of eastern provinces in the DRC between 1998 and 2003 was largely the result of military interventions by Rwanda and Uganda, and multiple local conflicts over the inclusiveness of Congolese citizenship and the rights of populations from so-called "Rwandan origins" to access land and mineral resources.[122]

Implications for conflict duration and severity

Beyond the likely type of conflict, this approach has also informed debates on the influence of resource sectors on the duration and severity of conflicts.

Conflict duration

The presence of valuable natural resources generally prolongs armed conflicts, but this effect depends in part on the type of resource, its location and the mode of exploitation.[123] Empirical testing of some of these hypotheses through quantitative studies suggests that longstanding rebellions tend to be associated with diffuse and distant resources,[124] and separatist conflicts with non-fuel mineral revenue from point resources.[125] Alluvial diamonds and narcotics are statistically associated with prolonged conflicts. Oil, in contrast, prolongs conflicts only when it is located within the conflict area (and even if it is not exploited), while oil exploitation outside the conflict zone tends to shorten conflict duration.[126] Arguably, oil revenue is more likely to be accessible and exploitable by the government than by rebel groups, although this depends in part on the accessibility of oil infrastructure and racketeering opportunities.

The basic factor is funding opportunity, which came to be of particular importance in the post-Cold War period when several guerrilla movements faced the withdrawal of support from foreign governments. In resource-poor Mozambique, the cash-strapped Renamo relied on an intergovernmental Trust Fund and adhered to the peace process in the early 1990s, whereas União Nacional para a Independência Total de Angola (UNITA) and the Movimento Popular de Libertação de Angola (MPLA)—awash with cash from diamonds and oil exploitation, respectively—twice returned to war. While Renamo had benefited from smuggling and protection rackets over the flow of goods from three neighbouring landlocked countries, there were few resources on which to build its war economy when these flows could be channelled through South Africa. To some extent, peace in El Salvador was partially the result of a lack of resources as foreign support was cut off, in contrast to Colombia, where local resources sustained the conflict.[127] Even prior to the end of the Cold War, revenue extorted by the Ejército de Liberación Nacional (ELN) from oil companies through kidnappings and taxation of their sub-contractors assisted the movement in recovering from a devastating government army offensive in 1973, and allowed it to grow from less than a hundred to more than 4,000 members by the mid-1990s.[128] In 1988, Khmer Rouge leader Pol Pot had stressed the "need to find ways to develop natural resources" to fight the Vietnamese.[129] Following the departure of Vietnamese troops in 1989, the Khmer Rouge succeeded in doing so by capturing gem mines and forested areas along the Thai border, allowing them to fight the government for six years beyond the termination of their Chinese sponsorship, even if reliance on logging and gem mining caused problems as discussed below and in Chapter 5.

If funding opportunity plays an important role on conflict duration, this influence depends in large part on which side benefits from such access: if the weaker party benefits, then prolongation and possibly escalation are likely. In contrast, when benefits flow to the stronger party a swift escalation and military victory by the dominant player is more probable. Profitable conflict stalemates are also frequent, whereby neither side seeks to conduct decisive combat operations to maintain a status quo that is mutually beneficial.[130] Resources can also influence conflict duration by acting as a divisive factor among international players, for example when some foreign governments veto a UN Security Council resolution. In addition, the ability of the belligerents to draw on private financial flows decreases the potential leverage of foreign donors.

A resource can also help shorten conflicts, by concentrating revenue in the hand of one party, financially motivating rebel groups to defect to the government, or providing an incentive in peace negotiations. As part of the Lomé peace agreement on ending the Sierra Leone conflict, the leader of the RUF, Foday Sankoh, was appointed Chairman of the Commission for the Management of Strategic Mineral Resources (CMRRD). Sankoh took up residence in the capital, which facilitated his eventual arrest after RUF guards in Freetown fired at people demonstrating against the movement in May 2000. His arrest contributed to widespread defections and the collapse of the RUF a year later.

Resource incentives can also undermine a rebel movement from within, as a result of "bottom up" revenue flows weakening discipline and chains of command.[131] As a Khmer Rouge commander noted, "the big problem with getting our funding from business [rather than China] was to prevent an explosion of the movement because everybody likes to do business and soldiers risked doing more business that fighting."[132] In order to prevent such "explosion," or fragmentation, the Khmer Rouge fully supported soldiers and their families while tightly controlling cross-border movements. The hierarchy also supervised business dealings by local units. In 1996, a new commander was sent to a local Khmer Rouge unit that had become too cozy with provincial authorities, as well as to settle a contractual dispute with the movement; fourteen workers and the boss of the logging company involved were captured and beheaded. Tensions also arose because of financial disparities between Khmer Rouge regional units, leading to a fragmentation of the movement, massive defections, and ultimately the demise of the movement. This process tracked the decline of gem mining revenue from reserve depletion and military attacks on mining sites, as well as the drying up of logging revenue as the Thai government closed its border to trade with the Khmer Rouge, following pressure from Global Witness and the US administration. The fall in logging revenue from mid-1995 onwards increased tensions and distrust within the leadership of the movement throughout 1996. In the southwestern part of the country—the most resource-rich among Khmer Rouge-controlled areas—local commanders resisted demands by the party elite in the north for more orthodox policies and increased revenue transfer. As both sides of the divided movement accused each other of embezzling money, the crisis led to infighting and to atomised negotiations with the government. Local Khmer Rouge commanders defecting to the government obtained partial control of their territory and its resources, as well as tax exemptions on fuel imports and financial aid to build schools. Government cronies also set up several casinos in the semi-autonomous territories in partnership with former Khmer Rouge elements.

The leadership may also retain authority through coercion, charisma and strong ideologies, or adopt radical measures, such as strict discipline, harsh sanctions, forced recruitment (especially of children), indoctrination inside the movement, and violent repression of the population. UNITA's security apparatus, the status of Savimbi as "all seeing" among many of the rank and file, as well as severe punishment, including summary executions for such offences as alcohol making or drinking, stealing diamonds or disrespect for officers, for long instilled fear and a culture of strict discipline within UNITA's ranks and the general population.[133] The torture and summary execution of diggers by UNITA soldiers or Congolese "collaborators" explains much about the movement's capacity to control and centralise the diamond business, and prevent fragmentation and corruption.

Finally, an armed group that exploits natural resources is vulnerable to losing popular support and political legitimacy in the event that its adversary portrays the group as mere bandits or criminals driven more by economic self-interest than by political ideals. Ignoring similar "criminal" practices on the part of government officials or paramilitary groups thus facilitates in turn the sanctioning and political isolation of rebel movements like the RUF, UNITA, MEND and the FARC. Such a policy can, of course, run the risk of marginalising a political resolution of the conflict in favour of a military solution. This, in turn, risks alienating local populations and drastically reducing their political support.

Conflict severity

Longer conflicts are likely to result in a greater number of victims, not simply through a larger number of direct victims of hostilities (in fact many prolonged conflicts have a low intensity) but through the indirect negative effects on population health, food security, and interpersonal violence. It does not automatically follow, however, that in the absence of resources a war would be shorter or have a more benign impact on populations. Belligerents lacking access to resource revenue may well be more predatory on local populations, or seek more violent ways of raising funds, for example through robberies and kidnappings. Greater abuses against civilians tend to be associated with armed groups relying on resources, rather than the contrary. There are several possible explanations for this pattern. The main one is that the funding context of rebellions shapes their organisation, with the end result that rebellions emerging out of wealthy contexts—arising from external sponsorship or valuable resources—will "commit high levels of indiscriminate violence."[134] Valuable resource contexts attract and reward financially motivated people. Seeking short-term rewards and low risks, these individuals may start or join "opportunistic" rebellions. Within "activist" or politically motivated insurgencies, these same individuals may progressively displace politically motivated ones as the "business side" of rebellion comes to dominate in such conditions of resource wealth. Accordingly, activist rebellions would turn into opportunistic ones, and whereas the former would seek the cooperation of local populations and carefully target violence directed at civilians ("traitors"), the latter would disregard the population and engage in indiscriminate violence.[135] Greater lack of discipline within opportunistic rebellions relying on "bottom-up" resource funding, as mentioned above, would have dramatic consequences in terms of rapes and widespread killings. Whereas this explanation warrants attention, there are wider factors implicated in the use of violence by armed groups and the severity of conflicts.[136]

To sum up, natural resources can play a dual strategic role in contemporary wars by motivating and financing them, both before a conflict begins and as it unfolds. Although there is no deterministic relationship, resources can participate in shaping the type of armed conflict taking place, objectives of territorial control, relations between belligerents and populations, and the duration and intensity of the conflict. Resources can also affect the internal cohesion of armed movements, frequently leading to their fragmentation, as well as to instances of collusion between adversaries. This strategic role therefore has significant implications for both conflict prevention and conflict resolution, as discussed in Chapters 6 and 7.

Conclusion

Critiquing perspectives on resource wars is a precarious exercise. The term itself is conceptually "reductionist"—and especially so when arguments exclusively relate conflicts to resources while adopting a narrow understanding of resources, which focuses on their exchange or use value and their physical location. Conflicting perspectives have also pitted theoretical and methodological approaches against each other. Early studies selecting resources as "proxy" variables for social processes have been criticised for their (de)politicising effects, particularly when emphasising the immediate financial aspects of resource "looting" at the expense of other dimensions. Resource war narratives have also been characterised by a high degree of essentialism, especially in the decontextualisation and denunciation of "greed-driven thugs looting resources" frequently reported in the public media. As a result, broader contexts, scales and interconnections have often been overlooked. Research on resource-related conflicts should therefore be self-reflective, and should question whose security interests are actually served by the perspective and methodologies adopted.[137] Although academic research has often lagged behind advocacy-oriented research, academic perspectives on resource wars continue to bear a responsibility for the interpretation of conflicts by policy-makers.

Engagement between different perspectives has contributed to novel approaches in the assessment of the significance of resources for conflict risk, duration, and resolution. Mainstream geopolitical perspectives have made the resource supply security of wealthy nations a priority—to the point of calling for military invasions abroad or resource autarky at home. There is little doubt that resource supply is a major concern of realpolitik, but geopolitical narratives have often been blinded by seductive (and sometimes dubious) supply and demand statistics, articulated by an oversimplified geographical understanding of power relations and representations of potential flashpoints. Critical geopolitical perspectives have rightly denounced such narratives, pointing to the vested interests involved, and built-in prejudices, calling for greater contextual sensitivity and nuance towards power relations between firms, communities, and authorities.

Econometric studies have striven for precision in the study of mechanisms linking resources and conflicts, and for methodological rigour within a mostly quantitative template, allowing for some more detailed comparative case studies. Yet the methodological approach taken by these studies has often limited the scope of their historical engagement, the form of violence studied, and the possible variables that could factor into the processes hypothesised. These studies have yielded major insights into the significance of resource dependence for conflict risks and patterns of conflicts relating to particular types of resources and modes of exploitation and regulation.

Finally, political ecology perspectives have emphasised contextualisation and multiscalar relations, pointing also to the specific material and social dimensions of resources. Through historically grounded studies of mostly individual case studies, political ecology has yielded nuanced analyses of power relations and insights into the material and social context of developing relationships between resources and wars. Certain resources have been found to increase vulnerability to certain types of conflict, and to affect the duration and severity of conflicts through shaping incentives and opportunities for belligerents. In this chapter, I have suggested that bridging and renewing conceptual and methodological approaches drawn from these three perspectives could yield yet further insights on so-called resource wars, and serve broad objectives of social and environmental justice. In the following chapters, I shall use the proposed analytical framework to examine specific resources frequently associated with armed conflicts, but first in Chapter 2, I outline the broader historical context of academic perspectives on resource wars.

2

MATERIAL MOTIVES

Although the term "resource wars" is relatively recent, resources have long attracted attention in the study of wars; accounts of resource plunder and destruction within war narratives date back to at least 3600 BCE. This chapter reviews accounts of resource wars from a historical perspective. Dominated by sociobiological and geopolitical explanations of struggles over resources, historical accounts of resource wars have often focused on simplistic material aspects of resources and failed to take their broader social dimensions into account. I argue that these approaches—which persist in popular interpretations of contemporary resource wars—posit an over-simplistic view of resource wars, in terms both of human nature (for example, soldiers motivated solely by greed) and of certain countries or regions as inherently and inevitably conflict-prone, because of either resource abundance or scarcity. While recognising the value of classic geopolitical perspectives, I point at the importance of critical geopolitical perspectives focusing on the influence of representations rather than simply the geographical "facts" on the ground.

Two often-intertwined explanations dominate historical accounts. The first explanation views resources as a motivational factor for war. Raiding, looting, pillaging, grabbing, capturing, annexing and conquering all carry a sense of violent dispossession and appropriation of resources. Such motivational dimensions can be mistaken for the consequences of social behavior during or after the conflict; state-led military annexation and house looting by individual soldiers are both forms of violent dispossession, but they differ in scale, intentionality, means and outcomes.

The second explanation is that some resources are crucial factors for warfare itself, thereby achieving a "strategic" status.[1] Resources that are strategic for warfare have long preoccupied military planners, including the anticipation of wars to obtain control over those resources. In the extreme, a war would be "preemptively" conducted to access resources necessary for warfare. Accessing such strategic resources and denying access to potential enemies have constituted one of the many "great games" of military strategists. But the strategic and security dimension of a resource needs to be considered in light of the corporate interests that can motivate, or at least benefit from, such association. For example, when US President Harry S. Truman approved the creation of a reserve of strategic raw materials in 1946, he suggested that corporate gain was trumping US national interests as the Buy American Act had prohibited the purchase of materials originating outside the US.[2]

In the next section, I explore how these two explanations—resources as loot and resources as a factor in military strategy—have provided the bedrock of the classic geopolitical accounts of resource wars, which dominate media, policy, and scholarly literature on resources and armed conflicts.

Resources and early warfare: Does resource availability matter?

Studies of resources and early warfare in pre-agricultural societies have largely focused on the role of material self-interest, the forms of conflict, and the organisation and the sedentarisation of social groups, as well as the relative availability, density, and predictability of resources.[3] Arguments from evolutionary ecology associate early warfare with the territorial control of abundant resources (mostly food) and uncertainty about resource access.[4] Much of the evidence is drawn from ethnographic studies of foraging or hunter-gatherer groups, with archeological evidence remaining relatively scarce.[5] Some studies also draw on comparative social ecology with other species, especially primates and cetaceans, where similar behavior—including intergroup aggression (warfare)—may relate in part to similarities in the variable spatial and temporal distribution of resources.[6]

The first general argument that may be drawn from this literature is that resource availability—relative abundance or scarcity—is a factor in conflicts. On the one hand, human groups appear to be less conflict-prone and more cooperative where resources are scarce and widely scattered (diffuse), rather than abundant but spatially concentrated (point). The relative nutritional value of resources, from this perspective, provides one of the bases of the stakes for competitive behavior (with, for example, grass ranking below fruits, roots and meat). Besides resources of nutritional value, resources are also prized as tools, as marks of status, and as objects of trade (such as flint, obsidian, shells). More broadly, while ecological theory "has been most concerned with how resource scarcity may generate war…subsistence orientations will have multiple consequences regarding the causes and practice of warfare."[7] And there will be variations in this respect among hunters, gatherers, horticulturalists and pastoralists.

Beyond increased warfare, this "dense abundance" relates to territorialisation, sedentarisation and social segmentation—three factors also associated with an intensification of early warfare.[8] This intensification can take place over space and time, with "dense abundance" being circumscribed in time (as through seasonal migrations, corridors of game or sparse but plentiful water points during dry season). These factors form the basis of the "economic defendability" hypothesis, according to which "territoriality is expected to occur when critical resources are sufficiently abundant and predictable in space and time, so that costs of exclusive use and defence of an area are outweighed by the benefits gained from resource control."[9]

According to this hypothesis, low population densities and resource scarcity would result in mutually beneficial cooperation, rather than conflict. Higher population densities and resource abundance result in territorialisation with "spontaneous conflicts over resources" occurring as a result of trespass or intrusion, often in border areas.[10] This latter type of conflict, in effect, responds to monopolistic appropriation of resource-rich areas, resulting in the avoidance of border areas. Whereas lethal violence reduces population density, this exclusion zone increases the density as no foraging from either side takes place there.[11] In short, conditions of scarcity within a general context of resource abundance, resulting in higher population density and social segmentation, would lead to more frequent and severe wars.[12]

Does the unpredictability of resource availability matter?

The second argument that can be drawn from studies of early warfare is that resource unpredictability, rather than scarcity or abundance per se, seems a factor in conflict. Specifically, unpredictability can increase both competitive and cooperative behavior, but evidence for pre-industrial societies is weighted on the side of higher conflict rates.[13] Among pre-state societies warfare would occur when scarcity was unpredictable; warfare did not address chronic and expected occurrences of scarcity.[14] Similarly, a study of warfare in Fiji since 1500 BCE suggests that "it was the richer—but less reliable—lower parts of the Sigatoka valley that were most fought over, leaving a patchwork of small defended claims, while the upper areas supported larger, co-operative land units."[15]

Yet some studies reach different conclusions. In the pre-Hispanic Philippines, for example, aggression was the main form of relation between coastal villages, in part because resources were predictable, dense, and easy to control. In contrast, alliance strategies prevailed between coastal and upland villages because resources were unpredictable, scarce, and hard to control.[16] More broadly, the transition to agriculture and the transformation in resources resulting from the relation of human groups with "nature" have often been understood as one of the main factors in the frequency of warfare.[17] In his study of early warfare, Raymond Kelly argues that

[p]aradoxically, it is not a paucity of resources that provides conditions favourable to the origination of war but rather reliability and abundance. It is under these latter circumstances that a society can afford to have enemies for neighbours. Prior to the development of agriculture, conditions compatible with the origination of warfare would be found only at particularly favourable locations within a few regional systems of unsegmented societies.[18]

Reviewing archaeological evidence of warfare, Jonathan Haas concurs, arguing that recorded instances of warfare sharply increase during the Neolithic, which he associates with sedentarisation, territoriality and a "concentration of resources."[19] Haas does note the negative impact of a fluctuating environment (pests and weather, for example) on the likelihood of warfare. His own research in the American Southwest and records from other regions suggest that warfare fits a pattern of "long waves" with extended periods (often several centuries) of relative peace or war. Warfare seems to be associated with the "initial transition from nomadic hunting and gathering to sedentary production (or intensified food procurement)."[20] Yet some critics have suggested the contrary: that the depletion of large game led gatherers to settle into agriculture and more peaceful relations,[21] and warfare only re-emerged later (with food surpluses, state formation, early forms of urbanisation and wealth accumulation, and a differentiated social order).

One tentative conclusion from this literature is that while abundance helped transform social groups demographically and organisationally (particularly through sedentarisation and segmentation), the ensuing resource dependence made them more conflict-prone in times of unpredicted scarcity. The unreliable abundance generated by agriculture (unreliable because of climate, disease or pests) and associated densification and segmentation of population fit this argument well. More generally, there is good evidence that prior to agriculture and state formation fights for resources often took place, especially in resource-rich locales, where competition could arise from population pressure and unexpected resource scarcity. Surplus generated by agriculture transformed warfare through the production of resource-rich locales, and the gradual evolution of social groups towards larger and more complex units. Thus, cooperation and competition for resources are not the outcome in any direct, deterministic way of either resource availability or predictability, which implies that we should reject simplistic views of environmental determinism that often characterise popular accounts of resource wars.

Resources, warfare, and state formation

As societies and warfare co-evolved, often around the availability, production, and control of agricultural resources, the emergence of states (political units encompassing populations larger than those defined by kinship and seeking to establish a monopoly of the legitimate use of violence) marked an important transition. Resource control was part and parcel of the process of segmentation, with leadership reinforced through consumption and redistribution of resources.[22] According to many scholars, resource abundance and dependence—resulting from agricultural innovation—formed part of the intensification and scaling-up of warfare associated with state formation.[23] Some even argue that states emerged out of the need to access resources for the purpose of warfare.[24] Even without active warfare, the accumulation of assets for warfare and (later on) for the maintenance of standing armies required access to resources. These state strategies, necessitating the control of labor power and trade routes—the basis of resource access—were themselves marked by violence.

An opposing view is that the importance of resources in early warfare gradually diminished in state-led societies as organisational and technological innovation removed limits on resources (through "substitution").[25] But as noted by Ferguson, "in chiefdoms and states, one's material interest depends more on position within the structure of society than on the general relationship of population to natural resources. Costs and benefits of war likewise depend on structural position... since the structure of inequality itself is key to prosperity for the elite, they will be vitally concerned with strengthening their position within that structure."[26] In other words, wars over resources may thus be motivated both by the goal of increasing resources for the group and by the goal of bettering one's position within the group itself. This can help explain in part the militarisation of states in relation to resources: successful military conquest of resources increases the size and importance of states, and the status of the military within them.

Whereas food was the main resource associated with wars, metals became a central preoccupation of emerging states, particularly copper, tin, silver and gold.[27] Metals had long been part of symbolic resources, but the rise of metal use, especially that of bronze (copper and tin alloy), starting around 3,000 BCE led to multiple social transformations, including transformations affecting warfare—not only through more deadly weapons but also through extended trade and warring expeditions.

According to many ancient writers of classical Greece, wars were fought for material gains, with wealth itself attracting military attacks.[28] Access to metal mines and markets were driving factors of imperialism, especially in Mesopotamia and Egypt, which lacked copper.[29] The shift to bronze weapons in the Early Dynastic period of Egypt, after 3100 BCE, led to military ventures in Sinai and Nubia to control sources of copper.[30] Some of the earliest documented centrally-ruled empires, such as that of the Akkadians around 2350 BCE, relied in part on bronze to equip their army, with metals being a prime target and booty of invasions. Athens funded its first navy in 483 BCE out of revenue from the nearby Laurion silver mines.[31] Macedonians found in the long disputed silver and gold mines near Amphipolis wealth they could use to finance further military campaigns. Silver and copper mines in southern Spain were an important dimension of the Punic Wars opposing Carthage and Rome between 264 and 146 BCE, with mining output financing military campaigns, paying war indemnities, and enriching military commanders.[32]

Beyond plundering stocks of metal, mining was actively pursued through state ventures and leases to private companies.[33] Military units were frequently stationed in important mining areas, as mining was vulnerable to both raiding by external armed groups and revolts by the labor force. The scale of mining declined after the fall of the Roman Empire, although some sources suggest that mining production peaked around 79 BCE and contributed to the fall of the empire through coin debasement, inflation and overtaxation.[34] The progressive demise of the Roman Empire saw a general decline in the scale of mining until the Renaissance, but metals were not representative of the scale of resource extraction in general; the mediaeval period between 900 and 1300 was characterised by high population growth, large-scale deforestation, and greater commerce.[35]

To summarise, for early empires, although wealth mostly consisted of land and slaves, it also included minerals. Metals, in particular, were necessary for military campaigns as both a source of finance and as raw materials for weaponry. Silver, gold, copper, tin and (to a lesser degree) more widely available iron played an important role in the military strategies and capacities of early empires.[36] The decision to go to war, and the nature of warfare tactics, are partly explained by the quest for metals. Fortifications were sometimes built to protect metal extraction and metal working areas, as well as trading routes, against fighting expeditions.[37]

Yet whereas most accounts of mineral resources focus on military conquest and centralised control of mines, these were not the only or even the main strategies. Plundering a mining area generates limited benefits as stocks are often low. Controlling a mining area without having the technical skills and labor force to exploit it is also useless. Securing resource access through alliances with local mining groups, however, could yield more benefits than conquest,[38] with the state focusing on the "efficient funelling of partially worked raw materials to the center, where finishing occurred," especially through the control of transport routes.[39] Intensive resource exploitation also took place outside elite monopolies, with control and access reflecting cultural mechanisms within relatively autonomous mining communities, able to restrict access and deploy mining and valuation skills. We should not hold a romantic view of mining "communities," however. Slaves, war prisoners, and convicts provided most of the labor during the classical period—mining being considered among the most arduous and dangerous of jobs.[40]

Competing views thus exist in literature regarding the relationship between state formation, resources and conflicts. They evoke some important hypotheses that will be explored in subsequent chapters. First, state governance can be shaped in important ways by the availability of, and dependence upon, resources and the revenues that they generate. Second, resources can play an important role in military strategy: both as target and as tactic in warfare. Of course, as we shall discover, the specificities of these relationships depend a great deal on historical and geographical context.

Resources, conflicts, and the rise of the West

In common with the classical period, contemporary Western geopolitical perspectives about resources have been dominated by the equation of trade, war and power.[41] Overseas resources and maritime navigation were at the core of this equation, with resources providing some of the means and motives of early European power expansion as a focus of inter-state rivalry and strategic denial of access.[42] Trade and war became intimately linked during the mercantilist period of the fifteenth century, as progress in maritime transport enabled the accumulation of "world riches," mostly in the form of bullion, upon which power was perceived to be determined.[43] Tropical slave-produced commodities were at the core of Western imperial extension,[44] with duties on sugar, tobacco, cocoa, cotton, coffee and opium providing "modernising" states with the finances to open new markets through warfare.[45] Since sea power itself rested on access to timber, naval timber supply became a critical preoccupation for major European powers from the seventeenth century onwards[46]—a situation comparable to the case of oil in the twentieth century. Given the strategic role of resources, concerns for resource scarcity and war received considerable attention from contemporary scholars. Malthus, for example, viewed war as a positive check against the limits of agricultural resources by raising the death rate ("vices of mankind and able ministers of depopulation"), usefully staving off (rather than resulting from) food scarcity.[47]

With growing industrialisation and increasing dependence on imported materials during the nineteenth century, Western powers intensified their control over raw materials, leading (along with many other factors such as political ideologies) to an imperialist "scramble for resources" both within Europe, and in much of the rest of the world.[48] Critiques of capitalism linked its rise and diffusion to imperialism and militarism, tying together the expansion of violent forms of "primitive accumulation" focused on raw materials (including labor in the form of slavery)[49] with the opening up of markets for commodities.[50]

The significance of resources in industrialisation and militarisation—especially coal, iron, and later oil—reinforced the idea of resource competition among European powers. It was the focus of much commentary, with respect to the geopolitical resource dimensions of the First and Second World Wars, and concerns over access to raw material distribution and inter-state conflicts, and resulted in a flurry of studies in the period between the two World Wars.[51] The geographical closure of imperialist territorial expansion, including the punitive seizure of German colonies after the First World War, augured a new era of economic intensification[52] but also renewed vindictive claims among industrialised powers without colonies, chiefly Germany, Italy and Japan.[53] Initiated through a series of meetings under the auspices of the League of Nations,[54] debates opposed the "haves versus have-nots" in the "raw materials race" that contributed to the preparation, onset and conduct of the Second World War.[55] While the "have-nots" (Germany, Italy and Japan) sought to achieve resource access through territorial redistribution, the "haves" (the United Kingdom, France, and the US) stressed the limits of raw material advantages derived from the colonies, the risks associated with territorial redistribution, and the positive impacts of free trade and of moving away from nationalistic views of the economy.[56]

Geopolitical perspectives informed by resource concerns were at work in both World Wars, whether in British and German efforts to own or control oil sources in Mesopotamia and Persia as they converted their navies from coal to oil in the 1910s,[57] in Hitler's failed Fall Blau military campaign in 1942 to capture and later to destroy oil fields in the Caucasus,[58] or in Japan's preemptive strike on Pearl Harbor in the face of an oil embargo by the US and its conquest of South East Asia to secure access to natural resources, including oil from the Dutch East Indies.[59] Less well-known examples include the destruction of British-controlled oil installations in Egypt by an Austro-Hungarian commando in 1915, the first oil-related military operation on the African continent,[60] or Japan's invasion of British Malaya in 1941 and capture of the world's largest rubber plantations, a strategic sector from which Japanese firms had been partly excluded during the First World War as Britain prohibited new rubber land acquisitions by foreign interests.[61]

Following the Second World War, international studies of resources and wars focused on resource supply geopolitics, the building up of stocks of critical materials, and foreign investment policies.[62] The growing assertiveness of Third World states during this period of rising independence transformed the political landscape of sovereignty over natural resources, for example through the nationalisation of resource sectors and the use of "resource weapons" (the political and economic leveraging of resource dependence among importing countries).[63] Resources also constituted the foundation for a more peaceful Europe through the 1951 Treaty of Paris, which established the European Coal and Steel Community. This treaty sought to turn these two sectors from a source of contention between France and Germany into one of cooperation.

Strategic thinking about resources during the Cold War continued to focus on the vulnerability arising from resource supply dependence and the potential for international conflicts resulting from competition over access to key resources.[64] Emphasis was placed on concepts of "resource security" (through strategic reserves and alliances with producing countries) and a military "balance of power" between the US and Soviet blocs. The decolonisation process, the 1956 Suez crisis, the 1973 Arab oil embargo, the 1979 Iranian revolution and subsequent Iraqi military invasions of Iran and Kuwait also increased Western strategic concerns (among states and businesses) over domestic and regional political stability and alliances,[65] as well as the threats presented by the more assertive countries in the Third World.[66] Areas identified as prone to armed conflicts, owing to both domestic and international factors, included those where external power involvement was likely due to economic resources.[67] Beyond the Cold War, such "resource supply" security continues to inform governmental and corporate decisions in the management of several minerals, particularly concerning high-tech minerals such as rare earths—now under the quasi-monopoly of China—and radioactive materials, with oil standing in its own category for its global strategic importance.[68]

By the 1960s, broader geopolitical conceptualisations of security had begun to incorporate issues such as population growth, environmental degradation, and social inequalities in poor countries.[69] The concept of "environmental security" was coined to reflect emerging ideas of global interdependence, illustrated through debates on global warming, environmental "limits to growth," and political instability caused by environmental scarcity in the South.[70] The concept has been criticised as representing a skewed and controversial "securitisation" of environmental issues, unfairly casting blame on the poor, uncritically legitimising support for military solutions, and constructing biased identities and narratives of endangerment.[71]

From this analysis we can surmise that, until the middle of the twentieth century, resources were still defined as they were in early historical periods: as loot or as military strategy. But by the end of the twentieth century, another view had become important: resources as part of the "global environment," comprising a potential threat not only to economic growth and political stability, but also to human survival. The resulting "securitisation" of environmental concerns within discourses of warfare resulted in concepts such as "green wars" (wars caused by worsening environmental conditions) and "environmental refugees."[72] In the next section, I investigate how the concepts of "environmental security" play an important role in contemporary debates over resource wars.

Resources in the post-Cold War era

With the end of the Cold War came greater attention to the internal mechanisms of war as the end of superpower clientelist politics and support for belligerents (often via "proxy wars") changed the conditions for armed conflict worldwide. A view emerged that violent scrambles for resources amongst local warlords, regional powers, and international actors were a major feature of contemporary conflicts, particularly given the "declining" role of ideology in regional or local conflicts.[73] Resource war narratives at first mostly interpreted conflicts in several African countries during the 1990s as "diamond wars," while by the early 2000s other narratives became concerned about international tensions over key resources, with the US-led invasion of Iraq putting the concept of resource war at the forefront of global anti-war activism.[74]

Like the Cold War, the US-led "War on Terror" at times rearticulated security threats and military strategies with corporate interests. In this case such rearticulation was aimed at regimes opposing the US, which were also reluctant to open their resources to Western or at least US companies, most prominently Iraq. As in the Cold War era, interventions have been framed around conflated concepts of freedom and security. Debates on oil and the American security agenda have significantly shifted as a result of the 9/11 attacks in the US. On one side, those opposing US military interventionism have argued that the "War on Terror" provided one more convenient cover for a renewed "imperialist oil grab" in the region; on the other, links between oil and terrorism pointed to problems of authoritarian (and warmongering) governance in several oil producing countries.[75] As the Bush administration reframed the "War on Terror" unleashed on Iraq as a war of liberation against select oil-funded dictatorial regimes, the US portrayed its Middle-East foreign policy as broadening from securing the free flow of oil out of the Persian Gulf, to promoting democracy in the region, as discussed in Chapter 3.[76]

Most accounts of future resource wars are associated with a combination of fast increasing demand for raw materials, growing resource shortages, and contested resource ownership.[77] From this perspective, increasing demand for raw materials is mostly associated with the rapid growth of emerging economies since the late 1990s, especially China but also India.[78] By the mid-2000s China accounted for nearly all the demand growth in non-fuel minerals, and about a third of the demand growth for oil.[79] Yet if most narratives stress the rapid industrialisation and rise of consumerism in China as driving demand, part of these resources are redirected at the rest of the world in the form of exported manufactured goods, thereby pointing at broader responsibilities for resource consumption.[80]

Growing resource shortages, in turn, result not only from demand growth, but from the depletion of many non-renewable resources. Peak oil output takes center stage here, even if other resources such as uranium or indium are also of concern.[81] Conventional oil production may have peaked in 2006, and oil supply growth will require tapping into unconventional oil, with low return on energy invested, and a higher carbon footprint.[82] Global oil demand estimates have been constantly revised downward since 2000, with a current scenario of about 100 million barrels per day by 2030, while many analysts expect a production plateau around 90 million barrels.[83] These downward estimates reflect in part previously unexpected price rises (in 2000, for example, the US Energy Information Agency had an "high oil price case" scenario of US$28 per barrel by 2020). More broadly they reflect widely recognised supply constraints linked to insufficient production capacity and uncertainties about physical reserves, given the lack of transparency among key producers, such as Saudi Arabia. The stakes are obvious in terms of energy supply security and affordability, if only for defence purposes (for example, a US$10 change in the price of a barrel of oil translates into a difference of US$1.3 billion for the Pentagon's budget).[84] Yet whether shortages and high prices depend on production restraints or physical constraints is important. Production constraints should lessen geopolitical tensions as companies and countries collaborate by pooling investments and expertise (noting that some actors in the oil sector rely on high prices rather than large volumes to increase revenues, and thus may contribute to tensions limiting supply). If physical constraints matter more, then there is simply not enough oil in the ground to go around, and geopolitical tensions will likely be exacerbated as countries and companies vie for the remaining reserves. Besides fuel and mineral shortages, climate change is also brought into the equation of future resource wars. Slow changes such as average temperatures can aggravate shortages of water and renewable resources such as food, while shortages in combination with extreme climatic events can act as a "threat multiplier" through its effects on migration and institutional breakdown.[85]

Finally, narratives of competitive resource control and contested resource ownership pit China against the US. Both countries, from such a perspective, are seen as deploying aggressive "resource diplomacy" supporting (or toppling) dictatorships, and bolstering their military capacities and international bases. Oil, again, has taken center stage with geopolitical accounts focusing on the Persian Gulf and Iraq's oil field dispute with Kuwait, the subsequent military invasion, and the US-led interventions.[86] Beyond the case of Iraq, the February 2011 uprising in Libya and ensuing NATO military intervention were portrayed by a few commentators as a geopolitical tug of war between Western and Chinese interests over the largest oil reserves in Africa.[87] Some US media interpreted the evacuation of 36,000 Chinese workers from Libya as signifying the vulnerability of China's supposed "non-interventionist" policy in "energy-rich pariah states."[88] Iran is now the US's chief target.

Besides the effect on relations with the US, the Chinese "global quest for energy" is also portrayed as a source of tensions with Japan, India, Southeast Asian countries, and possibly Russia.[89] One example of resource geopolitics bringing different sources of tension was the apparent instrumentation of China's near-monopoly on "rare earths" supplies to pressure Japan to release a Chinese fisherman, who was arrested after colliding with two Japanese patrol vessels in the waters of the disputed and potentially oil-rich Senkaku/Diaoku islands.[90] Among other prominently disputed areas are the Caspian region and Arctic Ocean. The Caspian Sea basin and Central Asia areas are depicted as the "cockpit for a twenty-first century energy version of the imperial "Great Game" of the nineteenth century": a cockpit in which the "dangerous vortex of competitive pressures" from US, Russian, Indian, and Chinese interests would play out through military bases, massive pipeline investments, and support for local autocrats.[91] The Arctic seabed, with an estimate 80 billion barrels of oil and vast gas resources, is another such area of potential conflict.[92] The planting of a flag under 4,000 meters of water by a Russian submarine at the North Pole—on the 1,800 km long Lomonosov ridge contested by Russia, Denmark, and Canada—was interpreted in this light as aggressive diplomatic posturing.[93] Besides these internationally contentious oil and gas areas, there is a vast array of domestic conflicts over resource ownership that fuel geopolitical concerns, as discussed in the following chapters.[94]

Conclusion

Historical accounts of resource wars have tended to be narrowly focused on material motivations and contributions to warfare. Classic geopolitical perspectives, in this regard, have sought to provide a "big picture" of current and future international tensions over "strategic" resources. These perspectives are important, because thinking ahead to the security implications of the "end of oil" scenario must be considered a priority. This is not only to avert international crises over oil, but also to ensure a transition away from oil that minimises environmental and social costs, including climate change and a deepening of poverty and income inequalities. If geopolitical perspectives on resource wars have tended to focus on oil, other resources are also of concern, such as rare minerals, farmlands and fisheries.

Geopolitical perspectives, however, suffer from several shortcomings. First, resources are not simply "materials" motivating or enabling the use of military force. Wars relating to resources are not only about obtaining or denying "materials." While the physical materiality of resources and their technical and economic functions need to be acknowledged, resources are also social processes embedding values, desires, and needs.[95] Geopolitical perspectives themselves contribute to how resources are represented, understood, and acted upon.

Second, classic geopolitical perspectives on resource wars inform and reflect dominant geostrategic policies and worldviews. As such, they bring about Manichaean constructs of places and identities, as well as biased conceptions of security. A focus on resources through a security lens not only leads to tunnel vision, blind to many other dimensions of conflicts, it also drastically reduces the type of understandings and relationships necessary to foster a broad peace. In other words, there is, for example, more to the Persian Gulf than oil. Resource sectors do influence the (un) making of places, political systems and social movements involved in conflicts. But understanding this influence solely through a classic resource war perspective narrows the range of explanations to "competitive struggles" for oil.

Third, the mere presence of resources should not be simply understood for the current or future stakes that they represent. From a classic resource wars perspective, some resource-exporting countries may seem intrinsically "unstable" and in need of foreign military intervention to preserve "vital" resource flows. Such justification is often provided without any reference to the historical role of resource sectors contributing to such instability. Oil's significance in contemporary conflicts in Iraq, for example, should be situated within the historical context of coercive British colonialism in the early twentieth century.[96] More generally, conflicts over resources are often played in a "repeated game" in which the histories of past conflicts inform present ones. Where the Western press portrays a maverick Saddam Hussein firing a rifle during official ceremonies, the Iraqi public recognises the symbolism of a President grasping historical legitimacy by firing a British rifle captured during the 1920–21 revolt against British rule. Hostilities do not occur in a vacuum, but build on collective memories and experiences of previous conflicts. Examining patterns of farmer-herder conflicts in the Sahel, geographer Matthew Turner points out that

the land-use conflict engaged in by herders differs significantly from the here-and-now conflict over scarce resources invoked by standard uses of the term "resource conflict." These are conflicts that are waged over the long term with the conflict's history being invoked and reworked to make moral claims in the present.[97]

Studies of so-called resource wars thus benefit from "thick" historical and geographical contextualisation, relating the past to the present, as well as resource locales to places of belonging and spaces of social relations. From this perspective, narratives of future conflicts over "increasingly scarce resources" and anthropogenic environmental change need to be considered in the light of particular geographies of vulnerability, threat and insecurity.[98] To conclude, geopolitical understandings of resources and wars have much to offer. Classic geopolitics can help identify major geographical factors and long-term historical patterns, while critical geopolitics helps identify representations influencing international relations over resource sectors. Yet the "realist" assessments and prognoses of classic geopolitics rest on narrow concepts of material scarcities and confrontational politics. Such narrow concepts risk raising unnecessary fears, exacerbating antagonisms, and contributing to hostilities rather than cooperation. In the following three chapters, I turn to specific resource sectors, namely oil, diamonds and timber.

3

OIL

From transport to food and plastics, oil is integrated into nearly every aspect of daily life. The world's largest internationally traded commodity and an essential component of modern economies and military supremacy, oil is associated with spectacular booms and busts, and with both extreme wealth and abject poverty.[1] Over the past few years, oil production has generated the largest corporate profits in history, and has faced some of the fiercest critiques faced by any industrial sector. Oil is a resource of contrasts and superlatives.

Oil is also one of the resources most commonly associated with armed conflict. Oil became more strategic than perhaps any other commodity during the twentieth century, and military dimensions are a factor in the geopolitics of oil. Arms transfers, military interventions, and overseas military bases in oil-producing regions have all been used by major powers over the past century.[2] Oil security considerations also extend to oil transport routes, motivating the control of maritime transport and pipeline routes, and contributing to a logic of militarised "imperialism"—the best examples being the history of the Suez Canal and, more recently, maritime transit through the Strait of Hormuz.[3] Oil has also been a feature of several international and regional conflicts, including territorial disputes over oil-rich areas, as well as a vast array of domestic conflicts.

Whereas the number of conflicts declined overall after the Cold War, it actually grew among oil producing countries.[4] In 1992, one in five countries at war was an oil producer; by 2006 this proportion was one in three.[5]

Conflicts making headlines between 2008 and 2011 have included many oil producing regions, such as Nigeria's oil production areas, Iraq's continued strife, violent unrest and repression occurring in the oil-rich Chinese Autonomous Region of Xingjian, Colombia's paramilitaries operating a resurgence in oil areas, Sudan and Chad—two recent oil producers—exchanging blows through proxy militias, and Gaddafi loyalists fighting with rebels for control of key oil infrastructure in Libya.[6]

A growing number of studies have argued that oil increases the risk of conflict. One set of arguments focuses on the fact that oil is "scarce," and oil reserves are highly concentrated; fewer than 30 countries are net exporters, and a handful of countries hold the vast majority of known conventional oil reserves. According to this argument, oil's strategic importance makes it a valuable "prize" over which importing states engage in intensely fought geopolitical struggles. This type of "oil wars" narrative tends to be most visible (at least within mainstream media sources) during major oil crises, typically marked by high prices, and thus amenable to scarcity-focused explanations. But in this chapter I argue that we must treat the scarcity argument with caution, although the geopolitical dimensions of the quest to control oil reserves must also be taken into account.

Another (more convincing) set of arguments pertains to oil production's uneven distribution of profits (and impacts). Controlled by states, dominated by large companies and employing relatively few people, oil production is often characterised by a highly skewed distribution of financial, social, and environmental costs and benefits. A capital-intensive sector with long-term horizons, oil pins down companies in specific locations, but it also facilitates a high degree of concentration. This has produced some of the largest corporate profits in history, and a high degree of political influence. At the same time, oil has enabled assertive governments to collect massive tax revenue and bring about extremely large wealth transfers between the North and selected countries in the South. Yet this argument also requires careful scrutiny, as critics have rightly pointed to many so-called petro-states' regime stability to argue that oil wealth can "buy peace." Equally, the question of profits merits careful study; for example, although oil imports represent a major financial burden for most countries, high taxes on oil consumption have nevertheless allowed some importing states to obtain even more revenue from oil flows than have been amassed by oil-exporting countries.

Building on the conceptual framework presented earlier, this chapter explores the three main hypotheses linking oil and armed conflict: (1) oil dependence creates vulnerabilities to armed conflict; (2) oil stakes and impacts create motivation for conflict; and (3) the accessibility of oil revenue creates opportunities for belligerents to scale up, sustain, or "criminalise" hostilities. I must stress from the onset that conflicts cannot be solely explained by oil, whether because of its supposed scarcity, high profitability, or socio-environmental impacts.

I first briefly review in this chapter the evidence for "oil wars," and then examine the characteristics of oil sectors, oil states, and oil-related conflicts before turning to the applicability of the vulnerability, risk and opportunity arguments for the oil sector. In turn, this discussion will shed light on the crucial question of why armed conflicts take place in some oil-producing countries and not in others. One of my major points in exploring this range of conflicts is that conceptual framings of oil wars, as driven solely or primarily by scarcity or greed, are overly simplistic. Rather, I argue that oil-related conflicts reflect the interplay of institutional setting with oil abundance, dependence and location of oil fields. In turn, these criteria influence the degree to which oil-related vulnerability, risk and opportunity shape the likelihood and course of armed conflicts.

Oil and wars

Oil figures in a wide diversity of conflicts, in a broad variety of contexts with a range of scales and degrees of organised violence. Four main types of conflict are generally recognised: (1) geopolitical struggles over oil sources (such as the 2003 US-led invasion of Iraq and US-China rivalry); (2) oil-funded political violence or "terrorism" by so-called rogue states (such as Libya and Iran); (3) territorial disputes over oil areas (for example over the Bakassi peninsula between Nigeria and Cameroon, or over the Ogaden region between Ethiopia and Somalia); and (4) the international dimensions of communal protests, insurgencies, and "criminality" affecting oil production and transport (as in Nigeria or Colombia). Some oil-related conflicts have also been among the most deadly since the Second World War, with about a million people dying in Biafra, the Southern Sudan, and during the Iran-Iraq war.[7] But in each case the context varied. Most deaths during the 1980–88 Iran-Iraq war were combat-related, reflecting the military might of oil-rich states long embroiled in the high stakes Persian Gulf geopolitics of oil. Most victims of the 1967–70 Biafra war and the 1983–2005 conflicts in Southern Sudan died as a result of forced displacement, hunger and diseases occurring in the midst of military repression. The Biafra war took place in Nigeria only about a decade after rising oil production, which exacerbated secessionism in an area already marginalised by its demographic minority status and lack of control over the military. Conflicts in Southern Sudan took place shortly after commercial oil discoveries as the autonomous Southern region came under threat of dispossession by the central Sudanese government, but before any actual production.

Western analysts do not have the exclusivity of mainstream geopolitical narratives. Similar accounts come from analysts in China and India, so that shared political imagination of a "scramble" holds practical consequences for the character of policy, however wrongheaded.[8] Of specific concern to China is its competition with Japan over East Asian oil reserves, and with Europe over Russian oil and gas resources.[9] Accounts from India focus more on gas, including competitive struggles over the Iran-Pakistan-India gas pipeline.[10] As in the case of Western energy policies, geopolitics do not have a stranglehold on official policy. Chinese energy specialists point out that while energy bears on both "economic and national security," China pursues a "new energy development approach with Chinese characteristics" resting not on geopolitical struggle, but on "energy-saving, high-efficiency, diversified development, environment protection, technology guidance and international cooperation."[11]

Several critical studies have pointed to the biases and limitations of a purely geopolitical perspective, which pits an "aggressive" China against the West.[12] Historically, this perspective is blind to the practices of Western companies, which, for example, adopted dubious approaches to securing oil deals in Africa (including corruption and the propping up of dictators). In this regard, the "Chinese" threat seems to push Western companies to promote *global* ethical practices in the oil sector that would ensure a level playing field and address concerns over trade competition.[13] In terms of oil production, at least on a project level, technical complementarities (and not solely outright competition) and collaboration are evident, at least for the moment.[14] In terms of global production, Chinese growth increases demand for oil, but Chinese investments in the oil sector also help put more oil on the market. The geopolitical struggle for oil is thus, in short, more complex than a zero-sum game for pieces of a scarce and ever-shrinking pie.

In Ecuador, by contrast, peasants and indigenous people speak of "slow death" from petroleum.[15] There, the forms of violence are more insidious than death in the midst of war. They consist of social, environmental and epidemiological ills, such as cancer, reported to be associated with oil exploration and production in the midst of Amazonian wetlands.[16] This "intrapersonal" violence, brought by one's own "polluted" body cells, contrasts with the intra-state and inter-state violence that is the focus of most academic studies. This type of violence is made visible by public protests, as well as prosecutions of oil companies and the Ecuadorian government.[17] More frequently, it is only visible to family and community members.

These examples suggest that oil-related violence is best understood as an umbrella term for a range of conflicts: colonial wars to gain control of oil regions; military campaigns to seize or destroy oil assets during broader conflicts; wars of independence taking place in a context of recent oil discoveries and production; foreign military invasions and territorial conflicts between regional oil producers; intra-state conflicts over national government or secessionism within oil rich regions; violent racketeering and oil trafficking; government and vigilante groups repression; communal conflicts; and the sorts of victimisation and criminalisation-related violence associated with oil production. While the bulk of conflicts took place in the Persian Gulf and Gulf of Guinea regions, no continent has been spared from oil-related violence.

With these caveats in mind, how widespread have oil wars been? An estimated 166 armed conflicts took place between 1945 and 2006 in countries where oil had been discovered, 60 percent of these overlapping with oil-producing areas (see Figure 3.1 and Figure 3.2).[18] The discovery or production of oil does not mean that all these conflicts were about oil, or that a statistical association can provide the right explanation.[19] Indeed, only one in four of the 166 armed conflicts seem plausibly related to oil (see Figure 3.1).[20] The majority of these forty cases were conflicts over territory (60 percent), rather than over the control of government. Most of these forty cases were "internal" conflicts (75 percent), yet half were "internationalised," for example through external military assistance. Moreover, these figures do not account for all forms of conflicts involving physical violence. A great deal of violence associated with oil exploration and production is expressed via cycles of repression, victimisation, and criminalisation that involve diffuse physical violence and do not fit the most commonly used definition of armed conflict (twenty-five battle deaths per year with government involvement).[21]

Are oil wars distinct, in any way, from armed conflicts more generally? The literature suggests that armed conflicts in oil countries have generally been less severe and shorter than elsewhere. Oil wealth is associated with so-called minor, or low-intensity, armed conflicts with between twenty-five and one thousand annual battle-related deaths, but not for "major" or "high-intensity" conflicts.[22] As already noted, there are exceptions, and conflicts are more severe and last longer (for fights over central government) when they take place in oil areas, while conflict in oil-producing countries occurring outside oil areas tends to be shorter and less severe than those in non-oil-producing countries.[23] Oil-producing status also generally favours government victory as a conflict outcome, although independence struggles and many coups d'état have been successful, and a few secessionist struggles have achieved at least a greater degree of autonomy.

Where do oil wars tend to occur?

Conflicts most closely associated with oil include the 1990 Iraqi invasion of Kuwait and the subsequent 1991 Gulf War, the 1967–70 Biafra secessionist war, recent Niger Delta insurrections, and the Cabinda secessionist struggle in Angola. Even if these conflicts support some of the three main arguments put forward in this book (vulnerability, risk and opportunity), oil cannot be singled out as the sole cause of hostilities. In reality, several characteristics of countries, conflicts, and oil influence the patterns of armed conflicts. In the next section, I discuss each of these characteristics in turn before assessing the three main factors: vulnerability, risk, and opportunity.

Arguments and evidence

Several characteristics of oil seem to influence armed conflicts. The first is the economic importance of oil within a national economy, which can be measured in terms of dependence or abundance. Most studies have found that oil dependence and abundance increase the risk of conflict,[25]

Figure 3.1: Location of oil fields and oil countries at war 1946-2006.

but very high oil revenue on a per capita basis seems to offset the risks associated with oil dependence.[26]

The second characteristic is oil location. Onshore oil production increases conflict risk, while offshore does not.[27] Overlapping oil and conflict areas are associated with longer governmental conflicts (over central government) but not with territorial (secessionist) ones.[28] The third is price levels and trends. Rising prices in high-rent and low-employment resource sectors such as oil can increase the likelihood and duration of conflicts, in contrast to low-rent and high-employment sectors such as cash crops, a proposition confirmed for the oil and coffee sectors in Colombia.[29] Yet oil booms do not negatively affect the durability of oil regimes, while negative economic growth shocks do increase the likelihood of conflict, oil-producing countries included.[30] During the 1960–2006 period, negative price shocks were statistically associated with separatist conflicts and positive ones only with governmental conflicts.[31] The fourth dimension is ownership structure, where majority state ownership in mineral and oil sectors is associated with a worse "resource curse" effect than sectors with less state involvement (and thereby a possibly higher risk of conflict), although this link has not been specifically tested.[32]

Overall, there is cross-national statistical evidence that oil can increase the onset, duration, and deadliness of armed conflicts. This effect depends,

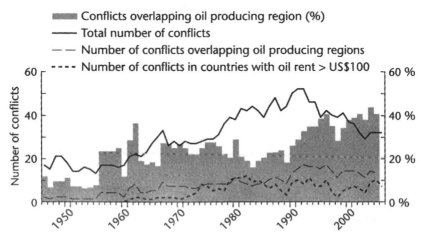

Figure 3.2: Number and ratio of oil countries at war 1946–2006.

however, on a set of conditions that include the characteristics of countries, conflicts, and oil sectors. To put it simply, populations in oil-rich states relying on offshore exploitation are less likely to be affected by armed conflicts than those of oil-dependent states with low oil revenues per capita derived from onshore exploitation.

In the next sections I examine, in turn, the three main factors potentially linking oil and armed conflicts—vulnerability, risk, and opportunity—that relate to the three main arguments central to this book. The oil curse argument suggests that oil dependence negatively affects the quality of institutions and results in economic shocks and long-term underperformance, thereby increasing vulnerability. The oil conflict argument posits that oil exploration, exploitation and consumption increase various forms of violence, ranging from disputes over national oil policies and rent allocation, as well as social and environmental impacts, to international hostilities over oil access and control; simply put, abundance creates the risk of conflict. Finally, according to the conflict oil argument, oil shapes the tactics, opportunities and behavior of belligerents by financing their activities and influencing their relations with local populations and external actors; oil, from this perspective, presents a series of opportunities for belligerents to engage in and sustain conflicts.[33]

The oil curse: Between abundance and dependence

Why do conflicts take place in some oil-producing countries and not in others? A first argument is that conflicts do not take place because of oil itself, but because of the institutional and economic context created by oil in some countries but not in others. There is a relatively solid consensus in the academic literature that poor quality state institutions—"state weakness" or "state failure"—increase the risk of conflict onset.

A number of arguments might be made about causal factors for "state weakness." The oil curse argument suggests that oil dependence negatively affects the quality of institutions and results in economic shocks and long-term underperformance.[34] In turn, this creates greater vulnerability to conflict. For example, a "weak state" would be less able to foresee and address potential sources of conflicts, and it would also constitute an easier target for armed rebellion or foreign intervention, in terms of both military action and political justification. Much of the evidence supports this hypothesis about the deleterious effects of oil on institutions,

Figure 3.3: Oil dependence, abundance and location (2000–8).

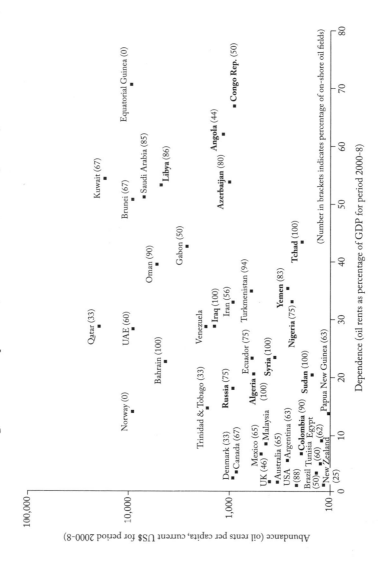

Source: World Bank and Uppsala conflict dataset.

but there remains some debate, including debate about the relative weakness of petro-states and the institutional effects on the likelihood of conflict. Here, we need to address two critical questions. First, are petro-states in fact characterised by weak institutions? And second, does state weakness necessarily lead to conflict?

In response to the first question, there is good evidence that oil dependence results in strong economic shocks and has resulted in poorer economic performance on the part of oil-dependent states, especially during the 1980s and 1990s.[35] Economic shocks result from rapid and massive price, production and contractual variations. Although the sector includes one of the last surviving commodity price regulation mechanisms—the Organisation of Petroleum Exporting Countries (OPEC)—the price of oil remains highly volatile. Terms of trade have recently followed an upward trend but with some sharp downward and extended low-price periods, such as the mid-1980s and during the 1990s.

We can also view the question of "weakness" through the eyes of investors: a survey of investors on the risks of expropriation and government contract repudiation has suggested that oil exporters are indeed weaker states in terms of per capita income.[36] Another argument, which favours the "vulnerability" hypothesis, is that past oil production is more strongly related to higher conflict onset risk than the mere presence of oil reserves (which should motivate "greedy rebels" and thus favour the "opportunity" hypothesis I discuss later).[37]

Nonetheless, these findings require qualification. For example, there is little support for the "weak state" hypothesis based on comparing conflict onset risk associated with onshore and offshore variables. If the institutional weakness of states were the main mechanism for conflict onset, then the location of production should not matter, as institutional weakness is supposed to come mostly from revenue effects. Yet both onshore production and fuel rents are associated with a higher risk than offshore rent.[38]

In summary, although many studies have suggested state weakness as a potential cause of oil-related conflicts, their interpretation remains open to debate. The question of state weakness is perhaps best approached historically. The 1970s, with much greater oil fiscal earnings from nationalisations, contract renegotiations and booming oil prices, marked a transition point; for after this point, windfalls brought greater financial strength yet new forms of weakness too, as fast-growing, overstretched and often fledging bureaucracies faced new or increased expectations from the population and ruling elites. Further, with the collapse of oil prices in the early 1980s states became doubly weakened. Financially, petro-states faced massive indebtedness—a debt "overhang" that resulted in part from the over-optimism and fast growth of the boom period.[39] Bureaucratically, petro-states faced new challenges of underfunding and accompanying structural adjustments. Debt, low prices, and a neoliberal agenda of privatisation further moved the balance of power in favour of foreign investors and new "civil society" organisations. This historical pattern does not apply to all oil producers, but its initial phases of oil windfall occurring in the midst of poor countries with low absorptive capacity are applicable to many new oil producers.[40]

The second key question is whether state weakness necessarily leads to conflict. There is strong evidence that negative economic shocks increase the risk of conflict onset.[41] Positive shocks may also increase conflict risk—with, for example, rising prices in high-rent and low-employment resource sectors such as oil increasing the likelihood and duration of conflicts, contrary to low-rent and high-employment sectors such as cash crops.[42] Some of these divergent effects may be explained by the capacity of the state to buffer shocks and maximise oil windfalls through broad economic growth. As explained earlier, the concentration of oil rents, little direct employment, and economic linkages make this a challenge for oil. Disproportionate effects on populations in production areas and the lowering of state capacity, as well as a pattern of authoritarian governments falling during economic crises, may thereby explain the greater frequency of separatist conflicts during negative oil shocks.[43] Higher fuel rents increase the risk of conflict onset, yet this higher risk is offset if fuel rents are translated into economic growth representing about double the value of the rent (a so-called positive multiplier effect).[44]

In summary, many academic studies find a statistical association between oil dependence or abundance and conflict onset. The issue is how this association should be explained. One key explanation relates to the political durability of oil regimes. Specifically, although economic shocks may increase the likelihood of conflict onset, they do not seem to negatively affect the durability of oil regimes.[45] Indeed, oil states appear particularly resilient to economic shocks, which may in fact partially explain the greater likelihood of conflict, as the absence of regime change could potentially be a motivating factor for armed conflict.

A paradox of the oil curse, in other words, is that oil fosters politically durable regimes overseeing volatile economies. This tension is often resolved through a set of repression, co-optation and redistribution mechanisms that characterise many "successful failed states."[46] The tight interconnections that arise between governments and the oil sector often reinforce the institutional weakness of the state vis-à-vis political responsiveness to its citisens (the taxation-representation nexus argument). However, this "success" often comes with armed conflicts if specific risks or opportunities arise. As discussed previously, negative economic shocks and long-term economic underperformance increase grievances and decrease the capacity of governments to deal with them, while positive shocks increase the appeal of taking control of the oil assets either through a government takeover or secession.

Oil conflicts: Beyond the specter of scarce oil

A second argument seeking to explain why conflicts take place in some oil-producing countries and not in others—the oil conflict argument—posits that the discovery and exploitation of oil motivates a broad range of armed conflicts aiming at controlling oil flows, revenue and conditions of exploitation. In contrast to geopolitical accounts emphasising oil scarcity as the central motive of oil wars, the oil conflict argument emphasises the conditions and outcomes of oil exploitation and their interpretation.[47]

A first factor in oil conflicts relates to broadly defined ownership issues at the international and sub-national levels. Much is made in geopolitical accounts of international level oil ownership, in particular the presence of foreign oil companies and military forces in oil producing countries. Conflicts associated with imperialist oil ventures, foreign sponsorship of coups d'état and insurrections to resist oil nationalisation in Iran and Iraq, Al-Qaeda discourses against the US presence in the Holy Land (that is, Saudi Arabia), all provide important examples of this. Yet there is also some evidence that protection by home governments of foreign oil companies can reduce risks by pre-empting or at least preventing, the escalation of conflicts, through diplomacy, aid, and military assistance.[48] Foreign oil ownership could thus potentially guarantee stability for oil regimes through such assistance. The key here is whether the regime itself is perceived as legitimate, a question that I address below. If foreign ownership has some advantages to political stability, domestic private ownership may more effectively deter governments from entering and prolonging armed conflicts by curtailing access to easy funding flowing from state ownership and control of mineral resources. Furthermore, domestic private ownership may also deter groups from seeking to violently capture oil revenues through controlling the state.[49] There may also be greater domestic and international leverage on private companies to address negative social and environmental impacts.[50]

At the sub-national level, a broadly defined oil ownership plays an important role in the allocation of oil revenues. Most frequently vested in the state, subsoil property provides a strong incentive for governments to assert sovereignty over areas with potential or proven oil reserves. The risk of conflict is thus high, particularly when territories are disputed, borders poorly defined, and local populations politically or economically marginalised. The presence of oil thus often plays an important role in the political imaginary of secessionist groups as a means of securing the economic independence of their future state. This was the case for Aceh and East Timor, both under Indonesian rule, Biafra (Nigeria), Kurdish areas (Iraq and to some extent Iran), Cabinda (Angola), and to a lesser degree for the southern part of Algeria during the war of independence. In many cases, these conflicts relate to domestic (although often internationalised) struggles over the control of oil revenue and exploitation practices. Simply put, these patterns of oil exploitation create political risks for the onset of conflict, although (as we shall see) these do not flow in a deterministic fashion from oil production practices.

A second, and related, factor results from the characteristics of the oil sector, one that generates few local jobs and direct connections with other local economic sectors.[51] Potential linkages with the oil sector thus consist, for the vast majority of populations in oil areas, in a share of oil revenue as well as the social and environmental impacts of oil production. Unsurprisingly, few jobs, a small revenue share, and a high degree of negative social and environmental impacts are likely to result in grievances among local populations. As discussed in the previous section, the absence of a benevolent developmental state willing and capable of addressing grievances and curtailing violence, including abuses by its own security forces, makes communities in oil-producing areas highly vulnerable to such risks. For example, the environmental and social effects of oil production, especially onshore production in wetlands, are frequently identified as a cause of physical violence.[52] Grievances and associated patterns of violence can, in turn, provide a "fertile ground" that increases the risk of armed insurrection. This risk relates not only to oil-related grievances but also to the instrumentalisation of these grievances by political and economic entrepreneurs, as well as to a cycle of resistance and repression that exacerbates and normalises violence.

In summary, oil countries do not face similar risks of armed conflict. Over the past few decades, countries faced a lower likelihood of violence if they had high income (over US$5,000 per capita), the protection of a permanent UN Security Council member (presence of military base), large social spending (for dictatorships) and low elite taxation (for democracies), lax checks on corruption, and large arms imports.[53] These factors are not necessarily ideal, as they evoke a "peace" marked by inequalities, domestic repression, external threats, and oil-for-arms deals. To these factors must be added considerations of political legitimacy, particularly in terms of democratic representation and accountability, and of the broad social and environmental impacts of oil exploitation.

Opportunities: Beyond conflict oil

The third major dimension relating to oil and wars consists of the opportunities that the oil sector can provide for belligerents to finance their struggle. According to the conflict oil argument, oil plays an instrumental role in the course of conflicts. This "opportunity" dimension of oil is critically important, as demonstrated by recurrent Iraqi military ventures under Saddam Hussein, Libya's recent turmoil and Gaddafi's long-time support for many insurrectional movements across the world (from Northern Ireland to Aceh in Indonesia), also the apparent expectation by senior US officials that reconstruction (if not the war itself) in Iraq would be "self-financed" through oil income.[54]

How and to what degree does oil provide opportunities for belligerents? And what lies below the surface of "conflict oil" narratives? Because of the structure of the industry, oil tends to mostly benefit governments, financing military ventures at home and abroad. In other words, oil revenues tend to be less accessible to rebel groups, at least when compared with more "lootable" resources such as alluvial diamonds or illegal resources such as narcotics.[55] Offshore oil exploitation, the burial of oil pipelines, and the military protection of oil infrastructures and staff tend to reduce the "lootability" of oil. Some onshore locations have many of the "unlootable" characteristics of offshore production, such those located in hard-to-reach areas with easy-to-defend terrain.

However, although oil is often portrayed as less lootable, there are multiple ways to derive revenue from oil or to deprive a government of access, and conflict oil narratives are replete with oil-funded militants. One way for opponents to access revenue is through "booty futures": the promise of future oil revenues for financial support. An early example is the assistance from ENI (the Italian oil company) to the Algerian FLN during the war of independence.[56] Another example is the alleged support by the French oil multinational Elf for its long-time ally ex-President Denis Sassou Nguesso against President Pascal Lissouba during hostilities in the Republic of Congo in 1997.[57] Having opened up the oil sector to (often American) competitors to French control, President Lissouba had "fallen from favour with the French."[58]

Another recent example is the failed 2004 coup attempt in Equatorial Guinea, a country of about half a million people that rapidly became one of the largest African oil producers after a massive offshore find in 1995.[59] The coup was aimed at deposing President Teodoro Obiang Nguema Mbasogo, who himself came to power through a coup in 1979 after a decade of murderous rule by his uncle Francisco Macias Nguema. In 2002, Obiang won elections that many observers considered fraudulent, as evidence accumulated that oil revenue was not reaching the population.[60] South African and British mercenaries who had operated in Angola and Sierra Leone organised the coup with the knowledge of the British government. Financing of at least US$3 million was allegedly obtained from British, South African, and Lebanese businessmen, including the son of the former Prime Minister Margaret Thatcher, who received a four-year suspended sentence in South African courts, and the Nigeria-born millionaire oil broker Ely Calil, who acknowledged connecting Equatoguinean political opponent Severo Moto with the mercenary group leader Michael Mann, but denied an intention to support a coup.[61]

Another key opportunity that oil provides to belligerents stems from the strategic vulnerability of oil infrastructure and personnel to attacks, sabotage, extortion and theft. Oil flows through pipelines can be obstructed, with rebel groups targeting the most crucial and hard-to-repair sections. Oil companies also employ expatriate staff, who can be kidnapped for high ransom. The scale of attacks against these targets is significant: half of 248 recorded "terrorist" and rebel attacks against the petroleum sector between 1968 and 1999 targeted pipelines and personnel.[62] Money can also be obtained through threats of future sabotage, or even by extorting compensation paid to local authorities and communities for environmental damage. Ransoms paid for the kidnapping of oil staff and ensuing "security contracts" provided by oil companies to prevent future hostage situations are also frequent ways by which belligerents (usually rebels) raise revenue. Armed groups also derive revenue from the higher budgets allocated to local authorities in oil areas, through collusion or extortion.

The case of the Ejército de Liberación Nacional (ELN) in Colombia is one example of how rebel groups can source financing by using these methods. After military defeats in the early 1980s, the ELN was able to resurrect itself as a viable guerrilla organisation through revenue streams from the oil sector, initially through ransoms and "*vacuna*" payments (literally "vaccination" against violence, or protection money) paid by the German company Mannesmann, which was laying down a major pipeline. The rebel movement was careful not to kill the proverbial goose that laid the golden eggs, in contrast to the Fuerzas Armadas Revolucionarias de Colombia (FARC), which could rely on other sources of finance and initially sought mostly to deny the state access to revenue by destroying oil infrastructure. The ELN also launched a political campaign to support the "nationalisation" of the oil sector in order to justify its military actions. ELN tactics and politics, however, were discredited after sabotage on the Ocensa pipeline that caused the death of seventy people, numerous injuries, and an oil spill.[63]

Large-scale oil theft of both crude oil and refined products circulating through pipelines is another strategy for generating revenue. This strategy requires networking with actors along the oil commodity chain, as the theft of oil requires access to sophisticated parallel markets and the collusion of buyers. Revenue is also generated from oil distribution, through trafficking in stolen refined products, import contraband, or extortion. In Colombia, for example, revenue derived by armed groups, especially paramilitaries, from the oil distribution network (or downstream sector) could have been higher during the early 2000s than that derived from oil production (or the upstream sector).[64] As discussed below, oil "theft" has taken place on an even larger scale in Nigeria.[65] Several oil companies and policy-makers have sought to curb such practices through proposing an international strategy for "oil fingerprinting," similar to some of the proposals made for "blood diamonds" detailed in the following chapter.[66]

In summary, despite depictions of oil as a less lootable resource, most rebel groups operating in oil-producing regions have been able to tap into oil revenue streams, by means ranging from oil theft and trafficking to "booty futures," protection rackets, extortion and kidnappings, as well as sub-contracting and access to oil funds allocated to local communities and authorities.[67] Similarly, governments have proved able to mobilise oil revenues in support of military campaigns both domestically and abroad. Oil, like other resources, thus provides important opportunities for belligerents to prolong conflicts.

An important, but often overlooked, dimension to the foregoing argument pertains to the opportunities that conflict offers to oil companies. Stability is arguably a favourable context for a capital-intensive industry with long time horizons. Instability for firms relates primarily to government policy changes (such as tax regime changes or nationalisation), erratic levels of corruption, and conflicts (for example communal unrest, civil wars, sanctions, and territorial disputes). Conflicts can directly affect a company's assets and oil flows, as well as the ability to secure financing. Oil and conflict overlaps are widespread.[68] Yet wars do not always affect negatively the contractual and infrastructural stability of oil exploitation.

Angola, in this respect, provides a major example with the same party in power since 1975, contractual continuity for oil companies since the late 1950s, and offshore oil infrastructures unaffected by conflicts for forty years.[69] Furthermore, war generally disadvantages governments in their negotiations with firms. War can also provide competitive advantages for specific firms[70] and attract risk-taking companies more inclined to use bribery, military force, and minimal corporate social responsibility measures. Peace, in turn, can paradoxically be interpreted negatively by financial markets.[71] In short, as I next demonstrate with the example of Nigeria, situations of conflict may also provide opportunities for oil companies; the shifting strategies of companies and governments, not just belligerents, influence the landscape of opportunity within "oil conflicts."

Nigeria

Nigeria has long been considered to be the "oil giant" of Africa, a continent that still had few known oil prospects by the early 1950s. Discovered in 1953, oil was first commercially produced in 1958. Since then, about US$450 billion worth of oil has come out of the ground.

Modest at first, oil revenue boomed as a result of production and price increases. Accordingly, Nigeria has been among the most oil-dependent countries in the world since 1974.[72] Three successive oil booms generated the bulk of revenue, creating price shocks (discussed in general terms at the outset of this chapter).[73] As with other oil-dependent countries, Nigeria's relative oil wealth thus reflects huge price swings that confronted the Nigerian government with massive revenue volatility and debts, as the government sought to sustain expenditure during the price doldrums of the 1980s and 1990s.

Nigeria has long been among the top ten oil exporters in the world and remains the largest producer in Africa. Yet Nigeria is not necessarily an "oil rich" country: with a vast population its average per capita oil revenue was only US$200 between 1960 and 2006, compared for example with US$1,500 for Gabon and US$6,600 for Saudi Arabia. Moreover, little of that money reached Nigeria's growing majority of poor people. After three decades of oil and debt dependence, the percentage of Nigerians surviving on less than US$1 a day had risen from 36 percent in 1970 to 70 percent in 2000, while income inequality had dramatically increased.[74] Better management, debt relief, and a third oil boom improved economic performance in the mid-2000s, but by 2008 about 54 percent of Nigerians still survived on less than US$1 a day.[75]

As a whole, then, Nigeria exhibits many of the economic ailments associated with oil dependence. Indeed, not only has the oil sector failed most Nigerians economically during the past fifty years but, as argued by the geographer Michael Watts, it has also created conditions that have "undermined the very tenets of the modern nation-state":

On the one hand, oil has been a centralising force that has rendered the state more visible and globalised, underwriting a process of secular nationalism and state building. On the other, oil-led development, driven by an unremitting political logic of ethnic claims making, has fragmented and discredited the state and its forms of governance ... [beyond] massive corruption, corporate irresponsibility or chronic resource-dependency ... the real deception [of oil] is the terrifying and catastrophic failure of secular nationalism.[76]

Cobbled together by British colonial interests, the Federal Republic of Nigeria has long faced recurring political tensions associated with processes of centralisation and fragmentation.[77] The number of constituent states of the Nigerian Republic increased tenfold between 1963 and 1996 (in part as a strategy of dividing the "spoils" from oil exports, because of the practice of allocating a large proportion of oil revenue through individual states). This multiplication of regional government institutions was, in large part, ethnicised. Ethnic tensions and rivalries persist, given that many state boundaries did not coincide with ethnic boundaries.[78] This situation is a factor of fragmentation, yet observers also argue that devolution in the context of a federal system has, along with federal government victory in the 1967–70 war with secessionist Biafra, enabled the Nigerian federation to formally "hold together"—a rare feat, given the number of federations that had broken apart since the First World War.[79] From the standpoint of most Nigerians, the influence of oil revenue on the practice of politics and the resulting weakness (both in terms of capacity and political legitimacy) of state institutions are expressions of an oil "curse" which has created systemic vulnerability to political and "ethnic" conflicts.

Oil conflicts

A second source of oil-related conflicts in Nigeria pertains to the risks of conflicts engendered by the living conditions of people living in oil production areas. Nearly all of Nigeria's oil has come from the Niger Delta region, where oil-related violence escalated during two main historical periods: in the late 1960s and since the late 1990s. Each followed a period of more peaceful protests.[80] In 1966, a revolt led by Isaac Boro proclaimed the "Niger Delta People's Republic" and was quelled within two weeks by the federal government. Broadly motivated by the poor outcomes of the Niger Delta Development Board initiatives instituted in 1962, Boro was part of the first ethnic militia in the oil region, the "Niger Delta Volunteer Force."[81]

Beyond oil impacts on Ijaw communities (the major ethnic group in the coastal areas of the Delta region where most of the oil is located), Boro's insurrection had much to do with disputes among ethnic groups for control of sub-national jurisdictions within Nigeria—and hence oil revenue. Specifically, Boro feared that the Igbos—the major ethnic group for the former Eastern Region in which the Niger Delta is located—would dominate the region after an Igbo-led federal-level coup in January 1966 (although this coup was unitarist and sought to keep Nigeria together).[82] This first post-independence insurrection in the Niger Delta was followed a year later by an Igbo-led attempt to turn the Eastern

Region into the independent Republic of Biafra (1967–70). This secession attempt followed on the creation by the Federal government of twelve states out of the existing four regions in Nigeria.[83] Although not the only factor in the onset of war, this new territorial arrangement threatened Igbos' access to oil revenue; while they had been the majority group in the former Eastern Region as a whole, Igbo dominance was now concentrated in the new East Central State and drastically reduced in the new Rivers State where most of the oil fields were concentrated.

The military defeat of the Republic of Biafra was followed by rising grievances yet only peaceful protests until the (re)emergence of militant groups deploying violence and a war rhetoric in the late 1990s. This (re)emergence, like the previous one, resulted in large part from state and corporate failure to address peaceful protests.[84] After those of the early 1960s, protests had coalesced again in the late 1970s as a result of changes in oil and budgetary legislation drastically reducing direct access to oil revenue for local communities.[85] Environmental factors also played a growing role, finding a powerful echo internationally by the early 1990s.[86]

Violence escalated in the Niger Delta through a cycle of protests and repression, a turning point being the massacre of villagers and protesters by a mobile police unit in Umuechem in 1990.[87] Adopting mostly non-violent strategies, these movements such as the Movement for the Survival of the Ogoni People (MOSOP), a smaller group than the Ijaw and Igbo located in some of the oldest and richest oil areas in the southeastern part of the Delta, challenged the status quo between international oil companies and the autocratic federal government.[88] Initially demanding from the federal government the "right to the control and use of a fair proportion of Ogoni economic resources for Ogoni development," MOSOP later directly required US$6 billion in past royalties and US$4 billion in environmental compensation from oil companies, an end to environmental degradation, and participation in future negotiations.[89] MOSOP organised mass protests and threatened to block oil production. Government repression and "inter-ethnic" violence ensued, as well as intra-Ogoni conflicts over MOSOP's strategy, leadership, and representation, while Shell departed from the area, citing staff security reasons.[90] The dictatorship's hanging of the MOSOP leader Ken Saro-Wiwa along with eight activists in 1995 resulted in an international public outcry and contributed to a shift from non-violent activism to armed militancy among the many emerging "civil society" movements.[91]

By the late 1990s numerous forms of militancy emerged, including sabotage and violent confrontation with corporate and state security forces. Such "hardened" strategies were expected to be effective, particularly in light of perceived foot-dragging by oil companies on promises made to local communities.[92] This shift to (particularly youth) militancy was exacerbated by intra- and inter-community conflicts, particularly over access to oil revenue, through territorial and chieftaincy claims, and a move to democracy in 1999 that brought in electoral violence in which competing politicians hired (and later protected) militant groups. Years of government repression against community representatives presented as a threat by oil companies have created a vacuum, leaving local communities cynical toward official authorities and oil companies' post-1999 overtures.[93] Interviews with militant youth group members suggest that the main motivations for advocating armed conflict stem from marginalisation, inequities and repression (which appear to be more important motivating factors than the attitude of oil companies and a desire for self-determination).[94]

In summary, the risks of conflict in the Niger Delta appear to be primarily related to distribution of the benefits of oil production (including the centralisation of oil revenue away from producing areas following the Biafra war) and its costs (such as rising socio-environmental impacts). Resulting grievances and unmet expectations leading to protests were addressed through repression and the radicalisation of militancy, itself instrumented by politicians and "parasited" by criminal gangs. The ensuing escalation of physical violence and declarations of "full-on wars" by some of the militant groups constituted and played out on the risk of armed conflict in the region. As I explore in the next section, the opportunities (financial and political) presented by the oil sector also constituted a major part of the connections between oil and armed conflicts in Nigeria.

Conflict oil, bunkering and offshore moves

What financial opportunities does oil offer for groups engaged in violent conflict in the Delta region? Some of these financial opportunities are indirect and stem from extortion or criminalised behavior. For example, most youth groups operate as "guards" for their communities as well as "thugs" for local strongmen, with some groups also receiving payments from oil companies for "protection."[95]

Direct financing from oil is also an important strategy, especially for armed militant groups more exclusively focused on political competition and the control of lucrative oil trafficking routes.[96] Such trafficking (or "illegal bunkering") operations have also taken place in Nigeria, many of them run by militias on behalf of local politicians and with the collusion of army personnel.[97] Estimated at 5 to 20 percent of national production during the mid-2000s,[98] the activities described as "bunkering" and their association with illegal armed groups have also been instrumented by some government officials to explain away production decline caused by other reasons, such as sabotage, that point at political rather than criminal dimensions of the conflicts.[99]

These militant groups acquired more weapons and influence, and they found a source of wealth and prestige in oil protection rackets, trafficking and sabotage. Yet, "infiltration of political elites, loss of focus and poor control have combined to turn the militias into perpetrators of crime, violence and insecurity and agents of private interests and greed."[100] The resulting heightened criminality and violence as well as oil production decline associated with youth militancy and militias have undermined initial support among local communities and made the militias a politically easier target for a large-scale military operation launched by the Nigerian government in May 2009.[101]

One way in which the Nigerian government and oil companies have sought to reduce opportunities for militant groups is a move to offshore areas. This move reflects a trend already long at work in areas such as Angola, where the relative safety of offshore sites is viewed favourably as compared with onshore projects vulnerable to insurgent attacks. However, although offshore oil production is rightly perceived as less prone to oil theft, offshore platforms have nonetheless been subject to protests, extortion, and attacks.[102] The "offshoring" move of oil production in Nigeria responded to geological opportunities associated with technological advances in deep-water oil production, as well as increasing community and militant pressure in the creeks of the Delta. Its implications are important for Delta states that receive 13 percent of the revenue generated by onshore fields through the "derivation" part of the revenue allocation formula. According to some, offshoring production thus further "dispossesses" Delta states.[103]

To assuage local politicians and "restive" populations, the Nigerian federal government passed the Offshore/Onshore Oil Dichotomy Abolition

Bill, which had a positive political effect for President Obasanjo but in fact only extended the onshore oil revenue derivation element of 13 percent for local states to offshore production at more than 200 meters depth.[104] Offshore oil production is now the object of deliberate attacks,[105] which are facilitated by the intricate coastal landscape of the delta and practices of insurgent groups which challenge, for example, the onshore and offshore criteria typically applied to "lootable" and "non-lootable" resources. Indeed, militant groups have promised to step up the attacks on offshoring, which is viewed by some as a means of escaping responsibility for meeting local demands for social and ecological justice—such as greater local employment and environmental remediation. Whether onshore or offshore, oil production facilities will continue to provide opportunities for militant groups and subsequent pretexts for military intervention, further entrenching the cycle of oil-related violence in the region.

Conclusion

There is strong evidence supporting connections between oil and wars. Assessing the applicability of the vulnerability, risk, and opportunities arguments for the oil sector, I found support for each of them—in contrast to diamonds, for which the opportunity factor predominates. As explored in this chapter, these connections reflect the specific context in which oil is discovered and produced. Levels of oil abundance and dependence, the location of oil fields, and the institutional setting all play a major role. The context is not fixed but evolves in concert with a variety of factors ranging from international oil price trends to local identity formation processes.

The overall perspective brought by this assessment differs from geopolitical perspectives on oil wars that stress the strategic dimension of oil as a military "prize" or as a national security issue, and through which conflict is perceived as an intrinsic result of competition over a scarce and profitable resource.[106] Connecting scarcity, conflicts and profitability points, in contrast, to the role of armed conflicts in the political economy of oil scarcity and the massive profits generated by insecurity in terms of oil rents and arms trading:[107] rebels are not the only ones "doing well out of war."[108] In this regard, critical geopolitics of oil wars can help deconstruct the narratives and practices linking conflicts, fears of scarcity, oil prices, and profits (for some), thereby going beyond the "facts and figures" upon which positivist analyses are based.[109] In short, this perspective suggests that the geography of "oil wars" is not simply that of "scarce oil." This geography is expressed on various scales, and through different forms of violence, which are differentially characterised as "war" according to distinct criteria employed by different constituencies.

Geopolitical constructs of oil wars based on misleading notions of "national interest" match the geography of "abundant oil"—places where the volumes of production and reserves (and thus the risks of scarcity, false promises of "energy security" and financial rewards) are greatest. The politicising effects of oil dependence amplify and distort imagined geographies of vulnerability, collusive friendship, enmity, and endangerment.[110] These imagined geographies, in turn, inform environmental, communitarian, and social perspectives from which emerge, for example, alternative geographies of "progressive" coalitions seeking to improve the human rights record of the oil sector through "good governance."[111] In the case of oil companies, corporate-led destabilisation efforts have targeted oil-nationalising governments (such as Mexico in 1938 and Iran in 1951), with stabilisation efforts similarly directed towards supportive ones.[112] Failure by governments and consumers to reduce oil demand reinforces scarcity, and an associated politics of tension around "strategic" oil areas, lead to the banalisation of the geopolitics of fear and force, such as that seen in the Middle East.

This "banal" violence is also expressed at the individual oil project level, with "communities" and political entrepreneurs shaping geographies of contestation and insecurity to improve access to revenues from, and conditions of, oil exploitation.[113] In the Niger Delta, such geographies have included street demonstrations and peaceful occupation of oil infrastructure, as well as stoppages, sabotage, kidnappings, illegal but licit oil bunkering, and separatism. The media's fascination with, and selective reporting of, violence makes this variable potentially more significant than other sources of scarcity and risk, such as OPEC oil cuts and production incidents. Yet selective reporting of violence—ranging from state repression to communal conflicts and poverty—reflects the symbolic violence of imagined geographies of producing regions, where oil wealth, corruption, poverty, and brutality are expected and banalised. Oil markets are quick to translate these selective geographies into financial opportunities, with discourses on the way the geography of wars is changing oil from a commodity of use to one of exchange, as conventional calculations of use value are filtered and transformed through discourses of violence propagated among analysts, traders, and investors.[114]

4

DIAMONDS

In the late 1990s, diamonds captivated the attention of conflict analysts and media outlets, largely because of their role in funding rebel movements in Angola and Sierra Leone. Many of these narratives depict war as a criminal project motivated by the "lust for resources" and facilitated by easily "lootable" resources.[1] Like other precious gems, diamonds are frequently portrayed as the primary motive of greed-driven wars led by rampaging warlords.[2] Even peacekeepers, the United Nations Secretary General Kofi Annan suggested, were not immune to the "poisonous mix" of diamonds and greed fuelling these wars.[3] War, from this perspective, is motivated largely by greed, and resources offer both motivation and opportunities for belligerents. Popularised in the media as "blood diamonds" and characterised as a "rebel's best friend," diamonds fit easily into this storyline.

In this chapter I question these conventional narratives of diamond wars and the assumptions about the political economy of diamonds that underpin them. I begin with the idea that these narratives obscure as much as they reveal. For example, numerous diamond companies profiteered from conflict diamonds, initially ducking and deriding attempts to curtail the trade. And although "greed-driven" warlords do mobilise diamond revenues and commandeer forced labor, the livelihoods of the hundreds of thousands of men, women, and children who engage in diamond mining—hoping, in a context of chronic poverty and widespread abuses, that their "luck is stronger than death"—also merit attention.[4]

These issues of livelihoods and industry regulation were of central importance to the debates over responses to "diamond wars." For example, international human rights campaigns were successful in exposing the complicity of the diamond industry, in part by successfully linking resource conflicts and livelihoods in diamond-producing countries with diamond consumers in the wealthy countries. By reframing diamond wars as an issue of consumer responsibility (and thus choice), often through inspired reworking of slogans (such as the controversial ad campaign "diamonds are a rebel's best friend"), campaigners were able to insert "the dystopian imaginary of greed, inequality, and brutality directly into the parlors of postindustrialism."[5]

The debate over appropriate responses to "diamond wars" is critical to understanding the broader debate over so-called conflict commodities, where diamonds played an influential role in reframing analyses of contemporary armed conflicts and conflict termination initiatives.[6] Accordingly, I shall return to the issue of responses (military, economic, and regulatory) to conflict resources in Chapter 6. In this present chapter, meanwhile, I focus on a critical analysis of the military interventions, economic sanctions, and regulatory initiatives that since the late 1990s have arguably succeeded in curtailing some of the major links between diamonds and wars. Throughout the chapter I seek to broaden analyses beyond spaces of resource exploitation to include the interrelationship between spaces of production, consumption, representation and governance.[7] Such analyses of commodity chains stress the importance of social relations that construct particular spaces and places of commodity circulation.[8] By doing so, I hope to bring out alternative understandings of causal factors and consequences of so-called diamond wars.

The analysis follows the vulnerability-risk-opportunity conceptual triad introduced in Chapter 2. Empirically, I draw from a wealth of studies on conflict diamonds, as well as personal experiences. I was first introduced to this issue in the mid-1990s through my collaboration with Global Witness, the first advocacy organisation to launch a major campaign on "conflict diamonds."[9] This was followed by fieldwork in several diamond-producing African countries, as well as interviews in diamond-processing zones and participant observation in policy forums dedicated to responses to diamond wars.

First, I query the extent to which a "diamond curse" exists, and caution that this concept must be constrained if it is to have any analytical relevance to the question of political and economic vulnerability to war. I then scrutinise the popular "blood diamonds" narrative, by asking whether and how diamond exploitation alters the risk of conflict. Here, I argue that the narrow definition of violence used in much of the literature—usually pertaining to armed conflicts resulting in at least twenty-five battle deaths per year—overlooks multiple forms and scales of violence enacted through resource exploitation and regulation. Recent work on the geography and political ecology of violence draws attention to expanded definitions of violence, encompassing non-physical forms of violence but also acknowledging the pervasive presence of (realised or implied) violence in resource (dis)possession regimes.[10] In other words, war is not the only (or even primary) type of violence associated with resource-extractive industries, and "resource war" arguments risk essentialising and depoliticising violence, thereby misreading its causal factors and impacts. Finally, I look at the claim that diamonds are a "rebel's best friend," pointing to the political and tactical ambivalence of the opportunities presented by diamond exploitation in the context of wars. More broadly, I stress that understanding of resource wars needs to look at geography beyond location, and avoid a sense of "geographical destiny" in struggles over resources. Here, the distinction made by geographers between the narrow sense of "location" (vector coordinates, distances) and the broader term "spatiality" (which asserts the social construction of spaces and scales) is useful. The latter perspective allows us to move beyond a narrowly deterministic view of location and to grapple with the social construction of space via the interrelationship of the biophysical aspects of resources, modes of production, and discourses of resource extraction.[11] This suggests that belligerents face significant constraints in mobilising diamonds within the context of resource wars, an understanding of which is critical for the successful regulation of resource wars.

As a caveat, I should note that the subsequent analysis remains largely focused on diamond-producing countries that experienced wars during the 1990s,[12] but also considers the broader historical context, particularly labor relations and the political economy of the diamond sector.[13]

Vulnerability: Is there a diamond curse?

To answer the question of whether (and to what extent) a "diamond curse" exists, I first examine the prevalence and occurrence of diamond wars. One

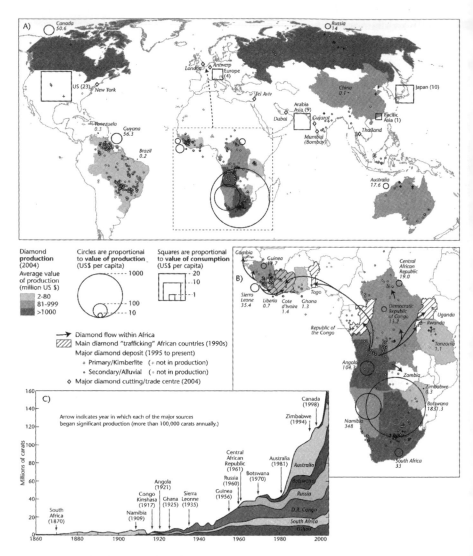

A. Diamond deposits and world production (2004).

B. Sub-Saharan Africa.

C. Historical trend of world production (1860–2005).

Figure 4.1: World diamond production.

Table 4.1: Quantitative analyses of diamonds and wars

Studies	Datasets	Resource variables	Findings	Vulnerability	Risk	Opportunity
Collier and Hoeffler (1998)	27 civil wars, 1960–92	Primary exports/ GDP	Increased conflict onset likelihood and conflict duration (curvilinear)	Weak	–	Strong
Buhaug and Gates (2002)	265 civil wars, 1946–2000	Natural resources, including diamonds, in sub-national conflict zone	Increased size of conflict zone	–	–	Strong
Fearon (2004)	128 wars, 1945–99	Contraband goods under rebel control, including diamonds	Prolonged conflict duration	–	–	Strong
Lujala et al. (2005)	127 wars, 1945–99	Diamond type, production, reserves	Secondary diamond production associated with increased onset likelihood of ethnic conflicts but not primary diamonds nor diamond reserves	Weak	–	Strong
Buhaug and Lujala (2005)	252 civil wars, 1946–2001	Presence of diamonds in conflict area	Prolonged conflict duration	–	–	Strong
Humphreys (2005)	122 wars, 1945–99	Diamond production	Increased conflict onset likelihood, but reduced duration (positively correlated with both military victory and negotiations)	Strong	Medium	Weak

Table 4.1 (contd.)

Studies	Datasets	Resource variables	Findings	Vulnerability	Risk	Opportunity
Ross (2006)	90 wars, 1960–99	Diamond type, production	Increased conflict onset likelihood for primary diamonds, but not secondary diamonds (reverse for separatist conflicts), no effect on conflict duration	Medium	Weak	Weak
Buhaug and Rød (2006)	Civil wars in Africa, 1970–2001	Diamond type, location	Increased governmental conflict onset likelihood, but reduced separatist onset likelihood for secondary diamonds	Strong	Medium	Strong

in six countries in the world currently produces diamonds, with a heavy concentration in Sub-Saharan Africa (sixteen out of twenty-eight producers and 60 percent of worldwide production value; see 4.1A, B). Since the 1980s, this has been the most conflict-affected region in the world.

As indicated in Table 4.1, quantitative studies have generally found conditional support for a relationship between diamonds and war; specifically, they provide conditional support for the opportunity argument but less for vulnerability and even less for risk. The small number of wars in diamond-producing countries should nevertheless caution against any generalising conclusions on the relationship between war and diamonds based on large-N studies.[14] Moreover, the relative significance of diamonds should also be weighed against other factors.[15] A review of the literature suggests that although an estimated twenty conflicts could plausibly be related to diamonds between 1946 and 2005 (see Table 4.1), in only four cases were diamonds strongly related to conflict either through vulnerability, risk, or opportunity factors: civil wars in Sierra Leone (RUF, 1991–2001) and Angola (UNITA, 1993–2002), the secession of South Kasai in Congo-Kinshasa (the Independent Mining State of South Kasai, 1960–62), and the independence struggle of Namibia (SWAPO, 1966–88).

Within this set of diamond-producing countries, what is the impact of "diamond wealth" on vulnerability to conflict? And how should diamond wealth be characterised in this respect? In order to answer these questions, we need to distinguish between diamond dependence, diamond abundance, and mode of exploitation (see Table 4.2).

Diamond dependence refers to the importance of the diamond industry within an economy, measured by diamond production as percentage of GDP. When simply considering GDP growth rates since 1960, the economies of diamond producers have generally outperformed those of non-diamond producing countries, particularly in the late 1960s and during the 1980s.[16] Since the early 1990s, diamond producers and non-producers have been, on average, on a par.[17] Not all diamond-producing countries performed equally. Botswana outperformed other diamond producers as well as the rest of the subcontinent over three decades of diamond production, it grew ten times faster than the Sub-Saharan Africa average. Among other diamond producers, a first group of countries including South Africa, Guinea, Tanzania, and to a lesser extent Namibia and Ghana performed on a par with the rest of Sub-Saharan Africa. A second group underperfomed, including the Central African Republic,

Table 4.2: List of diamond-related armed conflicts (1946–2010)

Country	Government (side A)	Rebel (side B)	Years	War-related deaths	Vulnerability factor	Risk factor	Opportunity factor (side)	Major rebel funding sources
Sierra Leone	Sierra Leone, ECOWAS, United Kingdom	RUF, AFRC	1991–2000	75,000	Strong	Strong	Strong (A,B)	Diamonds ($25–75 million/ year)
DRC	Congo/Zaire	Independent Mining State of South Kasai	1960–2	600	Strong	Strong	Strong (A,B)	Diamonds
Angola	Angola	UNITA	1991–2002	700,000	Medium	Medium	Strong (A,B)	Diamonds ($200–600 million/year)
Namibia	South Africa	SWAPO	1966–88	25,000	Medium	Strong	Medium (A)	Proxy
DRC	Congo/Zaire	AFDL, Rwanda	1996–7	230,000	Medium	Medium	Medium (A,B)	Proxy
DRC	Congo/Zaire, Zimbabwe, Angola, Namibia	RCD, MLC, Rwanda, Uganda	1998–2003	2.5 million	Medium	Medium	Medium (A,B)	Gold, coltan, coffee, diamonds

Table 4.2 (contd.)

Table 4.2 (contd.)

Country	Government (side A)	Rebel (side B)	Years	War-related deaths	Vulnerability factor	Risk factor	Opportunity factor (side)	Major rebel funding sources
Liberia	Liberia	NPFL	1989–96	200,000	Weak	Medium	Medium (A,B)	Iron, timber, rubber, diamonds
Liberia	Liberia	LURD, MODEL	2000–3	2,000	Weak	Medium	Medium (A,B)	Proxy
CAR	Central African Rep., Libya	Military faction	2001–2	500	Medium	Medium	Weak (A)	Proxy
Ivory Coast	Ivory Coast	MPCI, MJP, MPIGO, FN	2002–5	850	Weak	Weak	Medium (B)	Cocoa, timber, diamonds
Angola	Angola, Cuba	UNITA, South Africa	1975–91	500,000	Weak	Medium	Weak (A,B)	Proxy
Guinea	Guinea	Military faction, RFDG	1970, 2000–1	300; 1,100	Weak	Weak	Weak (A)	n.a.
Angola	Portugal	MPLA, FNLA	1961–74	90,000	Weak	Weak	Weak (A)	Proxy
South Africa	South Africa	ANC, PAC, Azapo	1981–88	20,000	Weak	Weak	Weak (A)	Proxy

Table 4.2 (contd.)

Table 4.2 (contd.)

Surinam	Surinam	SLA/Jungle Commando	1986–88	500	Weak	Weak	Weak (A) Proxy
Ghana	Ghana	Military factions	1966,81,83	100	Weak	Weak	Weak (A) n.a.

Source: Lacina and Gleditsch (2004); CSCW (2006); author.

Notes: AFDL (Alliance of Democratic Forces for the Liberation of Congo-Zaire), AFRC (Armed Forces Revolutionary Council), ANC (African National Congress), ECOWAS (Economic Community of West African States), FN (New Forces), FNLA (National Front for the Liberation of Angola), LURD (Liberians United for Reconciliation and Democracy), MJP (Patriotic Youth Movement), MLC (Movement for the Liberation of Congo), MODEL (Movement for Democracy in Liberia), MPIGO (Ivorian Popular Movement of the Great West), MPCI (Ivory Coast Patriotic Movement), MPLA (Popular Movement for the Liberation of Angola), NPFL (National Patriotic Front of Liberia), PAC (Pan Africanist Congress), RCD (Rally for Congolese Democracy), SLA (Surinamese Liberation Army), SWAPO (South-West Africa People's Organisation), UNITA (National Union for the Total Independence of Angola). Battle-deaths accounted for 460,000 lives.

Angola, Sierra Leone, Liberia, and the DRC. All of this second group have been affected by armed conflicts during the past decade. Furthermore, the level of economic dependence on diamonds does not seem to be associated in a general fashion with economic underperformance, at least within Sub-Saharan Africa, as both groups include countries with different levels of diamond dependence.

Diamond abundance can be defined in terms of per capita diamond production. The evolution of diamond abundance in terms of production should influence economic performance, especially when measured through GDP, which does not capture profit repatriation by foreign mining companies. This relation, however, runs counter to the economic underperformance argument. The level of diamond abundance also varies within these two groups, although to a lesser extent. The underperforming group seems to have a medium level of diamond abundance, with the exception of Liberia's low per capita value of diamonds.

The third issue is that of a "mode of exploitation," which refers to the technologies and associated socioeconomic systems used to exploit resources. A basic distinction for diamonds exists between two main types of deposits: alluvial and kimberlite. Diamonds found in alluvial deposits have been eroded from kimberlite volcanic pipes. While kimberlite mines are no more than a few square kilometers large and require industrial-scale exploitation that serves to concentrate revenue, alluvial mines are spread over vast areas and at minimum only require a shovel and a bucket for their extraction. Consequentially, exploiting primary or kimberlite deposits requires industrialisation. Secondary or alluvial deposits, however, are accessible by artisanal mining, which is widely practiced in poorer countries, with or without the official consent of authorities. The significance of this distinction is that, at least according to official statistics, industrial exploitation tends to be associated with stronger economic growth, especially for Botswana and Namibia. One must note, however, that the official contribution of artisanal production is frequently underestimated because of high levels of diamond smuggling. Therefore, it is difficult to assess whether a specific mode of exploitation—industrial or artisanal—predicts economic underperformance.

In short, when analysed independently, diamond abundance, dependence, and mode of exploitation do not seem to predict economic underperformance, and thus appear to lend little support to the "diamond curse" argument. The diamond sector compares positively with most other primary commodity sectors in terms of macro-economic development—particularly for Africa, where it is one of the few sustained commodity export sectors.[18] Unlike other commodities—and despite a huge increase in production volume (see Figure 4.1C)—diamonds have long been largely sheltered from massive price collapse or fluctuation because of the price regulating (and enhancing) monopolistic activities of De Beers until the early 2000s, and sustained expansion of demand.[19] The diamond sector thus appears relatively "privileged" by stronger terms of trade and lower volatility compared with most other commodity sectors.

This macro-economic and state-centered reading of the economic side of the "diamond curse" is, however, misleading for two reasons. First, it focuses on the nation-state scale and does not disaggregate economic performances in light of processes of marginalisation (or peripheralisation) and uneven development (see below). Second, it does not allow for the historic contextualisation of conflicts over resources, which provides additional insights into the construction of vulnerability.

These issues are of central importance in understanding the interrelationship of political and economic vulnerability to conflict. Take, for example, the problem of the governance of diamond rents within nation-states, which has been central to post-independence African regimes.[20] In the face of structural adjustments and declining terms of trade and market share for most other export sectors, diamonds rents have been remarkably resilient, yet with ambivalent political effects. Diamond rents are linked with state overextension, corruption, and capital flight.[21] Yet rents have also financed patronage politics and sustained the "stability" of political regimes. From this perspective, vulnerability to conflicts stems not only from the political impact of the rent, but more broadly from the governmentality of the diamond sector.[22]

Drawing on these insights, a second diamond curse argument relates to the quality of governance and political stability, which in turn would influence economic performance.[23] Specifically, resource wealth frequently undermines the quality of institutions, resulting in an overextension of the state and policy capture by vested interests,[24] ultimately weakening state capacity and legitimacy. The evolution of diamond rents is key to this argument, which must take into account the issue of ownership structure as well as levels of inputs and reserve depletion.

Control of and access to diamond revenue are also highly dependent on the mode of exploitation, which relates in part to the material specificities

of diamond deposits. Alluvial diamonds, retrieved with minimal technological input from vast areas of riverbed gravel, can unsurprisingly prove
to be a very "uncooperative commodity" for the bureaucratic state seeking
to capture rents.[25] Once retrieved from the soil, diamonds can easily evade
taxation (with the complicity of buyers). Control of and access to diamonds
then rely on the insertion of politicians into informal diamond trading, a
mode of governmentality defined as "shadow state" politics.[26]

Governing diamond rents thus relies in part on the spatiality of diamond
deposits and modes of exploitation. Since artisanal diamond mining is
harder to tax than industrial mining, this leaves poorer countries more vulnerable to weak state capacity.[27] Furthermore, industrial mining is frequently described as minimising "excessive" and "inefficient" labor inputs
and as being a less wasteful mode of exploitation (in terms of both reserve
recovery and environmental degradation) than artisanal mining.[28] Rising
resource prices, deposit discovery, or the legalisation of artisanal exploitation are often cited as drawing labor into mining with detrimental effects
on the rest of the economy and on tax revenue for the state. From this perspective poorer countries would thus be worse off again, because an artisanal mining boom would act as the precursor of economic and political
"troubles" that would leave a country more vulnerable to conflicts.

This perspective strongly favours industrialisation of mining sectors,
but it requires a more nuanced view of artisanal mining and its impacts.
First, artisanal exploitation provide tangible income and benefits at the
individual, communal and even national levels.[29] Few studies have systematically compared artisanal and industrial mining's relative benefits,
but those that did have pointed at some of the more positive outcomes
of artisanal mining, such as large local employment and inputs such as
tools and food, and even suggest fiscal advantage, especially when industrial ventures benefit from generous tax exemptions and even subsidies.[30]
There is also a need to distinguish between "push" and "pull" factors affecting labor mobility towards the diamond sector. Some artisanal mining
booms have been demonstrated to follow rather than precede economic
recession and to stabilise the economy, thereby reversing the resource
curse argument: it is not high diamond dependence that undermines economic performance, but economic underperformance that increases
dependence on diamonds.[31]

Artisanal mining, in this light, appears as a coping economy providing a potential source of income for the poorest. In many contexts, how-

ever, the predatory behavior of middlemen and officials in the diamond sector means that artisanal miners and local communities do not land much profit. In this regard, the food provided by local "supporters" financing artisanal mining schemes is a basic incentive to turn to artisanal mining, while more complex ones include the patronage that such "supporters" can provide in case of illness or security threat.[32] More broadly, one has to look at the desperation of populations facing failed and oppressive institutions, including colonial legacies and contemporary patterns of servitude and humiliation in agrarian spaces, shaping hopes of emancipation in the mining fields.[33] Such hopes are most often dashed, however, and most artisanal miners wish for alternative livelihoods.[34]

Second, there is a need to refine the link between weak taxation and political vulnerability to conflicts. Lack of fiscal grasp on diamond revenue generated by artisanal exploitation is a reality, and it does leave the state less capable of carrying out its role of public service provision, including social services, public infrastructure, and regulatory functions. Low state capacity can in turn reduce political legitimacy and increase vulnerability to conflicts. Some empirical evidence suggests that primary deposits are less frequently associated with civil wars than secondary deposits open to artisanal mining.[35] Moreover, there is some evidence that private industry expropriation in the diamond sector can aggravate resource curse effects.[36] In this perspective, Botswana's political stability is often presented as the result of its sound (public-private joint-venture) industrial exploitation and budgetary allocation of rich primary diamond deposits,[37] while the collapse of formal industrial mining in Sierra Leone since the early 1970s—which included the nationalisation and dismantling of the main diamond company—increased vulnerability to civil war in the early 1990s (see Figure 4.3).[38]

This institutional effect appears to vary according to the geographical and economic concentration of the resource involved, with more concentrated "point" resources having a more deleterious effect than "diffuse" resources.[39] In the case of diamonds, however, this effect seems to be reversed, as "diffuse" diamonds (that is, alluvial deposits exploited through artisanal mining) would undermine government institutions by making tax collection extremely difficult whereas "point" diamonds consolidate institutions.[40]

Accordingly, quantitative analyses of the diamond curse have recently begun incorporating these issues.[41] For example, while war is more prevalent in diamond-producing countries (74 percent experienced at least one armed conflict compared with 43 percent), the presence of diamond deposits or diamond production does not increase the risk of war onset when controlling for other factors, such as low income. Studies considering the characteristics of diamond deposits find that alluvial diamonds are associated with higher incidence (or relative frequency) of war, especially in poor countries, and with respect to ethnic conflicts and to the post-Cold War period. In contrast, primary or kimberlite deposits had a dampening effect on the incidence of war, while the discovery of diamond deposits alone had no effect.[42] These findings support the opportunity argument: lootable diamonds (secondary deposits) are more likely to increase the incidence of wars than non-lootable ones (primary deposits). The same findings cast doubt, however, on the vulnerability and risk arguments, in line with the majority of large-N studies.

How then, can we continue to claim that diamonds foster vulnerability to conflict, when there is little conclusive evidence for a diamond curse based on a general conception of diamond wealth or on an isolated examination of diamond dependence, abundance, and mode of production? One possible answer is that an assessment of the combined effects of these three dimensions might yield more support for a resource curse claim. Indeed, diamond-producing countries affected by growth collapse and political instability tend to exhibit a medium level of diamond dependence (5 to 20 percent) and abundance (US\$12 to US\$150 per capita),

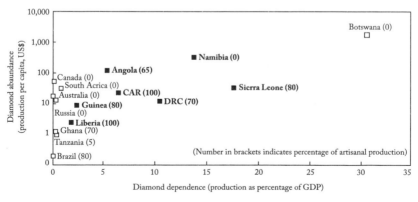

Figure 4.2: Diamond abundance, dependence and artisanal production.

as well as predominantly artisanal exploitation (60 to 100 percent) (Figure 4.2).[43] From this perspective, countries with such characteristics appear more vulnerable to armed conflict.

Comparing Botswana and Sierra Leone

Botswana and Sierra Leone are classic examples in debates over diamond wars, but their simplistic comparison as "diamond rich countries" is misleading as there are many differences between them. The first difference is that Botswana produces about US$2,500 worth of diamonds per capita, compared with US$150 for Sierra Leone. The economic and fiscal returns thus vary considerably.[44] Diamonds in Sierra Leone are mostly located in secondary deposits open to artisanal exploitation rather than exclusively in primary deposits as in Botswana. Thanks to well-negotiated contracts and easily controlled diamond extraction, the government of Botswana is able to raise US$1,500 per capita from the diamond sector, whereas the government of Sierra Leone receives a paltry US$8 from a sector that is largely dependent on artisanal mining. Entirely industrialised, Botswana's diamond sector generates only 8,000 jobs, whereas up to 150,000 people are working in Sierra Leone's diamond fields.

Historical factors also played a key role. In Sierra Leone, diamonds were exploited from the 1930s onwards under an exploitative British colonial regime that favoured British corporate interests. The late discovery of diamonds in a post-independence context meant that Botswana could bargain harder with foreign investors.[45] In turn, this allowed the government of Botswana to provide a greater degree of public services and infrastructure to its citizens, which in part compensated for the lack of direct access to diamond reserves (in contrast to Sierra Leone, less political manipulation and coercive policing was required, because of the necessarily industrial exploitation of primary deposits).

Having allegedly "beaten the resource curse,"[46] Botswana is frequently hailed as an "African success story." Contrary to this rhetoric, Botswana did in fact experience some resource curse effects as a result of its high diamond dependence,[47] but these aspects have not contributed to economic and political instability because of relatively sound macro-economic management, strong state capacity, and elite cohesion.[48] There are, however, some important caveats to this argument. Although Botswana has, so far, avoided the scourge of war, it has been ruled by the same party since independence in 1966, and much of its population has endured structural forms of violence, leaving the country with the second highest level of income inequality and second lowest life expectancy in the world.[49]

On the other hand, Sierra Leone's diamond curse has been particularly harmful.[50] Political power in Sierra Leone has long been maintained through predatory institutions resting on the reinforcement of the power of "customary" chiefs, especially at the district level. This system allowed the British mining company, the Sierra Leone Selection Trust (SLST), to rely on chiefs to minimise illegal mining (although granting them such power occasionally backfired, as it reinforced their ability to protect artisanal mining interests). SLST could also rely on Sierra Leonean police forces and its own paramilitary forces to stop illegal miners and repress the supporting local populations.[51] The chiefs' frequent misuse of delegated powers and privileged access to public revenue increased the frustration of a neglected population, and sidelined local central government officials.[52] The 1950s were marked by anti-chief and anti-tax riots, as well as the first large-scale "diamond rush" (see Figure 4.3). SLST's loss of effective control on the ground and demands for a radical shift in the control of diamond wealth in the context of active pro-independence movements led to the legalisation of artisanal mining in 1956, which greatly increased overall diamond production.[53]

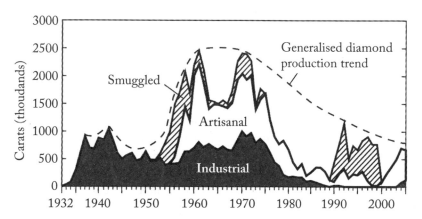

Figure 4.3: Official industrial and artisanal output and estimated smuggled output from Sierra Leone (1932–2005).

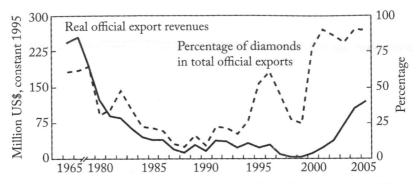

Figure 4.4: Diamond export dependence in Sierra Leone (1960–2005).

By 1961, a decade before any diamond production took place in Botswana, the artisanal diamond sector in Sierra Leone was officially exporting twice as many diamonds in volume than SLST, but brought in only half the tax revenue.[54] The diamond rush and renegotiation of the diamond mining regime had several effects.[55] At the national level, the transformations of the 1950s demonstrated the weakness and bias of a colonial regime and "native" government in dealing with a European company, as well as the tenuous nature of British colonial authority over local populations. Among mining communities, the diamond rush stirred a greater sense of ethnic identity (especially among the Kono), emancipation from chiefdom-based rule and identities, and political radicalism (including greater participation of the districts under Protectorate status in relation to the Sierra Leone Colony, Freetown).

By the early 1970s, the political status quo between British corporate interests, national political elites, and chiefs in the diamond-rich districts had again come under stress. Siaka Stevens, a former president of the Mines Workers Union, proved to be a successful political challenger to the ethnic Mende-dominated Sierra Leone People's Party (SLPP) that succeeded British rule at independence in 1961. Elected in 1967 on a populist platform through his All People's Congress (APC) party, Stevens nationalised SLST and reoriented diamond production towards clientelised (semi-industrial/artisanal) operations, while ensuring that local opponents involved in artisanal mining were marginalised or joined the APC. Diamond mining and revenue allocation were closely intertwined with corruption and the consolidation of a "shadow state," bringing diamonds into the private socioeconomic networks of the ruling elite while marginalising formal government institutions and bureaucracies.[56]

When Stevens personally appointed Brigadier-General Joseph Momoh as his successor in 1985, the diamond sector had been thoroughly informalised—mainly to the advantage of Stevens and his cronies. Momoh largely failed to gain the upper hand on diamond revenue, through either formal or informal means.[57] The Sierra Leonean diamond sector thus continued to induce two interrelated processes of peripheralisation. First, diamond smuggling (and thereby capital flight) continued, marginalising the country's official economy at the international level and the political control of the government at the domestic level (see Figure 4.4). Second, an increasing number of poor people moved into the mining sector as the rest of the economy collapsed.[58] The vulnerability of Momoh's regime was exposed when the RUF gained control of eastern parts of the country, and a year later when Momoh fled the country when confronted by disgruntled frontline government troops.[59]

From this perspective, vulnerability to conflict in Sierra Leone was not simply the result of the country's relative economic dependence on diamonds, the medium level of diamond abundance, the growth of artisanal diamond mining, or the partial nationalisation of the main diamond company. Rather, this historical configuration allowed for the progressive peripheralisation of the formal state by ruling elites and their cronies. In turn, this peripheralisation left official agencies unable to make legitimate political mandates operate effectively in a formal way, thereby deepening the informalisation of the sector. Forty years of political status quo favouring exploitative British and local elite private interests and resulting in major inequalities had contributed to making this peripheralisation possible.[60] From this historical background, the population had initially welcomed a shift in favour of artisanal mining and away from private foreign corporate monopoly. Because of the political character of this informalisation, however, artisanal mining and the nationalisation of SLST remained essentially beneficial to political networks rather than to mining communities and the government. This left the country in a political and economic situation that made it vulnerable to armed conflict. Beyond this vulnerability, Sierra Leone's civil war also related to a higher risk of war resulting from chronic conflict and violence in the diamond fields.

The contrasting cases of Botswana and Sierra Leone demonstrate several of my arguments with respect to vulnerability and the "diamond curse." First, an analysis of the spatial dimensions of uneven development is critical to a political and economic understanding of the causes of vulnerability. Second, in the case of diamonds, the peripheralisation of resource-based economies and the relative vulnerability of diamond-producing countries to conflict hinge not only on the mode of production (artisanal versus industrial) but also on the governance of diamond rents, which affect the degree to which diamond dependence and abundance are mediated by the state—which may be through "shadow" or parallel institutions under the supposed control of state rulers. Third, in order to understand vulnerability, we also need to examine the historical geographical contexts in which vulnerability is produced, as well as quantitative issues of diamond dependence, abundance, and modes of exploitation. Botswana and Sierra Leone have different levels of dependence, abundance and modes of exploitation. While these dimensions help explain very different trajectories, qualitative, historically informed analysis remains crucial to explaining the relative degree of diamond-producing countries' vulnerability to conflict.

Risk: Are diamond fields breeding grounds for wars?

Diamond mining areas are frequently referred to as "breeding grounds" for civil war.[61] But are there specific risks of conflict associated with diamonds, and what is the nature of the violence in the diamond sector? As in other extractive sectors, diamond-related conflicts are mostly associated with community relations, land rights and mining access, working conditions, and revenue sharing. One specific risk, for example, is that the price of a diamond is relatively subjective, much more so than gold for example, so that disputes over prices may occur more frequently.[62] Forms of violence include physical ones—such as repression by corporate security forces or interpersonal and inter-community violence around artisanal diamond mining—as well as structural and cultural ones.

More specifically, artisanal exploitation sites are portrayed as spaces of conflict and violence, in contrast with industrial mines described as "islands of modernity in a sea of civil war."[63] In turn, the difficulty of establishing a stabilising "industrial" order is explained by the diffuse physical geography of alluvial diamond fields. From this (de)fenceless physical geography emerges a threatening human geography of "swarming" and "dangerous" poor young men.[64] Thus, it is suggested, larger rebel movements emerge from mining teams (or "gangs"). According to this argument, alluvial diamonds and artisanal mining thus not only represent a weakening factor for the state and a financial opportunity for rebel movements, as I address below, but also shape a specific geography of risk.

Conflicts and various forms of violence are certainly involved in the diamond sector, but do chronic conflicts and violence in diamond mining areas increase the risk of war? Conflicts and violence arising from resource exploitation have occasionally acted as precursors to large-scale hostilities, especially through escalating processes of grievances and repression, but such scaling-up processes are rare.[65] Artisanal diamond mining is not simply a "violent" space characterised by anarchy (although it is frequently depicted this way). On the contrary, studies of artisanal mining have documented the existence of hierarchies that provide the levels of order and security necessary for successful resource extraction.[66]

Much of the physical violence, from this perspective, results from competing claims over diamonds between mining operators.[67] Whereas central authorities most often back industrial operators, it is frequent for local authorities to support artisanal operators. It is in part for this reason that self-defence groups protecting and regulating artisanal mining areas have a long history in the diamond sector. Although large-scale and violent demonstrations by artisanal mining groups are not uncommon, there is little evidence that these groups scale up their activities into "full-scale" wars. Rather, they frequently merge with wider conflicts, often through connections between mining groups and competing political entrepreneurs.

Rebel discourses are rarely novel, but transpose widely-shared "hidden transcripts" from aggrieved groups into the public realm.[68] The risk that diamond exploitation creates is, to a significant degree, discursively mediated by rebel groups, rather than emerging directly from the social and material practices of the diamond sector. The risk of war would thus result in part from the opening up of political space by risk-taking individuals seeking to achieve a radical and violent transformation. Indeed, this suggests that conventional arguments about the links between artisanal mining and resource wars can be reversed: given that artisanal mining often provides a space of relative social autonomy outside the traditional confines of chiefdoms and bureaucracies, eradicating artisanal mining (in the face of increased repression, diamond depletion, and growing competition in a context of generalised economic collapse) might increase rather than decrease the risk of conflict.

Relative deprivation, discontent, conflicts, and violence relating to the diamond sector have a long history in Sierra Leone, especially in the Kono district where SLST was present from the early 1930s. Radical social movements, such as the Kono Progressive Movement, emerged in the 1950s out of frustration with the behavior of SLST, customary chiefs, and the government in Freetown.[69] Its goals converged with those of illicit miners and Freetown-based pro-independence movements seeking "national" emancipation. Mining groups were frequently involved in (violent) political struggles. President Stevens intimidated local political opponents through youth groups also involved in mining, or replaced opponents with political appointees protecting the interest of his business cronies.[70] Appointees who had cracked down on "illegal" mining activities were later the target of artisanal mining groups more likely to have joined the RUF. In contrast, customary chiefs who had protected illegal mining activities maintained greater control of (mostly local) youths, drawing them into Civil Defence Force (CDF) local militias associated with initiation and "traditional hunter" societies such as the Kamajors.

Conflicts and violence reflected in part the wealth and character of diamond deposits.[71] The principal economic targets of central authorities were richer upstream alluvial diamond deposits around Kono that could be exploited industrially. In these areas, chiefs not siding with Stevens were more readily intimidated or replaced than chiefs in areas with poorer and shallower deposits around Kenema that were more suited for artisanal mining (see Figure 4.6A).

The spatiality of conflicts and violence was also shaped by local ethnic political affiliations. Mende chiefs around Kenema and Pujehun often supported the opposition party, and artisanal mining groups were drawn into violent demonstrations, often to support local candidates during electoral campaigns, for example during the Ndogboyosoi rebellion in 1982. More generally, brutal government "clean-out" operations since the 1950s had set a pattern of conflicts and acts of violence in Sierra Leone's diamond fields, although these did not directly initiate the 1991 civil war.

What, then, of the relationship between diamond mining and the initiation of insurgencies more generally? None of the rebel movements in Angola, the DRC and Sierra Leone started as insurrections in the diamond mining areas by diamond mining groups,[72] although some rebel leaders had a mining background, such as Laurent Kabila of the Alliance des Forces Démocratiques pour la Libération du Congo-Zaïre (AFDL)'s and the RUF's Sam Bockarie. All of these movements had broader constituencies, domestic and regional agendas, and geopolitical dimensions.[73] Yet homelessness, injustice, and corruption in the diamond sector did provide a cause—or at least a rationale—for some combatants to join and support the RUF in Sierra Leone.[74] Moreover, labor struggles, negative social and environmental impacts, highly unequal benefits, embezzlement by ruling elites, and abuses by security forces and mercenaries relating to diamonds, figure prominently in political discourses of emancipation and social mobilisation by radical organisations in Sierra Leone.[75] Beyond discontent relating to diamonds, however, the risk of war in Liberia and Sierra Leone—and individual acts of revenge committed during the conflicts—resulted from widespread and "deep-rooted" agrarian resentment by non-elite families lacking control over land and their own labor.[76]

These preceding examples qualify the claim that artisanal mining acts as an incubator for resource wars because of its inherently violent nature, and suggest that privileging industrial over artisanal mining has significant political consequences. Compared with artisanal exploitation, industrialisation concentrates power in the hands of the state, undermining state accountability to a population made more dependent on state handouts, thereby heightening societal vulnerability to state-level failures. The choice between industrial and artisanal mining also entails balancing fiscal revenue and direct employment opportunities, with consequences for political capacity and domestic political legitimacy. This choice additionally reflects the preferences of foreign extractive companies and their home governments seeking to foster industrial ventures. This, in turn, influences foreign relations as investments put a premium on "domestic political stability" and thereby on regime survival and the "sovereignty" of ruling elites[77]—often at the expense of local populations. Industrialisation may provide domestic rulers with external allies, but it may also attract competing mining interests seeking to undermine production or gain access to mineral rights through political destabilisation—not to mention companies disinvesting and sabotaging their own operations when faced with increased demands by states.[78]

This analysis also hints at an explanation of an apparent paradox with respect to diamond wars: secessionist wars involving diamonds have been extremely rare since 1946 (unlike the case of oil). Local populations' easier access to diamonds, in the case of secondary deposits, would reduce incentives to pursue diamond control through secession.[79] In the cases of the secessionist war in South Kasai (1960–62), and the independence struggles in Angola (1961–74) and Namibia (1966–88), diamond reserves included alluvial deposits, but colonial authorities and licensed corporations strictly prohibited access, effectively dispossessing local populations.[80] In these contexts, spatial struggles over the territorialisation of resource control constitute the major geographical dimension of "diamond conflicts" in relation to reserve ownership and production and also to livelihood options. This effectively limits the degree to which diamonds could, in these cases, "breed war."

Opportunity: Are diamonds a rebel's best friend?

The analysis to this point suggests that, in addition to vulnerability and risk, a third factor is central to resource conflicts: spaces of opportunity to rebel, which permit "radical" violence to be sustained in the face of repression. The "opportunity" argument is by far the most prevalent argument in the diamond wars literature. In conventional framings, simply put, diamonds are portrayed as the "ultimate loot," financing and rewarding rebel movements.

A key issue is the degree to which the extraction of diamonds presents an opportunity for financing belligerents. Small, low-weight, easily concealable, anonymous and internationally tradable, diamonds found in alluvial deposits are less easily amenable to government control. Empirical studies suggest that regions with alluvial diamonds are more likely to be embroiled in civil war than those with kimberlite diamonds, suggesting that, at least, alluvial diamonds represent a financial opportunity that can attract rebel movements. Indeed, in light of their significance in financing rebellion in Angola and Sierra Leone, diamonds have been dubbed a "rebel's best friend."

If revenues from diamonds did play a major role in the financing of some belligerents throughout the 1990s, including the provision of arms, local collusion, or foreign support for armed groups, diamonds were rarely the only available source of finance (see Table 4.1). Estimates remain imprecise, but "conflict diamonds" represented between 4 and 12 percent of the US$5 billion to US$8 billion annual international trade in rough diamonds throughout the 1990s.[81]

This, in turn, implies that the spatial dimension of rebel territory might be correlated with artisanal diamond mining areas. Indeed, a cursory glance at the territoriality of rebellions in Sub-Saharan Africa does suggest a correlation with the location of diamond areas (see Figure 4.5.AB). In Sierra Leone, diamond areas accounted for the largest number of recorded instances of conflict events.[82] Diamond areas were the focus of confrontation over the course of the conflicts (see Figure 4.6B). Yet diamond areas in Sierra Leone are not significantly related to the level of brutality against civilians (see Figure 4.6C).[83] Although brutalities were perpetrated against civilians in diamond areas,[84] many sought long-term refuge outside diamond mining areas, partly because these were the objects of recurring hostilities.

Opportunity stems largely from the material, spatial and social characteristics of diamonds: an easily mined and highly valuable commodity that is spread over vast areas when found in alluvial deposits, that is easy to conceal, transport, store and trade, and does not need any transformation before reaching international (rough diamond) markets. A rebel group can exert more effective control over alluvial diamond mining than governments because it can use direct physical violence with greater impunity—against miners to control labor and capture revenue, but also against state and corporate security services to allow illegal mining activities. While kidnappings and forced labor occur very frequently, in many cases poverty drives people to come "voluntarily" to mining areas to work under highly coercive conditions imposed by a rebellion.[85] UNITA's leadership retained control in the diamond sector through a mix of financial incentives and harsh punishment (including summary executions for such offences as stealing diamonds or disrespect for officers).[86] To protect diamond-mining operations and prevent diggers from taking for themselves high-quality stones that it systematically seized, UNITA set up a special force reportedly headed by the late UNITA Vice-president Antonio Dembo. The torture and execution of diggers by UNITA soldiers or Congolese collaborators, explain much about the movement's capacity to control and centralise the diamond business, and to prevent its own fragmentation and corruption.

Other valuable metals and minerals have similar lootability characteristics. During the early 1990s, sapphires and rubies provided the Khmer Rouge in Cambodia and the Karen in Burma (Myanmar) with significant revenue. In Afghanistan the late Ahmed Shah Massoud, the United

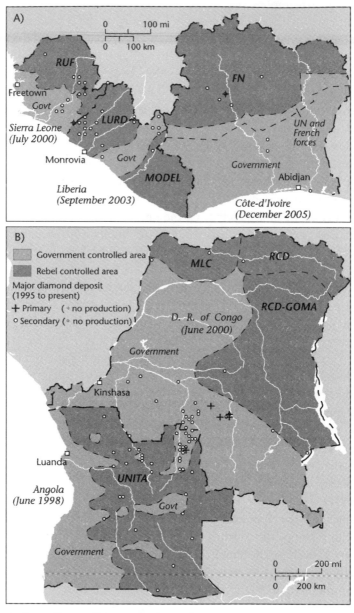

A. Sierra Leone, Liberia, the Ivory Coast.
B. Congo (DRC), Angola.

Figure 4.5: Diamond deposits and rebel controlled areas.

Front's commander, annually netted an estimated US$50 million from the sale of emeralds and lapis lazuli.[87] In the former Zaire, now the DRC, the mining and trafficking of alluvial gold in the hilly terrain of South Kivu province sustained Laurent Kabila's rebel movement, the Parti Révolutionnaire du Peuple, between the late 1960s and the creation of the AFDL in 1996. Gold and other alluvial minerals, such as coltan (a metal ore used in electronics, particularly mobile phones), appeared on the balance sheet of the Congolese "war economy" financing numerous armed groups operating in this region, from Ugandan troops to the "Mayi Mayi" local militia.[88]

We have seen that rebel access to diamond revenues is in part related to the type of deposits and associated mode of production, also to the military capacity of the government to secure the deposits and their relative location. In Angola, for example, UNITA's access to diamonds was largely facilitated by the existence of vast alluvial fields, but isolated industrial mining compounds also proved accessible through raids overwhelming army and mercenary protection. In turn, coercion and incentives were used by belligerents to reduce the "diffuse" character of diamonds once they had control of alluvial diamond fields, the impunity of belligerents enabling more drastic forms of disciplining.[89]

In Namibia, by contrast, alluvial diamonds buried under the sands of the southern coastline could also have constituted a lootable resource. But the South-West Africa People's Organisation (SWAPO), struggling for independence from apartheid South Africa, found it impossible to access the resource. Not only had previous German colonial authorities addressed the lootability problem by defining the area as a strictly enforced *Sperrgebiet* or "Forbidden Zone" in the wake of its genocide of the Herero, but the open terrain of the deserted coast also offered no cover to a guerrilla force. As explained by a former SWAPO fighter, now Director of Mines, "We could not have operated there—the South Africans would have simply bombed us."[90] This highlights the fact that the distinction between "point" and "diffuse" resources is to a large degree socially produced, with geographies of opportunity reflecting both physical and social conditions of control and access.

Spaces of opportunity are also shaped by the conditions of access to markets. The diamond market often starts in close proximity to the mines, often through "coaxers" and "bush" diamond-buying offices staffed by West African and Lebanese traders roaming the "diamond territory" from Guinea to Angola.[91] The diamond commodity chain continues through international connections hubs, bringing together local exporters with (multiple passport-holding) commodity brokers able to enter diamond trading centers (Figure 4.1A). The long-established culture of clandestine trading and "no questions asked" policy on the part of the diamond industry, as well as the strategic positioning of diamond-buying offices in countries neighbouring production areas, also allow multiple connections for both smuggled and conflict diamonds to be passed along the commodity chains and legally traded in international rough diamond markets such as that of De Beers, or the diamond bourses in Antwerp and Tel Aviv.[92]

Import statistics from Antwerp, the world's largest rough diamond market, demonstrate the complacency of the industry towards diamond trafficking. From the late 1980s to the mid-1990s as many diamonds arrived in Antwerp from "trafficking" countries as from producing ones in Africa, with no action taken during this period by Belgian authorities to address smuggling issues (see Figure 4.8).[93] While spaces of opportunity are shaped by connections with savvy companies and wealthy consumers, they also reflect a connection with poverty and coping economies, driving "civilians" to engage in diamond mining in rebel-controlled areas. Although forced labor and extortion were widespread, belligerents in Angola, Sierra Leone and the DRC also used economic incentives to draw workers into mining, including attracting them from neighbouring countries.[94] As succinctly stated by a Congolese miner when asked to explain his "complicity" with the rebellion in Angola, "there is no social welfare in Congo."[95]

Interconnections at the local and regional levels also reflect broader relationships and geographies that influence arms provision or diplomatic support.[96] Launched in 1991 from Liberian territory with the support of the Liberian warlord Charles Taylor, as part of a regional project supported by the Libyan and Burkinabe governments, the RUF insurgency continued to find in Liberia its main connections with diamond markets.[97] The Liberian government, and Charles Taylor personally, assisted in most "diamond-for-arms" flows between RUF mining sites and camps and Monrovia, as well as the port of Buchanan (see Figures 4.6A and 4.7). The RUF also relied on two other major types of connections. The first was with diamond buyers officially operating from government-controlled areas but using couriers crossing into rebel-held

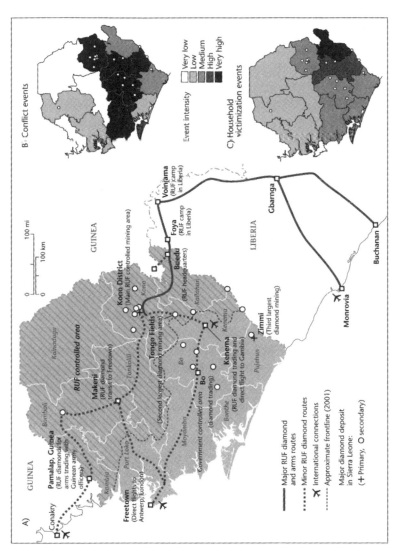

Figure 4.6: Diamond location, conflict intensity, and victimisation in Sierra Leone.

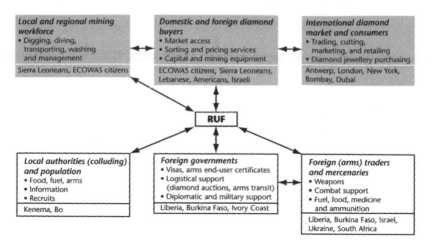

Figure 4.7: RUF diamond funded support network.

territories; as the diamond sanctions regime tightened controls, diamond buyers also set up "paper mines" in frontline areas to launder RUF diamonds.[98] The second was with colluding Sierra Leonean troops and with individual Guinean officers occasionally trading arms for diamonds.[99] As illustrated in Figure 4.6A, proximity to borders, transport infrastructure, diamond trading centers, and the collusion of authorities shaped the geography of these interconnections.

Because diamonds can be easily concealed, transported, stocked and (to some extent) marketed, they have been dubbed a "currency of choice" for

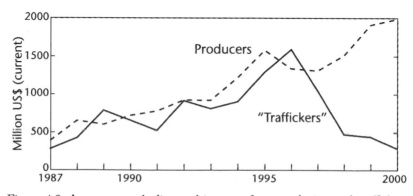

Figure 4.8: Antwerp rough diamond imports from producing and trafficking countries (1987–2000).

individuals and groups involved in money laundering and the financing of clandestine activities. In other words, the fact that diamonds are highly "fungible" may be an advantage for belligerents. Moreover, diamonds represent a relatively secure means of storing wealth, particularly when faced with volatile currencies, unreliable banking systems, regulatory scrutiny, or financial sanctions. Al Qaeda operatives, for example, are reported to have benefited from the sale in Liberia of millions of dollars of "conflict diamonds" mined under rebel control in neighbouring Sierra Leone.[100] Initial reporting confirmed the picture of West African warlords supporting Islamic terrorists. Deals had been conducted in Liberia under the protection of the warlord-turned-elected president Charles Taylor, an early supporter of the RUF also sponsored by Libyan authorities.[101] Such interconnections painted West Africa not only as a "wild zone" endangering the "locals" but also as a "rogue zone" threatening the West.[102]

The opportunities that diamonds (particularly alluvial) provide for combatants in mining and marketing are conventionally cited as reasons why diamonds are "conflict resources," as they are well suited, given their physical characteristics, to sustain armed conflict. Yet the role of the diamond sector as a "rebel's best friend" is a more ambivalent one than is generally portrayed. Diamonds have undeniably generated millions of dollars used to finance hostilities in Angola, the DRC, Sierra Leone, and to some extent Liberia and the Central African Republic (see Table 4.1). Although all three major diamond funded rebel movements—UNITA, RUF and AFDL—rapidly targeted diamond-mining areas, each also originally benefited from the backing of foreign governments and companies, even if some of that support was granted in part with the hope of gaining access to diamonds at a later date, as in the case of Liberian support of the RUF. So, the "financial opportunity" factor is thus broadly confirmed, but mostly after these conflicts were already initiated.[103] Furthermore this opportunity had ambivalent effects.

From a political standpoint, diamond financing facilitated the portrayal of rebellions as "greedy" criminal ventures, thereby undermining their political credentials. Access to diamond revenue also had a negative impact on trust and discipline within the movements, with accusations of private profiteering and widespread abuses against local populations.[104] Angolan and Sierra Leonean government troops abandoned their military duties to search for diamonds, with individual soldiers or officers trading with the enemy or leaving their posts after a significant find.[105] UNITA partly avoided this problem by prohibiting its soldiers from participating in mining and employing mostly Congolese diggers and foreign buyers.[106] Defending diamond areas is much more difficult than capturing them, which means frequent shifts of control between factions, or even local truces enabling both sides to mine.

The foregoing analysis suggests that diamonds, far from being a "rebel's best friend," pose a series of challenges—logistical, political, and even tactical—to belligerents. A key claim supporting this is that the distinction between "point" and "diffuse" resources is to a large degree socially produced, with geographies of opportunity reflecting political and social (as well as biophysical) conditions of control and access. In other words, the opportunities presented by diamonds in the context of resource wars are not only defined by simple notions of location (understood as vast and remote areas in the case of alluvial diamonds). They are also shaped by the commodity chain, which includes a range of interconnections defined by the material and commodity characteristics of diamonds: access to markets; transport and marketing infrastructure; and the domestic, regional, and international regulatory environment. This has profound implications for the successful regulation of resource-related armed conflicts.

Regulation, representation, and territorialisation

The assumptions that a "resource curse" exists, that artisanal diamond mining "breeds war," and that diamonds are a "rebel's best friend" have largely contributed to regulatory responses addressing conflict diamonds. Yet, as I have suggested, the limited conceptions of spatiality and violence underlying these arguments can misrepresent the role of the diamond sector in armed conflicts. In this section, I explore some of the implications for the regulatory strategies pursued to tackle diamond wars.

Four types of regulatory strategies have been adopted to address the role of commodities in fuelling war.[107] Three of these engage with the opportunity aspect of resource wars: targeted economic sanctions limiting market access for belligerents; military interventions restricting access to production areas by belligerents; and sharing agreements between belligerents reorienting financial incentives towards peace (that is, ensuring that opportunity is relocated into the realm of "peace" rather than war). The fourth strategy seeks to limit vulnerability and risk through resource management reforms (limiting the effects of the resource curse and reducing the risk of conflicts around resource exploitation).

In this section, I assess the adequacy of these mitigation responses. The analysis first considers the application of sanctions and international trade rules (the Kimberley Process), which have focused on limiting the opportunities afforded by conflict resources to belligerents through intervening in diamond commodity chains. I ask whether these measures, which have received the majority of attention from the media and NGOs, have had a significant effect, and I argue that military solutions to the risks posed by resource conflicts have played an important role that is often overlooked. The analysis then turns to a consideration of current mitigation initiatives, which are focused on vulnerability and risk pertaining to artisanal diamond miners, and explores the degree to which mitigation strategies engendered through an understanding of "conflict resources" operate spatially, creating spaces of legitimacy and criminality that may have unintended and undesired effects on conflict-affected countries and artisanal diamond producers.

From self(interested) regulation to international scrutiny

One of the particularities of the diamond sector is that it "has been largely self-regulating, operating outside the law of the state."[108] Reputation, trust, secrecy, and the superiority of private dispute resolution mechanisms have provided the regulatory tenets of the diamond trading sector. Since the late 1990s, however, the issue of conflict diamonds has brought about an unprecedented level of international scrutiny, with international diamond trade now coming under stricter national legislation in both exporting and importing countries. The role of diamonds in motivating or financing violence had long been acknowledged within industry circles. Measures such as UN sanctions had been slow to materialise because of the characteristics of the commodity, self-interest within the industry, foreign political support of diamond funded rebellions, and lack of public recognition of the problem.[109] Diamonds are easy to smuggle, and their geographical origin is also difficult to identify, once they are mixed in parcels with diamonds from other regions. Customary trading of diamonds smuggled out of producing countries to avoid taxation, and the lack of a paper trail and minimal external regulation of the industry, also reduce the prospect of effective sanctions.[110]

Attempts to address the problem of conflict diamonds in Angola in the early 1990s—such as Belgian MPs' 1993 proposed ban on Belgian imports of UNITA diamonds—were initially dismissed with such arguments, often by influential UNITA political backers.[111] However, momentum to address the problem of conflict diamonds grew in the late 1990s. Peace processes that had granted official responsibility over diamond sectors to rebel factions in Angola and Sierra Leone were failing. Moreover, the advocacy groups Global Witness and Partnership Africa-Canada launched public campaigns on conflict diamonds that resonated throughout the media.[112]

Three major initiatives were pursued. First, the UNITA Sanctions Committee of the UN Security Council drastically strengthened the implementation of the 1998 UN sanctions regime on UNITA diamonds through investigation panels "naming and shaming" sanctioned-busters, including the Presidents of Togo and Burkina Faso.[113] The Sanctions Committee also lobbied the diamond industry for prompt reforms and sent clear warnings about the consequences of a public boycott of diamonds, citing the example of the fur boycott in the 1980s. The UN later imposed sanctions on (non-certified) diamond exports from Sierra Leone in 2000, Liberia in 2001, and the Ivory Coast in 2005, with UN expert panels investigating the role of diamonds in these conflicts as well as those in the DRC.

The second initiative sought to consolidate the sanctions regimes by mobilising the industry and key governments in support of diamond trade reforms through public campaigns, international negotiations over certification of origin (the Kimberley Process), and legislative action. Campaigning NGOs denounced the complicity or inaction of the diamond industry and governments, yet they stopped short of calling for a complete diamond boycott that could affect hundreds of thousands of jobs (including diamond cutters in India) and diamond-dependent economies in Botswana and Namibia.[114] Nor did campaigners systematically launch judicial processes against corporate accomplices in war crimes and sanctions-busting. After initially denying any connection with conflict diamonds, major industry actors championed the creation of an international certification agreement to protect the carefully crafted image of their luxury product. By November 2002—after the end of war in Angola and Sierra Leone—thirty-eight countries adopted the international Kimberley Process Certification Scheme (KPCS). The scheme establishes a club within which participants commit not to trade in conflict diamonds. National legislation, peer review missions, and the possibility of exclusion back this commitment.[115]

The third initiative consisted of a set of "peace building" and "fair trade" programmes to improve the social conditions, political economy, and governance of diamond mining in conflict-prone countries. Recognising that the Kimberley Process did not address the concerns of artisanal mining communities, these programmes have been bringing together industry, governments, civil society organisations, and mining communities to address problems of poverty, corruption, political representation, and violence in diamonds areas.[116] The Diamond Development Initiative, founded by De Beers, Global Witness, Partnership Africa Canada, the international diamond valuator Martin Rapaport, and the World Bank, is seeking to "optimise the beneficial development impact of artisanal diamond mining to miners, their communities and their governments" throughout Africa.[117] In Sierra Leone, projects funded by the British and US governments aim to assist the government and communities in managing diamonds and to bring about "peace and prosperity" in mining areas.[118] Yet linking diamonds to terrorism and feeding the threatening image of "rogue" artisanal mining remain the best ways to get policy attention and funds from headquarters.[119] Most programmes, moreover, overlook the negative impacts of industrial mining on local livelihoods and community-related conflicts.[120]

Regulation as (punitive) representation and territorialisation

This set of three initiatives is often praised as a model for effectively regulating "conflict resources."[121] UN sanctions and the conflict diamond campaign undeniably undermined the strength of and support for rebel movements in Angola and Sierra Leone, and to a lesser extent in the DRC, mostly as a result of public shaming and valuable institutional and legislative changes within the diamond industry. The campaign also initiated new ethical dispositions and practices on the part of the diamond industry and diamond consumers, and by campaigners now refocusing this role towards "fair trade" artisanal diamond mining. Beyond the diamond sector, the campaign also inspired more ethical practices in other extractive industries, especially in terms of revenue transparency.

UN sanctions and expert panels, as well as the Kimberley Process Certification Scheme, have received the most media and scholarly attention.

Their role in ending the conflicts has often been overemphasised, compared with controversial military operations targeting the territorial dimensions of conflict diamond mining. Occasionally hailed for their effectiveness in curtailing rebel control over resource areas,[122] these operations were often marked by vested commercial interests on the part of intervening forces and widespread abuses, including the use of helicopter gunships against civilians in diamond mining camps.[123]

Moreover, the enactment of these regulatory initiatives can also be interpreted as a series of discursive representations serving to reposition corporate and political interests in diamond producing and consuming countries. Stricter international regulations have promoted "reputable" industrial companies at the expense of artisanal diamond diggers and petty traders, often associated with narratives of danger. The diamond industry successfully insulated itself from the potential financial costs of the conflict diamond campaign, and some companies even benefited by actively buying into the campaign and branding their diamonds accordingly. Prominent corporate interests championed diamond consumption through competing, and complementing, discourses of "prosperity diamonds" reasserting the contribution of the industry to the economy of several African countries such as Botswana and Namibia. What was lost through this strategy was a sense of historical accountability for past corporate practices. Ironically, for example, Sierra Leone's government called on British companies to resume mining activities in the country after the end of the conflict, yet during the British colonial period these companies had prohibited the possession of diamonds by "natives," underpriced Sierra Leone's diamonds, and in 1955 obtained the current equivalent of US$55 million from the public purse in "compensation" for relinquishing, after twenty years, the least valuable parts of a country-wide lease.[124] The discursive repositioning of diamonds as "conflict-free" and "ethical" also reinforced newfound advertising strategies based on corporate "integrity" and corporate restructuring around branding (for example, De Beers, Rand diamonds). The "purity" and "whiteness" of Canadian diamonds, for example, was evoked in contrast with tainted "blood diamonds" from Africa, invoking racialised images of Africa as synonymous with violence and primitivism.[125]

With the wars in Angola and Sierra Leone over, regulatory attention has been focused on "sustaining peace" in these countries, often with a view to enable large investments in industrial mining. The "conflict diamond" narrative conflating artisanal diamond miners with danger has informed "peace consolidation" strategies. Assuming the difficulties of taxation of the artisanal sector exploiting alluvial diamond deposits, revenue-concentrating modes of exploitation (through industrial means) and commercialisation (through trade licensing monopolies) are often presented as the best ways for a government to get income with which to sustain political stability.[126] In turn, however, securing peace in the diamond mining fields has been in part carried out spatially through military operations seeking to reinstate the "legitimate" claims of industrial mining companies—military operations that at times reek of wartime abuses.[127]

In Angola, "peace" has failed to bring about a "fundamental change in the pattern of exploitation in the diamond fields," while helping to pave the way for violent "clean-up" operations by government security forces and "to legitimise the status quo [of abuses and corruption] in the eyes of international observers and participants in the industry."[128] Although varying in their degree of physical brutality, violent processes of legalisation and (re)industrialisation have taken place in many post-conflict mining areas, including the eviction of freelance miners whose entitlements relied in part on conditions of chronic insecurity deterring industrial investments and enclosures.[129] Territorialising "peace," in other words, is proving to be a violent and marginalising process for many local mining communities.

Conclusion

My arguments in this chapter have suggested that we need to be cautious about conventional (and easy) arguments concerning the relationship between diamonds and war. Most important, if a "diamond curse" exists, it does so only in specific, constrained circumstances; diamond exploitation can be a factor for peace as well as a factor in increasing vulnerability to conflict. This reasoning implies that we need to look beyond simplistic arguments about diamond abundance or dependence to explain the role of diamonds in conflicts.

Equally, we should dismiss claims that artisanal diamond mining "breeds war." There is little evidence that so-called diamond wars directly emerged from lived experiences and social relations in diamond mining areas. However, it is equally true that the artisanal diamond sector is frequently rife with conflicts and violence, especially between (and within) local communities, migrant labor, companies, and authorities. Violent processes of dispossession, including forced displacement of communities and highly coercive "clean-up" operations against "illegal" diamond miners and traders in diamond fields, arguably increase the risk of war by raising grievances, undermining the probity and legitimacy of security forces, and drawing miners into wider conflicts. Thus, attempts to eradicate, displace, or control the revenues from artisanal mining may be the source of conflict (rather than the practice of artisanal mining itself).

Finally, we should be wary about arguments that diamonds are a "rebel's best friend." In fact, while diamond exploitation creates opportunities, it also sets up constraints and potential barriers (tactical, logistical, and even financial) to belligerents. Nonetheless, it is true that the diamond sector contributed to hostilities both financially (diamonds as source of revenue) and discursively (diamond-related grievances as source of rebellion justification) in several cases in the 1990s.

I have also attempted to explain, through a discussion of regulatory responses to diamond wars, why it is so important to nuance our views on the vulnerabilities, risks and opportunities created by diamonds in the context of armed conflicts. Conventional perspectives (in security studies and the public media) have often focused on military interventions and economic sanctions, with notable successes but also mixed effects. First, the deployment of troops into diamond mining areas often led to the involvement of armed forces deployed in diamond mining, collusion with rebel forces, and human rights abuses against local populations.[130] Second, there may be a tacit expectation that once resource locations are militarily "secured," the country will be at peace, yet renewed hostilities have followed government troops' and mercenaries' "successful" retaking of diamond areas, for example in Angola and Sierra Leone.[131] My analysis suggests that although the conventional emphasis on the spatial location and flows of resources helps with tracking diamond flows and reducing revenue access for rebel groups, measures to curtail conflict diamonds may have ambivalent effects on long-term peace-building.

This ambivalence ensues in part because mainstream perspectives on "resource wars" rest on narrow definitions of violence. By concentrating on the worst forms of human rights violations, conventional narratives of "resource wars" often succeed in grabbing the attention of policy-makers and consumers, and in promoting significant reforms, as in the case of rough diamond trading. Yet narrow definitions of violence, and ensuing policies focused on territorialising peace, overlook the violence implicit in regulatory interventions in resource governance, such as the forceful eviction of local populations and artisanal miners from diamond fields.

The selective representation of diamonds through their sites and modes of exploitation also contributes to (re)shaping spaces of legitimacy and criminality constitutive of (violent) processes of marginalisation. The idealisation of industrially-mined "Canadian" diamonds over artisanally mined "African" diamonds, for example, risked further marginalising one of the few commodities that has contributed sustained revenue to African economies in recent decades and aggravating the situation of artisanal miners. Ending diamond-related conflicts in Africa does not entail ending violence associated with diamond exploitation.

Broadening the definition of violence beyond armed conflicts and giving greater attention to violent processes of uneven development and territorialisation can help bring to light exploitative and exclusionary occurrences of "peacetime" diamond mining and trading. This expansion of the view, in turn, requires a critical re-reading of the selective geographies of post-conflict exploitation, regulation and consumption, (re)shaping spaces of legitimacy and criminality. Although nuanced accounts may undermine the strategic narratives of resource wars that have proved so effective in capturing public attention, these accounts should arguably help to bring about more durable, effective approaches to resource wars, a topic to which I shall return in Chapter 6.

5

TIMBER

From the deadly raids launched on Burundi's capital by Hutu rebels hiding in the nearby Tenga forest[1] to the multi-million-dollar exploitation of teak along the Thai-Burmese border by the Karen National Union,[2] insurgents have repeatedly used forests as a refuge or a source of finance. Located near roads and towns defined as military objectives or along border areas offering political sanctuary, forests provide some of the safest terrain from which to prepare or launch guerrilla operations. Forest products are also among the most frequent resources financing conflicts within a post-Cold War context in which business and predation have largely replaced foreign state support. As rebels take advantage of their location in forests to extort from or establish logging operations, underfunded or financially self-interested government forces deployed for counterinsurgency purposes frequently join in. Logging companies eager to access increasingly rare and valuable old growth forests are willing to take high risks and cut deals with whoever is in control.[3] Forests also provide a wide range of resources and environmental services, and changes in forest use result in frequent conflict between government authorities, local forest communities, recent forest colonisers, and resource companies.[4]

In this chapter, I briefly review the statistical evidence and literature on armed conflicts and forest resources before examining in turn the three thematic arguments of vulnerability, risk, and opportunity. I then turn to four main case studies—the Solomon Islands, Burma, Cambodia, and Liberia—to examine patterns and variations in war and forest relations. Finally, I discuss some of the livelihood and environmental dimensions of transition processes between war and peace.

Forests, timber, and wars

Forests have a prominent presence in wars as hideouts, sources of raw materials for warfare, and objects of conflict over their multiple uses.[5] As summed up by Hosny El-Lakany, FAO Assistant Director-General of Forestry:

There is so much about forested regions today that makes them perfectly primed to play host to war. It is in the forest where one often finds poor, isolated populations who are either ignored or mistreated and may need little encouragement to take up arms, and where there is usually valuable timber, minerals, oil and land that can easily be the source of tension. There is also the simple fact that forests can provide refuge, funds and food for fighters.[6]

But do forest resources increase the odds of armed conflict and influence its duration? Statistical studies testing these potential effects have yielded mostly negative results. Forest cover is not found to be significantly related to the likelihood of either onset or duration of armed conflict.[7] Conflict areas are found to be less forested than the average of the country in which conflicts occur.[8] A measure of forest export dependence does not yield robust statistical significance either.[9] Finally, forest conflicts could be related to changes in forest use. Tests based on deforestation rates have yielded mixed results, the most recent study finding no statistically significant relationship.[10] Overall, there is little statistically significant and robust evidence that forest cover, forest export dependence, or deforestation generally influences the onset risk or duration of armed conflicts. Such results do not mean, however, that no such relationship exists but that statistical tests, given the data available, cannot confirm a general pattern. Forests may matter to warfare, and in particular guerrilla warfare, but the existence of forest cover and forest product export dependence do not systematically affect conflict onset and duration. In over-simple terms, forests do not produce rebellions.

These results contrast with much of the literature on insurgencies, and with war studies more generally. Forests, along with swamps and mountains, have been the perennial "favourable grounds" of guerrilla warfare. In Classical Greece, Thucydides relates that the militarily weaker Aetolians defeated the "best soldiers of Athens" by getting them lost in pathless forests, blocked against ravines they could not climb and surrounded by a ring of fire. There are numerous records of insurgents making use of forests: Balkan Christians against the Turks, Americans fighting the British army during the War of Independence, Chouan royalists against French revolutionaries, Poles against Russians in the 1860s, Sandino's forces in Nicaragua during the 1930s, partisans in Nazi-occupied Ukraine, Mau Mau against British colonial forces, Viet Cong forces opposing US and South Vietnamese armies, or FARC units hiding from Colombian troops.[11] Forests have also been used for static defensive purposes, with citadels located within forests. Both kings and villagers have planted forests as a means of defence, with forest rings used for example around villages in the Sahelian savanna to create fortresses.[12]

Forests can stop cavalry and vehicles, provide cover to reduce the effectiveness of artillery or aerial bombardment, and facilitate ambush. Forests can also provide means of sustenance, and they have provided a refuge for some of the longest-running guerrilla movements. An anti-Communist highlander armed group was found in remote forested areas in eastern Cambodia in the mid 1990s, hiding from Vietnamese forces and thinking that the Vietnam War was still going on. Rebel groups frequently use contiguous forests as safe travel corridors, giving way to a parallel transport infrastructure. The frequent presence of forests in remote border areas also provides an advantage to transboundary military strategies for rebel groups, such as the famed North Vietnamese Ho Chi Minh Trail (or Truong Son Road). Many contemporary forests are classified as "protected areas," including transboundary "peace parks," which makes them choice locations for rebellions.[13] Under military pressure, the Ugandan rebel Lord's Resistance Army (LRA) in 2005 moved into the relative safety of the Garamba National Park's "dense and verdant forests" in the adjoining northeastern DRC.[14] The park was located across the border from the Lantoto Game Reserve in Southern Sudan. Eight UN peacekeepers died in 2005 during a failed attempt at capturing LRA leaders in Garamba. The UN operation, conducted by about eighty US-trained Guatemalan soldiers, had followed a US-backed helicopter attack on the main LRA camp in the park that dealt a blow to the rebel movement but also resulted in the deaths of many women and children.[15]

Most field manuals and war studies recognise the importance of forests in terrain analysis.[16] Ernesto "Che" Guevara made specific reference to the value of forests for rebel armies, and he considered them among the most favourable of settings for guerrilla warfare. Yet he also stressed that "[a]s soon as the survival of the guerrilla band is assured, it should fight; it must constantly go out from its refuge to fight" the enemy in more open terrain.[17] While forests are militarily secure and particularly suited to periods of consolidation or retreat, they are ineffective politically owing to the lack of contact with the population and engagement with the enemy army. As a Darfurian rebel in Sudan put it, "we cannot stay forever under the trees [hiding from Sudanese air forces]."[18] Forests also pose challenges such as access to food and medicine supplies, as well as poor living conditions, especially during the rainy season. Forest paths remain open to ambushes against rebel groups, especially by local militias with a superior knowledge of local conditions and hunting techniques such as the Kamajors in Sierra Leone.[19] So while forests still have importance, guerrilla warfare has shifted from "hiding in nature" to "finding cover in town," reflecting changes in demography, rising urbanisation, and more effective rural counterinsurgency, as well as changing political agendas.[20]

Recognising this strategic and tactical importance, forests have been destroyed for counterinsurgency purposes through fire, felling, or herbicides. Cambodians narrate how their capital Lovek fell to the Thai enemy in 1594;[21] while besieging the capital, Thai cannon fired silver coins rather than cannon balls into the citadel's defensive bamboo forest. The population cut the forest to get to the silver, and a year later the Thais returned to successfully assault the city. Russia's invasion and murderous "pacification" of the Caucasus in the first half of the nineteenth century faced resistance, as the Russian general Ermelov "conquered the mountains but the forests defied him."[22] After years of Chechen insurrection, Russian axemen protected by soldiers cut down forests in Chechnya's valleys. The motto of the US Air Force twelfth Air Commando Squadron in charge of defoliation in Vietnam (Operation Ranch Hand) was "Only we can prevent forests," asserting the effectiveness of Monsanto's Agent Orange herbicide over other deforestation techniques, such as aerial bombardment and clearing forests with bulldozers.[23] Between 1961 and 1971, the US spread 75 million litres of herbicides on "jungles" and forest regions,[24] but also on croplands and the perimeters of US bases and communication lines.[25]

Besides providing a hideout for militarily weaker parties, forests have also provided timber as a material for warfare and source of funding. Wood has been one of the longest used materials for weapons, defensive palisades, and warships.[26] Timber supply has been at times a major preoccupation of military strategists and a motive of colonial ventures.[27] A key concern of northern European states was naval timber, which led to legislation protecting oaks for their navies.[28] Seeking to address domestic shortages and break their dependence on timber coming from the Baltic, European powers sought sources in North America, Africa, and Asia.[29] Shipbuilding timbers and especially teak became a major concern during the Napoleonic wars.[30] The Spanish had found abundant supplies in the Philippines, the Dutch in Indonesia, and the British in India and Burma, while the French later signed a protectorate with Cambodia, partly on the false assumption of finding teak there. Colonial appropriation was generally followed by the application of European (mostly German) forest "scientific" management blueprints that created "forest reserves" exclusively geared at forest exploitation and conservation purposes.[31] The presence and practices of local populations—such as shifting cultivation involving "slash and burn"—were widely prohibited. Colonial appropriation of forests and logging practices, in turn, were a source of tensions among land users, local authorities, and empires as in the case of US mahogany logging operations in Honduras or that of British timber merchants pushing for war in order to access Lower Burma's best teak forests.[32]

Forests have also provided a source of funding for numerous armed groups either directly running logging operations or simply taxing them (see below). Besides timber, armed groups have tapped into non-timber forest products, such as wildlife and plants, and they have also used cleared forestlands for narcotics production.[33] From a contemporary perspective, forests and forest exploitation can influence armed conflicts in four main ways: by weakening governance; as a source of conflict over rights of use; by providing a safe haven; and as a source of funds for rebels and repressive governments.

Logging and the curse of timber booms

Is there a "timber curse," in the sense of a breakdown of governance and economic performance resulting in greater vulnerability to armed conflicts? The role of the forestry sector in sustaining corrupt, clientelistic and repressive rule has been suggested for many countries, at least at the subnational level.[34] Wood products represent a major export for about a dozen developing countries, most of them located in the inter-tropical band (see case studies below). These include most countries in South East Asia, with high level of export dependence in Indonesia, Malaysia, the Philippines and Thailand until the 1980s, and in Burma, Cambodia and Laos until the late 1990s. Africa's major exporters have included the Ivory

Coast, Nigeria, Cameroon and Gabon, as well as more recently the Democratic Republic of Congo. Forestry sectors in each of these countries have been affected by various forms of illegal logging which involved a high degree of collusion on the part of authorities.[35]

Like most other commodities, wood products experienced two major price booms, first for the decade following the 1973 oil crisis, and then again from 2003 onwards. By 2008, exports of global wood products were estimated at US$237 billion.[36] Some of the resource curse factors are not so prominent in the timber sector. The prices of forest products are generally less volatile than those of some other commodities, like oil or cash crops, in part because of the number of exporting countries, the relative resilience in the face of climatic events (unlike cash crops), and more limited opportunities for speculation.[37] Levels of wood product export dependence are generally much lower than for petroleum, minerals or agricultural commodities, and the rents thus have less distorting effects, at least at the macroeconomic level.[38]

Institutional breakdown in relation to forest-related activities during timber booms has been well documented in Southeast Asia.[39] As countries experienced successive logging booms, bureaucrats and politicians competed to increase and seize logging rents. This destroyed the institutions enabling sustainable forest exploitation and contributed to a downward price cycle as timber volumes ballooned. The timber booms in the Philippines and Malaysia not only saw the dismantling of institutional forestry safeguards, forest profits were also used to undermine broader institutions, by rewarding political supporters and co-opting or silencing opposition.[40] Logging contracts have also been a feature of patronage politics in Sub-Saharan Africa, especially Cameroon and the Ivory Coast.[41] Institutional breakdown worsened during Charles Taylor's rule in Liberia between 1997 and 2003, with foreign timber companies enabling the privatisation of rule by the former warlord—including security matters, with logging company militias staffed by Taylor's personal troops in effect displacing the army in some areas.[42]

There is also some evidence of the institutional legacy of colonial extractive sectors, including logging, in property rights and state building. Shifts in property rights from communal to state or private hands influenced local governance and power relations, not to mention being a source of conflict. Timber interests, and particularly those of the owners of timber trading companies, came to influence colonial policies, at times exacerbating conflicts as colonial forces were deployed to assert access to timber.[43] To facilitate resource exploitation, including timber stands, specific rights were assigned to (or left unaddressed in) resource areas, in effect creating a core area dominated by a politically and economically empowered group overseeing peripheral areas now peopled with "second-class" citizens. Burma, Cambodia, Laos, Liberia and Sierra Leone were archetypical situations in this regard, with coastal or riverine groups that had consolidated their power through agriculture and trade dominating "hinterland" populations in peripheral forested areas. These situations were not only the result of colonial politics, but also often reflected pre-colonial political geographies of domination.[44]

Forest exploitation also occurred in a context of nation-state building that included the political integration of peripheral populations (including forest dwellers) and economic modernisation (including the industrialisation of forest use). Such processes potentially reinforced the state through greater financial means and "national" politics, but also made it more vulnerable to dissent by overextending it and framing it as a threat to political "minorities." As we shall see, Burma is in this regard a prime case, with different policies for the ethnic majority Burmese "lowlanders" and ethnic minorities in the highlands. In short, timber can influence institutional performance and increase vulnerability to conflict, but this is often inscribed in much larger political geographies articulating populations and their territories—the historical constitution of "heartlands" and "borderlands," the latter frequently being forested regions.

Do forest dwellers have different institutions making them (or the central state) more vulnerable to armed conflicts? Arguably, many forest dwelling populations have a history of antagonistic relationship with central states. This relationship is frequently born out of state repression and predation, leading individuals and groups to seek refuge in remote and hard-to-control regions. There they develop institutions and livelihoods facilitating "state resistance," both from without and from within. As asserted by James Scott, the forested highlands of mainland Southeast Asia have been

peopled over the last 2,000 years largely by runaways from several state-making projects in the valleys, most particularly Han state-making projects. They have, in the hills, acquired, and shifted, their ethnic identities. Far from being "remnants" left behind by civilising societies, they are, as it were, "barbarians by choice," peoples who have deliberately put distance between themselves and lowland state-centers. It is in this context that their forms of agriculture, their social structures, and much of their culture, including perhaps even their illiteracy, can be understood as political choices.[45]

Vulnerability to conflicts in such areas as the Burmese, Laotian and Vietnamese highlands thus reflects in part the enabling institutional effects of forests as "hideouts" facilitating the institutional development of "anti-state" projects. Political opposition groups escaping from the lowlands have often found refuge with such groups, and sometimes inspiration in the institutional models of highlanders. In many cases, however, such opposition groups were pursuing state-building projects that clashed with the political choices of highland forest dwellers. The Khmer Rouge found in Cambodia's northeastern forests not only shelter from government security forces but also, in the initial years, a receptive and inspirational "indigenous" population.[46] However, the Khmer Rouge rapidly instituted Maoist centralisation measures. While some highlanders saw communism as an emancipatory and empowering project, many saw it as a state-building, subjugating one, from which they sought to escape— fleeing northward for the deep-forest areas along the Laotian border or eastward to Vietnam. Beyond Southeast Asia, hostilities have also focused on forested areas where "indigenous" groups perceived as supporting insurgencies were historically concentrated by the colonial practice of seizing the best lands. Military rulers in Guatemala, for example, targeted indigenous populations as state enemies, and the vast majority of massacres perpetrated between the late 1970s and the mid-1990s occurred in isolated and often forested highland areas where indigenous populations had been displaced by the Spanish conquest.[47]

Overall, there is good evidence that forests and timber booms can affect institutions and make them more vulnerable to armed conflicts. There is less evidence in favour of the "economic underperformance" argument, in part because of lack of studies and the often lesser importance of timber dependence compared with oil or mineral dependence. Evidence can be drawn from the ecological consequences of deforestation, especially on downstream agricultural productivity, with for example the well-documented benefits of protecting forested headwaters.[48] Evidence is scantier in terms of the macroeconomic consequences of forest revenue dependence (a timber version of the "Dutch disease"). Membership in the International Tropical Timber Organisation is associated with lower economic growth between 1975 and 2004, especially in the case of Africa.[49]

At the production area level, the renewable character of forests is supposed to enable stability, if not growth, among forest-dependent communities.[50] Mechanisation, capital intensification, and unintended or unpredicted forest depletion have nevertheless reduced the "sustainable" character of many forest-based economies.[51] Devastated landscapes and ghost logging towns (and, more frequently, simple base camps where workers settled at increasingly greater distances from logging sites) are testimony to the frequent unsustainability of logging for local development. In many cases, land use is restricted to timber production and does not allow other uses such as agricultural, industrial, or residential uses that would help diversify the economy. Agricultural forest settlements and the intensification of modes of production have opposed, for example, swidden agriculture (maintaining the forest), smallholder agriculture (such as shade-grown coffee, also maintaining the forest) and industrial plantations (such as for rubber or palm oil, leading to a drastic change in the "nature" of forests). Overall, there is some limited evidence that logging may undermine long-term growth while also opening forests to various forms of alternative land use that can result in high levels of inequalities. As I shall relate in the case of West Kalimantan, these changes can result in grievances and organised violence, yet they need to be contextualised in relation to other political and economic factors.

Forests and timber conflicts

Many conflicts are taking place over the exploitation and transformation of forested lands. Logging constitutes one of the most politicised forest-related activities, but forests have uses other than logging (some of which benefit from the access and deforestation resulting from logging activities). Mining, road building and forest clearing for agriculture and cattle ranching all involve major transformations of landscapes, environmental process, economies, and social relations. Major studies have documented conflicts occurring over changes in forest uses and rules of access to forest resources. Resistance to agrarian change in the forests of early eighteenth-century England, for example, resulted in the extension of state violence, with such extremes as the death penalty for acts associated with deer-stealing, including breaking down fences.[52] In turn, the struggles against Western colonial appropriation of forests and the imposition of Western forestry models have politicised populations,[53] as in the case of

Java's teak forests.[54] Peasant struggles around forest resources in the foot-
hills of the Himalayas have ranged from peaceful demonstrations to guerrilla fighting, and violent repression by the state and business interests.[55]
Harvesters of wild rubber in the Amazon opposed forest clearing by
ranchers during the 1980s, with some ranches violently quelling opposition, by means including targeted killings.[56] The Zapatista rebellion in
the Chiapas province of Mexico was largely related to land conflicts taking place over forested areas that were logged, converted for grazing and
agricultural purposes, or given protected area status, with indigenous
groups and poor migrant peasants being marginalised and abused.[57] Forest—and especially wildlife—conservation measures have often taken
the form of "war-like" rhetoric and practices since the 1990s, with "shoot-
to-kill" policies against poachers.[58]

The diversity of these conflicts begs the question of possible patterns
and processes relating them to large-scale armed conflicts. Arguably,
much of the physical violence associated with forest-related conflicts is
diffuse, involving an interplay of state repression and violent modes of
resistance seeking to challenge state (or corporate) rule. These modes of
resistance often accompany illegal but not always illicit—that is, socially
condemned—practices such as hunting, logging, non-timber forest product harvesting, and agricultural settlements. Historical stratification of
state and "popular" or customary rule lends various degrees of legitimacy
to these diverse practices, with international opinion being sometimes
mobilised to back certain claims over others (for example, indigenous
land rights in the Amazon but not hunting rights in the Congo Basin).

Conflicts over forest uses have broader political dimensions than the
forest resources themselves. In many parts of the world, processes of state-
formation and economic modernisation require the control of populations. As observed in the case of Southern Italy, and in other parts of the
world such as mainland Southeast Asia, "controlling people implied
changing their place in the landscape, and, thus, changing the landscape
itself."[59] Forests are "deforested" or put into exclusive use as "reserve forests;" upland livelihoods, involving a mix of trees, crops and animals, are
"improved" economically by shifting to other modes and locales of production; and remote villages are "relocated" to lowlands and main transport arteries. Such (mostly coercive) processes of enclosure allow for the
appropriation of forestlands, the provision and control of labor, and the
circumscribing of political spaces to those most amenable to state rule.[60]

A frequent example is the eradication of villages and displacement of populations located in logging concessions or protected areas.[61] The newly designated areas often come under the exclusive authority of forestry or conservation departments that allow coercive means such as the use of weapons. Justification for coercive means relates not only to the threat of violence from "illegal" forest users, such as illegal loggers and poachers, some of whom in fact seek to maintain pre-designation rights, but also to the perception of threat associated with forest-dwelling people. Hence, processes of state-making in forested areas often rapidly involve militarisation presented as counterinsurgency or an escalation of heavy-handed policing against "bandits" and "criminals."[62] The question of forest-related conflict escalation can, in this perspective, be framed as mobilisation against a state-led project of domination that quickly resorts to using military means to quell dissent, precisely because of the perception of state vulnerability resulting from the rebellious potential of forest landscapes and social institutions.

A second, associated framing relates to the migration of populations into forested areas, with conflict occurring between indigenous communities and migrants in search of land or forest resources. This process of colonisation is not exclusive to forest areas, but the characteristics of forest tenure—such as customary local commons, public land, or logging-oriented land use rights—make them prime targets for this type of population movement and settlement.[63] Such migration can respond to various push and pull factors, such as high demand for land and forest resources associated with poverty, a weak bureaucratic capacity unable to regulate migration flows or, on the contrary, a political project of settling forested areas with the "right" people in order to alleviate population pressure elsewhere, or undermine local populations.

In such contexts, the politics of identity can play a major role in conflicts. The politics of indigeneity have, for example, been at work in West Kalimantan in Indonesia, where recurring conflicts have pitted "indigenous" groups against various kinds of migrant populations.[64] The first victims consisted mostly of a long-established ethnic Chinese population suspected of communism during the late 1960s, and forcibly expelled from forest areas for the purposes of counterinsurgency by the Indonesian military, with the assistance of army-incited "indigenous" Dayaks. In the second category of victims were the Madurese people, who were successively targeted by Dayak groups in 1997 and by Malay groups in

1999. Stereotyped as violent, land-grabbing, recent migrants refusing cultural and social integration, the Madurese provided for the Dayaks in particular a convenient target group to reassert territorial claims and political strength at a time of institutional breakdown.[65] Stories of colonisation of "Dayak" forest areas by "Madurese," whatever the actual reality, were central to the politics of aboriginal rights assertion.

To sum up, there is some evidence that forests can increase the risk of conflict escalating into organised violence, not by reason of simply being forests, but through the resource stakes, identities and strategies associated with them. Forests do constitute particular landscapes in many cultural imaginaries of social strife. Association with forests thus constructs specific political identities that often, from a state perspective, include a notion of primitiveness and threat. Forests also provide tangible assets, including (but not solely) timber, the tenure of which is frequently challenged and in some respects easily contestable.

Conflict timber

Timber is a valuable resource, and not just for warfare: some hardwood species are valued at hundreds of dollars per cubic meter. This monetary value has made timber a major source of finance for many armed groups. Yet timber is bulky and hard to conceal, and existing river and road transport corridors often limit its shipment. In short, it is a resource for which shipment is relatively easy to control. With the exception of forests in border areas (including maritime shipment points) that are controlled by insurgents, timber should provide advantage to a government over a rebel group. Logging operations, however, are vulnerable to extortion schemes, particularly because of their location in forested areas. Threats can include: laying out mines along logging roads and bridges crossing creeks; ambushes along logging roads resulting in killing or kidnapping of staff; attacks on hard-to-defend logging camps; or sabotage of operating equipment. As I shall describe, armed groups in Burma, Cambodia and Liberia found timber a major source of finance during the 1990s. This was also the case in the Philippines for the New People's Army (NPA), the Communist Party of the Philippines' armed branch.[66] More recently, timber figures among Taliban funding sources, especially in Pakistan's Swat valley.[67]

If logging provides an apparently easy source of funding for insurgent groups, it is not without its challenges. Logging entails road construction and felling trees, which undermine the "hideout" qualities of forests by facilitating observation and transport. Rebel groups thus discriminate between logging in strategically benign areas and more sensitive ones. The NPA in the Philippines went as far as asking a few companies to reforest in 1990 and threatened some companies in order to obtain higher wages for reforestation staff.[68] Most of the few remaining forests in the Philippines were strategic guerrilla strongholds where rebel groups did not allow the construction of roads. Logging company staff can also act as informants to both sides in the conflict, providing security forces with the identity of key commanders and supporters, the location of camps and forest trails, and assessments of the relative strength of rebel forces.

Rebellions occurring in forested areas also acquire a specific identity via the language of counterinsurgency, denigrating them through rhetoric associating them with "wilderness" and "banditry." Rebels are merged with a space opposed to civilisation, represented as cruel bandits operating in the "dark woods" and savages fighting in the "jungles."[69] Growing environmental concerns among the public since the 1980s have also made rebels' association with logging a political liability, and many groups have sought to improve their image through declarations in favour of forest protection. This was particularly the case for "popular" rebel groups, such as the Karen National Union, which quite successfully portrayed itself as "green" by supposedly resisting logging perpetrated by Burmese forces and Thai companies. Finally, while timber has often been a source of funding for insurgents, it has also been used as an incentive for peace by governments through offering "legal" concessions and thus potentially massive financial rewards to armed groups, as the Philippines President Marcos did with Muslim rebels.[70] This strategy was widely applied in Burma in the 1990s, when—in a context of relative poverty, ethno-religious fragmentation of the Communist Party, rising military pressure, and increasing regional hostility—financial incentives provided an effective way to break apart some insurgent groups and increase the number of cease-fire agreements with the government.[71]

In short, timber is not the preferred "conflict resource" of rebellions for direct exploitation, but it has nevertheless been widely used because of its availability and the relative ease of extorting companies in areas under partial rebel control. As with the diamond sector—in which opportunities included a greater ease of recruitment (through voluntary or coerced recruitment of artisanal miners)—the forest sector also offers various opportunities, in this case terrain (or hideout) resources, and often receptive local populations with a history of state resistance.

Conflict and timber: Selected case studies

Prominent recent cases of armed conflict associated with timber include the Solomon Islands, Burma, Cambodia, and Liberia.[72] The question is not so much whether armed groups in these countries will seek to derive revenue from logging (they will), but how forests and the logging sector relate to armed conflicts and what consequences the availability (or "opportunity") of timber revenue will have on the conflict. The main argument is that timber facilitates the survival and scaling-up of insurgencies by providing access to funds.

These four countries attracted the most attention on timber and conflict relationships during the 1990s and early 2000s. Each country became highly reliant on timber exports and saw timber revenue financing both insurgencies and government troops, with logging issues grabbing the attention of international media and policy-makers. Timber export reliance was often exacerbated when the government was internationally isolated or in the early phase of a supposed transition to peace (when other sectors were yet to be rebuilt or developed). In this regard, timber exports played an important role in sustaining repressive regimes and insurgencies. Whereas the forest sector in these countries was not the only or even the main cause of conflict, timber at times drove the course of hostilities. This was particularly the case when both governments and insurgencies became effective logging partners, as both granted concessions and taxed logging companies. In Burma and to a lesser extent in Cambodia, logging revenues were used as an incentive by the government to end hostilities through cease-fire agreements or defections. In the best of cases, the situation led to a formal cessation of hostilities. However, this nevertheless resulted in low-level conflict involving local communities and logging companies over forest use and livelihoods. In the worst cases, the situation pitted contending parties against each other, vying for control of the logging sector, with intensified hostilities, a breakdown of chains of command within armed groups, the use of private militias by logging companies, and widespread human rights abuses against local communities. In most cases, logging and hostilities took place along border areas where rebel groups were most concentrated and timber stands could be most easily exploited and shipped. Neighbouring countries typically play a major role in this regard, through "resource diplomacy" strategies trading raw materials for military and political support.

Such patterns of forest exploitation came to an end through a combination of forest depletion, domestic and international outcry, and elites realising that they were losing control of logging activities to local strongmen and entrepreneurs. The ensuing crackdowns on "illegal logging" often targeted the most politically vulnerable logging operations, curtailing forest access by local communities, protecting select cronies, or shifting to alternative land use such as palm oil plantations.

Solomon Islands: Timber export dependence and vulnerability

The Solomon Islands provide an example of timber dependence potentially resulting in higher vulnerability to armed conflict.[73] The islands have a limited economic base, but by 1994, after a decade of dramatic increase, the logging sector provided about 56 percent of export revenues and 30 percent of government revenue. Such high dependence resulted in part from rising international demand in the face of a decline in timber exports from Thailand and the Philippines, with Malaysian, Indonesian and Korean companies turning to new sources such as the Solomons. The boom also resulted from a lack of regulations and massive tax exemptions, a situation that became politically volatile owing to widespread abuses on the part of companies and politicians, as well as powerful individuals declaring themselves landowners of commons.[74] A new prime minister was elected with the promise of a logging ban, but his government was prematurely brought down by politicians shifting sides— reportedly following bribes paid by logging companies.[75] A new government was again brought to power in 1997 under a forest reform agenda, but it was confronted by the Asian crisis and the associated collapse of timber prices. Rising tension escalated into a brief civil war between two main militias in 1998, followed by widespread social strife and opportunistic criminality. The 1999–2003 period further aggravated dependence on timber exports as many firms in other sectors left the Islands. In 2003, a bankrupt and powerless Solomons government requested military and administrative assistance from Australia.

Burma: Logging as profitable counterinsurgency

The largest mainland country in Southeast Asia, the former kingdom of Burma, came under British control following three successive wars between 1824 and 1886, with brutal "pacification" dragging into the late 1890s. With continuous insurgencies since independence in 1948, Burma remains today the most conflict-affected country in the world—not by the number of deaths or displaced persons but by the sheer number of insurgent groups involved and the longevity of these struggles.[76] Forests played a central role as a refuge for insurgent groups as early as the 1950s.[77] More broadly, many of the forest and highland "minority groups" in mainland Southeast Asia share a common history of escape from the state through relocation into remote and hard-to-control areas.[78]

Burma has also a long-established history of insurgency and military repression motivated or financed through logging.[79] British control of Burma became in part motivated by, and financed through its teak wealth.[80] The volume of teak harvested nearly doubled after the 1962 coup d'état, with logging revenue remaining one of the military regime's economic foundations.[81] From the 1960s onwards, the Burmese military encouraged the self-funding of semi-autonomous "home guard" militia groups through logging activities. This approach was extended to many of the armed groups benefiting from cease-fire agreements with the military regime.[82] Logging activities in Burma greatly increased after the withdrawal of international aid in 1988 following violent repression of a democracy movement, as the government sought to increase alternative sources of foreign currency. Logging bans in neighbouring Thailand in 1989 and China in 1998 (both after devastating floods) also intensified demand for Burmese timber.[83]

The Burmese military junta initially turned to Thai authorities and logging companies, with new logging contracts tripling the area of exploited forests and doubling government timber revenues.[84] Much of the logging was conducted in border areas where separatist insurgencies had long fought the regime and pro-democracy opponents had sought refuge after the 1988 and 1990 crackdowns. Roads built by Thai logging companies and the logistical assistance they provided to Burmese troops facilitated counterinsurgency, while much of the logging revenue went into arms purchases for the Tatmadaw (the Burmese state military). Lucrative logging concessions awarded by the Burmese military junta to politically influential Thais constituted a new "resource diplomacy" that favourably shaped Thailand's foreign policy towards the junta in Rangoon.[85] Intensive logging was a political blow to the insurgent groups such as the Karen, whose identity, struggle, and livelihoods were strongly associated with forests.[86] In response, insurgent groups sought to opportunistically tax some of the timber exports through their control of key border areas, or by awarding concessions of their own. This resulted in a massive rush on timber, overlapping concession areas, and competition both between armed groups and logging companies. So, by the early 1990s,

the sale of teak stands determined the course of the war. Teak and other tropical hardwoods were cut down at an unprecedented rate, without regard to sustainable management. In some cases trees were clear-felled even as battles were being fought. Territory changed hands, cash and arms flowed in, and the prospect of further gains intensified the war.[87]

Rapid logging and illegal practices also depleted forests and thus one of the assets sustaining the groups. The government cancelled Thai logging concessions in 1993 because of taxation by insurgent groups and contractual infringements by companies. Yet some of the counterinsurgency purposes of the logging deals were achieved, and by 1995 many insurgent groups had either signed cease-fire agreements, or seen their bases overrun by the Burmese army.[88]

Subsequent logging deals mostly involved China and took place in the context of prior cease-fire agreements, in effect sharing revenue between the State Law and Order Restoration Council (SLORC)/State Peace and Development Council (SPDC), the leadership of insurgent groups, and Chinese logging interests.[89] China has been a crucial supporter of the internationally isolated military junta in Burma since 1988, and in return for diplomatic and military support, Burma has become an important supplier of natural resources to China, including timber. Cross-border trade increased after the fall of the Communist Party of Burma in 1989, and logging increased following cease-fire agreements and the defection of insurgent groups to the government in the early to mid-1990s, as well as after the Chinese logging ban affecting Yunnan in 1998. Whereas local populations welcomed the cease-fire agreements, the logging boom that ensued provided little benefit to them, as Chinese companies employed Chinese labor for logging and road building and transformed logs in China. Most of the revenue generated for the Kachin States appeared to benefit local elites, including military groups.[90] Many of the major logging deals were on an "infrastructure-for-timber" barter basis, but many complained that "the only thing the Kachin people get is roads to get the trees out."[91] Massive losses in timber revenue due to illegal logging and smuggling, as well as international media coverage of the massive scale of Chinese logging in Northern Burma, led the SPDC to declare a logging ban in the northern part of the country in 2005, with Chinese authorities closing China's border to timber trade with Burma in 2006.[92]

Cambodia: Conflict timber and "post-conflict" corruption

A formerly powerful kingdom in decline since the fifteenth century, Cambodia came under French protectorate in 1863. Initially attracted by the prospects of a trading route via the Mekong River and a supply of teak (both of which proved delusory), the French considered the country a "backwater" of Indochina.[93] Ravaged by US bombing and the murderous rule of the Khmer Rouge led by Pol Pot, Cambodia became emblematic of links between forests, armed groups, and logging companies in the 1990s, as the Khmer Rouge survived financially on timber exports to neighbouring Thailand. Cambodia was among the first countries to come under a UN Security Council sanctions regime, which specifically targeted the main source of finance of rebel groups, in this case log exports. Logging's role in sustaining war in Cambodia was also the first campaign of Global Witness, the leading NGO on resources and conflict issues, which carefully collected and widely publicised evidence on the role of the logging sector in financing the war, demonstrating the complicity of neighbouring state authorities, the collusion of Cambodian political parties in power, and the massive costs this entailed for the population and the environment.[94]

Since Vietnamese military forces routed the Khmer Rouge regime in 1979, Thai border areas and forests had provided a refuge for the Khmer Rouge and other insurgent groups. From the early 1980s, Thai military personnel entered into logging deals with armed factions located along Cambodia's western border in exchange for arms and the protection of refugees. The presence of Vietnamese troops inside Cambodia until 1989 greatly confined such activities. Logging remained of minor importance to the different warring factions as they continued to receive financial backing from their foreign sponsors (such as China in the case of the Khmer Rouge).[95] In 1988, three years before the withdrawal of major

Chinese sponsorship, the Khmer Rouge leader Pol Pot stressed that the long-held policy of autarky was no longer suitable for Cambodia and that it was "imperative that we find ways to develop the natural resources that exist in our liberated and semi-liberated zones as assets to be utilised in the fight against the Vietnamese aggressor enemy."[96] The departure of Vietnamese forces in September 1989 tipped the local balance of power in favour of the Khmer Rouge and other factions along the Thai border. Furthermore, a logging ban was declared in Thailand in the same year following a devastating landslide. This conjunction of military opportunity and economic demand set the scene for a sharp increase in logging deeper inside Cambodia.

From the signing of the Paris Peace Agreement between opposing Cambodian factions in 1991 to the end of the first term of the newly elected government in 1998, a minimum of US$2.5 billion worth of timber was exported from Cambodia—roughly equivalent to the nation's average annual GDP for that period. By the mid-1990s, timber earnings represented an estimated 43 percent of Cambodian export revenues, more than the comparable revenues of any other country at that time.[97] Logging provided the main post-Cold War source of finance for the remnants of the Khmer Rouge.[98] Forests, more generally, were also the subject of numerous conflicts and accommodations between a vast range of actors, including farmers, military personnel, politicians, international agencies, and transnational resource companies.

Ironically, the importance of the forest sector in Cambodia was in part the result of previous hostilities. Despite massive bombing and chemical defoliation in the eastern half of the country by the US, Cambodian forests had not faced the logging onslaught experienced in many other parts of Southeast Asia during the logging boom of the 1970s and 1980s. Much could be earned from logging these largely "pristine" forests, and while all-out war would have been likely to prevent logging, the "neither war nor peace" stalemate that lasted during much of the 1990s created a situation propitious for illegal logging.

Several dimensions made forests a significant factor in Cambodia's arduous and lengthy transition out of war in the 1990s. The first dimension is geopolitical: most forests are located at the periphery of the country, along the borders with Thailand and Vietnam—two countries that have often supported opposing Cambodian factions in order to increase their respective influence over Cambodia. Forests thus have a long history of involvement in insurrections and politics; providing a refuge for opponents to central authorities and a safe conduit to the lifelines secured from neighbouring sponsors (such as the provision of arms, equipment, drugs, or food).[99]

Second, the logging revenue controlled by politico-military factions became particularly important as the financial backing of foreign sponsors declined in the late 1980s, and social status in society became increasingly tied to financial wealth. Logging revenue thus played an active role in enabling the prolongation of the conflict. Again, the location of forests was important for providing a spatial continuity between the site of struggle and the source of support (the market)—in this case, by enabling Thai companies to access Cambodian forests controlled by particular factions. The capture of this economic rent also expanded military objectives to include the control of forested areas and transport routes. Opportunistic local commanders and politicians imposed their rule, often violently, upon local populations and forestry officials. In this way, the behavior of the government army in the 1990s was not very different from that of the early 1970s, when Lon Nol's army used its wide-ranging powers during the conflict against communist forces to log and export timber.

A third dimension is the socio-political effects that logging had on participants in the conflict. More than money, logging provided networks of support reaching important military and political figures in Thailand and Vietnam. Thai politicians used bribe revenue to enhance their electoral slush funds. In Vietnam, the collusion of the provincial ruling elite and the absence of transparent government or civil institutions also provided an enabling regional environment. Direct contacts developed at the local level between military commanders, politicians and businessmen also nurtured the personal economic interests of faction members, as well as cooperative arrangements between ostensible enemies. In this way, these socio-economic relations "diluted" the orthodoxy of individual Khmer Rouge members' political commitments, and weakened military factions' general chain of command.[100] This was particularly true when logging activities criss-crossed political divides that required accommodation by the different sides; such divides included for example export routes under the control of different factions, or logging and export licenses required from bureaucracies controlled by different political parties.

Fourth, the availability of windfall revenue from large-scale logging operations had a significant politico-economic effect on the structure of power in a country as impoverished as Cambodia. A source of corruption and a means of patrimonialism, the forestry sector weakened formal governance, reducing it to profit-taking by individual and factional interests. Logging provided opportunities for peripheral actors, mostly provincial strongmen and politicians, to benefit from the conjuncture of economic liberalisation and political uncertainty. It strengthened their power base by increasing their financial wealth and by building local production networks. In turn, the central leadership counteracted this decentralisation of resource control and political power with a concessionary framework ensuring more secure control and capture of forestry rents through foreign companies or cronies.

A fifth dimension was the antagonism that this mode of forest exploitation created between the government of Cambodia and the local population, as well as the international community. The local population and international community perceived the government of Cambodia as corrupt, and the administration of the forestry sector reinforced this impression. Much of the antagonism between these various actors resulted from the confrontation of pragmatist and idealist perspectives regarding the transition process itself. In this regard, the "rationalisation" of forestry reduced that antagonism and helped the government win back a degree of support from the international community.

The international community played a dual role through its discourse on sustainable and accountable resource management, as it enabled open criticisms of skewed and illegal practices, but also pushed practices further underground. The tenets of a "green reconstruction" were deeply contradictory given the *Realpolitik* at play in Cambodia. The apparent failure of the government to control and effectively tax logging can be interpreted as resistance to the demands of the international community for greater apolitical or non-partisan development of resources. Illegal logging was not only a tactic of resistance, however; it was used by politicians and military to line their pockets and further their ultimate objective of regime and individual security. Faced with such conditions for (re)establishing governance (strict but poorly enforced logging and taxation guidelines) neither of the co-prime ministers, beyond deceptive pronouncements, had strong incentives to consolidate the rule of law and public services to the detriment of their own clientele and particular interests. The international community's "public transcript" of legalisation and rationalisation of the forestry sector also entrenched the legitimacy of foreign transnational companies, until adequate independent monitoring demonstrated that they were no better than local loggers.

Finally, the case of logging in Cambodia suggests that neoliberal prescriptions during "post-conflict" transition can be accommodated and redirected by state elites in ways that have profoundly negative implications for the general population. While politico-military elites and their circle of clients have benefited from Cambodia's logging sector and the rise of palm oil plantations, the population has seen its access to forest resources and logging revenue drastically reduced. Cambodia remains one of the least developed countries in the world, even though hundreds of millions of dollars have been generated from logging in the last decade, and the plunder of forests has continually been justified in the name of "development." The failure of democratisation in the 1990s played a role in this plunder, as ruling elites remained largely unchallenged.[101] The main responsibility of international agencies dealing with the logging issue was to emphasise an industrial/corporate approach rather than a community-oriented one. In combination with biased neo-liberal reforms and the imperative of drawing fiscal revenue from forests, this approach came to accommodate and ultimately serve the political and economic interests of a tiny minority, with disastrous consequences for Cambodia's environment and the livelihood of the population at large.

Liberia: Logging and the Warlord-President

Established by freed slaves from the US in the 1820s, Liberia was ruled until 1980 by a very small minority of Americo-Liberians constituting about 3 percent of the population. Following a coup led by 29-year-old Sergeant Samuel Doe, this West African country continued to benefit from the assistance of the US until the end of the Cold War. The withdrawal of US support left a kleptocratic, inept and clientelist government vulnerable to attacks started at the end of 1989 by Libyan-trained and Ivorian-backed rebel groups. Led by Charles Taylor, a former Doe associate jailed in the US on charges of embezzlement in Liberia, the National Patriotic Front of Liberia (NPFL) succeeded in capturing most of the country except the capital, Monrovia, which was protected by a regional peacekeeping force.[102]

Given the devastation of the economy and the wealth of timber in Liberia, it is unsurprising that timber was to play a major role in the conflicts affecting this country. Revenue derived from the logging sector financed some of the belligerent groups during the conflicts in 1989–97 and 1999–2003. Logging revenues were also one of the main sources of financing for Charles Taylor during his presidency between 1997 and 2003, with Taylor's brother Robert controlling the forestry authority in charge of logging concessions.[103] Timber production peaked in 2000 with recorded annual exports close to a million cubic meters and an estimated value of US$186 million, out of which only US$6.6 million was officially collected as taxes.[104]

As summed up by Liberia's Truth and Reconciliation Commission, the logging sector affected the conflict in several ways:

Logging revenue was unlawfully used by political elites and warring factions to fund armed conflict. Logging companies shipped, or facilitated the shipment of, weapons and other military material to warring factions. Logging companies also facilitated, and contributed to, the movement of suspicious funds and illegal economic gains out of Liberia and utilised security forces that operated as, or were, in fact, militia units that committed grave human rights abuses in Liberia and throughout the region. Lastly, the companies unintentionally contributed to conflict when logging operations were looted by warring factions.[105]

Most significantly, the logging sector provided some of the hard currency and much of the logistical infrastructure, through which weapons could be purchased and transported, especially for the RUF in neighbouring Sierra Leone during the late 1990s.[106] Logging companies also created private militias with Taylor's backing. This established a parallel security apparatus that contributed to the survival of his regime and was implicated in numerous human rights abuses, often perpetrated against local communities resisting the logging of their forests.[107]

The logging sector provided a veneer of legitimacy to the economic activities of the Taylor presidency. This furnished a cover for criminal activities, including arms and drug trafficking as well as money laundering. Claims of large-scale employment, tax revenue, and "modernisation" were used to justify continued timber exports. Whereas diamond imports from Liberia came under sanctions in 2001, timber imports from there were not prohibited until July 2003.[108] China and France faced criticisms for opposing UN sanctions on the logging sector, with human rights organisations pointing out that the two countries were the main importers of Liberian timber (46 percent and 18 percent respectively in 2000).[109] By the time sanctions against logging were in place, the civil war was so widespread in Liberia that many logging companies had withdrawn from forest areas.[110] By August 2003, rebel groups were closing in on Monrovia; Taylor left for exile in Nigeria, and his government collapsed. The transitional authority placed forestry matters under the responsibility of the Ivorian-backed rebel group MODEL. To avoid a repeat of the situation in Cambodia (where timber sanctions were lifted by the new government, and new revenues benefited the Khmer Rouge for another round of conflict) sanctions in Liberia were to be maintained until three conditions had been met: security throughout the country; no timber being used to finance conflict; and legitimate forest management. Sanctions were lifted in 2006, but none of the logging operators could provide evidence of a legally established concession, and so all contracts were cancelled.

Peace and the fate of the forest

Countries facing the challenge of transition from war to peace in the turbulent early 1990s also faced a dilemma for natural resources extraction. Natural resources were generally perceived to be the springboard of economic reconstruction, while vast social needs clamored for the rapid sale of resources and immediate investment in health, education, shelter and food. Natural resource exploitation, however, remained a largely contested solution, given the growing importance of environmental and sustainable development issues in the global political agenda since the late 1980s. This contestation was most acute in the case of forests as an emblematic ecosystem for the preservation of biodiversity, but also an important source of livelihoods, building materials and foreign currency.

Countries long affected by armed conflicts often hold major remnants of so-called primary forests, hostilities having to some extent sheltered forests from exploitation (as seen in the case of Cambodia). In turn, the timing of intensified logging often coincided with the early stages of post-conflict transition processes, when a modicum of accommodation between belligerents could prove highly rewarding financially. Questions thus arose over which type of forest exploitation or protection, if any, was preferable during the transition to peace; what development policies were best suited to respond to the needs of populations and states emerging from conflicts; and who would benefit.

As a result of these dilemmas, forest exploitation has come under scrutiny for its effect upon the environment and populations. For some analysts, mostly those within domestic governments and some international development agencies, forest use would be best rationalised through a programme of management that emphasises "national" prosperity. Peacebuilding success is often measured economically by criteria such as foreign direct investments, volume of exports, and rising fiscal revenue, while militarily it is perceived by the degree to which "jungles," peopled by potentially dangerous individuals and groups, are "tamed" as uninhabited forests or newly cleared lands, settled by the "right" people. Massive population movements thus occurred, for example in Laos ethnic minority highlanders were moved to the lowlands with the assistance of international aid agencies, under the pretence of improving their security, and the help of the government, which made way for logging concessions and national parks; or in Indonesia, where some social groups were expelled, such as ethnic Chinese accused of communism in the late 1960s, while others, such as retired members of the Javanese military, were brought in.[111]

In contrast, some policy analysts see a transition to peace as presenting clear threats to forests that had been spared from logging and conversion to agriculture because of hostilities. As argued by David Kaimowitz at the Center for International Forestry Research (CIFOR), "no one is saying 'let's start a war so we can save the forest' but the fact remains that in many areas of conflict, forest ecosystems fare better in war time than they do in peace time …Wars can discourage logging and other resource depleting activities… Look at Colombia. Largely because of years of conflict it has more forest acreage than it did several decades ago."[112]

There is thus frequently a rush to establish or enforce environmental protection measures. About 19 percent of the Cambodian territory, mostly forests, was designated as protected areas briefly after the UN-sponsored transition in 1993. This move was not only motivated by the opportunity to push the conservation agenda at a point when institutions were still being consolidated, but was also intended to counterbalance the rapid awarding of logging concessions, which by 1996 covered about a third of Cambodia.

Grassroots social movements have been wary of both exploitation and the conservation agenda, arguing that both are destructive—although in different ways—of existing relationships between local communities and their environments and often end up further marginalising vulnerable forest dwellers. In Mexico, while conservationists accused peasants of using the conflict in Chiapas to move to forests in protected areas, peasants claimed that conservation projects served counterinsurgency purposes, with peasant eviction from forests a tactic used to reduce the number of rebel bases.[113]

Conclusion

There is no statistical evidence that forests make much difference to the onset risk and duration of armed conflicts. Yet there is considerable anecdotal evidence that insurgent groups will opportunistically use forests as advantageous terrain for guerrilla warfare and as a source of finance, mostly through taxing logging companies. Beyond these opportunistic dimensions, links between forests and rebellions also include the particular histories, institutions, and capabilities of forest-dwelling populations. Rarely originating from such populations, contemporary rebellions have nevertheless found a source of inspiration and sustenance among these people, typically after crushing repression in urban centers. Many forest-dwelling populations have long been neglected or oppressed by central state authorities and economic elites, and often consist of an uneasy mix of "indigenous" populations with a longer history of presence in forested regions combined with poor peasant families in search of land. When combined, these factors have made forests and forest-dwellers the frequent target of counterinsurgency activities.

There is also strong anecdotal evidence that institutional distortions and political de-legitimation of authorities occur as a result of breakneck and corrupt forest exploitation. This is particularly the case when conflicts over indiscriminate logging, the seizure of cleared land for grazing or plantation purposes, or the establishment of protected areas pit local communities against state authorities and businesses. The mix of institutional breakdown and forest-related conflicts can give way to other hostilities, especially when combined with a broader context of unfair land distribution and economic downturn, pushing more people into forested areas.

6

SPOILING WAR

The international community has made considerable efforts since the mid-1990s to end conflicts funded through natural resources.[1] The strategies adopted have reflected greater interventionism by the UN Security Council since the end of the Cold War and a consensus that insurgents' access to resource revenue tends to prolong conflicts.[2] The UN Security Council, for example, has taken an unprecedented number of measures to curtail access to revenue by targeted groups, and to help foster a durable transition to peace in several countries. Chief among these were so-called commodity sanctions, and the mandating of expert groups charged with investigating, and publicly reporting on, commodity-related sanctions-busting and illegal activity.[3]

A critical analysis of these conflict termination strategies is the focus of this chapter (Chapter 7 examines conflict prevention and peace-building more broadly). The analysis is structured around the three more prevalent approaches to curtailing belligerents' access to resource revenues. The first conflict termination strategy is that of military intervention, which seeks to interdict armed groups' access to resource revenue. This generally occurs via the coercive control of production and main transport areas as a means of "capturing" resource areas, thereby depriving belligerent forces of access. This was the case, for example, in Angola and Sierra Leone, where the South African mercenary group Executive Outcomes targeted rebel-controlled oil and diamond areas.

The second conflict termination strategy consists of economic sanctions (or "commodity sanctions" in the case of resources). An alternative sanctions strategy involves restricting investment in resource sectors or the provision of resource production technology to the sanctioned party. Individual countries, regional organisations, and the UN Security Council have imposed sanctions targeting resource sectors and specific armed groups in a large number of countries, with the governments of oil-producing states such as Iraq, Libya and Sudan, or diamond-funded armed groups such as UNITA and the RUF, figuring most prominently.

The third (and perhaps most controversial) strategy consists of "buying peace" through using resource revenues as incentives for belligerents to adhere to conflict termination conditions. A variety of revenue-sharing agreements have been implemented with various degrees of success, from awarding individual resource concessions or government ministerial portfolios to direct control of, or a share in, resource revenue. Such agreements largely failed in Angola, with UNITA being granted the portfolio of Minister of Mines in the 1994 Lusaka protocol and a scheme to legalise its mines, and in Sierra Leone, with the RUF leader Foday Sankoh given Chairmanship of the Commission for the Management of Strategic Mineral Resources, as mentioned earlier.[4] In Burma and Sudan, by contrast, these schemes were more effectively implemented (see below).[5]

These initiatives have resulted in some important successes. Overall, there has been much improvement in curtailing belligerent access to resource revenue at the international level. But these conflict termination strategies have also been criticised for interpreting war as driven by economic motives, for ambivalent impacts on local livelihoods, and for limiting peace to policing belligerents rather than broadly addressing the causes of conflict.[6] Other critiques focus on the insufficiently developed international regulatory framework (as evidenced by the absence of an internationally agreed legal definition of "conflict commodities"), the lack of a systematic framework for UN Security Council investigations and responses, and relatively weak (or absent) legal framework to guide the behavior of resource companies operating in conflict-affected countries.

The three types of instruments mentioned here are not the only ones deployed to address the role of resources in prolonging conflicts. For example—although it is still rare—litigation against resource companies or individuals suspected of trading in conflict commodities has occurred in order to implement and give future credibility to UN sanctions. More than a dozen "conflict resource" traders have faced trial, mostly in national courts, with some receiving jail sentences.

Another example is that of transparency instruments—especially the Extractive Industries Transparency Initiative (EITI)—which have been deployed to reduce the likelihood of corruption and revenue embezzlement. Industry regulatory schemes have been debated in several sectors, most prominently in the diamond sector with the Kimberley Process Certification Scheme seeking to curtail the "conflict diamonds" trade (as discussed in Chapter 4). Many of these instruments focus on conflict prevention as well as termination and have objectives (such as human rights and accountability) beyond conflict termination specifically. Accordingly, they are addressed in Chapter 7, whereas this chapter focuses more narrowly on conflict termination through curtailing access to resources and resource revenues.

Why is this analysis merited? Within the literature, there exist relatively few comparative assessments of the most effective way of ending armed hostilities financed by resources. In this chapter, I provide a retrospective analysis of instruments targeting resource-financed hostilities since 1989, focusing on their effectiveness. After identifying 26 armed conflicts in which at least one strategy was used between 1989 and 2006, I attempt to assess their relative effectiveness, especially in relation to the types of conflicts and resources involved. This study is complemented by two broader ones looking at the effects of resource-focused initiatives on peace duration.

A first (and still preliminary) study also examines the three main options of military intervention and wealth-sharing, for the post-Second World War period up to 2006. Testing for post-conflict peace periods for sixty-three resource-related conflicts that took place in thirty-nine countries, the study tentatively finds that none of these three options have major peacebuilding effects on resource-related conflicts. This general assessment does not apply when focusing on specific types of contexts and conflicts, with the most robust findings associating military interventions and wealth-sharing with increased peace duration for severe conflicts (those with over 300 battle-related deaths per year).[7]

A second study examines 552 documented international attempts at resolving 154 cases of conflicts related to disputes over oil, water and diamonds occurring between 1997 and 2007.[8] Assessing the relative impact of eleven types of international interventions, the study finds that regulating market access through sanctions or positive incentives is the most effective immediate measure. It is also the second most frequently used, behind

153

financial aid, which does not reduce resort to violence in a statistically significant way.[9] A wide array of measures, including anti-corruption initiatives, resource sector monitoring, capacity building, reporting requirements and commodity prize stabilisation—in decreasing order of statistical significance—are positively related to greater cooperation. Finally, military mobilisation and intervention at first negatively affect dispute outcomes by aggravating the use of violence, but over time are statistically associated with the strongest positive outcome of all initiatives.

Why is this sort of analysis useful? First, analyzing the success or failure of resource-focused conflict termination instruments may help us to refine our arguments about the role of resources in prolonging conflicts. Second, if (as I will argue) specific conflict termination instruments are more effective with respect to some types of resources than others, more effective responses to resource wars can be designed through "matching" specific termination strategies with particular resources and conflicts.

Before embarking upon the analysis, it is important to note that the assumption that resource revenues prolong conflicts and undermine peacebuilding efforts is not universally accepted and requires careful qualification. Although several empirical studies have suggested that the availability of valuable resources in a conflict area tends to prolong hostilities and undermine peacebuilding efforts,[10] others suggest that oil or diamond production is in fact associated with shorter conflicts.[11] This suggests that the relationship between resource revenues and conflict duration is by no means straightforward, given the diversity of mechanisms at play.[12] In some instances, resources may prolong wars by making conflict more feasible for belligerents, particularly when resources are easily accessible to the weaker party, or when economic agendas are central goals for belligerents or for regional or international actors—particularly when neighbouring states may economically benefit from a conflict. But in other cases, resource revenues may provide drivers to shorten conflicts, particularly when resources are exclusively available to the stronger party, when resource revenues provide incentives to participate in and abide by peace processes, or when disputes over resource revenues fragment and thereby weaken military groups (for example, through fostering of discord, a breakdown of discipline, and allegiance-switching because of distrust over resource revenue sharing).[13] This process applies equally to other actors in the commodity chain; major commercial interests, for example, may seek to end conflicts in order to protect or access resources.

The complexity of the mechanisms at play underscores the importance of distinguishing among different types of resources and different types of conflicts, as well as carefully differentiating the parties accessing resources and the mechanisms prolonging or shortening conflicts. This complexity suggests, in turn, the need for a refined set of strategies, as some conflict termination initiatives may be more suited to some types of mechanisms and resources than others. Hence a central argument of this chapter: the more carefully one matches conflict termination strategies to the types of actors, resources, and conflicts in any given situation, the greater the chance of success.

Resources and conflict termination: Capture, sanction, or share?

Curtailing wartime access to resource revenues can take two main forms: military interventions to capture resource production areas ("capture") or economic sanctions preventing investments, technical inputs or the trading of resources ("sanction"). A third strategy, revenue-sharing ("share"), does not imply curtailment of access to resource revenues as such, but rather uses them as leverage in conflict cessation or peace negotiations. I consider each of these strategies in turn.

Capture: Strategies of military intervention

Natural resource assets constitute a classic target of military campaigns. Military interventions typically aim to secure access to strategic resources such as petroleum, derive revenue from (future) resource exploitation, and/or destroy assets under enemy control. Such military interventions can target resource production areas, infrastructure and project staff, or transport networks. In a post-conflict setting, interventions may involve creating or maintaining a military presence in resource production areas and along transport corridors.

There are three main categories of military interventions relevant to this discussion: (1) those conducted by domestic forces as part of the general conduct of war; (2) those conducted by external mercenary forces (private military companies, or PMCs) working under contract with one of the belligerents; and (3) those conducted by external military forces under a mandate from the United Nations, a regional organisation, or in the form of a "coalition of the willing."[14] In this analysis, I focus on the second and third categories.

Table 6.1 lists seventeen military interventions that occurred between 1989 and 2006 in conflicts selected for the involvement of resources; five of them involved mercenaries. The PMCs are frequently brought in with a precise mandate to prop up local governments and regain control of resources from rebel forces. These interventions, although not benefiting from the military capacity of major foreign states, are rarely constrained by their mandate and are able to make full use of their military capacity.[15] As a result, many interventions have been successful from a tactical perspective, such as those of Executive Outcomes in Angola and Sierra Leone in the mid-1990s.[16] Typically, the primary goal is to retake control of key resource production sites, such as onshore oil fields or key diamond mines, from belligerents, and the critical role of PMCs is in the retraining and backing of local governmental or paramilitary forces.

Although PMCs can act independently, they seek to operate under some degree of international legitimacy.[17] In many cases, they receive the backing of their home governments, even if only tacitly; in others, they may even act as a proxy for foreign powers. But the local legitimacy of PMCs is often questioned. For example, the hiring process for a PMC by the government of Papua New Guinea, aimed at quelling the 1989 rebellion in Bougainville, unintentionally triggered a military and political crisis that opened the way to a negotiated settlement of the conflict.[18]

Interventions by PMCs are also marred by controversies over their timing, methods and motives. PMC combat activities may undermine peace negotiations and result in human rights abuses. A UN commission denounced their impact on the "independence, economies, democracy and self-determination" of affected populations.[19] Backlashes have occurred, as in Sierra Leone where a conflict between national army personnel and paramilitary forces supported by a PMC degenerated into a coup in 1997. Furthermore, although PMC operations are generally far cheaper than UN peacekeeping operations, capacity for funding by local governments is generally limited and could not be sustained in several cases without mortgaging future resource revenue, thereby threatening the future economic viability of the government.

Moreover, their controversial presence often legitimates demands by rebel parties for their withdrawal and departure. Negotiated settlements, such as the 1996 Abidjan Agreement for Sierra Leone, have included the departure of PMCs. In cases where the contested legitimacy of PMCs results in a failure to maintain a military presence on the ground, resource

Table 6.1: External military interventions, 1989–2006

Countries	Intervening forces	Targeted groups	Resource objectives
Afghanistan	US/NATO	Taliban, Al Qaeda	Heroin revenue (2001)*
Angola I	PMC	UNITA	Oil fields and diamond mines (1993)
Cambodia	UNTAC	Khmer Rouge	Timber export points (1992–93)
Colombia	US forces and PMC	FARC, ELN	Cocaine production and trafficking (1999), oil pipelines (2001)
Congo, Rep.	Angola	Congolese government	Oil revenue, diamonds trafficking (1997)
D.R. Congo	PMC	Uganda, Rwanda, ADFL	Copper and diamond mines (1997)
D.R. Congo	Angola, Namibia, Zimbabwe	RCD, Uganda, Rwanda, Burundi	Copper and diamond mines (1998)
D.R. Congo	MONUC	Militias	Diamond and coltan mines (2002)
East Timor	Australia, UNTAET	Militias	Oil revenue (1999)
Iraq-Kuwait	UN mandated coalition	Iraqi government	Oil fields (1991)
Iraq	US-led coalition	Iraqi government	Oil fields (2003)
Lesotho	South Africa, Botswana	Lesotho Defence force mutineers	Water dam (1998)
Liberia I	ECOWAS forces	NPLF and other rebel groups	Iron ore and timber shipping route, rubber plantation, diamonds (1990)
Liberia II	UNMIL	Militias	Idem (2003)
Papua New Guinea	Regional peace-keeping forces, PMC	BRA	Copper mine (1997-aborted)
Philippines I-II	US forces	NPA, MNLF	Extortion from logging firms (2001)*

| Sierra Leone | PMC and ECOWAS forces | RUF | Diamond areas, bauxite mine (1995) |
| Sierra Leone | British forces and UN peacekeeping troops | RUF | Main diamond trading areas (2000)* |

Note: * Military interventions in which resource control represented a minor objective or indirect consequence.

production sites may fall back into the hands of rebel forces. This was especially the case with respect to alluvial diamonds in Angola and Sierra Leone in the mid-1990s, when a PMC was asked to leave as part of a negotiated settlement including a wealth-sharing mechanism (see below). PMCs have also been involved in narcotics eradication campaigns by the US in Afghanistan, Colombia and Peru.

Military interventions by foreign government forces often see their immediate resource control objectives successfully achieved through superior military capability. These forces, however, rarely declare resource control officially to be a major objective, given the broad scope of their interventions and the political sensitivity of the apparent military pursuit of commercial interests. For example, the US-led and UN-approved intervention in Kuwait in 1991 enabled control of Kuwaiti oil fields to be regained from Iraqi forces, although renewed production was delayed by the torching of well heads (with significant environmental impact). Angolan forces' 1997 intervention in the oil-rich Republic of Congo, backing ex-President Sassou Nguesso, is another example.[20]

Not all full-scale interventions have achieved rapid success, however. The US-led invasion of Iraq in 2003 illustrates this point. Even though control of the oil sector was apparently a high military priority, oil production plummeted, owing in part to persistent sabotage. Intervention by Uganda and Rwanda in the former Zaire in 1996 resulted in one of the world's deadliest conflicts since the Second World War. Furthermore, the long-term sustainability of peace resulting from military interventions is also questionable. The 2003 invasion of Iraq resulted in continued armed resistance against occupying forces and the new Iraq authorities as well as a quasi-civil war. Intervening forces' corruption and commercial resource interests have occasionally contributed to the prolongation of some conflicts, as in the case of some ECOMOG[21] troops in Liberia during the early 1990s and regional forces in mineral rich areas of the DRC since the late 1990s.

Moreover, some initiatives by external governmental forces are more akin to training and assistance than full-scale intervention, and generally have more limited results, as demonstrated by US military involvement in Colombia against drug trafficking and extortion in the oil sector, both of which are sources of income for rebel groups.[22] The limited operational success and counterproductive effects of opium eradication campaigns in Afghanistan is also a case in point.[23] Finally, many foreign interventions occur through United Nations mandates that do not provide for the full use of force and involve the participation of countries whose parallel objective is also to limit the risks taken by their troops. Therefore, only those UN peacekeeping missions specifically mandated to control resource sectors are considered here.

UN peacekeeping troops have very rarely engaged directly in, or supported, combat missions to curtail resource access by belligerents. By 2010, the most explicitly mandated UN mission had been UN mission in the DRC (or MONUC, by its French acronym, Mission de l'Organisation des Nations Unies en République Démocratique du Congo). Established in 1999, the mission has repeatedly confronted conflict-related resources issues. During the first war (1996–97), the second war (1998–2003), and the aftermath of the second war, mineral resources financed both local and foreign armed groups, especially in the eastern part of the country. Although the UN has used expert-panel investigations and public reporting to address this connection, it did not impose sanctions on conflict resources (see below), and officially mandated its peacekeeping forces to target conflict commodities only in 2008.[24]

In a subsequent resolution, the UN Security Council extended the list of individuals and companies subject to travel sanctions, financial sanctions, or both, thus sending a signal to companies involved in trading in conflict resources.[25] In the same resolution, the UN Security Council also requested that MONUC, governments in the region, and the UN Experts Panel (or Group of Experts) "cooperate intensively, including by exchanging information regarding … the illegal trafficking in natural resources." However, military cooperation between MONUC and the Congolese government has not been straightforward or stable: for example, in a joint Congolese-Rwandan operation undertaken in January and February 2009 against the Forces Démocratiques de Libération du Rwanda (FDLR) MONUC was largely excluded from planning and implementation.

Implementation of UN Security Council resolution 1856 involved some major difficulties. First, the resolution calls for MONUC to work "in close collaboration" with the Congolese government and to intervene "in support of" Forces Armées de la République Démocratique du Congo (FARDC) led operations, which has occasionally resulted in delays in conducting operations.[26] More important, many of the new FARDC officers are former members of armed groups that continue to have a stake in illegal exploitation, and some FARDC units are directly involved in such exploitation. As noted by Global Witness, "in parts of Mwenga and Kalehe, Congolese army units ... have started taking over mining sites after dislodging the FDLR."[27] In response to criticism of such actions, the President of the DRC, Joseph Kabila, ordered all military personnel to vacate mining sites.[28]

Second, the situation in the DRC is complicated by the fact that natural resources are not the only source of finance for armed groups. Some militias also derive income from illegally taxing the local population. Curtailing access to resource revenue may therefore, at least in the short term, increase predatory behavior towards local populations—which might, in turn, increase the workload of the UN mission, whose main task is to protect the civilian population. MONUC has limited capacity, and needs to prioritise its activities, concentrating on the protection of civilians and limitation of the activities of armed groups (chiefly the FDLR), even if curtailing armed groups' access to resources would improve medium-term prospects of security.

Third, not all mining sites and links in the trading network can be brought under control. Systematic mapping of mining and mineral trade routes in the two Kivu provinces (in the eastern DRC) identified 215 mining sites, forty-five trading houses, ten airports, and six major border crossings.[29] In July 2009, a MONUC military spokesperson noted that while Kimia II, the latest joint FARDC-MONUC military operation, "aimed at recovering the main mining sites ... there are other sources of income [still available] for the FDLR and the armed groups."[30] A report from Global Witness also stressed that while Kimia II:

appears to have temporarily disrupted the FDLR's mining activities in certain other areas, ... the longer-term effect is not yet clear. The FDLR have abandoned some mines in parts of Mwenga (South Kivu), in anticipation of the deployment of [Kimia II], only to continue mining in nearby areas. The FDLR have turned increasingly violent against the civilian population since the start of [Kimia II][31]

Fourth, despite nearly a decade of journalistic, NGO, and UN expert panel reports stressing the importance of conflict resources, and despite the UN Security Council resolutions of late 2008—which encouraged MONUC, more strongly than ever before, to cooperate with the FARDC to curtail the illegal resource trade—the UN has not taken the step of imposing sanctions, which would have made it easier to distinguish between legal and illegal resources, exploitation, and trade. In the absence of official sanctions, many resource companies, faced with accusations of complicity in war crimes, have stopped importing minerals from conflict zones in the DRC, in particular tantalite from the eastern DRC. Thus, a poorly implemented de facto sanctions regime is currently in place, which tends to favour the most informal (and criminal) trading networks.

A related problem is the involvement of Congolese military, political and business leaders in "illegal" trade—an issue that is rendered even more complex by the difficulty of defining legality in the DRC, where political legitimacy is uncertain and where international, national, provincial, and customary laws may simultaneously apply.[32] A 2009 UN report noted that "conducting random checks at port, airport or border posts can … have serious consequences for the Mission's relations with the Government and the FARDC."[33] In 2008, a UN expert panel argued that "targeting companies complicit in systematically trading minerals with FDLR and promoting due diligence within the international minerals supply chain represent effective ways of cutting off the financial support of FDLR."[34] Such efforts are complicated, however, by the fact that many of the businesspeople involved in conflict resources are also major subcontractors or landlords for MONUC and aid agencies. Thus, MONUC is in a somewhat difficult position: to accomplish its mandate, it must maintain a good relationship with the government of the DRC, but it may not always be in the interests of the government to have MONUC on board.

To address these problems, MONUC personnel have recommended the following strategies: training MONUC staff, especially military observers and civil police, in the monitoring of conflict-resource trade (for example, how to identify trade vectors—vehicles, planes, companies—and how to recognise legal documentation); deploying military observers at key locations (including airports), and providing support for unannounced inspections (of aircraft for example) by Congolese security forces; removing armed groups' and army checkpoints that are illegally taxing the resource trade; assisting with capacity building for Congolese police, military personnel, and customs officers, through the provision of training and equipment; profiling peace spoilers and key economic actors likely to be involved in commodity conflict production and trading; undertaking satellite observation of mining sites and transport corridors; undertaking centralised data gathering and analysis; building awareness, among local businesses, of illegal exploitation; engaging in broader collaboration with development agencies and local authorities to regulate and bring trade into the formal economy.

The Congolese government has also given attention to resource issues as part of its Programme of Stabilisation and Rebuilding of Former Conflict Zones (STAREC). This programme calls for Congolese security forces to monitor mining sites operated by armed groups; for government services—specifically, the mining registry; the Centre of Evaluation, Expertise and Certification (the DRC's regulatory mining body); and the Ministry of Mines' antifraud office—to be strengthened in the provinces, and for controls to be established on airfields and roads leading to mine sites.[35] The Congolese Prime Minister asked MONUC to assist in the transport and deployment of mining inspectors, but MONUC staff considered that such an effort could not be undertaken until road projects were completed and police forces and credible public administrators were in place in areas where mines are located. As discussed in the conclusion, there is some scope for improving the contribution of UN peacekeepers in this respect.

Overall, the military capture of resource regions from rebel forces appears to be a deceptive quick fix. Successful implementation often forces the targeted party into a settlement but ultimately fails to dovetail into a stable peace. Accordingly, military capture requires significant follow-up to avoid the recurrence of hostilities, including peacekeeping, negotiations, and effective demobilisation. Security forces can help in establishing and maintaining credible traceability systems enabling legitimate trade and curtailing peace spoiler financing. Yet military intervention poses major ethical dilemmas when intervening forces (troops from foreign countries or mercenaries) are suspected of commercial interests. For example, the record of the Executive Outcomes PMC in South Africa has been tarnished by allegations of vested commercial interest, while distrust among Iraqis about US troops relates in part to the suspicion of an oil grab.[36]

How then might one evaluate the relative success of military interventions? I shall return to this question shortly, to examine the relative effectiveness of military interventions in creating peace with respect to conflicts involving both lootable and non-lootable resources. A number of other strategic questions arise. For example, are military interventions more successful when they are followed by a military settlement, or when they follow costly wars? Before turning to these questions, let us take a brief look at the two other major types of conflict termination strategies: sanctions and sharing.

Economic sanctions and expert panels

Economic sanctions (or commodity sanctions) seek to undermine the production and/or exports of resources by the targeted party. Sanctioned parties have included governments (often through a country-wide sanctions regime) or non-state groups (mostly rebel movements). Sanctions aimed at particular commodities (commodity sanctions) can be applied to a country, but in effect they only target the actor that benefits most from that commodity. Generally used to influence the policies of targeted governments, sanctions have also been increasingly deployed to curtail the financial means available to rebel groups.

How do sanctions work?

Under Article 41 of the UN Charter, the UN Security Council may impose restrictions on economic relations by UN members with targeted countries or groups. While sanctions have generally been used as an economic leverage to promote negotiations or policy change, UN sanctions regimes have increasingly aimed at putting targeted belligerents "out of business" by prohibiting commodity exports upon which they rely economically. The logic of sanctions has thus evolved from containment and influence to policing. Prior to 1990, only Southern Rhodesia had been subject to a commodity export embargo. Since then, seven countries or armed groups have had their commodity exports prohibited or limited by the UN (see Table 6.3).

Sanctions targeting resources have been also been imposed by regional associations of states. For example, the Economic Community of West African States (ECOWAS) imposed economic sanctions against NPFL-controlled areas in Liberia in 1993, after its military arm, the ECOWAS Monitoring Group (ECOMOG), had organised a military blockade and takeover of Taylor's leading port in Buchanan, from which the National Patriotic Front of Liberia (NPFL) had imported arms and exported timber, rubber and iron ore. Although Taylor lost a significant portion of his income as a result, unimpeded diamond and timber trafficking allowed him to maintain his military strength until he was elected president in 1997. A political and trade embargo was imposed for more than two years on Burundi by neighbouring countries after a military coup in 1996. Much criticised for its macro-economic and humanitarian impact, the embargo was systematically violated by participating states, allowing for the export of all key commodities from Burundi, particularly the smuggling of coffee, which was also encouraged by the low prices offered by the parastatal marketing board.[37] The UN Security Council remains the most potentially effective source of sanctions because of the global reach that its decisions convey, yet its actual effectiveness relies on enforcement.

Individual countries have also imposed commodity export sanctions. In the US, the federal administration, state governments, and even municipalities have multiplied unilateral sanctions against countries or individuals—sometimes with extra-territorial reach, as through the Iran and Libya Sanctions Act of 1996. The US administration was among the first to impose sanctions against Iraq immediately after its invasion of Kuwait. It also targeted the military regime in Burma in 1995, through an investment moratorium affecting mostly US energy companies. However, that measure fell short of requiring disinvestment, or even deterring reinvestment in existing projects. In the context of civil strife and the hanging of Ogoni activists by the Abacha regime in 1995, the Nigerian Democracy Act banning new investment was presented to Congress, but was rejected after lobbying from US business associations and the Nigerian government. European governments also generally opposed such sanctions, on the grounds that they could have jeopardised debt repayment, risked expropriation of oil-business assets, and further undermined the Nigerian economy; they preferred instead to adopt non-economic sanctions.

How are sanctions enforced?

To enforce sanctions, the UN Security Council relies on its members to prohibit trading in target commodities through regulatory or military means. According to Article 25 of the Charter, members must abide by and implement these sanctions. Although member states may themselves be sanctioned for non-compliance, there is general reluctance to propagate so-called "secondary sanctions." Only Liberia, under Charles Taylor, came under this type of sanctions for its role in supporting the RUF rebellion in neighbouring Sierra Leone and threatening Guinea.

However, enforcement is variable. The lack of adequate national legislation and enforcement by some governments has left many sanctions with a merely rhetorical effect, as with the sanctions against the Khmer Rouge in Cambodia in the early 1990s. Such ineffective enforcement can favour criminal groups by forcing more legitimate companies out of resource sectors, with potentially negative consequences in terms of conflict prevention. Recognising this dynamic in the context of sanctions against UNITA, the UN Security Council specifically urged "all States… to enforce, strengthen or enact legislation making it a criminal offence under domestic law for their nationals or other individuals operating on their territory to violate the measures imposed by the Council."[38]

Very few sanctions measures have involved ground troops. Iraq is one exception. Immediately after the Iraqi invasion of Kuwait in 1990, the UN Security Council imposed a sanctions regime to block Iraqi-controlled oil exports. The Multinational Interception Force (MIF), led by the US Navy, acted under UN Security Council Resolution 665 (1990) to interdict all maritime traffic to and from Iraq, to ensure a strict implementation of sanctions.

At the time these sanctions were imposed, Iraq was highly dependent on foreign trade and had large external debts. As a result of the sanctions and associated military enforcement, Iraqi oil exports were reduced by 90 percent between 1990 and 1995, crippling the country's economy. Yet Saddam Hussein proved sufficiently resilient (or unconcerned by the plight of his population) to withstand the sanctions, which were progressively eroded by the successive "Oil-for-Food" programmes and oil smuggling; for example, Iranian authorities sold "transit permits" to smugglers to pass through their territorial waters.[39] Furthermore, political "realism" led the US to avoid a confrontation over smuggled oil with "friendly regimes" such as Jordan and Turkey, which were importing vast quantities of smuggled Iraqi oil (the US itself was one of the main importers of officially exported oil). By the late 1990s, smuggling was estimated to bring annual revenue in excess of US$500 million. Major as well as small oil purchasers and companies were involved, suggesting that sanctions-busting was widespread, and in some cases flagrant.

Another well-known example of conflict resources-related sanctions is that of Cambodia. In 1992, the UN Security Council asked the UN Transitional Authority in Cambodia (UNTAC) to impose a log export ban, mostly targeting the Khmer Rouge. The UNTAC mission was 22,000 strong, but although extensive, its mandate did not include the use of force under Chapter VII (proactive combat involvement). Its leadership was wary that any military move to control the logging sector could get out of hand, given the extensive profits at play.

Accordingly, instead of militarily confronting illegal logging, and possibly requesting authorisation for the use of force from the UN Security Council, UNTAC deployed military observers without power of arrest to monitor Cambodia's international border. The Khmer Rouge refused to allow monitoring in its territories, and the Thai government denied access on its side of the border. Despite holding documentary evidence of log trade from Khmer Rouge territories into Thailand, UN Secretary-General Boutros Boutros-Ghali took a "quiet diplomacy" approach towards the new Thai government, which had just replaced a military junta. Even though he carried the matter personally to the Foreign Minister of Thailand, the Thai government remained reluctant to act against the pro-Khmer Rouge Thai military and provincial officials who profited from ties with the rebel group. Although all log exports were eventually prohibited by Thailand, the Cambodian government lifted the ban after nine months, undermining its overall impact. In the end, Thai timber imports for 1993 were only 20 percent lower than in 1992 and 1994, while the gems trade, which also benefited the Khmer Rouge, continued largely unabated. As in Iraq, the ban consolidated corruption and political actors' control of illicit economic activities.

How effective are sanctions?

Some sanctions regimes have had positive results. For example, the imposition of sanctions against the government of Liberia progressively eroded its support for the Revolutionary United Front in Sierra Leone. But the Iraqi example previously outlined suggests that most sanctions are difficult to enforce, even with extraordinary (if partial) efforts.

Indeed, research on sanctions (the most intensively studied conflict termination strategy of the three types examined in this chapter) suggests that sanctions most often fail to change the behavior of their targets,[40] although some argue that sanctions can have positive impacts in terms of stigmatising targets and reducing their funding opportunities.[41] Economic sanctions have a generally poor overall record in terms of implementation and impact. Resource smuggling has remained widespread under most sanctions regimes, in part because of a lack of enforcement on the ground and of effective judicial action against sanctions-busters. The natural characteristics of resources have also influenced the effectiveness of sanctions through their relative ease of transport and concealment, or low traceability. Yet with the collusion of local authorities on both sides of an international border, the bulkiness of a resource is not a prohibiting factor in sanctions-busting, as illustrated by the smuggling of vast quantities of Iraqi oil or Cambodian logs in the 1990s. The end result has been that poorly enforced sanction regimes have a perverse effect: they favour less law-abiding businesses, including politically connected criminal groups, with potentially negative consequences in terms of conflict termination.

Nevertheless, there remains some potential for more effective enforcement of sanctions; for example, the unique physical characteristics of oil fields and the availability of databases allow for the identification of oil transported to the international market. Shell was fined US$2 million by the UN for such dealings after one of its tankers was "fingerprinted" as transporting Iraqi oil in April 2000.[42]

Furthermore, the use of sanctions has much evolved since the end of the Cold War, with a greater use of better targeted and implemented UN sanctions.[43] Major improvements have been noted since the late 1990s.[44] Sanctions regimes have also become increasingly sophisticated and diverse; for example, sanctions regimes in some cases may exempt commodities certified by a government once a credible system is in place. This allows for licit revenues to be received by governments, while they are denied to rebel groups. So-called smart sanctions have allowed for selective targeting to maximise the impact on the sanctioned group, while lessening the effects on the general population. Sanctions on timber in Liberia were finally decided after resistance from two timber-importing UN Security Council members (China and France), especially because figures of effect on employment, backing the argument of a widespread negative impact of sanctions, proved to be much lower than anticipated.

UN Security Council sanctions-compliance measures have also been aimed at the identification and conviction of sanctions-busters, often through specially convened "expert panels." Following past UN failures in Angola, including the failure to implement sanctions, lobbying by NGOs and Canadian officials in 1999 resulted in a new approach under which international agencies, governments, and businesses were directly enlisted to help implement sanctions. Along with media reporting and advocacy work by NGOs such as Human Rights Watch, Global Witness and Partnership Africa Canada, the UN publicly "named and shamed" sanctions-busters—including heads of states—shattering the law of silence generally characterising relations within the UN. For example, the Presidents of Togo and Burkina Faso were among those named by the expert panel on UNITA sanctions. Indeed, UNITA lost logistical and diplomatic support in 2000 and 2001, following exposure by UN expert panel reports.

Key to the success of public naming and shaming was the UN's innovative use of expert panels, involving independent experts, whose work was not hampered by diplomatic protocol, and who were given the time and budget to conduct in-depth investigations. As noted by the chair of the UN expert panel for the DRC, the goal of this strategy was "to shock" countries the panel suspected of benefiting from the "looting" of eastern DRC.[45] The first reaction from named countries (Rwanda and Uganda) was to protest and even threaten disengagement from the Lusaka peace agreement. However, a more conciliatory tone was adopted in the medium term, and may have contributed to the subsequent realignment of Ugandan-backed rebels with Kinshasa. Critics of this policy have argued, however, that "naming and shaming" is useless against people without shame, a position supported by a record of continued predatory practices by elite networks in the region.[46]

Another objection to sanctions is that they often have a negative humanitarian impact on local populations. This argument should be treated with caution. The idea that commodity export sanctions should be avoided or lifted to promote positive economic engagement that benefits populations does not easily hold with respect to extractive industries. This is primarily because the targeted belligerents often control the rent of the extractive sector, and secondarily because extractive industries generate little local employment. In Angola, for example, the oil rent is controlled through the presidency, the ministry of finance, and the parastatal oil company Sonangol. The sector has generated only about 10,000 local jobs, and very little revenue trickles down to the general population. UN sanctions against the Liberian logging sector under UN Security Council Resolution 1478 (2003) have been heavily debated. UN expert panel members and Global Witness have claimed that timber revenue supported the RUF, while the humanitarian coordinating branch of the United Nations (OCHA) has argued that too many jobs would be lost in an already very weak economy. France and China—the two main importers of Liberian timber—initially opposed sanctions, taking their cue from the humanitarian argument and demanding indisputable evidence of the link between logging and arms, but they eventually agreed to sanctions. This was probably because of pro-sanctions advocacy, strong US backing for the ousting of Taylor, and the deteriorating security situation in the neighbouring Ivory Coast.

In summary, sanctions represent a potent but problematic strategy. Often difficult to enforce, sanctions remain subject to the vagaries of UN Security Council members' politics, poor enforcement by most states, and the complacency of many businesses. The most thorough attempt to manage resource revenues under a sanctions regime, and redirect them to humanitarian purposes—the UN Oil-for-Food Programme for Iraq—was supposed to alleviate the plight of many Iraqis in the face of unyielding political forces, but was marred by corruption and political instrumentalisation.[47] Nonetheless, targeted sanctions, the creation of independent investigative panels under the UN Secretariat leading to the "naming and shaming" of sanctions-busters, the imposition of "secondary" sanctions (as against Liberia), and judicial trials have improved the effectiveness of sanctions, which remain an important strategy for conflict termination.

What happens in the absence of sanctions?

Many conflict-affected countries do not see their conflict-commodities come under sanctions. As mentioned above, there are many possible reasons for this. In the absence of alternative revenue sources and precise targeting, sanctions are often more likely to undermine the government than the rebellion. In most of these cases sanctions are not imposed, because the government is not targeted and is not interested in receiving the assistance of the UN Security Council in this matter. A good example is the petroleum sector in Colombia, which finances rebel movements but is not the object of sanctions. Rather, the US gave military assistance to the government of Colombia to decrease the vulnerability of its oil infrastructure, an approach that does not fully address the sophisticated collusion or extortion schemes through which rebel groups can derive funding from the sector.[48] Sanctions can also affect foreign commercial interests, and there are many proponents of a "constructive approach" asserting that continued investment and trade are more likely to provide a way out of the conflict (see below). Finally, sanctions may be deemed as logistically impossible to implement, often because of the lack of cooperation from neighbouring countries, or because they impose too high a cost on local populations deriving a livelihood from conflict resources.

The importance of natural resources in financing belligerents in the DRC has been well documented since the late 1990s, by UN expert panels among others. Yet after more that a decade of calls to impose commodity sanctions—particularly on coltan, the main mineral financing multiple armed groups in the eastern DRC—no such specific sanctions have been formally imposed.[49] Three main reasons motivated the absence of sanctions: concerns about their feasibility given the DRC's massive size, the number of neighbouring countries, and those countries' limited capacity or lack of support; concerns about the embargo's effects on livelihoods and the overall economy; and the implication of local and regional political-cum-economic elites upon which the political process as well as UN mission logistics relied. Strategies of "naming and shaming" through UN expert panel and media reports and NGO campaigns did deter some companies from transporting or trading in coltan, such as the Belgian-Swiss airline Sabena/Swissair which voluntarily suspended transporting of "coltan and all related minerals" from Eastern Africa.[50] Several European NGOs launched a "No blood on my cellphone! Stop the looting of Congo!" campaign to force mobile phone companies to stop using components including minerals from conflict areas in the DRC. Advocacy groups have also used corporate social responsibility mechanisms such as the OECD Guidelines for Multinational Enterprises, following Global Witness' complaint against some companies for their alleged contribution to the financing of belligerents.[51] Despite their relative success, these initiatives have been occasionally decried for undermining local livelihoods and have remained largely ineffective given the collusion of regional authorities and the absence of an overarching sanctions regime.[52]

Revenue-sharing: "buying peace"

A third, important and controversial strategy for addressing the linkages between resources and wars is the sharing of resource revenue between "former" belligerents, rather than seeking to curtail revenue access. Sharing resource revenue, in other words, can "buy peace." This is possible insofar as resources constitute divisible goods, especially in terms of revenue and to a lesser degree in terms of ownership (especially if considering state sovereignty); they are thus amenable to self-enforcing sharing agreements.

How are resources to be shared or divided? Division can be arranged according to territorial, organisational or commercial criteria, corresponding to the three main options for revenue-sharing. A first option is to simply leave the armed group in (at least partial) control of the territory and resources it is holding (for example, as part of a local autonomy or secession agreement, or even as part of a sanctions regime as in the case of the Oil-for-Food Programme in Iraq). A second option is to offer the armed group new resource concessions, the control of resource businesses, or lucrative government positions overseeing resource sectors, as was done in Angola with the diamond sector. A third option is to establish a broad agreement on sharing resource revenue, as in Sudan.

Sudan's oil industry development stems partly from the Yom Kippur war and the oil crisis of 1973 that led Chevron to explore in Southern Sudan following the 1972 Addis Ababa Peace Agreement that ended nearly two decades of secessionist struggle in the region.[53] Chevron's oil discoveries in the South led the Sudanese central authorities in Khartoum to renege on the Peace Agreement, redrawing provincial borders and creating a new "Unity" province around the main oil fields.[54] This move contributed to the resurgence of rebellion in the South, with a Southern secessionist group killing three Chevron employees in 1984. Following Chevron's departure, "junior" oil companies (Canadian, Swedish and Austrian) moved in, often partnering with Asian state oil companies (Chinese, Malaysian, and Indian).[55] In 1997, the Khartoum Peace Agreement provided for oil revenue sharing between the central authorities and local Southern secessionist military factions around some of the oil fields partly suspended hostilities, enabling companies to operate more easily.[56] Ultimately, military opposition by the Sudan People's Liberation Army (SPLA), repression by government forces and its allies against local populations, infighting between Southern factions, and the reluctance of Sudan's government to respect the agreement led to renewed hostilities.[57] Fast rising oil revenue resulting from oil exports after 1999 consolidated the Government of Sudan's security apparatus, but also provided incentives for peace negotiations among Southern groups.[58] The resulting 2005 Comprehensive Peace Agreement provided for oil wealth sharing between North and South, and authorised a referendum that granted Southern Sudan its independence in 2011.[59]

To some degree, any conflict settlement could be considered to involve sharing resource revenue as long as opposing parties are allowed to have an input into governing. However, in this analysis, I only consider the cases in which natural resources constituted a major financial stake in the conflict, and in which agreements had an important resource dimension (although not always incorporated into formal documents, see below). These agreements can take place at various levels, concerning an entire rebel movement (as part of a comprehensive peace agreement) or only regional units (as part of a local ceasefire or defection process).

Revenue-sharing and post-conflict 'recovery'

To be effective, revenue-sharing agreements should be undertaken in a broader context of post-conflict economic "recovery" during the transition to peace. Why is this important? First, in the early post-conflict period, international actors often enjoy greater (if temporary) leverage as a result of additional funding, political transition, institutional flexibility, and in many cases a strong military presence. Second, the domestic economy of poor countries may rely heavily on primary commodity sectors and aid. It is therefore crucial for donors and development agencies to work with the private sector to promote an economic diversification strategy as early as possible, which requires cooperation with donors, development agencies, and the private sector. This also implies that the flows from revenue-sharing do not flow simply to belligerents, but also to the state and the general population.

Key to this strategy is a set of practical regulatory frameworks that can be set up to deprive belligerents of revenue they could use to follow a double agenda of peace transition and rearmament, as in Angola, Cambodia or Sri Lanka. For example, internationally supervised tax collection and budgetary allocation using escrow funds help to ensure that populations and public institutions benefit from resource revenue. Direct payment of resource revenue to the population has also been proposed, including the case of Iraq.[60] This would have the advantage of distributing a "peace dividend" to the needy, and partly addresses the problems of the lack of representation and accountability through broad-based taxation, affecting many resource-dependent countries. Businesses themselves may be deterred from operating outside the scheme through a system of incentives and sanctions. If this is successful, and in the absence of alternative sources of support, opting out of a peace process would become prohibitively expensive for belligerents. As with all instruments of control, the effectiveness of such schemes depends partly upon the characteristics of the targeted resource sector, the economic incentives attached, and the political motivations of belligerents. So far, such schemes have had at best a very mixed record, as illustrated earlier through the cases of the Oil-for-Food Programme in Iraq, or the Chad-Cameroon Petroleum Development and Pipeline Project.

Barriers to successful revenue-sharing

As the cases of Sudan (1997 Khartoum Agreement), Liberia (1995 Abuja Accord), Sierra Leone (1999 Lomé Agreement), or Angola (1994 Lusaka Protocol) illustrate, revenue sharing initiatives involve important risks of failure. The parties to the sharing agreement may not encompass all actors with a capacity to prolong the conflict. The inability of a party to enforce the agreement within its own ranks can lead to a resumption of the conflict by new factions rejecting the agreement. Finally, a party can be duplicitous and use such agreements to rearm, reorganise, or relocate troops to achieve its objectives by military means.

These barriers arise in part because, while military demobilisation and electoral monitoring characterise most contemporary peace processes, war economies are rarely "demobilised" and "monitored" in order to mitigate the risk of renewed insecurity. International financial institutions and donors intervene increasingly early in conflict termination processes, and with greater political sensitivity. The political economic aspects of peace processes, however, have remained relatively neglected, leaving the initiative to belligerents looking for the most lucrative position in the new government, for personal enrichment, or for the chance to embezzle funds to rearm.

There are also practical challenges to implementing revenue-sharing agreements. For example, for revenue-sharing agreements to work, fraud needs to be prevented. Accordingly, there is a need to review all resource-related contracts passed during the conflict and transition period, in order to hold accountable those responsible for fraud, sanctions-busting, and other grave abuses. But the cases of Uganda and the DRC illustrate how difficult this is in practice. For example, the Porter judicial commission in Uganda investigated charges of war profiteering against Ugandan officials operating in the neighbouring DRC. Although Judge Porter recommended disciplinary action against the two most senior army officers in charge, no such action was apparently taken. Similarly, in the Congo, the special National Assembly commission led by Christophe Lutundula found dozens of illegal or dubious contracts signed between 1996 and 2003. Its report recommended renegotiation or cancellation of sixteen contracts, judicial investigation of twenty-eight Congolese or international companies, and prosecution of seventeen persons on fraud charges. The Congolese Parliament, however, has repeatedly delayed an official consideration of this report, with some senior politicians implicated in these deals hoping to bury it.[61]

Moreover, as with military interventions and economic sanctions, there are ethical dimensions to the use of sharing agreements since those benefiting from these agreements (or at least negotiating them) include individuals or groups bearing responsibility for war crimes and occupying positions of power through force rather than consent and popular representation. Buying peace, in other words, may be perceived as rewarding violence.[62] The trade-off is of course curbing further abuses that could result from the absence of such agreements. Although sanctions and military interventions should have the ethical advantage of punishing rather than rewarding war criminals, in practice both often increase the sufferings of the general population.

Accordingly, there remains much debate about the effectiveness of these strategies and more generally about the use of force, sanctions, or negotiations.[63] In the following section I present an assessment of individual initiatives conducted between 1989 and 2006 before discussing possible factors influencing their relative effectiveness.

How well do resource-focused instruments work?

How should the effectiveness of the three types of strategies I have just reviewed be assessed? In this section, I present an analysis of the effectiveness of resource-focused conflict termination initiatives over the period from 1989 to 2006. Within this period, I identify twenty-six armed conflicts in which at least one resource-focused conflict termination initiative was used. In total, for these armed conflicts, I survey forty-five resource-focused initiatives. Within this sample, external military intervention is the most frequent type of intervention, followed by revenue sharing and UN sanctions. Two conflicts were addressed through all three types of instruments and nine through two types of initiatives.

To assess their potential effectiveness in terms of conflict settlement in general, I use three criteria: effective implementation; status of the conflict after one year; and status of the conflict after five years. Implementation success represents the achievement of operational objectives, specifically institutionalisation of the agreement in the case of sharing; curtailment of trade in the case of sanctions; and control of resource production area in cases of military intervention. Effectiveness is assessed through a review of UN situation reports and expert panel investigations, as well as think-tank, civil society, and press reports. As such, these assessments remain tentative and at times subjective. The one- and five-year lags assess the immediacy and sustainability of a potential effect on conflict termination. I do not argue that peace is the result of the implementation of instruments, but simply assess the occurrence of both events.

A number of caveats and limitations to this dataset should be mentioned. First, I only consider external military interventions that were publicly reported. I include major mercenary interventions and foreign government-mandated interventions (Table 6.1). Second, with regard to revenue-sharing initiatives, I only consider the cases in which a reference to the control of a key resource by the opposing party is included in a publicly available settlement agreement. Yet revenues are generally fungible, and other types of economic incentives may be offered in addition to, or as a substitute for, resource revenue in a sharing agreement. Furthermore, not all financial deals appear publicly; no confidential agreement would appear in this dataset. The selection criteria thus reflects the difficulty of identifying other types of agreements, either because they are clandestine, or because they occur on a smaller scale and fail to be reported. The fourteen selected revenue-sharing initiatives are listed in Table 6.2. These initiatives were concluded between opposing armed groups, with the exception of three cases that were set up unilaterally by central governments, in part to address secessionist agendas—in Angola for the Frente para a Libertação do Enclave de Cabinda (FLEC) and in Indonesia for both the Gerakan Aceh Merdeka (GAM) and the Organisasi Papua Merdeka (OPM). Finally, I assess the effectiveness of these initiatives through only three main criteria: successful implementation; conflict outcome after one year; and peace stability after five years.

Third, I limit the analysis of economic sanctions to those mandated by the Security Council, because UN sanctions are currently the sole means of legally and internationally imposing a market access denial, except for prohibition of specific commodities through international agreements, as in the case of narcotics, or voluntary agreements and peer monitoring, as in the case of the Kimberley Process Certification Scheme. UN sanctions can thus be considered more comprehensive than other types of sanctions and related initiatives, even if they have often been less strictly implemented than sanctions originating from individual states (for example, US sanctions). NGO advocacy was often key in bringing about a more effective implementation of UN sanctions, as in the case of "conflict diamonds." Table 6.3 lists seven sanctions initiatives, one of which only involved a ban on the export of production material to the targeted group—the Taliban in Afghanistan—since narcotics were already illegal on the international market.

Findings

Which type of conflict termination initiative was most successful? Those most successfully implemented were military interventions (89 percent) and revenue-sharing mechanisms (83 percent), while sanctions lagged at 57 percent.[64] This result is not surprising since revenue-sharing involves willing, if sometimes duplicitous, parties; military intervention is generally used when there are reasonable chances of success, especially in the case of military intervention by Western powers; and sanctions represent a limited instrument of coercion which has been used as a default policy option, and furthermore has been criticised for being poorly enforced.

When examining the potential effect of instruments on the resolution of a conflict, however, peace was achieved within a year for about half of

Table 6.2: Revenue-sharing initiatives, 1989–2006

Conflicts	*Instruments*	*Parties*	*Resources*
Angola I	Lusaka Protocol (1994)	Government/ UNITA	Diamonds, minerals
Angola II	Cabinda "special budget" (1996)*	Government/ Provinces	Oil
Cambodia	Unofficial (1996–98)	Government/PDK defecting units	Timber, gems
Chechnya	Khasavyurt Joint Declaration and Principles for Mutual Relations (1996)	Russian Security Council/Chechen Armed Forces	Oil and oil pipeline revenue (tacit recognition of independence)
Colombia	Putumayo agreement (1998)	Government/ FARC	Cocaine
Indonesia (Aceh, West Papua)	Laws 22/99 and 25/99 (implemented 2001)*	Government/ Provinces	Oil, gas, minerals and timber
Iraq-Kuwait	UNSC resolution 986 (1995)	UN/Iraq	Oil
Liberia I	Abuja Accord (1995)	Factions	Timber
Myanmar/ Burma I-IV	Various (1989–97)	Government (SLORC)/various	Minerals, timber, heroin
Papua New Guinea	Bougainville Peace Agreement (2001)	Government/ BPG-BRA	Copper and other resources
Philippines II	Peace Agreement (1996)	Government/ MNLF	Mines and minerals
Sierra Leone	Lomé Peace Agreement (1999)	Government/ RUF	Gold and diamonds
Sudan	Khartoum Peace Agreement (1997)	Government/ UDSF	Oil and metals
	Naivasha Agreement (2004)	Government/ SPLM	Oil and non-oil revenue

Note: * revenue-sharing agreements unilaterally passed by the government and not officially negotiated with the rebel groups.

Table 6.3: UN sanctions and other initiatives targeting resources, 1989–2006

Countries	Resolutions and targeted resources
Afghanistan	S/RES/1333 (2000) banned the provision to Taliban-controlled areas of acetic anhydride used in heroin production.
Angola I	S/RES/1173 (1998) on all diamonds outside governmental Certificate of Origin regime and the provision of mining equipment and services to non-government-controlled areas; S/RES/1237 (1999) establishment of expert panels; S/RES/1295 (2000) establishment of a sanctions monitoring mechanism.
Cambodia	S/RES/792 (1992) on log exports, requests adoption of embargo on minerals and gems exports, and requests implementation measures by UNTAC.
Iraq-Kuwait	S/RES/661 (1990) on all resources; S/RES/665 (1990) calls for halt, inspection, and verification of all maritime shipping in the Gulf area to ensure strict implementation of S/RES/661.
The Ivory Coast	S/RES/1584 (2005) establishment of a group of experts; S/RES/1643 (2005) on all rough diamonds, and re-establishment of group of experts.
Liberia II	S/RES/1343 (2001) on all rough diamonds, and establishment of an expert panel; S/RES/1408 (2002) establishment by government of Liberia of transparent and internationally verifiable audit regimes on use of timber industry revenue; S/RES/1478 (2003) on all round logs and timber products.
Sierra Leone	S/RES/1306 (2000) on all rough diamonds pending an effective governmental Certificate of Origin regime, and creation of expert panel on the implementation of sanctions.

the successfully implemented revenue-sharing agreements (53 percent), sanctions (50 percent), and military interventions (47 percent). This proportion increases for all instruments after five years, but sanctions were associated more frequently with durable peace (66 percent) than with revenue-sharing (57 percent) and military intervention (50 percent). This suggests that whereas military intervention is the most frequently used and successfully implemented, their potential contribution to peace seems lower than that of the two other instruments, when these are also successfully implemented. Military interventions were more successfully implemented against states than non-state groups, but these successes were more frequently followed by war than for non-state armed groups. Sanctions seem to have been more successfully implemented and followed by peace in the cases where they targeted whole countries or governments, rather than non-state groups. Sharing agreements all involved state and non-state groups (or the separatist government).

What reasons might underlie the variable effectiveness of conflict termination initiatives? Here, I highlight two possible factors influencing the effectiveness of commodity-focused measures: the type of resources and type of conflicts involved.

Resource type

Two main criteria can help define financial opportunities afforded by resources to belligerents in conflict situations: the legality of a resource and its accessibility or "lootability".[65] The legality of a resource refers to its legal status in domestic and international markets. This legal character shapes specific opportunities for belligerents. In the case of an illegal resource, a rebel group is advantaged compared with a government that risks losing its international legitimacy and associated sources of support if it engages in trafficking. In the case of a legal resource, a government is advantaged since the market will offer higher prices to a recognised authority than to an illegal one.

The accessibility (or lootability) of a resource is defined by the ease with which an armed group can generate revenue from it through exploitation or theft, as well as by taxation or extortion (see Table 6.4).[66] Several factors influence this accessibility. Some relate to the production and commercial characteristics of a resource: a resource is more accessible when its exploitation requires fewer financial, technological or labor inputs, and when the high price-per-volume ratio facilitates transport (see also below). Other factors relate to the geographical context and mode of exploitation of a resource: a resource is more accessible when it is spread over a vast territory, in a terrain propitious to insurgency, and along an international border, as well as when it is exploited by a high number of businesses vulnerable to protection rackets and protected by ineffective or corrupt security forces.[67]

Together, the legality and accessibility criteria may be used to define four categories of resources: illegal lootables (for example narcotics), legal lootables (such as alluvial diamonds), legal non-lootables (like off-shore oil), and illegal non-lootables. Illegal non-lootables could include uranium, exploitation of which is mostly conducted by tightly controlled industrial mines while trade in it comes under regulation through the Nuclear Non-Proliferation Treaty and the national legislation of Nuclear Suppliers Group members (akin to the voluntary agreement of participants to the Kimberley Process Certification Scheme). In practice, however, uranium from the DRC was identified by a UN group of experts as both "lootable," through artisanal exploitation, and somewhat "legal" given the total absence of control on the site and at the porous borders of the country.[68]

Five other criteria can also be considered when targeting conflict resources.[69] The first is the level of investment and technological inputs

Table 6.4: Resource categories and risk of accessibility by rebel forces

Resources	Risk of accessibility by rebel forces			Price range (US$/Kg)
	Exploitation	Theft	Extortion	
Illegal lootables				
Drugs	High	High	High	5,000–6,000
Other lootables				
Alluvial gems and minerals	High	High	High	20,000—500,000
Timber	Medium	Medium	High	0.1
Agricultural goods	Medium	Medium	Medium	1.5 (coffee)
Onshore oil	Low	Medium	High	0.12
Non-lootables				
Kimberlite diamonds	Low	Medium	Medium	20,000—500,000
Deep-shaft minerals	Low	Low	Medium	2 (copper)
Water dams	Low	Low	Medium	n/a
Offshore oil	Low	Low	Low	0.12

Note: Approximate prices in producing countries during the 1990s, adapted from industry sources, personal communication from Gavin Hayman at Global Witness, and Richard Auty, "Natural Resources and Civil Strife: A Two-Stage Process," *Geopolitics*, 2004, 9(1): 29–49.

required for production. When the level required is high, sanctions can aim at investors and technology providers, as for example in the case of offshore oil. A second criterion, also related to lootability, is that of ease or transport and concealment. If it is low, "on the ground" sanctions implementation, for example through border control, may be effective. A third is the level of revenue available to belligerents, and also the state. Sanctions should have a greater impact if this level is high. Another criterion is the redistribution of revenue. If it is redistributed locally, as is frequently the case for oil producing regions, insurgents are likely to tap into it via local authorities through extortion or collusion. Measures should thus be in place to minimise such leakages without turning the local population against authorities. The last criterion is the elasticity of demand for the resource—that is, how much consumption responds to prices or other criteria. If this is high, the threat of consumer boycotts may be effective in getting the industry to react, as was the case for diamonds. If it is low, as in the case of oil, targeted divestment and product purchasing on individual companies may still offer a potential leverage. I apply this framework to the three resources examined in this book—oil, diamonds, and timber—with opportunities for interventions underlined (see Table 6.5).[70] I then review each type of instrument in turn, since some commodity-focused instruments may better address specific resources given these distinctions.

Table 6.5: Economic features of oil, diamonds and timber

	Investment required	Ease of transport and concealment	Levels of revenue	Revenue distribution	Demand elasticity
Oil	High	Medium	High	High	Low
Diamonds	Medium	High	Medium	Medium	High
Timber	Low	Low	Low	Low	Medium

Revenue-sharing agreements have been used for all three types of resources. Their implementation success rate is highest for illegal lootables and non-lootables, but their association with a stable peace is strong only in the case of illegal lootables. More generally, it seems that wealth sharing works when belligerents remain in control of their area. The relative successes in Southern Sudan and in Burma contrast in this respect with the failures in Angola and Sierra Leone, where insurgents had to relinquish territorial control to the central government (even if they were formally part of it). Furthermore, wealth sharing rested on formal agreements over resource exploitation or revenue sharing in Burma and especially in Sudan. This contrasted with agreements allocating cabinet positions in the cases of Angola and Sierra Leone, where such arrangements rested on a mix of political agenda (measures to reduce rural poverty through extractive sector revenue, for example) and assumptions of corruption (such as accessing resource wealth through the control of a ministerial portfolio).

Second, sanctions have also been used for all three types of resources, but mostly for lootable goods. Sanctions failed to be implemented in the only case of an illegal lootable resource, and have a low implementation success rate for other lootables, and a medium one for non-lootables. Association with peace stability is also nil for illegal lootables but medium for the other two categories.

Third, military interventions have also been used for all three types of resource categories. Military intervention has been successfully implemented in most cases but most strongly for non-lootable resources—a result that also appears to be associated with peace stability.

Overall, this survey of instruments indicates that illegal lootable resources have been most successfully dealt with through revenue-sharing mechanisms.[71] The only successful case of military intervention recorded seems to be that of the US-led military campaign against the Taliban in 2001, but US policy prior to 2005 was not to actively target heroin revenue.[72] In the case of legal lootable resources, sanctions appear to be the most successful with regard to peace stability, despite a low implementation success rate. Although sharing appears as a second best option, with a higher rate of implementation success, all successful cases were only part of broader negotiated peace agreements, rather than anterior to conflict settlement. Revenue-sharing in Papua New Guinea, for example, was part of a comprehensive agreement signed after a three-year truce between belligerents. Military interventions to control legal and lootable resources, while highly successful in terms of implementation, were very often followed by a resumption of the conflict within the next five years. In the case of non-lootable resources, military intervention was most successful, followed by sanctions. This could be explained by the fact that these resources were controlled by central governments unwilling to respond to sanctions (as in Iraq) or facing politically motivated secessionist groups with which sharing agreements were not respected or proved unsatisfactory (as in Aceh in 1999, Chechnya in 1996, and Sudan in 1997).

Conflict type

Previous work on primary commodities and armed conflicts has suggested a possible relation between resources (their location, characteristics, and modes of production) and types of armed conflict.[73] For example, as found by Paul Collier and Anke Hoeffler, rebellions in oil regions almost always have a secessionist character.[74] In turn, this has implications for conflict termination, as the type of conflict involved may play a part in the effectiveness of a specific initiative. If a rebellion in an oil region is secessionist, for example, a sharing agreement may be more successful than a military intervention.[75]

Revenue-sharing agreements have been used in both types of conflict—territorial and governmental—with a higher rate of success in the former case. Sanctions have rarely been used for territorial incompatibilities (except for Kuwait) and have rarely been successful in governmental ones (with the exception of Angola and Iraq). Military interventions have been mostly used in governmental incompatibilities, and have been relatively successful in both types of conflict in terms of implementation. Peace stability records, however, are only positive in the case of territorial incompatibilities. Moreover, these cases appear deceptively successful, as the only occurrences of stable peace took place in an international war context (Kuwait) or came as the result of an unintended political crisis triggered by the recruitment of a foreign mercenary group by the government (Papua New Guinea).

Overall, these preliminary findings suggest that secessionist conflicts (the UN's "territorial incompatibilities") appear to be best addressed through revenue-sharing, while non-secessionist civil wars (the UN's "governmental incompatibilities") are best addressed through sharing and sanctions. This suggests a potential dilemma in the choice of initiatives, given Ross' argument that lootable commodities are more generally associated with governmental incompatibilities, and non-lootable commodities with territorial incompatibilities.[76] Hence territorial conflicts would be best addressed through revenue-sharing, but the non-lootable commodities financing or motivating them would be best addressed through capture or sanctions. The sequencing of different initiatives may solve part of this dilemma.[77]

Multiple mechanisms are at play in resource-related conflicts.[78] Accordingly, it is important to take into account the impact that resource-focused initiatives may have upon these conflicts in all of their complexities. Most important, it is necessary to grapple with the multiple mechanisms at work in order to anticipate cases when conflict termination agreements may be undermined, or have unexpected effects.

As outlined here, for example, revenue-sharing agreements can serve to reduce the need to use violence to access resources and thus shorten hostilities. They might also hasten a transition to peace through fostering fragmentation of belligerent forces by selectively rewarding some groups (and thereby employing a strategy of "divide and rule"). Moreover, revenue-sharing could also help create economic linkages across divided communities (though arguably revenue may remain at the mercy of predatory belligerent elite groups); however, revenue-sharing may also facilitate resource access to a weaker opposition group that could prove to be duplicitous (regrouping and rearming while pledging peace).

Similarly, while sanctions can be used to reduce the revenue available to belligerents and their international commercial backers, they might also play a more negative role through creating fragmentation, criminalising the resource sector, and promoting conflict-dependent (rather than peace-building) economic linkages between groups. Targeted sanctions, of course, can avoid some of these impacts, for example, through promoting the positive role of balance of power by selecting which parties can legally export resources and which ones cannot, or by redirecting economic activity away from resource sectors towards other ones with more linkages. Sanctions could also play a negative role by preventing peace-buying, although their removal or re-imposition could become a tool to ensure that peace-buying arrangements are followed through and applied.

Military interventions may also have an ambiguous effect. For example, military defeat may disperse violent actors in the absence of adequate disarmament, demobilisation and reintegration programmes. Military interventions may also fuel nationalist mobilisation, thereby escalating the conflict.

In short, this analysis of the relative "success" of different conflict termination initiatives should be balanced with recognition of the complexities at stake. The types of resources, types of conflicts, and the broad range of underlying mechanisms all complicate the task of successfully bringing about peace. This implies that conflict termination strategies should take these factors into account, in part through the strategic association of different types of conflict resolution mechanisms, so as sustain or amplify the positive impacts of instruments on a possible return to peace. Simply put, the question is not, "Capture, share, or sanction?" but rather, "What is the right combination of conflict termination instruments?"

Conclusion

So can war be ended by instrumentalising resources, either through sanctions, military capture, or revenue sharing? The analysis in this and previous chapters has suggested that we should not over-emphasise the degree to which resource revenues prolong conflicts. First, mostly on the basis of a review of the literature and anecdotal evidence from case studies, the analysis provides qualified support for the argument that conflicts involving resources tend to recur more frequently, and that access to resource revenue by belligerents generally prolongs armed conflicts. This argument is supported here by the relatively short timespan within which a number of conflicts are settled after resource-focused initiatives are implemented. Yet renewed hostilities after many of these "successful" interventions indicate that curtailing financial opportunities is not a panacea. It suggests, rather, that the importance of resource revenue for the viability and motivation of rebellion in these conflicts may be over-emphasised. In this regard, resources are rarely the only source of revenue and motivation for belligerents, who often find ways to adapt their struggle to more difficult economic conditions resulting from effective resource-focused initiatives.[79]

Second, resource-focused initiatives have been differently associated with successful interventions and a stable peace. The military capture of resource areas from rebel forces appears to be a deceptive quick fix: successfully implemented, it often forces the targeted party into a settlement, but ultimately fails to usher in a stable peace. Military capture requires significant follow-up to avoid the recurrence of hostilities. This calls for a mix of robust (if challenging) peacekeeping and reforming domestic security forces.

Revenue-sharing is as successful as military intervention in terms of implementation, and is more rapidly followed by conflict settlement, but is also rarely followed by a stable peace. This finding, however, may reflect a timing issue, since agreement on revenue sharing is often concluded as part of a conflict settlement. Given the asymmetry between belligerents and the risks of duplicity characterising many of these revenue-sharing agreements, third parties may also have a role in guaranteeing these arrangements. Adequately mandated peacekeeping forces and an international supervising mechanism for the resource sector can help provide such guarantees.

Sanctions have a poor overall record in terms of implementation for the period examined, but major improvements have been noted since the late 1990s in terms of monitoring and enforcement. Sanctions, furthermore, are generally lifted only once a conflict is settled and the security situation is under control. This possibly contributes to a lasting peace by reducing the likelihood that "peace spoilers" (often splinter groups from rebellions or the army) use resource revenues to restart hostilities, as well as by minimising the risk of conflicts within resource sectors (for example between the militias of logging companies and the self-defence groups of local communities).

The effectiveness of individual instruments is difficult to assess in isolation from other factors. On the one hand, military intervention and revenue sharing have a more successful implementation record than sanctions. But, on the other hand, sanctions and revenue-sharing agreements have a stronger correlation with durable peace than military interventions. Effectiveness also varies according to the type of conflicts and resources involved. Accordingly, I suggest that the choice of conflict termination instruments should reflect the characteristics of commodities, the structure of the resource sector, and the motivations and capacities of actors along the commodity supply chain.

Third, I suggested earlier that the characteristics of the resource sectors targeted and the type of conflict involved may affect the effectiveness of these instruments. The relative effectiveness of these three types of initiatives appears to respond in part to the characteristics of the targeted resource. Resources most accessible to rebel forces (such as alluvial diamonds or timber) seem to be best addressed through sanctions, while military capture is most effective for resources like oil, which generally fall more easily under government control. Controversially, illegal resources (such as narcotics, which are not examined in detail here) appear to be best dealt with through revenue-sharing arrangements between belligerents. Such a realpolitic approach to conflict resolution can easily prove controversial if not counterproductive, as suggested by the cases of Burma, Colombia, and more recently Afghanistan.

These findings not only lend support to arguments in favour of contextualising responses, but also point to some of the dilemmas and limits of resource-focused instruments. Conflicts involving primarily illegal lootable resources seem best addressed by revenue-sharing arrangements, those involving legal lootable resources by sanctions, and those involving non-lootable resources by military intervention. Responding to conflicts related to narcotics poses a dilemma: revenue-sharing arrangements are rarely an official option for governments and even less so for countries seeking to intervene in a conflict. However, as noted earlier, a number of governments have taken this option unofficially to secure a conflict settlement or to support local allies, as initially in the case of the post-9/11 intervention in Afghanistan, hoping that once a clear victor emerges subsequence assistance in curtailing drug trafficking will solve the problem—a position that seems to fly in the face of most cases such as Burma or Colombia.

This analysis is admittedly tentative, as it does not address the many other conditions that affect the settlement of a conflict and the likelihood of war recurrence.[80] A more comprehensive analysis would require an examination of the effectiveness of military interventions by domestic groups; a more detailed analysis of different types of economic revenue-sharing agreements, considering different scales; and an examination of regional and unilateral sanction regimes. Analyses could also examine the influence of the timing and complementarity of these various initiatives, as well as the influence of resources on the capacity and will of external interveners (including the question of commercial interests among interveners).[81] Finally, further research could focus on the means by which to establish a credible and enforceable revenue-sharing agreement, and examine how credibility and enforceability might vary according to the type of resources involved. Learning more about the context in which conflict termination instruments are deployed may improve their effectiveness and reduce the risk of renewed conflicts.

By strategically addressing the broader context in which commodity-focused conflict termination initiatives are to take place, their effectiveness could be improved. For example, agencies seeking to curtail revenue access for belligerents should also consider the structure of the industry, as well as the capacity and motivations of intermediaries and authorities along the resource supply chain—as demonstrated in the case of "conflict diamonds" and the creation of the Kimberley Process.[82] More generally, there is a need to reshape resource sectors in the interest of peace and economic recovery. I return to these issues in Chapter 7.

7

RESOURCES FOR PEACE

Putting an end to resource-funded hostilities is a major task, as seen in the previous chapter. But how to make resource sectors work for peace? Resource sectors can boost economic recovery, provide much-needed jobs, help rebuild infrastructure, and raise large tax revenues. Yet civil wars involving resources not only often last longer, they are also more likely to restart than those that do not.[1] Judging from this record, the relationship between durable peace and "post-conflict" resource exploitation is thus far from straightforward. Advertising that a country is now "open for business" may help to bring in Foreign Direct Investment by firms eager to tap into resources long inaccessible because of hostilities, but it is not a panacea to ensure by itself a lasting "peace dividend" for local populations. So-called "post-conflict" situations provide a challenging context for effective resource management.

First of all, resource sectors tend to attract armed groups in search of economic opportunities. Peace spoilers tend to hold on, or hang around, resource areas in the hope of accessing funding for renewed hostilities. Former combatants and army units frequently engage in illegal resource exploitation and extortion schemes targeting resource companies and workers. Corporate-sponsored military units and private militias also frequently expel local residents, artisanal miners and loggers to make way for new resource concessions. Resource production areas and trade routes are thus common "hot spots" for various types of conflicts and forms of violence, from land dispossession and forced labor to pitched battles between competing mining or logging groups.

Second, local authorities often suffer from a lack of knowledge about the resources available for exploitation and recent developments in the sector—due, for example, to lapses in surveys, undocumented wartime resource exploitation, death or flight of qualified personnel, and outdated training. As a result, local authorities often fail to maximise revenue collection, especially when negotiating with better-informed companies.[2] Meanwhile, the population may have unreasonable expectations of extractive sector revenue and, unsurprisingly, attribute low official revenue to high government corruption. A major challenge is thus rapidly acquiring and spreading knowledge about potential resource revenue in order to inform both policy decisions and public opinion. As a general principle, international organisations assisting in the post-conflict and reconstruction process should therefore support resource surveys, revenue flow analyses, tax structures, and information dissemination.

Third, breaking the vicious cycle between high risks and low fiscal returns represents a major challenge. The risk of renewed conflict, degraded infrastructure, and uncertainties in the regulatory environment may disadvantage the government in its negotiations with investors.[3] Governments often offer major tax incentives to attract large-scale investments. The companies attracted to "post-conflict" countries are frequently those willing to take the most risks but also those more inclined to use bribery, deploy private armed protection, and take short cuts in terms of corporate social responsibility. Financial institutions and donor governments eager to fast-track Foreign Direct Investment may turn a blind eye to the backgrounds and records of these companies.[4] As a general principle, transitional authorities should not be granted the right to award long-term contracts for extractive projects. International assistance should provide for budgetary and security support both to lower risks and to help maximise fiscal returns.

Fourth, owing to limited large-scale investment, resources are often first exploited through small-scale ventures that offer livelihood opportunities for local populations but usually prove difficult for the government to tax. This is frequently the case, for example, with logging and alluvial mining. A major challenge in such cases is to balance local livelihood opportunities and fiscal revenue maximisation. As a general principle, a comprehensive assessment of options for each sector and exploitation area should clarify objectives, outline possible scenarios, and help increase broad developmental benefits. Assessments and policies need to be based on the participation of local entrepreneurs and workers (including the poorest) as well as local communities' free, prior, and informed consent.

Finally, budgetary allocation in post-conflict environments often presents special difficulties. The ephemeral character of political and bureaucratic appointments in transitional governments usually heightens incentives for corruption. Political priorities often trump economic ones, thereby affecting budgetary processes, often through arrangements for revenue sharing between former belligerent parties. Corruption may be tolerated by both politicians and donors for the sake of "political stability." Donor support for social services can weaken pressure on the government to allocate revenue to these high priority areas. Some donors may tie their nominally "unconditional" assistance to privileged access to resource sectors, such as granting resource projects to home companies or preferential treatment in resource supply access.[5] A major challenge is thus to ensure that the path of revenue allocation consolidates both economic recovery and good governance. As a general principle, revenue allocation mechanisms should foster a sense of entitlement over revenue amongst the population, building incentives and mechanisms to protect revenue from abuses by governments and extractive industries.[6]

I present in this chapter several proposals for resource sector contributions to peacebuilding—noting furthermore that many proposals are also relevant in areas of peacemaking, peacekeeping and peacebuilding in order to address resource curse, resource conflict and conflict resource issues (see Table 7.1). I first discuss proposals relevant to resource exploitation management, focusing on the potential contributions of peacekeeping missions as well as the prevention of resource-related land conflicts and the promotion of domestic entrepreneurship and employment. The second set of proposals deals with the management of resource revenue, including the recovery of looted wealth, post-conflict resource contract reappraisal, direct revenue disbursement to the population, and the creation of special funds. The final set of proposals speaks to resource governance more broadly, focusing on relevant international initiatives. I come back to these various policy options, their prioritisation and their timing in the last section before the conclusion.

Table 7.1: Resource/conflict linkages and peace initiatives[7]

	Resource curse	Resource conflict	Conflict resource
Peacemaking	Integrate resource governance reforms into peace agreements	Resolve resource ownership and revenue sharing issues	Address revenue incentives of belligerents
Peacekeeping	Regulate the post-conflict resource rush, prevent awarding of unfair long-term resource contracts	Deploy peace-keepers in resource areas to pre-empt human rights abuses and conflict escalation	Use investigations, sanctions, certification and military deployment to curtail resource financing and profiteering
Peacebuilding	Cancel or renegotiate "odious" resource contracts and improve developmental outcomes through governance reforms and capacity building	Promote inclusive forms of resource ownership, control, and access	Consolidate the demilitarisation of resource sectors and set up long term certification scheme

Managing resource extraction

A rush on natural resources often characterises post-conflict transitions as local populations need jobs, governments need revenue, and companies strive to secure the most attractive resource prospects.[8] Undue haste is especially characteristic when elites are driven by short-term personal interests and when donors actively promote Foreign Direct Investment. Four main extraction-management challenges arise in such contexts: regulating the post-conflict rush on resources; recovering looted assets and dealing with the legacy of "odious contracts" signed previously by belligerents or transitional governments; striking a balance between fiscal and other socioeconomic objectives; and averting conflicts over new resource developments.

Regulating the "post-conflict resource rush": Can the UN help?

Extractive businesses are among the most resilient to armed conflicts. Often they are the last to depart from conflict areas and the first to return after the end of hostilities.[9] Rapid recovery in the extractive sector is thus often possible. Although restarting an industrial mine may take years, many local entrepreneurs and international "juniors" (mid-size companies) handling small and medium-scale projects can rapidly increase output (as demonstrated by diamond rushes in Angola in the mid-1990s and Sierra Leone in the early 2000s). These activities can help "quick-start" the economy, but their effect on post-war state building can be ambivalent. Tax evasion, environmental degradation, labor abuses, conflicts with local communities, and collusion with peace spoilers controlling resource production areas are frequent challenges, difficult to regulate.

Not only are resource sectors subjected to overlapping and sometimes transient authorities, resource companies also frequently deploy their own private security forces.[10] Furthermore, policies and legislation are rarely clear as old regulations are revised, often through divergent donor-sponsored initiatives, leaving companies and regulating authorities in a state of uncertainty favouring discretionary power and corruption. The ranks, capacity and legitimacy of resource management institutions are also frequently depleted, as in several resource management offices in Cambodia where only a handful of professional foresters had survived. The challenge is thus to fast-track regulatory policies and institutions alongside—or preferably ahead of—the post-conflict rush. Regulations, however, need to be sensitive to local populations' livelihood opportunities. Priority should thus be placed on regulating large-scale extractive projects with long-term consequences, while artisanal and small-scale activities should be supported through legalisation and capacity building.

Multidimensional peacebuilding missions, including their peacekeeping forces, can be mandated and deployed in resource production areas and key transport hubs to better control resource exploitation and address resource-related conflicts. Such mandates can be backed by a commodity sanctions regime that is conditional upon adherence both to peace process benchmarks and legal practices in the resource sector. A logging sector, for example, can be closed for exports until sound regulatory institutions are in place, and until the security and political situation can ensure that these are effective on the ground.

Peacebuilding missions have often been hesitant about such roles, viewing these as high-risk burdens and distractions from their main mandates. In Sierra Leone, the UN mission (UNAMSIL) actively engaged in diamond-sector regulation only in the last stages of its operation. Initially, it was wary of breaching its mandate, antagonising local interest groups, exposing its troops to criminal violence, and reinforcing rumors of peacekeeping forces' involvement in diamond trafficking.[11] Some of these concerns were legitimate, yet reports from military observers about the importance of diamond-related conflicts—including ongoing armed skirmishes—and assistance requests from the government and from donors funding diamond reforms led to UNAMSIL's eventual engagement. From 2003 onwards, UNAMSIL conducted aerial surveys, foot patrols, and targeted conflict-settlement interventions in the diamond sector, often jointly with the Ministry of Mines but also occasionally in a supervisory capacity.

UN peacebuilding missions have accumulated much experience as transitional authorities and in implementing sanctions regimes, experience that could be collected and analyzed to improve future missions. In the transition phase, peacekeeping forces should focus on curtailing access to resource revenue for potential "peace spoilers." This can be done by identifying players in the extractive industries, demilitarising resource production areas, and closing down activities benefiting spoilers by targeting key trading intermediaries and transport bottlenecks, such as bridges and ports. Peacekeeping forces can also intervene to prevent the escalation of resource-related conflicts, as in the clashes between local youths and demobilised rebel soldiers during the 2001 "diamond rush" in Koidu (Sierra Leone's "diamond capital").

During the peacebuilding phase, mission staff should seek to address broader linkages between resource revenue and conflicts by assisting local authorities and international agencies in charge of resource sectors. Monitoring activities, logistical support, and the "good offices" of the UN Secretary General's Special Representative can all contribute in this regard. In the DRC, for example, the UN mission (MONUC) shares information collected on illegal logging with several UN agencies, NGOs, and government authorities.

In the case of UN trusteeship, foreign transitional authorities have a much broader mandate that generally include the management of resource sectors. Transitional authorities, whether local or international, should not be granted the right to award long-term contracts in extractive sectors.[12] Revenue from resource sectors should be put under international trusteeship or at least supervision.[13] Even as foreign trusteeship authorities relinquish their power to domestic ones, it is desirable to maintain external supervision and a capacity to intervene in revenue management, possibly for as long as a decade. Given sensitivities over sovereignty, such efforts risk raising questions about the motives of intervening parties, thus strict independence and an absence of vested interests must be demonstrated. With regard to the opening up of oil fields, the Australian intervention in East Timor and the American intervention in Iraq offer cautionary examples.

Renegotiating "odious" contracts

Wartime looting results in tax losses, but even greater plunder can result after the war through inequitable contracts and new investment laws that favour resource companies. International aid can initially mask these losses, but they become more apparent when donor fatigue sets in and countries are most in need of sustained revenues. *Ex post facto* policies are needed for reappraising and renegotiating contracts, as well as recovering "looted" resource revenue.[14] Wealth recovery seeks to identify and repatriate the proceeds generated by illegal resource exploitation, as defined by domestic legislation or international sanctions regimes. This can include the assets of rebel groups and members of unconstitutional governments, as well as the proceeds of companies that participated in illegal commercial activities. The objective is not only to recover money to bolster fiscal revenue but also to signal the end of impunity and discourage extractive companies and banking institutions from participating in wartime resource looting.[15]

Contract reappraisal and renegotiation can increase public revenue, provide greater transparency and accountability, and support the regulation of the social and environmental impacts of resource sectors. By cancelling speculative or poorly run resource projects, reappraisal can also attract higher-quality investments that are more fiscally advantageous for the government and can better benefit local communities. Finally, a well-run reappraisal scheme that yields demonstrably successful development outcomes can strengthen trust in, and improve the legitimacy of, the government. Yet contract reappraisal initiatives should be carefully conducted so as not to act as a deterrent against legitimate future investment. Adoption of international standards providing contractual guidelines would help in this regard (see below).

For contractual reappraisal, a first step is full disclosure of contracts, corporate structure, and ownership. Confidential commercial clauses should not be considered legally valid, given that the review is legally mandated for all contracts in the country. Tax evasion and abusive practices—including tax holidays, transfer pricing, biased commodity-pricing mechanisms, and liability sheltering—need to be revoked. This requires a systematic review of extractive sector activities and contracts, including those involving state companies, with a concept of "odious contracts" being applied to cancel existing contracts if necessary.[16] Tax reappraisal for company activities conducted during the war should be considered, as well as penalties imposed on companies that knowingly traded in conflict resources (see below).

Donors should foster such reappraisal through technical assistance and support for civil society organisations demanding and monitoring changes. To gain the cooperation of domestic authorities, donors should consider providing funds to make up for potential losses in revenue during review periods. In order for this process to be meaningful, reviews must be open and their findings and contractual revisions made public. If necessary, disciplinary measures against reluctant companies and governments should be considered, including resort to targeted reactivation of UN Security Council sanctions.

Tracking down assets requires extensive expertise, judicial support, and collaboration from financial institutions.[17] The focus in such cases should be on major investors, traders and exporters. Possible measures include building domestic or foreign investigative capacity (and ensuring that these are not co-opted or dismantled by powerful political interests), following due judicial process to avoid convictions being quashed (maybe in a foreign court where standards of procedure and evidence may be higher), and the disarmament and demobilisation of militias protecting suspected entrepreneurs and politicians that could interference with policing.

Needless to say, these requirements pose serious challenges, especially in highly politicised and volatile environments with weak state capacity. The record of post-conflict contract reappraisal is thus very mixed, but with some notable successes. Many dubious logging and mining contracts were signed in the DRC as the Mobutu regime collapsed in the 1990s and the country became engulfed into a series of regional and local conflicts. The formal Congolese mining industry has been in disarray since the late 1980s and the fragility of the Congolese state has been clear to see over the following two decades. A National Assembly commission led by Christophe Lutundula identified dozens of illegal or dubious contracts signed between 1996 and 2003, and its final report recommended both contract renegotiations and judicial prosecutions (as discussed above).[18] Contracts signed under the new Mining Code passed by the Kabila government in 2003 to attract mining interests (and secure the support of their home governments) were not considered despite their minimal tax revenue return. Following repeated calls by civil society and opposition politicians for contractual reviews, a second government commission, examining this time the 1996–2006 period, concluded in late 2007 that out of sixty-one mining contracts reviewed—many of them signed during the "transition" period—thirty-eight contracts had to be renegotiated and twenty-three cancelled because of irregularities.[19] Still, mining revenue for the state remained minimal compared with the wealth generated by the sector.[20] Overall, contractual reappraisal initiatives appear to have yielded limited long-term benefits for the DRC, while further undermining the credibility of the political class and government. In some cases, the DRC's inability to bring the reappraisal and renegotiation process to a positive conclusion increases the risk that international arbitration will vindicate the ousted companies that have challenged the decisions of the Congolese government.[21]

In Liberia, forestry concessions were cancelled, and President Ellen Johnson-Sirleaf was able to renegotiate a rubber concession contract with Firestone and an iron ore mining contract between Mittal Steel and the previous transition government that had, among other abusive clauses, allowed the company to determine the price of iron ore and thereby its own taxation rate. Public exposure of inequities in the contract by Global Witness assisted by the Tax Justice Network, engaged leadership by President Johnson-Sirleaf (Africa's first elected female president), a collaborative and unified government negotiation team, and "world-class" technical assistance contributed to substantially improved terms in the new contract (see Table 7.2).[22]

Revisiting liberalisation policies

Extractive sectors have been liberalised since the late 1980s, particularly in post-conflict countries. Liberalisation policies often increased foreign

Table 7.2: Fiscal aspects of Mittal contract renegotiation in Liberia[23]

Initial Contract	Renegotiated Contract
Mittal sets iron ore price, and thus effective royalty rate and tax rate	Iron price set by international market price
Five year tax holiday, with unlimited extension	No tax holiday
Obligations guaranteed only by concessionaire (Mittal's subsidiary)	Obligations guaranteed by parent company
Transfer to Mittal of main national railway line and deep-sea port	No transfer, no exclusive right
Extended and backdated equitable treatment clause	Equitable treatment clause limited to iron ore sector and no backdating
Concessionaire rights to all minerals in the concession area	Rights to iron ore only
Contract governed by United Kingdom law	Contract governed by Liberia law
Minimal social obligations	National senior managers and health care obligations

investment and economic output, using reduced taxation rates as a core incentive. The overall fiscal impact has varied among countries, but observers have pointed to long-term risks associated with lower fiscal returns on non-renewable resources.[24] Fiscal regimes have privileged income tax and production sharing agreements (PSAs) that grant the government a proportion of resource earnings, rather than contracts based on royalties or direct exploitation through publicly owned companies, which both ensure a greater degree of control by the government.[25] One problem is that the terms of the resulting agreements reflect the limited bargaining power of post-conflict states. A second problem is that politicians often take decisions with long-term impact based on short-term considerations. Politicians may be more eager, for example, to privilege a foreign company able to jump-start a project and offer a large cash bonus on the signature of the resource contract, over the development of a domestic industry. Both strategies offer different risks and opportunities, ignoring the downsides of locking the resource sector into foreign control and exacerbating its "enclave" character.

Attracting foreign companies to the extractive resource sector is frequently the major priority of the government and aid donors alike. Low taxation rates remain the main incentive for FDI, and tax holidays abound in the mining codes drafted since the early 1990s. Taxation stability clauses, and the fear of deterring investment, mean that such generous tax breaks and low royalty rates are rarely challenged by local authorities, even as resource prices rise sharply. Such situation leaves governments with a meager portion of resource revenue, and the growing discontent of an increasingly better-informed population. Zambia provides a typical case where the government finally imposed a windfall tax in 2008 after coming under much public pressure, only to lift the measure following the 2008–09 economic crisis that (briefly) sent copper prices down, pressure from mining companies, and criticisms from some opposition parties.[26]

Domestic benefits may be better secured outside fast-tracked FDI projects. For instance, some resources, such as timber and surface deposits of high-grade ore, can be exploited through labor-intensive methods requiring minimal technological and capital inputs. These modes of exploitation (artisanal or small-scale) may have lower tax potential, but they often have higher net national value added than capital intensive projects (see Table 7.3). Domestic ownership allows for higher rates of taxation than those imposed by the "global norm" of foreign investment.[27] Domestic ownership can be public, private, or a mix of both. Private ownership can help to hold the state accountable, but the state must also hold the private sector accountable. In practice, governments have frequently sought to bail out private companies—for example, through tax exemption—when faced with the prospect of large-scale unemployment or when key political supporters are at risk.

Table 7.3 compares FDI-industrial and domestic-artisanal (or small-scale) resource extraction. Industrial exploitation generally provides higher resource recovery rate than artisanal methods. Yet the net national product (NNP) of industrial production falls below that of domestic artisanal extraction because of higher imported inputs, expatriate wages, depreciation, and profit repatriation. The potential advantage of industrial exploitation is higher tax revenue—but only assuming that there are sound tax policies in place. Attention should also be given to indirect economic effects of both modes of production, such as indirect jobs and spending on domestic inputs such as food and tools. Domestic small-scale operations can also generate crucial financial capital for rural economies and more local economic development. Beyond the private/public and foreign/domestic divides, measures such as contract and revenue transparency and firewalls between regulators and regulated companies are necessary to prevent crony capitalism, asset stripping, and capital flight. What matters, in short, is effective governance through strong regulatory mechanisms.[28]

Table 7.3: Foreign-industrial versus domestic-artisanal resource extraction[29]

	FDI-industrial	Domestic-artisanal
Value of resource deposit	100	100
Resource recovery (gross output)	95	70
Material inputs		
• Imported	20	3
• Locally produced	7	1
Gross Domestic Product	68	66
Wages and payments		
• Expatriates	7	0
of which repatriated	*3.5*	–
• Nationals	14	50
Tax payments	20	4
Depreciation	9	1
Repatriated profits	18	11
Gross National Product	46.5	55
Net National Product	37.5	54

Preventing resource exploitation conflicts

As discussed in previous chapters, many different conflicts can arise from resource exploitation. Resource management should emphasise reducing potential sources of tensions and violence within the country. The core area in resource conflict prevention is dealing with land-related issues. These include potential for tensions over land ownership, land use, resource control and access rights, land degradation or environmental effects.[30] Post-conflict settings are particularly prone to land-related conflicts, due in part to large population movements, including those of returnees who may find their land occupied.

Local authorities also frequently award large land concessions, and occasionally implement vast land tenure reforms. Motivations behind these concessions and reforms include for example the needs to increase fiscal revenue, to "kick start" the economy through large-scale investment, and to free up land for key infrastructure such as roads and housing. Other motivations, however, include corruption, the desire to please certain donor countries through investment opportunities, and a strategy of state consolidation through centralising resource activities. The single largest direct impact of extractive sectors is the loss of land-based resource access for local communities, most often through the privatisation of commons and resource concessions or activities prohibiting previous land use. In this respect, forest-related resource activities may have the largest footprint as vast logging or tree plantations such as palm oil are awarded over hundreds if not thousands of square kilometers. Mineral exploitation comes second, with relatively medium-sized affected areas around a few square kilometers—with the exception of placer or secondary deposits, for which artisanal mining activities can be prohibited over vast areas if not the entire country. Lastly, oil activities tend to have a relatively small footprint in terms of exclusive land and maritime domains, generally a few hundred meters around oil infrastructures, but transport infrastructure and incidents such as spills can have large-scale impact (as in the case of some mining activities, especially where water pollution is an issue). Several broad policies and specific measures can help prevent resource-related conflicts involving land issues.

First, resource management should have broad developmental outcomes. This means prioritising not only large investments and high fiscal revenue, but also local livelihoods and long-term social and environmental impacts. As a principle, a moratorium should be placed on large-scale resource exploitation until policy and legal reviews of existing systems and concessions are conducted and robust institutions with satisfactory management and governance standards are in place (including land titling procedures, independent monitoring of resource sectors, transparent and accountable revenue flows, and credible impact assessments).

Second, resource managers ought to identify high-value resources, land ownership, and user rights. This includes documenting existing resource activities, locating and assessing resource reserves, and presenting likely options for future resource development. Such information should then be put in dialogue with existing land ownership and user rights. Existing and potential land-related conflicts should be assessed in collaboration with communities and resource companies; the process ought to include risk evaluation, information sharing, and providing early warnings to concerned parties on an ongoing basis. Third, multipurpose land use and access to land-based resources should be promoted through participatory land-use planning involving local communities. The key concept of free, prior and informed consent should provide the basis of such a participatory approach, with a fair process of negotiation over compensation, possible veto rights by local communities, and long-term participation in control over resource exploitation.

Fourth, broad developmental outcomes for local communities ought to be encouraged, with priority placed on reducing the risk of renewed conflict and on improving the lives of conflict-affected populations. In this respect resource-related land use should foster activities that positively contribute to the income and wellbeing of populations while reducing land disputes. This can be done in several ways, including helping to inform local communities about their land rights and the developmental potential and pitfalls of high value natural resource exploitation; assisting local communities in their negotiations with state agencies and resource companies to formalise their land ownership and use rights (through community land rights legislation, for example); facilitating the negotiation of surface use agreements between (subsurface) resource lessees, land owners, and land-based resource users (including agreements for resource access, resource exploitation footprint minimisation, and adequate compensation); promoting land uses that can cohabit with or complement resource exploitation (with maintaining of land access as a priority); engaging with resource companies and local communities to foster mutually beneficial economic activities as well as social and environmental benefits; and ensuring fair and timely compensatory, conflict resolution, and judicial litigation mechanisms for mining affected communities, especially in matters of relocation.

Land policies should also help strengthen pro-poor land and land-based resource rights, paying attention to customary and user rights, particularly those of indigenous populations. Such rights can be better balanced with fiscal revenue needs by promoting synergies between poor household needs and resource exploitation, for example through joint development, multiple land-use, land reclamation, pollution abatement, and economic linkages, such as added-value activities (or beneficiation) and the diversification of economic activities. Courts should be accessible and judicial processes affordable to allow communities to defend land ownership and usage rights, while ad hoc conflict resolution mechanisms can complement statutory and customary laws. Land-based environmental and social impacts of resource exploitation should regularly be monitored in resource projects, and communities and the broader public should be kept informed. Particular emphasis should be place on maintaining communication with affected communities, especially as resource exploitation often affects remote communities. Beside officials and journalists, humanitarian and development workers can help report abuses through a variety of channels including local authorities, media and international advocacy organisations.

To sum up, decisions to develop resource sectors should take into consideration not only potential fiscal revenue, but also broader goals of poverty reduction and conflict prevention. Land rights, and especially the recognition of local populations' customary rights, are an import factor in this respect. Such rights can provide the basis for fairer outcomes and help prevent conflicts arising from the diverging interests of landowners, resource users, and resource lessees. Customary rights are not a panacea, however, and they can bring their own set of inequalities and conflicts within and between communities, especially when formalisation procedures (such as statutory titling) entrench power differentials within communities.

Collecting and channelling resource revenue

The collection and use of revenue from extractive sectors are major political and economic issues. Politically, this revenue can undermine the transition to democracy and exacerbate identity politics. Economically, it can retard economic diversification and jeopardise sustainable economic recovery from conflict. Both sorts of risk are particularly acute in divided low-income states facing high levels of "horizontal" inequalities between social groups with distinct identities.[31] Two key challenges in post-conflict revenue management are therefore how to address resource-related identity politics and how to ensure that revenue contributes to a sustainable and diversified economy. Before addressing these matters, however,

203

I first look at revenue recovery and financial compensation for wartime exploitation.

Recovering "looted assets" and claiming compensation

Wartime and post-conflict "looting" of high-value natural resources can lead to significant losses of public revenue. Such looting is frequently accompanied by human rights abuses, including complicity in war crimes and crimes against humanity (not only through violent predation but also, more indirectly, through the funding of further violence and long-term effects of dispossession). The goal of asset recovery is to track down and repatriate the proceeds generated by illegal resource exploitation, as defined by domestic legislation or international sanctions regimes.[32] The UN Security Council has made increasing use of asset freezing (making assets inaccessible to their illegitimate "owners" to curtail opportunities for funding further hostilities) and asset recovery (an additional step enabling the reallocation or return of assets to their rightful owners or to victims requiring compensation), often on the basis of investigations conducted by sanctions committees and panels of experts. As mentioned above, a primary goal is to recover money to recapitalise state coffers,[33] but a secondary one is to end impunity for war profiteering and promote better practices among banks and resource companies—goals that can be further reinforced by suing individuals and companies that profited from conflict resource exploitation, to raise funds that can be used to compensate the host government and the victims of human rights abuses.[34]

Finding and freezing assets are critical initial steps in the recovery process. More difficult, however, are identifying assets' rightful owners and determining the conditions for their repatriation. Indeed, many governments as well as the courts and, in some cases, the UN Security Council impose conditions on the repatriation of funds. In Liberia, for example, the UN Security Council required that guarantees of proper fiscal governance be in place before allowing some extractive sectors (such as logging) to restart, while the Liberian Act to Establish the Truth and Reconciliation Commission enabled the commission to make recommendations to the Head of State regarding reparations to victims of human rights abuses. Despite the difficulties involved, post-conflict political transitions offer a major opportunity for asset recovery because of the confluence of a number of factors, including a change in regime; the presence of international security forces and international courts; and financial and diplomatic support from international donors—not to mention media coverage.

Tracking down assets requires expertise, judicial support, and collaboration from financial institutions.[35] Recovery is often slow and costly, and efforts are frequently ineffective—often because of a lack of material evidence; the high speed of funds transfers; lack of collaboration between jurisdictions; the immunity of perpetrators still in power (or protected by current governments); and legal loopholes and inconsistencies. Even when the assets are within the country and there has been a change in government, seizure may be difficult.[36] The government of Liberia, for example, was for a long time reluctant to freeze the domestic assets of Liberian politicians for fear of political backlash from profiteers' supporters.[37] Major contemporary examples include cases of looting and profiteering in the war-torn DRC and Liberia, Iraq during the sanctions and the Oil-for-Food Programme, and the identification of Gaddafi's family assets.

A landmark 2005 civil case in the International Court of Justice (ICJ), brought within the context of increasing attention to "conflict commodities" in policy circles. The UN Sanctions Committee in particular, has revitalised attention to the potential for prosecuting companies for pillage of natural resources under charges of war crimes. In "Democratic Republic of the Congo v. Uganda, Armed Activities on the Territory of Congo (DRC v. Uganda)," the ICJ found that although there was no evidence of a state strategy to use its military to pillage DRC's resources, the Ugandan state nevertheless failed in its obligation as an occupying power to prevent pillage of natural resources by its armed forces and their non-state collaborators in the occupied gold- and mineral-rich Congolese province of Ituri. For evidence, the court relied heavily on the findings of the Judicial Commission of Inquiry into Allegations of Illegal Exploitation of Natural Resources and Other Forms of Wealth in the DRC, set up by the Ugandan government in May 2001 and headed by Justice David Porter. However, the damages due to the DRC pursuant to this ruling are still under bilateral negotiation because the court did not award damages, and analysts say it will be nearly impossible to enforce a compensation ruling. Experts warn that the negotiation could be so protracted that a settlement might take many years to conclude, but believe that the case nevertheless represents a positive step towards peace (Uganda accepted the judgment) and was therefore also a step toward legal accountability—albeit as part of a larger process.

In Liberia, the Truth and Reconciliation Commission (TRC) Act gives the Commission the power to make recommendation to the Head of State for reparations towards victims of gross human rights abuses, as mentioned above. In its final report, the TRC recommended that:

The [Government of Liberia] should also hold responsible individuals and entities that were responsible for committing tax evasion. In particular, the TRC recommends that corporate officers in the timber, mining and telecommunications sector be prosecuted for their willingness to avoid the payment of tax revenues to Liberia during the civil conflict in Liberia. Government agents that knowingly facilitated and colluded in tax evasion must also be held accountable.[38]

The TRC called for the Government of Liberia to set up a Reparation Trust Fund financed through:

judgments against economic criminals through three ways: (1) recovering tax arrears from timber, mining, petroleum and telecommunications companies that evaded tax liability under the Taylor regime; (2) obtaining funds from economic criminals that are sentenced by Liberian courts to pay restitution or other fees; and (3) utilising criminal and civil confiscation schemes in foreign jurisdictions to repatriate Liberian assets.

Lastly, one of the most ambitious ongoing compensation schemes is the attempt by the Republic of Iraq to sue multinational corporations for having "conspired with the former regime of Saddam Hussein to corrupt the United Nations Oil-for-Food Program."[39] Companies are alleged not only to have paid kickbacks to Saddam Hussein's regime, but to have benefited from bargain deals over oil prices, thus in effect stealing from the Iraqi people while busting sanctions.

The return of stolen assets is a central principle of the UN Convention against Corruption (UNCAC), which came into force in 2005.[40] Since 2007, this principle has received further backing from the Stolen Assets Recovery (StAR) Initiative, a joint effort of the World Bank and the UN Office on Drugs and Crime.[41] Although StAR's main focus so far has been on policy analysis for the regulatory reform of the international financial system, it has also developed training materials, undertaken some capacity building, and developed programmes in about half a dozen countries.[42] StAR collaborates with the main international corruption and money-laundering initiatives, such as the Financial Action Task Force, as well as with specialised organisations, such as the International Centre for Asset Recovery.[43]

Generally speaking, asset recovery focuses on investors, traders and exporters and banks who have profited from conflict resources. Other targets include politicians, government officials and leaders of armed groups that have been linked to human rights abuses. Given the risk that some actors, such as armed group leaders, may "spoil the peace" to avoid facing justice, preventive measures—such as disbanding their closest military units and armed supporters—are required. Asset freezing and, to a lesser extent, asset recovery (which demands a higher level of evidence regarding ownership) also risk breaching the presumption of innocence and the right to judicial review, as decisions to freeze assets are taken outside court and are not easily challenged by courts.[44]

As of this writing, most post-conflict asset recovery has focused on allegedly corrupt heads of state rather than on businesses or rebel groups funded by conflict resources, while most recent asset-freezing by the UN has been directed at suspected financiers of terrorism. Among political leaders who ruled during armed conflicts, successful asset-recovery procedures have been undertaken against Mobutu Sese Seko (DRC), Alberto Fujimori and Vladimiro Montesinos (Peru), and Saddam Hussein (Iraq). Procedures are under way against Dos Santos (Angola), Charles Taylor (Liberia) and most recently Muammar Gaddafi (Libya). Although a number of rebel groups are believed to have accumulated funds, little information is generally available on their whereabouts.[45]

Addressing resources and identity politics

A key distinction between resources and resource revenue is that the territory where resources are located may be indivisible, but resource revenue can be easily divided. This difference was built into the peace agreement in Southern Sudan, a compromise in which the ownership of oil reserves was left outside the scope of the agreement (until a referendum could take place) while the focus was instead on oil revenue sharing and petroleum sector management. The difficulty, however, is in creating a revenue sharing arrangement that is as secure as a territorial division would be.[46]

With respect to resources, populations in producing regions have claims related not only to ownership, but also to the socio-environmental impact associated with resource extraction. But, while there is a wealth of experience in dealing with such impact, lessons learned from post-conflict situations are only emerging.[47] One example comes from Sierra Leone's diamond sector, in which a scheme was established to allocate a portion of the diamond export tax revenue to local communities to compensate them for the negative impact of mining, and to demonstrate that some of the revenue was flowing back to production areas. This scheme promoted the formalisation of artisanal mining ventures, helping to raise taxes while returning some of the revenue to local communities. However, the scheme suffered from several shortcomings: it was not implemented for large industrial ventures (though these often had the largest socio-environmental "footprint") and much of the revenue initially went to traditional chiefs, many of whom were not accountable to communities. Things improved over time and the scheme also had indirect positive effects, including mobilisation of local communities around budgetary governance.[48]

With respect to resource revenue, experiences over the past two decades suggest that revenue sharing agreements between governments in a divided state, or between ruling parties in a coalition government, have a poor record in terms of risk of renewed conflict (as noted in the previous chapter). Wealth sharing may facilitate the positive conclusion of a peace negotiation, but this does not guarantee a positive outcome over the medium term. Indeed, such agreements can have several negative consequences. First, revenue sharing negotiated under false pretences can enable belligerents to rearm. In Sudan, as detailed in Chapter 6, oil fields were developed under the terms of the 1997 Khartoum Peace Agreement, which granted several Southern armed factions a share of oil revenue in exchange for a cessation of hostilities. This agreement eventually collapsed and conflict in the region reignited, this time with a much wealthier Sudanese government. Second, resource revenue allocation may be perceived as rewarding the belligerent party, providing incentives for other groups to follow suit. The Sudan Liberation Army in Darfur, for example, is perceived as motivated in part by the example of the oil revenue sharing deal negotiated with the government by the Sudan People's Liberation Army in Southern Sudan.[49] Third, sectarian divisions of resource revenue risk aggravating tensions among communities. In Nigeria, state-based revenue allocation relying on identity politics undermined secular modern governance through the reshaping of incompatible community identities.[50] In Iraq, securing oil revenue allocation based on population rather than territory is a preoccupation for Sunni Arab political parties in areas with little proven oil reserves, and the regional autonomy promoted by oil-rich Shiite and Kurdish political parties thus promotes mistrust.[51]

Some central governments have sought to address antagonistic identity politics through fiscal decentralisation, with mixed results.[52] The process through which decentralisation is achieved seems to matter as much as its economic outcomes. The best results, as in South Africa or Mozambique, have been characterised by broad popular participation (including that of minority groups), bargaining between government and sub-national groups, state outreach in remote areas, trust-building among groups participating in local governance institutions, and revenue redistribution across regions. Building on these experiences, direct disbursement of revenue to the population can be proposed as a way to reframe the institutional and economic relationships among resources, governments, and the people.

Directly allocating revenue to populations

As an alternative to channelling resource revenue through regional and local governments and the parties that control them, direct disbursement to the population offers several advantages.[53] Direct revenue allocation provides tangible evidence of a "peace dividend" for the population. Recent studies show that direct cash payments contribute positively to poverty alleviation and disaster recovery, including in conflict-affected environments.[54] Direct disbursement to the population also sends a signal that resources are owned by the people, not by the government or the parties that control it. This can increase pressure on companies and governments to maximise public revenue. If the choice is made to distribute the revenue equally across the entire population, this can contribute to a sense of national identity and common destiny. Last but not least, direct disbursement is less subject to political manipulation and associated grievances than the government budget.

Are direct revenue transfers unrealistic given low state capacity, lack of information on citizens, and rudimentary financial and fiscal systems in many post-conflict countries? Direct payments of oil revenue have been suggested in the case of Iraq, only to be quickly dismissed owing to continued insecurity and weak bureaucracy.[55] But the situation in Iraq is not yet "post-conflict." Logistical challenges remain in most developing countries, but they can be overcome. Moreover, tackling such challenges can provide benefits beyond putting money in the hands of individual citizens. For example, the tasks of peacebuilding missions often include voter registration. This "political entitlement" process could be matched with an "economic entitlement" process, whereby a system of citizen identification is set up. The basis for income tax collection can also be strengthened, by providing an incentive to enter into a formal financial relation with the state. Direct disbursement can also help to consolidate local financing through cash inflows into community-level saving and investment schemes.

Direct revenue transfers do pose problems, but they may not be insurmountable. First, financial transfer may be prohibitively expensive and risk, for example, making a vast number of small cash transfers in a high insecurity environment unviable. One possible option here would be to channel payments through mobile phone banking.[56] Another issue is what people may actually do with these payments. If spent on non-productive imported goods, payments could simply act as a short-term consumer welfare measure, be detrimental to the trade balance and undermine local production. Spending options may be limited to maximise both household and macroeconomic efficiency, while payments can also be tied to conditions such as the schooling of children, to promote broader social goals.[57] Third, payments can be politically manipulated, for example electoral candidates promising increased revenue disbursement. Here, payment levels could be "frozen" by law following a defined set of criteria. Fourth, payments may exacerbate tensions over the particularistic claims of populations in production regions. Still, many grievances in producing areas result not so much from the lack of transfer payments to production regions, as from corruption and wastage reducing their positive impact for local populations. Such direct payments would help solve these two problems.

Yet another issue is that in the absence of adequate alternative sources of revenue, direct disbursement may also reduce the state's ability to provide public goods and services. If direct disbursement of revenue were used to justify and legitimate privatisation reforms of public services, this could have a regressive impact on the poor. Given the need for state revenue, one option is a hybrid scheme, whereby part of the revenue is distributed to the population directly and the other part goes to the government for public investment and social expenditure. An alternative way to address the need for state revenue is to not only transfer revenue to the population but also tax it according to recipients' income levels.[58] This would have a progressive income effect, leaving more revenue in the hands of the poor. At the same time, it would inform citizens about both the revenue generated by the extractive sector and the funding requirements of the state. While direct transfer payments risk turning into a populist measure decreasing the accountability of the ruling regime, this system could help close the taxation-representation gap that afflicts many resource-dependent regimes, leading citizens to demand that the state justify its taxation and be accountable to the people.

Donor support for such a scheme could help to advance the economic objective of poverty reduction and the political objective of state-building. Donors could step in to compensate for taxation losses resulting from delaying resource projects, and thereby provide an incentive for the government to support this scheme. This budgetary support could be phased in to respond to the absorptive capacity of the government and phased out to incentivise the state to develop its fiscal autonomy and foster economic diversification.

Contributing to a sustainable and diversified economy

Economic recovery is a priority in post-conflict contexts, and years of violent dispossession, neglect, and curtailed opportunities also make it a moral imperative. Moreover, tangible peace dividends, reduced unemployment, and channelling efforts into "business" rather than divisive politics can consolidate peace. It would be naïve, however, to think that economic recovery is not political, or that it is inevitably conducive to building a durable peace. Rather, attention needs to be paid to the ways and means through which the recovery is achieved.

The channelling of resource revenues should ideally foster a diversified and sustainable economy that insures against future growth collapse and thereby reduces the risk of a renewed outbreak of hostilities. But extractive sectors present several challenges to sustainability and diversification. First, extractive sectors often rely on non-renewable resources. Investments in prospecting and more efficient technologies can augment the status of reserves, but these are ultimately finite. Dividend savings funds, as in the case of Norway, may be part of the solution to resource depletion. But in post-conflict countries, reconstruction and social needs militate against setting aside a substantial fraction of resource revenue (see below).

Second, extractive resources tend to create a "resource trap" or "staple trap," locking countries into dependence and exposing them to future revenue instability.[59] Revenue windfalls resulting from booming prices or one-time bonuses may generate unsustainable expenditure and policy "myopia," delay reforms, and create unrealistic expectations within the population. Revenue collapses may induce governments to borrow beyond their means.

Third, resource revenue faces a high risk of capture by ruling elites unless robust institutions are in place to prevent this. There is good evidence that extractive-sector revenue is especially vulnerable to embezzlement and that resource wealth is correlated with higher levels of perceived corruption in low-income countries.[60] There is also some evidence that levels of corruption increase in post-conflict situations, possibly because of increased opportunities coupled with competitive politics and economic liberalisation.[61]

Regulating resource revenue management

Recent international efforts to address these challenges have been devoted mostly to transparency issues. Examples include the Extractive Industries Transparency Initiative (EITI), the Publish What You Pay (PWYP) campaign, the IMF's Guide on Resource Revenue Transparency (GRRT), and section 1504 of the US Dodd-Frank Wall Street Reform and Consumer Protection Act.[62] Overall, these efforts have improved the level of transparency over resource revenue. Although it operates relatively slowly, the EITI was able to validate the compliance of eleven countries by 2011 since its start nearly a decade earlier, while twenty-four other countries worked towards validation.[63] Yet long-term positive impact will depend on sustaining these efforts and turning these voluntary standards into global and more mandatory norms so that all companies and countries meaningfully disclose revenue and improve their accountability.[64]

Besides transparency, several international aid programmes have attempted to address some of the resource curses and especially poor resource revenue management issues. Norway, through its Oil for Development programme, has been at the forefront of this approach, but also the United States Agency for International Development (USAID), the UK's Department for International Development (DfID), and the World Bank.[65] Yet these programmes have been limited in scope, with little chance of affecting power dynamics, such as informal decision-making structures, that exacerbate the resource curse. Many of these programmes have also been selectively deployed in countries, reflecting donor interests rather than need. While one should not paint too bleak a picture, even in places where seemingly comprehensive measures were taken—such as the Chad-Cameroon Petroleum Development Project—regulatory loopholes and oil-boosted sovereignty have left populations at the mercy of their rulers and the corporate sponsors.[66]

Revenue volatility, a crucial dimension of the resource curse and source of popular grievance, has been exacerbated rather than resolved over the past two decades. International revenue stabilisation mechanisms have spectacularly faltered, mostly for lack of support within a neoliberal economic establishment privileging free trade and financial deregulation.[67] With the exception of OPEC, which proved rather limited in its impact, most commodity producer organisations have given up their price stabilisation activities, in part because of the promotion of invidualistic and competitive strategies by international financial institutions within a globalised world.[68] The massive financial crisis of 2008–09 sent a strong signal to the governments of global financial centers, but several banking institutions, among the most influential of these, ended up winning out of the crisis, while most commodities showed no sign of decreased volatility.[69]

Domestic "revenue management laws" generally define the principles and objectives of resource revenue management. Transparency, accountability, representation and equity are major issues these laws must address in order to avoid revenue capture by narrow interest groups and to reduce risks of (renewed) armed conflict. They can also create three major types of fiscal instruments. First, revenue volatility-smoothing instruments seek to reduce sharp variations in the level of revenue resulting from up-and-downs in resource production or resource prices. This can be achieved through stabilisation funds setting aside revenue that exceeds forecasts or the government's absorption capacity, then releasing reserve funds when revenue decreases. Savings funds serve a similar function but with a longer-term horizon, seeking not to buffer variations but to build a future source income, in particular when the resource will be exhausted. Ironically, these have generally been introduced where they least needed; that is, where sound fiscal policies are already observed and resource revenue represents only a small part of fiscal inflows.[70] Stabilisation funds should be encouraged in a post-conflict context given the major volatilities in resources revenue, provided that they are well integrated into budgetary management and secured from embezzlement. Saving funds, in contrast, are not a priority given post-conflict economic recovery and social needs; establishing a saving fund can be part of a programme of institution building, but allocating significant amounts of money to it in the early phase of the transition may be more a source of tension than a contribution to state consolidation.

Finally, revenue management laws can establish allocation mechanisms, such as an annual fund withdrawal ceilings and ratios of revenue allocation to areas (such as provinces) and sectors (such as health and education). Introducing or consolidating such legislation and the administrative and oversight bodies needed to implement it should be a priority of post-conflict state-building. One option in such consolidation is to put the proposed legal framework to a referendum. Not only would this grant stronger legitimacy, it would also help mobilise community involvement in debating the draft. The absence of flexibility in budgetary allocation, however, can also be a source of tension, as demonstrated in the Chadian crisis over oil revenue allocation.[71]

Strengthening resource governance

Robust institutions can address some of the deleterious economic and political impacts of resource dependence and thereby help to consolidate peace. Many of these institutions directly relate to domestic state-building. The state does not operate in a vacuum, however, and the international institutional environment and the behavior of multinational extractive companies are central to post-conflict recovery. Three proposals for strengthening resource governance are presented below, all of which require the support of international as well as domestic actors: a transitional trusteeship arrangement; a national extractive-sector compact on resource governance; and an international agreement on extractive sectors, including an international revenue management agency.

One recurrent issue is that of the role of transitional authorities in reforming resource sectors and allocating resource contracts. In short, much depends on the specific nature, legitimacy and capacity of transitional authorities. If the interim administration consists of a national unity government bringing together former armed groups with short-term interests in mind (including amassing electoral campaign funds, or rearming in the case of peace spoilers) then resource management reforms and exploitation contracts should be postponed until a democratically elected government is in place. On the contrary, if there is strong sense by the population and international community that the democratically elected administration may not be able to deliver within a reasonable time frame the types of reforms that will consolidate a "just, equitable, and prosperous peace," then the interim administration should have to step in at an early stage. In terms of broad principles, I think that a strong regulatory framework should be set up at the earliest under an internationally and domestically scrutinised interim administration while there is maximum transparency, civil society participation, an open political field, and donor leverage in order to ensure that the best rules for the interest of the local population are in place. The final validation through parliament, and the implementation of these rules (for example in the allocation of concessions), should be left to the democratically elected government. In any case there should not be an abrupt and safeguards-free transition from transitional to elected government rule. It is important to maintain a degree of civil society and international supervision, capacity building and accountability via formal mechanisms such as the Governance and Economic Management Programme (GEMAP) in Liberia.

Foreign assistance and donor conditionality are important but time-sensitive instruments of governance in post-conflict contexts.[72] Host country aid dependence means that donors can exert much influence over the pace and nature of reforms, including playing an active role in supporting and supervising local authorities. Donor conditionality is especially time-sensitive in resource rich context, as the leverage provided by aid dependence is undermined by increasing resource revenue. As local authorities shift from a situation of aid dependence to one of resource revenue dependence, the influence of donors decreases. This relationship is complicated when donors are also seeking to further the interest of their home resource companies, in which case they can tend to self-undermine (or downplay) their influence to win the favours of local authorities negotiating resource contracts. In many instances, donors will also prioritise a rapid increase in public revenue. When resources are available there can be a temptation to bypass difficult reforms and protracted capacity building in the hope that fast rising resource revenue will help fix things. This is frequently a major error, as weak institutions during resource booms are one of the main aggravating factors of the resource curse. This suggests that donor conditionality should be more sensitive to, and focused on, resource sectors.

The major objectives of intervention by external actors have been to promote foreign investment, strengthen budgetary processes, curb corruption, and improve local livelihoods. Reaching these objectives has often proved challenging. To start, there is the classic issue of donor coordination and vested interests—an issue that is particularly acute in the natural resource sector and came to prominence with the mix of China's policy of "non-interference in domestic affairs" and the rise in competition between Western and Asian resource companies. The first implications resulting from such competition are positive. A host government should be able to benefit from increased competition between foreign resource companies; Chinese corporations often present resource-for-infrastructure deals that under the right conditions can reduce the risk of corruption and wastage in spending of resource revenue, thereby maximising public good returns on resource exploitation; the fast pace of resource exploitation and infrastructure projects can rapidly create tangible peace dividends consolidating the transition to peace; and Chinese companies are perceived as getting things done, with mid-level managers and technicians sometimes giving cheap hands-on training to local workers. However there are major concerns. Poorer governance standards may be accepted by resource companies, including widespread human rights abuses; the Chinese "non-interference" policy tends to reduce leverage to improve governance standards for most donor countries, international agencies and (hypothetically) resource corporations; cheap Chinese labor costs and the low local employment in resource projects and associated infrastructure work can create resentment among the local population, while related Chinese immigration and commercial competition result in increasing social tensions and grievances; and limited resource opportunities for Western companies can have a negative indirect effect on Western donor support (as donors are less inclined to support relatively well-funded countries that do not offer major trade opportunities). This suggests that Western companies, possibly in association with major donor agencies, need to compete through resource-for-infrastructure deals, and that Asian governments and companies need to support more broadly a "good governance" agenda, via international agreements, bilateral relations, and corporate social responsibility practices.

Another issue is the limited will or capacity of donors to improve contractual agreements between companies and host governments, which has often resulted in generous tax incentives for the extractive industry, lack of transparency, allegations of corruption, and local community-level conflicts—as was at times the case for the DRC.[73] Yet another is that donors push for reforms without providing the capacity of the government to carry these out. While bilateral agencies have large budgets, often little of that money ends up actually strengthening government; for example, less than 10 percent of the US$13 million spent by US and UK aid agencies on diamond reforms in Sierra Leone was spent on directly improving government capacity.[74]

Creating a resource compact

Incentives are a major driver of policy outcomes. Because resource sectors and post-conflict contexts are highly specific, finding the right balance of incentives is less a matter of applying a blueprint than of overcoming particularistic interests opposing the public interest. The public itself needs to get informed and involved, through support and contributions from civil society organisations, reform-minded politicians and bureaucrats, aid donors, and progressive extractive companies. One striking feature of post-conflict resource reforms is the frequently confrontational engagement of civil society organisations with companies and authorities, or their cooptation. Another is the criminalisation of extractive activities by local populations, leading to a mix of open protests and informalisation.[75] In the best cases, this leads to progress in the right direction, but on many occasions the outcome is greater secrecy and repression. Another common feature is an outdated, ineffective, or corrupt regulatory environment. The resource compact should thus allow for both constructive engagement among stakeholders and improved regulatory capacities in terms of legislation, implementation, and monitoring.

The heart of the compact is an extractive sector forum that should bring together citizens, politicians and companies into public debates that are reported by the media and considered by institutions such as parliamentary commissions, relevant ministries, donor agencies, and extractive companies. Timing is crucial here, in order to bank on the climate of relative openness and security provided by a transition period under peacekeeping forces. A main priority of the forum is to identify and spell out the nature, objectives and operational principles guiding the extractive sector.[76] The forum should play an active role in informing the general population about resource sectors, including the potential value of reserves, options for modes of production, forecast revenue streams, socio-environmental impacts, and chains of accountability. To this end, the forum should have a secretariat capable of acquiring, analyzing, and diffusing information. A second priority of the forum should be providing a public platform for extractive sector stakeholders, particularly those that are likely to be marginalised or at risk if taking an isolated stand on their own. Such a platform could facilitate representation and negotiations in shaping sectoral policy and legislative affairs and contribute to filling the regulatory vacuum of post-conflict transition.

The resource compact should establish an independent extractive sector monitoring body. Arm's-length relations are key to credible monitoring, and should be strengthened through financing by a donor trust fund and diversity in monitoring team membership. The monitoring body should enjoy freedom of access to information and field sites (including company sites), and its findings in turn should be reported to the public. Support should also be provided for the complementary state-monitoring agency so that the state's capacity to exercise its regulatory role can be consolidated. Overall, the challenges and limitations of such a forum should not be underestimated, especially in terms of cooptation risk, prevailing power dynamics, and weak accountability leverage. Yet such a forum can provide an important avenue to enhance information flow and relative protection for advocates of improved resource management.

International standards for resource sectors

Conflict situations have focused the attention of the international community on resource governance, opening political space for creating international standards for extractive industries that could over time evolve into an international agreement. The development economist Paul Collier initiated such efforts in 2008 through the creation of the Natural Resource Charter.[77] Based on a set of twelve principles defined by a group of academics, the Natural Resource Charter suggests to governments that resource development should take place under open and accountable management, backed by robust fiscal regimes that maximise sustainable broad benefits for citizens, and minimise negative social and environmental impacts; that contracts should be awarded competitively and all relevant actors—including (national) resource companies, their home governments and financial institutions—should operate transparently, competitively, and according to best practices; and that resource revenue should be smoothed to reduce volatility and invested domestically in a gradual way to foster economic diversification and value added operations, while public spending should strive for efficiency and equity.

The Natural Resource Charter is neither the first nor the only initiative seeking to set international principles and standards for resource sectors. Several initiatives have taken place since the mid-1990s, for example through international initiatives at industry level with the Mining, Minerals and Sustainable Development project, through international financial institutions with the World Bank extractive industries review, through tripartite industry-government-civil society collaboration such as the Kimberley and EITI processes, and domestically, as in the Canadian Government roundtable on extractive industries. There are also many civil society initiatives, such as the Publish What You Pay campaign or the UN Committee on World Food Security, CIDSE and Oxfam programmes on extractive sectors and poverty.

One possible normative evolution is towards an international agreement that would in effect set mandatory standards for natural resource sectors. Such a comprehensive agreement will undeniably take time to develop. Yet previous voluntary initiatives that took on mandatory dimensions and achieved a broad international reach, such as initiatives on conflict minerals certification and extractive sector revenue disclosure, suggest that such an agreement may come to light. An international task force including national governments, relevant international organisations, industry associations, and civil society organisations is needed to negotiate such standards, drawing on relevant existing international law and codes of conduct.[78] National ratification of the standards could be backed by incentives as well as by peer and consumer pressure. This standard would have the potential to achieve the status of a widespread mandatory norm.

Among its key elements, the agreement should define "conflict resources" and set clear ethical norms and reporting procedures regarding revenue generated in conflict-affected countries, in order to deter activities that risk prolonging or reigniting violent conflicts. One definition, proposed by Global Witness, is "natural resources whose systematic exploitation and trade in a context of conflict contribute to, benefit from, or result in the commission of serious violations of human rights, violations of international humanitarian law or violations amounting to crimes under international law."[79] Resources suspected of meeting such a definition should be subject to independent investigations, such as those of UN expert panels, and the activities and assets of companies involved in these sectors ought to be made liable to international sanctions, fines, and criminal procedures.

Second, the agreement should set contractual standards, particularly in terms of imposing public bidding procedures for resource contracts, tax assessment (in order to avoid transfer pricing and other tax avoidance mechanisms), and transparency and accountability in revenue collection and allocation. The agreement also needs to address resource revenue risk, specifically by facilitating access to revenue smoothing instruments, and by better sharing of risk between companies and governments.

Third, an International Revenue Management Agency should be created as part of the agreement. The mandate of this agency would be to ensure that the "revenue pipeline" between companies, governments and populations is tight, and that revenue—whether in the form of direct disbursement, public services, or both—reaches the population. In effect, the agency would provide international insurance mechanisms in a manner analogous to the role that export credit and receivables management agencies now play in reducing investment and revenue risks for extractive companies. There is considerable expertise available for companies to recover lost revenues following currency or political crises, yet little of that expertise has been deployed on behalf of the interests of local populations in producing countries. The people of low-income producing countries should not bear more risks than large and highly profitable companies.

The agency could protect populations from revenue volatility linked to unforeseen events, currency devaluation, and resource price variations, using revenue stabilisation instruments and direct budgetary assistance to support and complement the role of existing institutions (such as producers' associations and international financial institutions). The agency could also respond to tax evasion and corruption, addressing complaints by citizens and civil society with regard to fiscal management. It could conduct budgetary audits to assess the "spending" side of revenue management and track down irregularities, which could then be publicly reported and addressed through local or international institutions. In exceptional cases, government revenue could be directed towards a trust held by the agency. Financing for the agency could be secured through a consortium of donors, companies, and producing governments. Incentives for all parties would include greater stability and greater legitimacy for the resource sector activities.

Conclusion

Post-conflict situations provide a promising but challenging context for managing extractive sector revenues—promising because much of the context for resource exploitation can be improved, but also challenging because of the incentives and limits of existing institutions. A central question for peace building is whether revenues should be shared among parties in a coalition government or among authorities in a divided state. The record of wealth sharing agreements in the past two decades has been poor. As seen in the previous chapter, wealth sharing may enable the positive conclusion of a peace negotiation, but it does not guarantee conflict settlement over the medium term. Efforts to mainstream the management of extractive sectors into conflict resolution and peacebuilding initiatives should not focus only on drafting agreements sensitive to extractive sector issues, but also on providing the guarantees that extend from rights over natural resources to accountability mechanisms in revenue allocation. Without such guarantees, wealth sharing is insufficient, and in the wrong political context it can even prove counterproductive. In addition, the rights of transitional governments to allocate long-term resource exploitation contracts should be curtailed, and the resource revenue generated under transitional governments should be under external supervision.

A second question is whether extractive sectors should be rapidly developed during the post-conflict transition period, and under what conditions. Extractive industries can spur economic recovery and contribute to political stability, but relevant institutions should be sufficiently strong before exploitation occurs, or at the very least proactive measures should be taken to consolidate these institutions as resource exploitation proceed forward. A second requirement is for new resource policies and contracts to be appropriately timed, so that long-term economic benefits are maximised, particularly in terms of fiscal revenue, employment, and economic diversification. Rather than rushing to involve foreign companies, domestic entrepreneurship should also be developed to the fullest. Comprehensive options assessments should be systematically conducted, and resource exploitation should be the subject of prior, free, and informed consent by local communities. To these ends, I noted the importance of carefully considering the timing of contract awarding in relation to institutional capacity, political legitimacy, and economic opportunities. I also noted the importance of reappraising "odious" extractive resource contracts and seeking to reappropriate looted assets. More broadly, I emphasised the importance of an international agreement on extractive sectors but also the importance of detailed contextualisation.

A final central issue is that of revenue allocation mechanisms, including responses to the instability and exhaustibility of resource revenues. Revenue stabilisation funds should be promoted with the support of donors and extractive companies. Savings funds, in contrast, are not a priority in poor countries, and if introduced they should be limited to a small amount of revenue, the management of which could help build institutional capacity for long-term financial planning. Direct payments of resource revenue to the population should also be given serious consideration, particularly where poverty rates are high and resource revenue is sufficient to make a difference for the poor. An international agreement, including an international revenue management agency, should seek to reduce the economic and political risks faced by populations in the poorest and most resource dependent producing countries.

The objectives and behavior of international agencies play an important role in reforming extractive resource sectors. Intergovernmental organisations and donor agencies should provide assistance to maximise revenue collection and to ensure transparent, fair and accountable allocation. Revenue and socio-economic forecasting should be provided and the results widely broadcasted, so as to build realistic expectations in the government and among the population. Donors should not systematically promote FDI-related extractive policies and projects—at present a central goal of their export and credit agencies—over domestic entrepreneurship. Rather, donors should support host authorities in allocating resource reserves according to broader social and environmental criteria, including protecting and strengthening of local livelihoods. Given that greater resource revenue eventually reduces donor financial leverage as the relative importance of aid diminishes, extractive companies should enter into agreements with donor agencies to ensure the durability of reforms. An incentive to do so could be provided by making such agreement a condition of access to the services of export credit agencies. An international extractive industries agreement would help to curtail competitive behavior among donors eager to promote their resource interests and provide a legal environment guiding the behavior of extractive companies and governments.

The proposals advanced in this chapter are not equally applicable for all cases of post-conflict extractive resource management. The specifics of the setting—the sectors involved, the capacity of institutions, and broader political and economic aspects of post-conflict recovery—play a major part in deciding which options are most appropriate to pursue. As demonstrated in previous four chapters, the specific characteristics of resources, their location, mode of exploitation and the structure of their value chain all represent important considerations. Just as important, the pursuit of these initiatives will require champions and the appropriate set of incentives.

CONCLUSION

Natural resources have long been a strategic concern for states. Military conquest, support for local dictators, and stockpiling were key tools of the trade to secure resource supplies and corporate profits. These concerns were somewhat eased in the aftermath of the Cold War. Growth in international trade supposedly augured an age of resource plenty.[1] Resources were cheap, trading more flexible, and supply reliable. This brief era is mostly over, in large part because of rising resource nationalism, physical limits to production, growing resource demand in Asia, increasing markets and demand worldwide as a consequence of cheaper manufacturing, and reduced investment in resource sectors during the 1990s.[2] Concurrently, tensions over key resource areas such as the Persian Gulf are not simply about the need to ensure the "free flow" of strategic resources, as a much broader agenda of "good governance" is selectively put to work to balance emancipation and stabilisation. Accordingly, the conceptualisation of resources as a "strategic imperative" needs to move beyond both traditional state-centric perspectives stressing the risk of wars driven by dwindling resource supply and neoliberal market-centric perspectives emphasising the promises of growing resource demand.

As I have sought to argue in preceding chapters, the "geopolitical" and "neoliberal" views are both incomplete and dangerous. Geopolitical narratives centered on the risk of international resource wars driven by Asian growth need to be interpreted cautiously; such strategic geopolitical perspectives tend to reinforce warmongering logic even while denouncing militarised resource nationalism. Neoliberal narratives presenting market laissez-faire as a panacea to resource woes also warrant caution. Increased demand will not simply be resolved by the market, nor will it translate into prosperity for the populations of producing countries. Fast-growing and wasteful mass-consumption requires vastly more resource-efficient lifestyles, and a collective response to growing scarcity that does not take the shape of a "free for all" scramble for resources. For sure, a scramble can bring about greater competition among resource companies, a competition that would afford greater leverage for governments in resource producing countries to negotiate more favourable terms and obtain larger revenues. Yet such resource bonanzas are no guarantee of long-term and broadly shared prosperity. Entrenched resource dependence has set most countries on a path of recurrent developmental failure. Even well-governed countries have found it difficult to break out of resource dependence when faced with an unfavourable geography and a legacy of resource-based public welfare.[3]

This means that "getting resource management right" is a strategic priority and a responsibility to be shouldered by resource companies, political authorities, financial institutions, and consumers along a resource value chain, so that the long-term benefits of resource dependent populations in low-income producing countries are maximised. As this book has made clear, several resource strategies can help avoid the pitfalls of "militarised nationalism" and "market fundamentalism" that leave populations worse off; although no single measure can reduce the prevalence of resource-related conflicts, a number of steps can assist in preventing conflicts and fostering a stable peace.

From strategic resources to resource strategies

Following on the framework in this book, I briefly review for the main strategies to address conflicts and resources linkages.

Strategies against conflict resources

The first and most pressing strategic issue is that of conflict resources sustaining armed groups. Accessible and internationally marketable resources such as diamonds and timber, not to mention narcotics, figured prominently in conflicts in about twenty countries during the 1990s. Given the high incidence of war in poor countries with few foreign earning sources, natural resources are likely to remain an economic focus for belligerents, even if conflict resources come under greater regulatory pressure. This study has examined some of the reasons, processes, and possible solutions relating to these issues, with a focus on the characteristics and role of "conflict resources" in war. The cases examined in preceding chapters suggest that the vulnerability of populations and the need for political and economic accountability in resource management should be taken seriously at both local and international levels.

A first step is to better understand the significance of resources in war economies and the motivation of belligerents. War economies are essentially destructive and exploitative, cornering people into fuelling the very violence at the heart of their torment. Yet war economies can also bring about social innovations and progressive outcomes. Some "barefoot entrepreneurs" can thrive in a war context, redefining rules and social rankings.[4] War can also bring about a massive redistribution of wealth, particularly through land reform. Yet there should be no idealisation of the transformative potential of violence. A better understanding of war economies and their impact requires extensive investigation of the conditions of production, identification of the actors, assessment of the distribution of costs and benefits along the commodity chain, and finally assessment of impacts on military activities, livelihoods, and tax revenue.

With a better grasp of the workings of war economies and their impact, a second step is to identify synergies and trade-offs arising from within war economies and their regulation. Should curtailing rebel revenue, increasing government income, or sustaining livelihoods be a priority? Are these goals reconcilable, or is it a zero-sum game? As development economist Chris Cramer argues, the challenge is to maximise the progressive changes arising in the course of armed conflict—not just to minimise its damage.[5] This is a difficult but not impossible task.

In this regard, let me make a few comments. "Coping economies" that sustain hostilities should not be prioritised, especially if these livelihoods are rife with abuses (such as forced labor) and alternatives for survival can be found, for example in agriculture, crafts or trading within areas better insulated from rebel influence. Counter-insurgency approaches like moving populations into "strategic hamlets" to sever links with insurgencies have proven their limits and massive humanitarian costs, however. Governments, advocacy groups and businesses have come up with an array of measures to deal with war economies, including targeted sanctions, resource-specific military interventions, and resource wealth sharing. As reviewed in Chapter 6, these measures need to suit both resource and conflict contexts. As a general rule, revenue-sharing appears to be an illusory solution in the absence of belligerents' genuine political commitment or third-party military deterrence. Similarly, military interventions are often a short-term fix with many negative impacts. A well-phased combination of these three measures—backed by tangible enforcement outside the targeted country—is the most effective approach.

Strategies for resource conflicts

The second set of strategies concerns the diversity of conflicts and forms of violence associated with resource control and exploitation, broadly framed under the concept of resource conflict. As shown in Chapter 2, some relations between resources and conflicts are very direct and involve highly visible forms of violence. Resource conflicts that fall into this category typically pit resource companies and state security forces against local communities and "militants" opposing extractive ventures. Of course, one should not underplay the complexity of social relations involved, as illustrated in the case of oil-related conflicts in the Niger Delta. Other relations are more indirect and result in less visible forms of violence and suffering, such as interpersonal physical abuse and entrenched inequalities. The relative visibility of violence matters because public opinion and policy makers tend to focus on the more direct relations and visible forms of violence. As a result, some structural factors may remain unaddressed, at least from the perspective of preventing further violence.

Most of these conflicts are peacefully resolved or limited to social protest movements and small-scale skirmishes. However, in some cases, such as that of Bougainville in Papua New Guinea, a vicious circle of resistance and repression leads down the path of full-scale war. Political opportunism and a radicalisation of ideologies also greatly contributes to such violent outcomes. Growing opposition to unbridled forms of economic globalisation on one the hand and rising demand for raw materials on the other often result in adversarial politics. In this regard, there is a need not only for more effective dialogue between "stakeholders" but also (as explored below) for a set of enforced rules guaranteeing fairness and accountability.

Strategies for the resource curse

The last—but arguably most significant—set of strategies seeks to address the resource curse. Many resource dependent countries face a similar pattern of growth collapse, corruption, and delegitimised state authority. Often sustained through a mix of redistributive policies and repression, these regimes can give rise to "successful failed states" with enduring leadership.[6] Translating resource exploitation into political emancipation (rather than simply political stability) and broad human development (rather than narrow economic growth) remains a major challenge, but there is growing pressure—both domestic and international—to address them.[7]

Beyond understanding and regulating war economies, an array of policies is also needed to prevent future resource-related conflicts, as discussed in Chapter 7. This third set of strategies often takes place during the "post-conflict" phase of political transition and reconstruction. Arguably, it could take place earlier in peace negotiations, squarely putting the "economic" agenda into the political one.

Although post-conflict countries are often heavily reliant on foreign assistance, developing countries as a group have greatly reduced their level of resource dependence over the past few decades. However, many of the poorest and most unstable countries are likely to remain resource-dependent for decades to come. It is thus imperative to maximise resource-exporting countries' revenue capture, while strengthening the quality of governance and thereby institutional legitimacy. Such a policy entails broad goals, such as "deep" democratisation processes that build robust checks and balances within society and consolidate state legitimacy and capacity, as well as sector-specific goals such as improved communication among different stakeholders, greater respect for human rights, and effective mechanisms of transparency and accountability at the project level. Realistically these institutions must focus on key nodes in the upstream value chain, such as contract awarding, conditions of production, and revenue allocation, but they should also permeate all the way down to final customers to ensure greater and more diverse leverage.

What global regulatory regime for natural resource sectors?

A global governance regime for resource sectors is required to level the playing field for populations, governments, and businesses. To take the example of accountability in the oil sector the demand of the local population for full fiscal transparency is more likely to be conceded by the host government if it is legally imposed on oil companies by stock-exchange regulators, and subject to moral suasion by individual consumers and consumers' groups.

Such a global regime would bring about fairness and accountability throughout the value-chain linking resource extraction to waste disposal. Inspiration for such schemes can be found in the regulatory initiatives on diamonds, the Forest Stewardship Council certification of "sustainable timber harvesting," and the fair trade movements for coffee and garments. In other words, mass consumerism in the twenty-first century needs to be "strategic" if it is not to sustain mass poverty, authoritarian rule, and war in the developing world. Many of these schemes are limited in scope and do not constitute a panacea. If the moves that major brands and retailers are making towards fairer and more sustainable products in response to consumer demand offer the possibility of "scaling-up" these schemes, such moves can turn out to be a cooptation, defusing risks to corporate profit margins and displacing negative impacts.[8]

International financial mechanisms and trade rules are giving renewed attention to the stabilisation of primary commodity prices. Opening the markets of rich countries to processed commodities from developing countries is another priority. A radical move in this direction would be the inversion of trade tariffs that have long protected the wealthiest economies. An international trade agreement imposing tariffs on the importation, by industrialised countries, of raw materials rather than processed goods would motivate investors to consider more seriously downstream processing in resource-dependent and poor countries. Capital-intensive and technology-intensive downstream industrialisation, however, has a poor record in developing countries and moves in this direction should be made with particular caution and deliberation. In some cases, a diversification strategy targeting value-adding industries outside the resource sector might often be preferable. Light manufacturing and service exports, in particular, have recently helped many countries to move out of resource dependence.

What regulations for extractive companies?

Extractive companies are both victims and beneficiaries of the politically sensitive environments in which many operate. They have to cope with higher risks, but they also reap higher profits from the effects these risks have in deterring competitors, and in lowering taxation by host governments.

Left to its own devices, the current process of economic globalisation risks following the colonial tradition of distinguishing between "useful" and "useless" areas in resource-dependent countries, creating commercially driven enclaves around the most profitable resource reserves and ignoring the rest. Engaging with autocracies has long represented little risk for extractive industries, but democratic pressure is challenging this arrangement, sometimes with dramatic consequences after years of predatory regimes. Isolating countries by branding them "pariah states" is not a long-term solution, either. Reinforcing an exclusionary form of "globalisation" that bars countries with pariah status from investment and legitimate trade will only further promote their re-inclusion in the international arena in the form of illicit trafficking, illegal immigration and fraud, and set the context of further political instability and greater abuses.

This situation has become untenable. Businesses and international regulators need to promote an alternative framework in which trade comes to reinforce governance. If outside involvement is to succeed in mitigating the economic vulnerability of resource dependence and its dampening effects on domestic politics in producing countries, the former UN Secretary-General Kofi Annan's call "to unite the powers of markets with the authority of universal ideals" must be heeded. So far, this call has led to the value-based platform of the UN Global Compact, which mostly hoped to show the "good will" of businesses, and the more stringent yet voluntary UN guiding principles on business and human rights developed by UN Special Representative John Ruggie.

What priorities?

Several broad-based initiatives are required to reform the global architecture of commodity regulation, promote more ethical trade and bring about greater corporate social responsibility. Judging by the evidence reviewed in this book, corporate or consumer-driven voluntarist ethical trade initiatives to date have significant shortcomings, and are likely to be insufficient in the long term. The global architecture of commodity regulation should be a central focus for policymakers. Three areas are particularly important: resuscitation of and reengagement with commodity trade agreements; tighter domestic and international regulation of resource-derived revenue, focusing on transparency; and a change in the culture of impunity in international resource trade.

In the first case, producing countries and the international community should reconsider their disengagement and withdrawal from most international commodity agreements, and consider how revitalised commodity agreements might mobilise investment and contribute to positive economic and political improvements. Accordingly, revisiting commodity agreements should take place in tandem with an international framework for the regulation of resource revenue, which would seek not only greater stability in revenue, but also greater transparency and increased accountability to local populations. Finally, international instruments used to prevent or terminate conflicts financed by natural resource exploitation would move from "shaming" international actors to formalising punishments and sanctions against individuals as well as corporations. These measures will take time to develop. In the interim, confronted with the likelihood of continued resource-fuelled wars, the international community should seek to develop and apply frameworks through which the "economic demobilisation" of combatants could break the pernicious and persistent relationships between natural resources, political underdevelopment, and armed conflict.

Resources and the future of war

To conclude, I would like to briefly discuss speculation about future "resource wars," through two anecdotes. One is based on popular geopolitics for futuristic conflicts and the other on speculation about the fate of Afghanistan, a country that has—along with Iraq—experienced the most protracted and internationalised series of wars over the past three decades.

As I was writing this book, the biggest-grossing film in history, *Avatar*, was released. A colleague teaching at Singapore National University told me that one of his students had asked him if he had "read any of Philippe Le Billon's work on resource wars and conflict diamonds, because the movie is a lot like what he talks about."[9] This is not to claim any input into the *Avatar* story line, but rather to suggest that the fantasy anti-mining struggle of the *Na'vi* in *Pandora* resonated, at least with this student, with themes in this book. *Avatar* was exemplary of recurring struggles by indigenous peoples to protect their relationship with nature against violent corporate greed. As a student of mine confided, she greatly enjoyed the film and felt that it resonates with a wider generation raised on the ideals of "fair trade" and "sustainability"—burdened by a sense of responsibility and experiencing bipolar swings between individual impotence in the face of corporate control and geographical distance and the highs of "do-gooding" with their wallets at Starbucks. Avatar spoke to that fantasy of shedding privilege—to the radical extent of shedding one's body—and being ABLE to stand on the side of right and fight the good fight in a reassuringly alien world with no logical middle ground, where ideology was as simple as nature-versus-greed, and where there were no ambiguous motivations or outcomes… and win.[10]

The film could have been a public relations disaster for extractive companies. Some environmental and human groups used it to raise awareness about indigenous struggles against mining, alleged corporate involvement in the killing of anti-mining community leaders, and the environmental devastation of tar sands (which was denounced by *Avatar*'s director James Cameron in the press). A pro-mining conservative columnist, in turn, described James Cameron's work as "lurid anti-capitalist, anti-mining fantasies that provided the psychic substructure for [a] mega-grossing but Oscar-short movie."[11] In the end, companies' share values did not seem to register any dips as a result of *Avatar*, but popular geopolitical visions of militarised resource extraction have most likely been reinforced among a generation of young consumers.

While resource wars, as I have sought to demonstrate, are not simply about violent corporate greed, that aspect is undeniably the one that captures the most popular attention.[12] Rather than fight over resources, will future resource-related wars be over environmental rights? This would entail a scaling-up of environmental struggles that has so far rarely occurred.[13] The radicalisation of environmental activism is certainly on the radar screen of security agencies. Violent repression, including the murder of environmental and community leaders, could contribute to polarisation and conflict escalation.

The second anecdote revolves around the "discovery" of up to a trillion dollars' worth of mineral reserves in Afghanistan by a US team led by the Deputy Under Secretary of Defense and Director of the Task Force for Business and Stability Operations.[14] News of this discovery was released in June 2010 through the *New York Times* (timing perhaps prompted, some speculated, by the Obama administration needing a "good news" story for Afghanistan).[15] Judging from many of the 1,460 comments posted on the *New York Times* website, this announcement was far from being interpreted as straightforward "good news." The discovery and its announcement raised lots of questions. Was this known beforehand? Would this explain why there was so much international interest in Afghanistan in the first place (gas pipeline politics from Central Asia to Pakistan and India providing a complementary resource rationale)? Will this mineral potential exacerbate the conflict or help bring about peace? Will Chinese companies reap the benefits after the sacrifices of Western troops? What will populations gain from this potential mining boom given the corruption and ineptness of the Afghan government?

There is no doubt that such questions will continue to be asked, for Afghanistan and elsewhere. I hope that this book has contributed to providing some answers.[16]

NOTES

PREFACE

1. The number of armed conflicts in the world peaked in 1992, then fell until 2003, and has been rising since. Lotta Harbom, Erik Melander, and Peter Wallensteen, "Dyadic Dimensions of Armed Conflicts, 1946–2008," *Journal of Peace Research* 46, no. 4 (2009).
2. The efforts were led by H.E. Mok Mareth, Minister of Environment, David Ashwell from IUCN and Gregory Woodsworth from IDRC. See Royal Decree No. 126, "Creation and Designation of Protected Areas," signed on 1 November 2003 by H.M. King Norodom Sihanouk.
3. Global Witness, *Forests, Famine and War: The Key to Cambodia's Future* (London: Global Witness, 1995). Global Witness held press conferences in Phnom Penh and Bangkok on 24 and 25 May 1995. The Thai government closed the border to logs from Cambodia on 26 May; see Christopher Connell, "Q&A with Patrick Alley, Co-Founder of Global Witness, Winner of the 2007 Commitment to Development Ideas in Action Award" (Center for Global Development, 2007). For a detailed account of the war and the political economy of logging at the time see Philippe Le Billon, "Power is Consuming the Forest" (unpublished DPhil thesis, Oxford University, 1999). For a summary, see Philippe Le Billon, "The Political Ecology of Transition in Cambodia 1989–1999: War, Peace and Forest Exploitation" *Development & Change* 31, no. 4 (2000).
4. The intervention initially prevented the military defeat of the rebels and thus prolonged the conflict, yet from past record external military support for the rebels should shorten the conflict: P. Collier, A. Hoeffler and M. Soderbom, "On the Duration of Civil War," *Journal of Peace Research* 41, no. 3 (2004). A selective embargo by the European Union, in effect only authorising rebels to export oil, should also strengthen their position. On the "Arab Spring" see J.P. Filiu, *The Arab Revolution: Ten Lessons from the Democratic Uprising* (London: Hurst Books, 2011).

INTRODUCTION

1. I.O. Lesser, *Resources and Strategy. Vital Materials in International Conflict, 1600–Present Day* (New York: St. Martin's Press, 1989); A.H. Westing (ed.) *Global Resources and International Conflict: Environmental Factors in Strategic Policy and Action* (Oxford University Press, 1986). Armed conflict refers to the deployment of organised physical violence and includes coups d'état, terrorism, and intra- or inter-state armed conflict. In this respect, the criterion of annual battle deaths (e.g. 25 or 1,000) and that of state involvement and political motivation are not always helpful, since the number of violent deaths can be higher in "peacetime" than in "wartime" (e.g. El Salvador), and economic motives play a significant role, with in some cases a continuum between banditry, organised crime, and armed conflict.

2. Looking more broadly, about half of all armed conflicts between the end of the Second World War and 2006 were affected by natural resources, either through rebel financing, disputes over resources, or resource-related context: see Siri A. Rustad and Helga M. Binningsbo, "Rapid Recurrence: Natural Resources, Armed Conflicts and Peace," in *PRIO* (Olso: 2011). See also Chapters 2 and 6.

3. Mats Berdal and David Malone (eds) *Greed and Grievance: Economic Agendas in Civil Wars* (Boulder, CO: Lynne Rienner Publishers, 2000). Other major sources of funding include criminal proceeds from kidnappings or protection rackets, diversion of relief aid, diaspora remittances, and revenue from trading in commodities such as drugs, timber or minerals: François Jean and Jean-Christophe Rufin (eds) *Economie des Guerres Civiles* (Paris: Hachette, 1996). For a review of the literature on war economies and the political economy of war in the late 1990s, see Philippe Le Billon, "The Political Economy of War: An Annotated Bibliography" (London: Humanitarian Policy Group (HPG), Overseas Development Institute, 2000). The "War on Terror" has led to a rebounding of foreign military assistance, but most of this funding has been directed at states rather than rebel groups, thus maintaining the commercialisation of war economies. This growing importance was relative, as in absolute terms the number of resource-related conflicts apparently declined after the mid-1990s: see Rustad and Binningsbo, "Rapid Recurrence: Natural Resources, Armed Conflicts and Peace."

4. David Keen, "The Economic Functions of Violence in Civil Wars" (London: International Institute of Strategic Studies (IISS), 1998).

5. Presidential statement dated 2 June 2000 (S/PRST/2000/20).

6. Gavin Bridge, "Mapping the Bonanza: Geographies of Mining Investment in an Era of Neoliberal Reform," *Professional Geographer* 56, no. 3 (2004); James M. Otto, "Global Changes in Mining Laws, Agreements and Tax Systems," *Resources Policy* 24, no. 2 (1998).

7. Daron Acemoglu and James A. Robinson, *Economic Origins of Dictatorship and Democracy* (Cambridge University Press, 2006).

8. The collapse of oil prices was partly the result of a deliberate US policy to economically undermine the Soviet Union. See Robert W. Strayer, *Why Did the Soviet Union Collapse? Understanding Historical Change* (New York: M.E. Sharpe, 1998).

9. J.F. Bayart, Stephen Ellis and Béatrice Hibou, *The Criminalization of the State in Africa* (Oxford: Currey, 1999); M. Duffield, *Global Governance and the New Wars: The Merging of Development and Security* (London: Zed Books, 2001); W. Reno, *Warlord Politics and African States* (Boulder, CO: Lynne Rienner Publishers, 1999).

10. The rise in commodity prices was also the result of a lack of investment in resource production and financial speculation on commodities; see Philippe Le Billon and Alejandro Cervantes, "Oil Prices, Scarcity and Geographies of War," *Annals of the Association of American Geographers* 99, no. 5 (2009).

11. This was not always the case, as liberalisation reforms had reduced taxation rates. Overall the "government take" (or proportion of revenue taken by the state) was higher for oil producers such as Angola than for solid mineral producers such as Zambia. On progressive taxation schemes for resource sectors, see Bryan Land, "Capturing a Fair Share of Fiscal Benefits in the Extractive Industry," *Transnational Corporations* 18, no. 1 (2009). On royalty tax optimisation for minerals, see J. Otto, *Mining Royalties: A Global Study of Their Impact on Investors, Government, and Civil Society* (Washington, DC: World Bank Publications, 2006).

12. See Luke A. Patey, "Crude Days Ahead? Oil and the Resource Curse in Sudan," *African Affairs* 109, no. 437 (2010). Angola made progress, especially in terms of infrastructure, primary education and child and maternal health, but extreme poverty and income inequalities remained major issues, see http://mirror.undp.org/angola/MDGs-Angola.htm

13. Michael Klare, *Rising Powers, Shrinking Planet: The New Geopolitics of Energy* (New York: Metropolitan Books, 2008); Ian Taylor, "China's Oil Diplomacy in Africa," *International Affairs* 82, no. 5 (2006).

14. Deborah Brautigam, *The Dragon's Gift: The Real Story of China in Africa* (Oxford University Press, 2009). Several types of corruption are recognised: among officials, petty corruption (or facilitation payments, in effect illegal user fees) and grand corruption (or political corruption, in effect illicit or illegal political influence); corruption can take three major forms in relation to rents: *rent creation*, whereby a company bribes an official to create opportunities of extraordinary profits (such as obtaining a monopoly); *rent extraction*, whereby an official threatens a company to obtain a illegal payment (such as imposing costly regulations); and *rent seizing*, whereby officials

compete among themselves to capture and allocate part of the rent. See Michael L. Ross, *Timber Booms and Institutional Breakdown in Southeast Asia*, 1st edition (New York: Cambridge University Press, 2001). See also James M. Buchanan, Robert D. Tollison and Gordon Tullock (eds) *Toward a Theory of the Rent-Seeking Society* (College Station: Texas A&M University, 1980); Susan Rose-Ackerman, *Corruption and Government: Causes, Consequences and Reform* (Cambridge University Press, 1999).

15. For a general overview, see Svante Cornell, "Narcotics and Armed Conflict: Interaction and Implications," *Studies in Conflict and Terrorism* 30, no. 3 (2007). For comparisons with oil and diamonds, see Paivi Lujala, "Deadly Combat over Natural Resources: Gems, Petroleum, Drugs, and the Severity of Armed Civil Conflict," *Journal of Conflict Resolution* 53, no. 1 (2008); Michael L. Ross, "Oil, Drugs, and Diamonds: How Do Natural Resources Vary in Their Impact on Civil War?," in Karen and Jake Sherman Ballentine (eds) *Beyond Greed and Grievance: The Political Economy of Armed Conflict* (Boulder, CO: Lynne Rienner Publishers, 2003). On narcotics in the Andes, see Francisco E. Thoumi, *Illegal Drugs, Economy and Society in the Andes* (Baltimore, MD: Johns Hopkins University Press, 2003). On Asia, see Pierre-Arnaud Chouvy, *Opium. Uncovering the Politics of the Poppy* (Cambridge, MA: Harvard University Press, 2010).

16. Forecasts of future "water wars" have been made by, among others, John Bulloch and Adel Darwish, *Water Wars: Coming Conflicts in the Middle East* (London: Gollancz, 1993); Marq De Villiers, *Water Wars: Is the World Running out of Water?* (London: Phoenix Press, 1999); Nasrullah Mirza, *Water, War and India-Pakistan Relations* (London: Routledge, 2011); Joyce R. Starr, "Water Wars," *Foreign Policy* 82 (1991). Among those taking a circumspect view, because of positive institutional factors among other reasons, see Undala Z. Alam, "Questioning the Water Wars Rationale: A Case Study of the Indus Waters Treaty," *Geographical Journal* 168, no. 4 (2002); A.T. Wolf, K. Stahl and M.F. Macomber, "Conflict and Cooperation Within International River Basins: The Importance of Institutional Capacity," *Water Resources Update* 125 (2003). On the availability of "virtual water" (imported water-intensive goods) see J.A. Allan, "Hydro-Peace in the Middle East: Why No Water Wars? A Case Study of the Jordan River Basin," *SAIS Review* 22, no. 2 (2002). Statistical studies of armed conflicts over international waterways disprove the 'water wars' argument, see N.P. Gleditsch *et al.*, "Conflicts over Shared Rivers: Resource Scarcity or Fuzzy Boundaries?" *Political Geography* 25, no. 4 (2006), and Aaron T. Wolf, "Conflict and Cooperation Along International Waterways," *Water Policy* 1, no. 2 (1998). However, drought is statistically related to a greater risk of conflict: E. Miguel, S. Satyanath and E. Sergenti, "Economic Shocks and Civil Conflict: An Instrumental Variables Approach," *Journal of Political Economy* 112, no. 4 (2004).

17. For a retrospective analysis of "rural insurrections," see Eric R. Wolf, *Peasant Wars of the Twentieth Century* (University of Oklahoma Press, 1999). For one of the latest works, see Elisabeth Jean Wood, *Insurgent Collective Action and Civil War in El Salvador* (Cambridge University Press, 2003). On environmental security debates, see John Barnett, *The Meaning of Environmental Security: Ecological Politics and Policy in the New Security Era* (London: Zed Books, 2001); S. Dalby, *Environmental Security* (Minneapolis, MN: University of Minnesota Press, 2002. On resource scarcity and conflicts, Thomas F. Homer-Dixon, *Environment, Scarcity and Violence* (Princeton University Press, 1999).

18. For a review of this debate, see Indra de Soysa, "Ecoviolence: Shrinking Pie, or Honey Pot?" *Global Environmental Politics* 2, no. 4 (2002).

19. Resource dependence can be measured in different ways, including as a percentage of GDP, exports, or government revenue. The IMF, for example, qualifies a country as "resource dependent" if resource sectors represent more than 25 percent of GDP and 25 percent of state revenue. National-level figures, however, can be misleading, as resource dependence may characterise only subnational areas and may not account for the importance of some resources in subsistence livelihoods, cultural beliefs, or identity formation.

20. On the concept of structural violence, and the cultural violence that legitimates or renders it "invisible," see J. Galtung, "Cultural Violence," *Journal of Peace Research* 27, no. 3 (1990); Johan Galtung, "Violence, Peace and Peace Research," *Journal of Peace Research* 6 (1969). A basic definition of structural violence is the "physical and psychological harm that results from exploitive and unjust social, political and economic systems": Robert Gilman, "Structural Violence," *In Context* 4, no. Autumn (1983).

21. Fair because they often have to address conflicting interests and engage in cost-benefits allocation; technically competent because resource projects are technologically, economically and legally complex; robust because they are likely to come under political pressure to serve the vested interests of ruling elites but also popular/populist demands, see Terry L. Karl, *The Paradox of Plenty: Oil Booms and Petro-States* (Berkeley: University of California Press, 1997); J.A. Robinson, R. Torvik and T. Verdier, "Political Foundations of the Resource Curse," *Journal of Development Economics* 79, no. 2 (2006); Michael L. Ross, "The Political Economy of the Resource Curse," *World Politics* 51, no. 2 (1999). Whether institutions are "producer-friendly" or "grabber-friendly" matters a great deal for economic outcomes: H. Mehlum, K. Moene, and R. Torvik, "Institutions and the Resource Curse," *Economic Journal* 116, no. 508 (2006). On the greater importance for civil peace of state capacity for cooperation with civil society versus its capacity for co-optation and coercion, see Hanne Fjelde and Indra de Soysa, "Coercion, Co-Optation, or

Cooperation? State Capacity and the Risk of Civil War, 1961—2004," *Conflict Management and Peace Science* 26, no. 1 (2009).

22. Two narratives dominate debates about environmental violence and security. The first understands environmental violence as violence perpetrated on the environment and indirectly as violence perpetrated on human health and wellbeing through polluted environments. Security is thus a matter of environmental regulation. The second perspective understands environmental violence as violence perpetrated for environmental motives, with "eco-terrorism" a catchword frequently used by the media. Security, from this narrative's perspective, is thus a matter of political inclusion and policing to prevent "radical environmental activism."

23. This physical basis should not exclude the psychological trauma and memories of violence associated with conflict. As discussed in Chapter 2, memories of violent dispossession can play an important role in conflicts.

24. These include DFAIT, ODI, IISS, World Bank, ITCJ, Transparency International, Global Witness, International Peace Academy, UN-Habitat, ELI-UNEP.

25. I must acknowledge again in this respect my debt to Global Witness.

26. These include Michael Ross at UCLA, as well as Halvard Buhaug, Paivi Lujala, and Siri Rustad at PRIO.

27. These include Angola (1998, 2001), Cambodia (1992–2001), Colombia (1991, 2001, 2009), the DRC (2001), Sierra Leone (2001, 2006), and the former Yugoslavia (1994–96).

28. C.N. Brunnschweiler and E.H. Bulte, "The Resource Curse Revisited and Revised: A Tale of Paradoxes and Red Herrings," *Journal of Environmental Economics and Management* 55, no. 3 (2008); Mehlum, Moene and Torvik, "Institutions and the Resource Curse."

29. See Daron Acemoglu, Simon Johnson and James A. Robinson, "The Colonial Origins of Comparative Development: An Empirical Investigation," *American Economic Review* 91, no. 5 (2001).

30. The number of wars declined from fifty-two in 1992 to twenty-nine in 2003, and until 2006 stabilised at thirty-two: L. Harbom and P. Wallensteen, "Armed Conflict, 1989 2006," *Journal of Peace Research* 44, no. 5 (2007).

1. RESOURCE WARS REFRAMED

1. E.W. Zimmermann, *World Resources and Industries; a Functional Appraisal of the Availability of Agricultural and Industrial Materials* (New York: Harper & Bros., 1951).

2. Thomas R. De Gregori, "Resources Are Not; They Become: An Institutional Theory," in Marc R. Tool (ed.) *Evolutionary Economics: Foundations of Insti-*

tutional Thought (Armonk, NY: M.E. Sharpe, 1987). Institutional political economy emerged in part from evolutionary economics, which gave much attention to the concept of scarcity and the creation of resources, see C.E. Ayres, *The Theory of Economic Progress* (Chapel Hill, NC: The University of North Carolina Press, 1943); Robert L. Bradley, "Resourceship: An Austrian Theory of Mineral Resources," *Review of Austrian Economy* 20 (2007).

3. Such claims narrow the broad and emotionally charged concept of "land" to that of surface rights.

4. E. Swyngedouw, "Modernity and Hybridity: Nature, Regeneracionismo, and the Production of the Spanish Waterscape, 1890–1930," *Annals of the Association of American Geographers* 89, no. 3 (1999).

5. A. Appadurai (ed.) *The Social Life of Things: Commodities in Cultural Perspective* (Cambridge University Press, 1988).

6. See also J. Baudrillard, *Le Système des Objets* (Paris: Gallimard, 1968).

7. Matthew Paterson, *Automobile Politics: Ecology and Cultural Political Economy* (Cambridge University Press, 2007): John Urry, "The "System" of Automobility," *Theory, Culture and Society* 21, no. 4/5 (2004).

8. Raymond C. Kelly, *Warless Societies and the Origin of War* (Ann Arbor: University of Michigan Press, 2000).

9. As argued by Stathis N. Kalyvas, *The Logic of Violence in Civil War* (Cambridge University Press, 2006).

10. Galtung, "Cultural Violence." Most of the quantitative analysis in this book uses the PRIO/Uppsala definition of war as armed conflict involving a state and resulting in at least 25 battle-related deaths per year.

11. E. Staley, *Raw Materials in Peace and War* (New York: Council on Foreign Relations, 1937).

12. W.J. Broad, "Resource Wars: The Lure of South Africa," *Science* 210, no. 4474 (1980); M.T. Klare, "Resource Wars: On the Navy's Case for Unlimited Expansion," *Harper's Magazine* 262 (1981).

13. A. Gedicks, *The New Resource Wars: Native and Environmental Struggles against Multinational Corporations* (Cambridge, MA: South End Press, 1993); T. Perreault, "From the Guerra Del Agua to the Guerra Del Gas: Resource Governance, Popular Protest and Social Justice in Bolivia," *Antipode* 38, no. 1 (2006).

14. Timothy Edward Josling and Thomas Geoffrey Taylor (eds), *Banana Wars: The Anatomy of a Trade Dispute* (Wallingford: CABI, 2003); Steve Striffler and Mark Moberg (eds), *Banana Wars: Power, Production, and History in the Americas* (Duke University Press, 2003); Maury Bredahl, Andrew Schmitz and Jimmye S. Hillman, "Rent Seeking in International Trade: The Great Tomato War," *American Journal of Agricultural Economics* 69, no. 1 (1987); Julian Alston, Richard Gray and Daniel A. Sumner, "The Wheat War of 1994," *Canadian Journal of Agricultural Economics* 42, no. 3 (2005).

15. Michael Klare, *Resource Wars: The New Landscape of Global Conflict*, 1st edition (New York: Metropolitan Books, 2001).

16. Resources have also attracted much attention as a factor for peace, particularly through trade. For a critique of the liberal argument of trade fostering international peace, see Katherine Barbieri, *The Liberal Illusion: Does Trade Promote Peace?* (Ann Arbor: University of Michigan Press, 2005).

17. G. Baechler and K.R. Spillman, *Environmental Degradation as a Cause of War* (Zurich: Ruegger, 1996); Homer-Dixon, *Environment, Scarcity and Violence.*

18. K. Conca and G.D. Dabelko, *Environmental Peacemaking* (Baltimore: Johns Hopkins University Press, 2002); Norman Myers, *Ultimate Security: The Environmental Basis of Political Stability* (New York: Norton, 1993).

19. Homer-Dixon, *Environment, Scarcity and Violence.*

20. N.P Gleditsch, "Armed Conflict and the Environment: A Critique of the Literature," *Journal of Peace Research* 35, no. 3 (1998).

21. N.L. Peluso and M. Watts, *Violent Environments* (Ithaca, NY: Cornell University Press, 2001).

22. Dalby, *Environmental Security.*

23. Clionadh Raleigh and Henrik Urdal, "Climate Change, Environmental Degradation and Armed Conflict," *Political Geography* 26, no. 6 (2007).

24. Paul Collier, "Doing Well Out of War: An Economic Perspective," in Mats Berdal and David M. Malone (eds) *Greed and Grievance: Economic Agendas in Civil Wars* (Boulder, CO: Lynne Rienner, 2000); see also de Soysa, "Ecoviolence: Shrinking Pie, or Honey Pot?"

25. Christopher Cramer, "Homo Economicus Goes to War: Methodological Individualism, Rational Choice and the Political Economy of War," *World Development* 30, no. 11 (2002); Roger Mac Ginty, "Looting in the Context of Violent Conflict: A Conceptualisation and Typology," *Third World Quarterly* 25, no. 5 (2004); Roland Marchal and Christine Messiant, "De L'avidité des rebelles: L'analyse Économique de la Guerre Civile Selon Paul Collier," *Critique Internationale* 16 (2002); James Ron, "Paradigm in Distress? Primary Commodities and Civil War," *Journal of Conflict Resolution* 49, no. 4 (2005); M.L. Ross, "What Do We Know About Natural Resources and Civil Wars?" *Journal of Peace Research* 41 (2004).

26. See for example M.L. Ross, "How Do Natural Resources Influence Civil War? Evidence from Thirteen Cases," *International Organization* 58, no. 01 (2004).

27. M. Humphreys, "Natural Resources, Conflict, and Conflict Resolution: Uncovering the Mechanisms," *Journal of Conflict Resolution* 49, no. 4 (2005); Michael L. Ross, "A Closer Look at Oil, Diamonds, and Civil War," *Annual Review of Political Science* 9 (2006).

28. J.D. Fearon, "Primary Commodities Exports and Civil War," *Journal of Conflict Resolution* 49, no. 4 (2005).

29. Paivi Lujala, "The Spoils of Nature: Armed Civil Conflict and Rebel Access to Natural Resources," *Journal of Peace Research* 47, no. 1 (2010); Ross, "A Closer Look at Oil, Diamonds, and Civil War."

30. James D. Fearon, "Why Do Some Civil Wars Last So Much Longer Than Others?" *Journal of Peace Research* 41, no. 3 (2004); P. Lujala, N.P. Gleditsch and E. Gilmore, "A Diamond Curse?: Civil War and a Lootable Resource," *Journal of Conflict Resolution* 49, no. 4 (2005).

31. On the importance of forests in armed conflicts, see Will de Jong (ed.), *Extreme Conflict and Tropical Forests* (New York: Springer, 2007). For statistical findings, see Siri Camilla Aas Rustad *et al.*, "Foliage and Fighting: Forest Resources and the Onset, Duration, and Location of Civil War," *Political Geography* 27, no. 7 (2008).

32. Humphreys, "Natural Resources, Conflict, and Conflict Resolution: Uncovering the Mechanisms."

33. Lujala, "Deadly Combat over Natural Resources: Gems, Petroleum, Drugs, and the Severity of Armed Civil Conflict."

34. Adapted from Humphreys, "Natural Resources, Conflict, and Conflict Resolution: Uncovering the Mechanisms."

35. Richard Auty, "Natural Resources and Civil Strife: A Two-Stage Process," *Geopolitics* 9, no. 1 (2004); Richard Auty (ed.) *Resource Abundance and Economic Development, Wider Studies in Development Economics* (New York: Oxford University Press, 2001); Philippe Le Billon, *Fuelling War: Natural Resources and Armed Conflicts, Adelphi Paper No. 373* (London: Routledge, 2005); Philippe Le Billon, "The Political Ecology of War: Natural Resources and Armed Conflicts," *Political Geography* 20, no. 5 (2001); Ross, "How Do Natural Resources Influence Civil War? Evidence from Thirteen Cases"; Ross, "What Do We Know About Natural Resources and Civil Wars?"

36. Philip Verwimp, "The Political Economy of Coffee, Dictatorship, and Genocide," *European Journal of Political Economy* 19, no. 2 (2002).

37. Cullen Hendrix, "Leviathan in the Tropics: Geography, Bargaining, and State Extractive Capacity" (University of North Texas, 2007).

38. R. Snyder and R. Bhavnani, "Diamonds, Blood, and Taxes: A Revenue-Centered Framework for Explaining Political Order," *Journal of Conflict Resolution* 49, no. 4 (2005).

39. Richard Snyder, "Does Lootable Wealth Breed Disorder? A Political Economy of Extraction Framework," *Comparative Political Studies* 39, no. 8 (2006).

40. See Samuel P. Huntington, *Political Order in Changing Societies* (New Haven: Yale University Press, 1968). For recent econometric testing see Leonardo R. Arriola, "Patronage and Political Stability in Africa," *Comparative Polit-*

ical Studies 42, no. 10 (2009). On corruption, resources, and armed conflicts, see Hanne Fjelde, "Buying Peace? Oil Wealth, Corruption and Civil War, 1985—99," *Journal of Peace Research* 46, no. 2 (2009); Philippe Le Billon, "Fueling War or Buying Peace: The Role of Corruption in Conflicts," *Journal of International Development* 15, no. 4 (2003).

41. William Reno, *Corruption and State Politics in Sierra Leone* (Cambridge University Press, 1995); Snyder, "Does Lootable Wealth Breed Disorder? A Political Economy of Extraction Framework."

42. P.J. Luong and E. Weinthal, "Rethinking the Resource Curse: Ownership Structure, Institutional Capacity, and Domestic Constraints," *Annual Review of Political Science* 9 (2006).

43. Collier, "Doing Well out of War: An Economic Perspective."

44. Krijn Peters and Paul Richards, "'Why We Fight': Voices of Youth Combatants," *Africa* 68, no. 2 (1998).

45. Jeremy M. Weinstein, *Inside Rebellion: The Politics of Insurgent Violence* (Cambridge University Press, 2007).

46. Ross, "How Do Natural Resources Influence Civil War? Evidence from Thirteen Cases"; Ross, "What Do We Know About Natural Resources and Civil Wars? "

47. Le Billon, "The Political Ecology of Transition in Cambodia 1989–1999: War, Peace and Forest Exploitation."

48. Le Billon, "The Political Ecology of War: Natural Resources and Armed Conflicts."

49. S. O'Lear and P. Diehl, "Not Drawn to Scale: Research on Resource and Environmental Conflict," *Geopolitics* 12, no. 1 (2007).

50. Homer-Dixon, *Environment, Scarcity and Violence.*

51. H. Buhaug and P. Lujala, "Accounting for Scale: Measuring Geography in Quantitative Studies of Civil War," *Political Geography* 24, no. 4 (2005).

52. C. S. Simmons, "The Political Economy of Land Conflict in the Eastern Brazilian Amazon," *Annals of the Association of American Geographers* 94, no. 1 (2004).

53. Michael Watts, "Antinomies of Community: Some Thoughts on Geography, Resources and Empire," *Transactions of the Institute of British Geographers* 29, no. 2 (2004).

54. B. Korf and H. Fünfgeld, "War and the Commons: Assessing the Changing Politics of Violence, Access and Entitlements in Sri Lanka," *Geoforum* 37, no. 3 (2006).

55. Peluso and Watts, *Violent Environments.*

56. Galtung, "Cultural Violence." See also C. McIlwaine, "Geography and Development: Violence and Crime as Development Issues," *Progress in Human Geography* 23, no. 3 (1999).

57. On Central American cases, see Jenny Pearce, "From Civil War to 'Civil Society': Has the End of the Cold War Brought Peace to Central America?" *International Affairs* 74, no. 3 (1998).

58. N.L. Peluso, *Rich Forests, Poor People: Resource Control and Resistance in Java* (University of California Press, 1992).

59. J.C. Ribot and N.L. Peluso, "A Theory of Access," *Rural Sociology* 68, no. 2 (2003).

60. On the violence of property rights, see Nicholas Blomley, "Law, Property, and the Geography of Violence: The Frontier, the Survey, and the Grid," *Annals of the Association of American Geographers* 93, no. 1 (2003).

61. Jonathan Goodhand, "Frontiers and Wars: The Opium Economy in Afghanistan," *Journal of Agrarian Change* 5, no. 2 (2005).

62. R.P. Neumann, "Moral and Discursive Geographies in the War for Biodiversity in Africa," *Political Geography* 23, no. 7 (2004).

63. See on gold E. Hartwick, "Geographies of Consumption: A Commodity-Chain Approach," *Environment and Planning D: Society and Space* 16 (1998). On timber Le Billon, "The Political Ecology of Transition in Cambodia 1989–1999: War, Peace and Forest Exploitation."

64. M.D. Smith, "The Empire Filters Back: Consumption, Production, and the Politics of Starbucks Coffee," *Urban Geography* 17, no. 6 (1996). J.M. Talbot, "Information, Finance and the New International Inequality: The Case of Coffee," *Journal of World-Systems Research*, VIII, 2 Spring (2002): 214–50.

65. W. van Schendel and I. Abraham (eds) *Illicit Flows and Criminal Things: States, Borders, and the Other Side of Globalization* (Bloomington, IN: Indiana University Press, 2005).

66. Philippe Le Billon, "Geographies of War: Perspectives on 'Resource Wars,'" *Compass* 1, no. 2 (2007).

67. D. Leslie and S. Reimer, "Spatializing Commodity Chains," *Progress in Human Geography* 23, no. 3 (1999).

68. F. De Boeck, "Domesticating Diamonds and Dollars: Identity, Expenditure and Sharing in Southwestern Zaire (1984–1997)," *Development and Change* 29, no. 4 (1998).

69. Philippe Le Billon, "Diamond Wars? Conflict Diamonds and Geographies of Resource Wars," *Annals of the Association of American Geographers* 98, no. 2 (2008).

70. Philippe Le Billon, "Fatal Transactions: Conflict Diamonds and the (Anti) Terrorist Consumer," *Antipode* 38, no. 4 (2006).

71. N. Castree, "Commodity Fetishism, Geographical Imaginations and Imaginative Geographies," *Environment and Planning A* 33, no. 9 (2001).

72. Gavin Bridge, "Resource Triumphalism: Postindustrial Narratives of Primary Commodity Production," *Environment and Planning A* 33, no. 12 (2001);

I. Cook and P. Crang, "The World on a Plate: Culinary Culture, Displacement, and Geographical Knowledges," *Journal of Material Culture* 1 (1996).

73. S. Freidberg, "The Ethical Complex of Corporate Food Power," *Environment and Planning D: Society and Space* 22, no. 4 (2004).

74. Paul Richards, "To Fight or to Farm? Agrarian Dimensions of the Mano River Conflicts (Liberia and Sierra Leone)," *African Affairs* 104, no. 417 (2005).

75. K. Dodds, "Licensed to Stereotype: Popular Geopolitics, James Bond and the Spectre of Balkanism," *Geopolitics* 8, no. 2 (2003).

76. Le Billon, *Fuelling War: Natural Resources and Armed Conflicts.*

77. Auty, "Natural Resources and Civil Strife: A Two-Stage Process"; de Soysa, "Ecoviolence: Shrinking Pie, or Honey Pot?"; Fearon, "Primary Commodities Exports and Civil War"; Le Billon, "The Political Ecology of War: Natural Resources and Armed Conflicts"; Ross, "The Political Economy of the Resource Curse."

78. Christopher Blattman and Edward Miguel, "Civil War," *Journal of Economic Literature* 48, no. 1 (2010); James and David Laitin Fearon, "Ethnicity, Insurgency and Civil War," *American Political Science Review* 97, no. 1 (2003).

79. Auty (ed.) *Resource Abundance and Economic Development*; Mehlum, Moene, and Torvik, "Institutions and the Resource Curse"; Michael L. Ross, "Extractive Sectors and the Poor" (Boston, MA: Oxfam America, 2001); Jeffrey and Andrew Warner Sachs, "The Curse of Natural Resources," *European Economic Review* 45, no. 4–6 (2001).

80. E. Neumayer, "Does the "Resource Curse" Hold for Growth in Genuine Income as Well?" *World Development* 32, no. 10 (2004); A. Rosser, "The Political Economy of the Resource Curse: A Literature Survey" (Brighton: University of Sussex IDS, 2006).

81. Carlos Leite and Jens Weidmann, "Does Mother Nature Corrupt? Natural Resources, Corruption, and Economic Growth," in George T. Abed and Sanjeev Gupta (eds) *Governance, Corruption, and Economic Performance* (Washington, DC: International Monetary Fund, 2002); Mick Moore, "Revenues, State Formation, and the Quality of Governance in Developing Countries," *International Political Science Review* 25, no. 3 (2004); Ross, "The Political Economy of the Resource Curse."

82. For a review, see Fearon, "Primary Commodities Exports and Civil War"; Ross, "What Do We Know About Natural Resources and Civil Wars?"

83. David Harvey, *The Limits to Capital* (University of Chicago Press, 1982); G. Lanning and M. Mueller, *Africa Undermined: Mining Companies and the Underdevelopment of Africa* (London: Penguin, 1979); Neil Smith, *Uneven Development: Nature, Capital, and the Production of Space* (Oxford: Basil Blackwell, 1984).

84. Gavin Bridge, "Exploiting: Power, Colonialism and Resource Economies," in Ian Douglas, Richard Huggett, and Chris Perkins (eds) *Companion Encyclopedia of Geography* (London: Routledge, 2006).

85. Acemoglu, Johnson and Robinson, "The Colonial Origins of Comparative Development: An Empirical Investigation."

86. Rebecca Roberts and Jacque Emel, "Uneven Development and the Tragedy of the Commons: Competing Images for Nature-Society Analysis," *Economic Geography* 68, no. 3 (1992).

87. G. Bridge and P. McManus, "Sticks and Stones: Environmental Narratives and Discursive Regulation in the Forestry and Mining Sectors," *Antipode* 32, no. 1 (2000); Stephen G. Bunker, *Underdeveloping the Amazon: Extraction, Unequal Exchange and the Failure of the Modern State* (Urbana, IL: University of Illinois Press, 1985).

88. Barnett, *The Meaning of Environmental Security: Ecological Politics and Policy in the New Security Era*; Dalby, *Environmental Security*.

89. Homer-Dixon, *Environment, Scarcity and Violence*; Peluso and Watts, *Violent Environments*; Simmons, "The Political Economy of Land Conflict in the Eastern Brazilian Amazon"; Matthew D. Turner, "Political Ecology and the Moral Dimensions of "Resource Conflicts": The Case of Farmer-Herder Conflicts in the Sahel," *Political Geography* 23, no. 7 (2004).

90. Klare, "Resource Wars: On the Navy's Case for Unlimited Expansion"; Philippe Le Billon and Fouad El Khatib, "From Free Oil to 'Freedom Oil': Terrorism, War and US Geopolitics in the Persian Gulf," *Geopolitics* 9, no. 1 (2004); Lesser, *Resources and Strategy. Vital Materials in International Conflict, 1600-Present Day*.

91. Roger Hayter, "'The War in the Woods': Post-Fordist Restructuring, Globalization, and the Contested Remapping of British Columbia's Forest Economy," *Annals of the Association of American Geographers* 93, no. 3 (2003); Michael Klare, "The New Geography of Conflict," *Foreign Affairs* 80, no. 3 (2001); Neumann, "Moral and Discursive Geographies in the War for Biodiversity in Africa"; Perreault, "From the Guerra Del Agua to the Guerra Del Gas: Resource Governance, Popular Protest and Social Justice in Bolivia."

92. UN General Assembly resolution 55/56 adopted on 1 December 2000.

93. See the definition proposed by Global Witness: Global Witness, "The Logs of War: The Timber Trade and Armed Conflict" (Oslo: Programme for International Co-operation and Conflict Resolution, Fafo Institute for Applied Social Sciences, 2002).

94. Neumann, "Moral and Discursive Geographies in the War for Biodiversity in Africa"; Peter Vandergeest and Nancy Lee Peluso, "Territorialization and State Power in Thailand," *Theory and Society* 24, no. 3 (1995).

95. Ross, "Oil, Drugs, and Diamonds: How Do Natural Resources Vary in Their Impact on Civil War?'

96. Le Billon, "The Political Ecology of War: Natural Resources and Armed Conflicts."

97. R. Duffy, "Peace Parks: The Paradox of Globalisation," *Geopolitics* 6, no. 2 (2001), for example, notes the contribution of "peace parks" stretching across weakly controlled border areas to networks of "criminal" activities—potentially linking with the spatial structure of insurgency.

98. See also Auty (ed.) *Resource Abundance and Economic Development*; Anne D. Boschini, Jan Pettersson and Jesper Roine, "Resource Curse or Not: A Question of Appropriability," *Scandinavian Journal of Economics* 109, no. 3 (2007).

99. Ross, "Oil, Drugs, and Diamonds: How Do Natural Resources Vary in Their Impact on Civil War?"

100. Le Billon, "The Political Ecology of War: Natural Resources and Armed Conflicts."

101. Paul Collier and Anke Hoeffler, "The Political Economy of Secession," in Hurst Hannun and Eileen Babbitt (eds) *Negotiating Self-Determination* (Lanham, MD: Lexington Books, 2006); Le Billon, *Fuelling War: Natural Resources and Armed Conflicts*.

102. Roland Pourtier, "1997: Les Raisons d'une Guerre "Incivile,"" *Afrique Contemporaine* 186 (1998); interview with Pascal Lissouba, London, January 2002. Controlling the north of the country, Sassou Nguesso could also have benefited from logging revenue from timber exports via Gabon and Cameroon (*La Lettre du Continent*, 13 January 2000).

103. Ibid.

104. Nkossa was the name of an oil field recently awarded to French oil company Elf Aquitaine. Rémy Bazenguissa-Ganga, "Les Milices Politiques dans les Affrontements," *Afrique Contemporaine* 186 (1998).

105. Cited in Stephen Ellis, *The Mask of Anarchy: The Destruction of Liberia and the Religious Dimension of an African Civil War* (London: Hurst, 1999).

106. Marites Dañguilan-Vitug, *Power from the Forest: The Politics of Logging* (Manila: Philippine Center for Investigative Journalism, 1993).

107. Tony Hodges, *Western Sahara: The Roots of a Desert War* (Westport, CT: Lawrence Hill, 1983).

108. Sjamsuddin Nazaruddin, "Issues and Politics of Regionalism in Indonesia: Evaluating the Acehnese Experience," in Lim Joo-Jock and S. Vani (eds) *Armed Separatism in Southeast Asia* (Singapore: Institute of Southeast Asian Studies, 1984).

109. Cited in P. Polomka, *Bougainville: Perspectives on a Crisis* (Canberra: Strategic and Defence Studies Centre, Research School of Pacific Studies,

Australian National University, 1990). See also Volker Boge, "Mining, Environmental Degradation and War: The Bougainville Case," in Mohamed Suliman (ed.) *Ecology, Politics and Violent Conflicts* (London: Zed Books, 1999).

110. Karl Claxton, *Bougainville 1988–98: Five Searches for Security in the North Solomons Province of Papua New Guinea, No. 130* (Canberra: Strategic and Defence Studies Centre, Australian National University, 1998).

111. Cited in S.E. Hutchinson, *Nuer Dilemmas: Coping with Money, War, and the State* (Berkeley, CA: University of California Press, 1996).

112. See Chapter 3.

113. H. Peimani, "Turks Threaten: 10,000 Fighters in Kirkuk," *Asia Times* 21 December 2002.

114. In contrast, sovereign rights afforded East Timor the opportunity to regain its independence from Indonesia in 1999. Ironically, this was made possible by Australian military intervention, one of the few countries that had officially recognised Indonesia's illegal sovereignty over East Timor, in part to obtain a (more favourable) settlement of territorial claims over petroleum resources in the Timor Sea: B. Dubois, "The Timor Gap Treaty: Where to Now?," in *Briefing Paper (Community Aid Abroad, Australia) no. 25.* (Oxfam Australia, 2000).

115. L. Horton, *Peasants in Arms: War and Peace in the Mountains of Nicaragua, 1979–1994* (Athens: Ohio University Press, 1998).

116. Alain Labrousse, "Colombie-Pérou: violence politique et logique criminelle," in François Jean and Jean-Christophe Rufin (eds) *Economie des Guerres Civiles* (Paris: Hachette, 1996).

117. Maj. Rodney Azama, "The Huks and the New People's Army: Comparing Two Postwar Filipino Insurgencies" (Quantico, VA: Marine Corps Command and Staff College, 1985).

118. Thomas Pakenham, *The Boer War* (London: Weidenfeld and Nicolson, 1979).

119. A. Aissaoui, *Algeria: The Political Economy of Oil and Gas* (Oxford University Press, 2001).

120. Alexander A. Arbatov, "Oil as a Factor in Strategic Policy and Action: Past and Present," in A.H. Westing (ed.) *Global Resources and International Conflict: Environmental Factors in Strategic Policy and Action* (Oxford University Press, 1986).

121. This was the case for US corporate interests linked to Belgian companies and close to Eisenhower, while the Kennedy administration had ties with investors seeking to replace the Belgians, see David N. Gibbs, *The Political Economy of Third World Intervention: Mines, Money, and US Policy in the Congo Crisis* (University of Chicago Press, 1991). For a general history of

conflicts around resource exploitation in the DRC, see Samuel Solvit, *RDC: Rêve ou Illusion. Conflits et Ressources Naturelles en République Démocratique du Congo* (Paris: L'Harmattan, 2009).

122. Interview with Prof. Séverin Mugangu, Université Catholique de Bukavu, April 2002. On the importance of local-level conflicts see Séverine Autesserre, *The Trouble with the Congo: Local Violence and the Failure of International Peacebuilding* (Cambridge University Press, 2010).

123. This positive relationship is valid for a number of resource measurements, including resource prices—Collier, Hoeffler, and Soderbom, "On the Duration of Civil War"—and the presence of resource deposits in conflict areas: Halvard Buhaug, "Geography, Rebel Capability, and the Duration of Civil Conflict," *Journal of Conflict Resolution* 53, no. 4 (2009).

124. For example, "contraband goods" in Fearon, "Why Do Some Civil Wars Last So Much Longer Than Others?" On alluvial or secondary diamonds in Lujala, Gleditsch, and Gilmore, "A Diamond Curse?: Civil War and a Lootable Resource."

125. With the possible exception of alluvial diamonds, see Ross, "A Closer Look at Oil, Diamonds, and Civil War."

126. Lujala, "The Spoils of Nature: Armed Civil Conflict and Rebel Access to Natural Resources."

127. Interview, Terry Karl, Stanford University, June 2002.

128. Nazih Richani, *Systems of Violence: The Political Economy of War and Peace in Colombia* (New York: SUNY, 2002).

129. Cited in Nate Thayer, "Rubies Are Rouge: Khmer War Effort Financed by Gem Finds," *Far Eastern Economic Review*, 7 February 1991.

130. Keen, "The Economic Functions of Violence in Civil Wars."

131. In contrast to "top-down" revenue flows, with revenue being generated by foreign governments or by (violently) centralised remittance networks channelling funds from diaspora, as in the case of the Tamil Tigers/LTTE in Sri Lanka and the ELF in Eritrea, see Katrin Radtke, "From Gifts to Taxes: The Mobilisation of Tamil and Eritrean Diaspora in Intrastate Warfare," in *Working Papers Micropolitics No. 2* (Berlin: Humboldt University, 2005).

132. Interview with the author, Cambodia, January 2001.

133. Interviews with Congolese diamond buyers in Angola, 2001; "Violations of Security Council Sanctions Against UNITA," S/2000/203, p. 27; Filip De Boeck, "Garimpeiro Worlds: Digging, Dying and 'Hunting' for Diamonds in Angola," *Review of African Political Economy* 28, no. 90 (2001).

134. Weinstein, *Inside Rebellion: The Politics of Insurgent Violence.*

135. It is also noted that many civilians often use the context of war to settle personal scores (Kalyvas, *The Logic of Violence in Civil War*) or engage in

economically motivated crimes (Keen, "The Economic Functions of Violence in Civil Wars").

136. For a critique, see Sydney Tarrow, "Inside Insurgencies: Politics and Violence in an Age of Civil War," *Perspectives on Politics* 5, no. 3 (2007). For an in-depth review of violence in civil wars and evidence that violence is highest at the margins of disputed areas, see Kalyvas, *The Logic of Violence in Civil War*. Weaker groups challenged by indiscriminate counterinsurgency tactics seem to the most prone to violence against civilians: R.M. Wood, "Rebel Capability and Strategic Violence against Civilians," *Journal of Peace Research* 47, no. 5, September 2010.

137. Simon Dalby, *Security and Environmental Change* (Cambridge: Polity Press, 2009).

2. MATERIAL MOTIVES

1. Such "strategic" resources have included timber, iron, coal, and more recently oil, uranium, and rare earth minerals.

2. "It is only because of the overriding importance of this purpose that I am able to overcome my reluctance to signing a bill which reaffirms the application to stockpile purchases of the provisions of … the Buy American Act. Those provisions will not only materially increase the cost of the proposed stockpiles but will tend to defeat the conservation and strategic objectives of the bill by further depleting our already inadequate underground reserves of strategic material": Truman speech on the occasion of his signature of the Strategic and Critical Materials Stock Piling Act, 23 July 1946 (Public Law 520, 79th Congress (60 Stat. 566)). A first Stockpiling Act was passed by the US Congress on 7 June 1939: OTA, "An Assessment of Alternative Economic Stockpiling Policies" (Washington, DC: Office of Technology Assessment, 1975), http://www.trumanlibrary.org/publicpapers/index.php?pid=1671&st=&st1=.

3. See R. Brian Ferguson, "Introduction: Studying War," in *Warfare, Culture, and Environment* (Orlando, FL: Academic Press, 1984); Azar Gat, *War in Human Civilization* (Oxford University Press, 2006), raises the ethical question of considering females as "resources"—see also the discussion on "slaves" in this chapter.

4. Rada Dyson-Hudson and Eric Alden Smith, "Human Territoriality: An Ecological Reassessment," *American Anthropologist* 80, no. 1 (1978); Carol R. Ember and Melvin Ember, "Resource Unpredictability, Mistrust, and War: A Cross-Cultural Study," *Journal of Conflict Resolution* 36, no. 2 (1992); Julie S. Field, "Environmental and Climatic Considerations: A Hypothesis for Conflict and the Emergence of Social Complexity in Fijian Prehistory," *Journal of Anthropological Archaeology* 23, no. 1 (2004).

5. Kelly, *Warless Societies and the Origin of War*.
6. Lori Marino, "Convergence of Complex Cognitive Abilities in Cetaceans and Primates," *Brain, Behaviour and Evolution* 59 (2002); B. Wursig, "Occurrence and Group Organization of Atlantic Bottlenose Porpoises (Tursiops Truncatus) in an Argentine Bay," *Biological Bulletin* 154, no. 348–359 (1978). Chimpanzees are one of the rare species of mammals to engage in warfare, with some evidence suggesting that warfare does succeed for the dominant group in reducing resource competition: Michael L. Wilson, William R. Wallauer and Anne E. Pusey, "New Cases of Intergroup Violence among Chimpanzees in Gombe National Park, Tanzania," *International Journal of Primatology* 25, no. 3 (2004). Attacks frequently occur during territory boundary patrolling by males, with group, fraternal warrior band, and individual warrior benefits including range extension and increase in food amount and quality: David P. Watts and John C. Mitani, "Boundary Patrols and Intergroup Encounters in Wild Chimpanzees," *Behaviour* 138 (2001).
7. Jonathan Haas (ed.) *The Anthropology of War* (Cambridge University Press, 1990).
8. Ethnographic or archaeological records studies included, in relation to fisheries and in particular to river estuaries in the American Northwest, bison migration routes in the North American Great Plains, seasonal waterholes in the Australian interior, and wild pigs in New Guinea. One hypothesis of transition to warfare is revenge killing by fraternal interest groups for deaths occurring as a result of "shoot-on-sight" behavior by competing groups during hunting parties: Kelly, *Warless Societies and the Origin of War*. Within early agriculture, warfare has been linked with competition over secondary growth forest for swidden agriculture.
9. Dyson-Hudson and Smith, "Human Territoriality: An Ecological Reassessment."
10. Kelly, *Warless Societies and the Origin of War*, suggests that "warfare is typically rare to inexistent within and between unsegmented foraging societies inhabiting environments characterised by low resource density, diversity and predictability at densities below 0.2 persons per square mile [0.08 per square kilometer]."
11. This is particularly the case when space is circumscribed, as in the case of islands (see the case of the Andaman Islands, where some groups succeeded in establishing peace and exploited the whole surface while others did not, leaving vast areas as "no-man's land"): Kelly, *Warless Societies and the Origin of War*.
12. The economic defendability hypothesis has been criticised for lacking consideration of cognitive and cultural aspects of territorial defence, whereby, for example, social boundary defence is more cost effective than perimeter

defence in large territories. Elizabeth Cashdan, "Territoriality among Human Foragers: Ecological Models and an Application to Four Bushman Groups," *Current Anthropology* 24, no. 1 (1983).

13. Ember and Ember, "Resource Unpredictability, Mistrust, and War: A Cross-Cultural Study."

14. Mikhail S. Burtsev and Andrey Korotayev, "An Evolutionary Agent-Based Model of Pre-State Warfare Patterns: Cross-Cultural Tests" (Moscow: undated).

15. Julie S. Field, "Land Tenure, Competition and Ecology in Fijian Prehistory," *Antiquity* 79 (2005).

16. Mary M. Gunn, "Aggression and Alliance: The Impact of Resource Distribution on Exchange Strategies Chosen by Prehispanic Philippine Chiefs," *Indo-Pacific Prehistory Association Bulletin* 14 (1996).

17. Quincy Wright, *A Study of War* (University of Chicago Press, 1983).

18. Kelly, *Warless Societies and the Origin of War.*

19. Jonathan Haas, "Warfare and the Evolution of Culture," in Gary M. Feinman and T. Douglas Price (eds) *Archeology at the Millenium: A Sourcebook* (New York: Springer, 2007).

20. Gat, *War in Human Civilization*; Haas, "Warfare and the Evolution of Culture."

21. Keith F. Otterbein, *How War Began* (Texas A&M University Press, 2004).

22. Jonathan Haas, *The Evolution of the Prehistoric State* (New York: Columbia University Press, 1982).

23. Gat, *War in Human Civilization.*

24. On the case of Europe see Charles Tilly, "War Making and State Making as Organized Crime," in Peter Evans, Dietrich Rueschemeyer and Theda Skocpol (eds) *Bringing the State Back In* (Cambridge University Press, 1985).

25. Cited in Haas, *The Evolution of the Prehistoric State.*

26. R. Brian Ferguson, in Jonathan Haas (ed.) *The Anthropology of War.*

27. Raymond L. Smith, "The Impact of Metals on Society," *Journal of the Minerals, Metals and Materials Society* 50 (1998).

28. John Rich and Graham Shipley, *War and Society in the Greek World* (London: Routledge, 1993).

29. William James Hamblin, *Warfare in the Ancient near East to 1600 BC: Holy Warriors at the Dawn of History* (London: Routledge, 2006).

30. Such as the Serabit el-Khadim, near Wadi al-Mughara in southwestern Sinai, a mining area for malachite, turquoise, and copper.

31. As written by Herodotus (VII.144), "when the Athenians, having got large sums of money in the public treasury, which had come in to them from the mines which are at Laurion, were intending to share it among themselves, taking each in turn the sum of ten drachmas. Then Themistocles persuaded

the Athenians to give up this plan of division and to make for themselves with this money two hundred ships for the war, meaning by that the war with the Eginetans: for this war having arisen proved in fact the salvation of Hellas at that time, by compelling the Athenians to become a naval power."

32. Smith, "The Impact of Metals on Society." See Champion, "Roman wars were wars of plunder, at least in the sense that plundering was a normal part of them": Craige Brian Champion, *Roman Imperialism: Readings and Sources* (Wiley-Blackwell, 2004). Romans considered minerals as some of the main spoils of victory (*pretium victoriae*), in particular because of the paucity of known mineral resources in Italy apart from iron: David Stone Potter, *A Companion to the Roman Empire* (Wiley-Blackwell, 2006).

33. J.C. Edmondson, "Mining in the Later Roman Empire and Beyond: Continuity or Disruption?" *Journal of Roman Studies* 79 (1989).

34. Malcolm W. Browne, "Ice Cap Shows Ancient Mines Polluted the Globe," *New York Times* 9 December 1997. http://www.nytimes.com/1997/12/09/science/ice-cap-shows-ancient-mines-polluted-the-globe.html, accessed on 31 May 2011.

35. Ibid.; Robert Sabatino Lopez, *The Commercial Revolution of the Middle Ages, 950–1350* (Cambridge University Press, 1976); M. Williams, "Dark Ages and Dark Areas: Global Deforestation in the Deep Past," *Journal of Historical Geography* 26, no. 1 (2000).

36. The shift from bronze to iron was also marked by a deep social transformation, because of the increased availability of metal weaponry to a larger number of groups.

37. F.M.V.R. Queiroga, *War and Castros. New Approaches to Northwestern Portuguese Iron Age* (Oxford: Archaeological Reports, 2003).

38. G. Nakou, "The Cutting Edge: A New Look at Early Aegean Metallurgy," *Journal of Mediterranean Archeology* 8, no. 2 (1995).

39. Elizabeth Bloxam, "Miners and Mistresses: Middle Kingdom Mining on the Margins," *Journal of Social Archaeology* 6, no. 2 (2006); M.W. Spence, "The Social Context of Production and Exchange," in J.E. Ericson and T.K. Earle (eds) *Contexts for Prehistoric Exchange* (London: Academic Press, 1982).

40. Enrico Dal Lago and Constantina Katsari, *Slave Systems* (Cambridge University Press, 2008). Mining slaves were typically shackled in classical Athens: Peter Hunt, "The Slaves and the Generals of Arginusae," *American Journal of Philology* 122, no. 3 (2001). Mining was one of the sectors with the highest proportion of slaves in the Roman economy: William D. Phillips, *Slaver from Roman Times to the Early Transatlantic Trade* (Manchester University Press, 1985).

41. Ronald Findlay and Kevin H. O'Rourke, *Power and Plenty: Trade, War, and the World Economy in the Second Millenium* (Princeton University Press, 2007);

Edward D. Mansfield, *Power, Trade and War* (Princeton University Press, 1995).

42. J. Evelyn, *Navigation and Commerce, Their Original and Progress* (London: B. Tooke, 1674); A. T. Mahan, *The Influence of Sea Power Upon History, 1660–1783* (London: Low and Marston, 1890).

43. Lesser, *Resources and Strategy. Vital Materials in International Conflict, 1600-Present Day.*

44. W.G. Clarence-Smith, *The Third Portuguese Empire, 1825–1975: A Study in Economic Imperialism* (Manchester University Press, 1985).

45. David Armitage and Michael J. Braddick (eds) *The British Atlantic World* (Basingstoke: Palgrave Macmillan, 2002).

46. Robert Greenhalgh Albion, *Forests and Sea Power: The Timber Problem of the Royal Navy, 1652–1862, Harvard Economic Studies Vol. XXIX* (Hamden, CN: Archon Books, 1926).

47. Thomas Malthus, *An Essay on the Principle of Population* (St Paul's Church-Yard: Johnson, 1798).

48. Aron, *War and Peace: A Theory of International Relations* (London: Doubleday, 1962).

49. Karl Marx, *Capital: The Process of Production of Capital* (1867 [1887]).

50. Rosa Luxemburg, *The Accumulation of Capital* (1913).

51. Edwin Clarence Eckel, *Coal, Iron and War: A Study in Industrialism, Past, and Future* (New York: Henri Holt, 1920); Scott Nearing, *Oil and the Germs of War* (Ridgewood, NJ: Nellie Seeds Nearing, 1923); Westing (ed.) *Global Resources and International Conflict: Environmental Factors in Strategic Policy and Action* (Oxford University Press, 1989).

52. I. Bowman, *The New World: Problems in Political Geography* (New York: World Book Company, 1921).

53. K. Haushofer, *Geopolitik Der Pan-Ideen* (Berlin: Zentral-Verlag, 1931); E. Obst, "Wir Forden Unsere Kolonien Zurück!," *Zeitschrift für Geopolitik* 3 (1926).

54. C.K. Leith, *World Minerals and World Politics: A Factual Study of Minerals in Their Political and International Relations* (New York: Whittlesey House, 1931). C. Gini, Report on the Problem of Raw Materials and Foodstuffs (Geneva: League of Nations, 1921); C.K. Leith, World Minerals and World Politics: A Factual Study of Minerals in Their Political and International Relations New York: Whittlesey House, 1931; IIIC, *Peaceful Change: Procedures, Population, Raw Materials, Colonies. Proceedings of the Tenth International Studies Conference* (Paris: International Institute of Intellectual Co-operation, 1938).

55. Jonathan Marshall, *To Have and Have Not: Southeast Asian Raw Materials and the Origins of the Pacific War* (Berkeley: University of California Press, 1995).

56. N. Angell, *Raw Materials, Population Pressure and War* (Boston, MA: World Peace Foundation, 1936); Staley, *Raw Materials in Peace and War*. (RIIA 1936). In the area of resources for peace, a first "peace park" was inaugurated in 1932 between Canada and the US: S.H. Ali, *Peace Parks: Conservation and Conflict Resolution* (Cambridge, MA: MIT Press, 2007).

57. William F. Engdahl, *A Century of War: Anglo-American Oil Politics and the New World Order* (London: Pluto, 2004).

58. Joel Hayward, "Too Little, Too Late: An Analysis of Hitler's Failure in August 1942 to Damage Soviet Oil Production" *Journal of Military History* 64 (2000).

59. Scott D. Sagan, "The Origins of the Pacific War," *Journal of Interdisciplinary History* 18, no. 4 (1988).

60. Jacob Rosenthal, "Georg Gondos, an Heb Jewish Combatant on the Middle-Eastern Front," *Qatedrah le-tôldôt Eres Yísra'el el we-yiššûbah* 117 (2005).

61. Yuen Choy Leng, "Japanese Rubber and Iron Investments in Malaya, 1900–1941," *Journal of Southeast Asian Studies* 5, no. 1 (1974).

62. S.D. Krasner, *Defending the National Interest: Raw Materials Investments and US Foreign Policy* (Princeton University Press, 1978). In US policy circles, see for example the 1952 Paley Commission report "Resources for Freedom," in *Communication from the President of the United States, Transmitting the Report of the President's Materials Policy Commission* (Washington, DC: US Government Printing Office, 1952).

63. In 1962, the UN General Assembly passed resolution 1803 (XVII) to ensure "Permanent Sovereignty Over Natural Resources." S.J. Kobrin, "Diffusion as an Explanation of Oil Nationalization (or the Domino Effect Rides Again)," *Journal of Conflict Resolution* 29, no. 1 (1985), Hanns Maull, *Oil and Influence: The Oil Weapon Examined, Adelphi Paper 117* (London: Routledge, 1975).

64. R.W. Arad and U.B. Arad (eds) *Sharing Global Resources* (New York: McGraw-Hill, 1979); R.D. Lipschutz, *When Nations Clash: Raw Materials, Ideology, and Foreign Policy* (New York: Ballinger Pub. Co., 1989); Westing (ed.) *Global Resources and International Conflict: Environmental Factors in Strategic Policy and Action*

65. B. Russett, "Security and the Resources Scramble: Will 1984 Be Like 1914?" *International Affairs* 58, no. 1 (1981).

66. C.F. Bergsten, "The Threat From the Third World," *Foreign Policy* 11 (1973).

67. S.B. Cohen, *Geography and Politics in a World Divided* (New York: Random House, 1973).

68. E.W. Anderson and L.D. Anderson, *Strategic Minerals: Resource Geopolitics and Global Geo-Economics* (Chichester: John Wiley & Sons, 1997); European Commission, "Critical Raw Materials for the EU" (Raw Materials Supply Group, 2010), http://ec.europa.eu/enterprise/sectors/metals-minerals/files/

fiches_raw_materials_supply_group_en.pdf, accessed on 31 May 2011; US Department of Energy, "Critical Materials Strategy" (2010).

69. R.A. Falk, *This Endangered Planet: Prospects and Proposals for Human Survival* (New York: Random House, 1971); Bjorn Ola Linnér, *The Return of Malthus: Environmentalism and Post-War Population-Resource Crises* (Cambridge: White Horse Press, 2004); H. Sprout and M. Sprout, "Environmental Factors in the Study of International Politics," *Journal of Conflict Resolution* 1, no. 4 (1957); L. Timberlake and J. Tinker, "Environment and Conflict," in *Earthscan Briefing Document* (London: International Institute for Environment and Development, 1984).

70. L. Brown, *Redefining National Security* (Washington, DC: World Watch Institute, 1977), Donella H. Meadows *et al.*, *The Limits to Growth* (New York: Universe Book, 1972); Richard H. Ullman, "Redefining Security," *International Security* 8, no. 1 (1983).

71. Dalby, *Environmental Security*.

72. Ibid.

73. Klare, "The New Geography of Conflict," Reno, *Warlord Politics and African States*.

74. M.T. Klare, *Blood and Oil: The Dangers and Consequences of America's Growing Dependency on Imported Petroleum* (New York: Metropolitan Books, 2004); Linda McQuaig, *Its the Crude, Dude: Greed, Gas, War, and the American Way* (Thomas Dunne, 2006).

75. An irony when considering the Texas-based and oil-linked Bush-Cheney administration, see for example McQuaig, *Its the Crude, Dude: Greed, Gas, War, and the American Way*.

76. Le Billon and El Khatib, "From Free Oil to 'Freedom Oil': Terrorism, War and US Geopolitics in the Persian Gulf."

77. Klare, *Rising Powers, Shrinking Planet: The New Geopolitics of Energy*.; J.H. Kunstler, *The Long Emergency: Surviving the End of Oil, Climate Change, and Other Converging Catastrophes of the Twenty-First Century* (New York: Grove Press, 2006).

78. Peter S. Goodman, "Booming China Devouring Raw Materials," *Washington Post*, 21 May 2004; David Zweig and B. Jianhai, "China's Global Hunt for Energy," *Foreign Affairs* 84, no. 5 (2005).

79. Marian Radetzki, *A Handbook of Primary Commodities in the Global Economy* (Cambridge University Press, 2008).

80. This includes both the exported goods and the waste and air emissions generated by their production: Ming Xu and Tianzhu Zhang, "Material Flows and Economic Growth in Developing China," *Journal of Industrial Ecology* 11, no. 1 (2008).

81. David Cohen, "Earth Audit," *New Scientist* 194, no. 2605 (2007); Richard Heinberg, *Peak Everything: Waking up to the Century of Declines* (Gabriola

Island: New Society Publishers, 2007); Michael Montgomery, "Indian Steel Producers Aggressively Seek Raw Materials," *Manganese Investment News*, 11 January 2011.

82. IEA, "World Energy Outlook" (Paris: International Energy Agency, 2010).

83. The 2002 IEA scenario estimated that US$3 trillion should be invested to satisfy a predicted demand of 120 million barrels per day in 2030. This was revised down annually to 99 million barrels per day in 2010.

84. Military Advisory Board, "Powering America's Defense: Energy and the Risks to National Security" (Centre for Navy Analyses, 2009).

85. The security implication of climate change are not discussed here: see James Randerson, "UK's Ex-Science Chief Predicts Century of 'Resource' Wars," *The Guardian*, 13 February 2009; UN Secretary General, "Climate Change and its Possible Security Implications" (New York: United Nations, 2009). For example, conflicts in Darfur were often interpreted in light of climate change: Stephan Faris, "The Real Roots of Darfur," *The Atlantic Monthly*, April 2007.

86. See Stephen Pelletiere, *Iraq and the International Oil System: Why America Went to War in the Gulf* (Wesport, CT: Praeger, 2001).

87. See for example the claim that "Oil is the "trophy" of US-NATO led wars" and that the NATO "military campaign directed against Libya is intent upon excluding China from North Africa," a claim that was relayed in some media such as the RT (previously Russia Today) television network: Michel Chossudovsky, *"Operation Libya" And the Battle for Oil: Redrawing the Map of Africa* (Centre for Research on Globalization, 9 March 2011: http://www.globalresearch.ca/index.php?context=va&aid=23605, accessed 18 March 2011.

88. David Pierson, "Libyan Strife Exposes China's Risks in Global Quest for Oil," *Los Angeles Times*, 9 March 2011.

89. Yi-huan Lang and Li-mao Wang, "Russian Energy Geopolitic Strategy and the Prospects of Sino-Russia Energy Cooperation," *Resources Science* 29, no. 5 (2007); Pak K. Lee, "China's Quest for Oil Security: Oil (Wars) in the Pipeline?," *Pacific Review* 18, no. 2 (2005).

90. See Leslie Hook, "China Reins in Rare Earth Exports," *Financial Times*, 19 October 2010.

91. Klare, *Rising Powers, Shrinking Planet: The New Geopolitics of Energy*.

92. On the Arctic, see Eric Posner, "The new race for the Arctic." *Wall Street Journal*, 3 August 2007: http://online.wsj.com/article/SB11861091588668 7045.html?mod=googlenews_wsj, accessed 31 May 2011.

93. C.J. Chivers, "Russia Plants Underwater Flag at North Pole," *New York Times*, 2 August 2007.

94. For example on "Chindia," see Nancy Macdonald, "So Much for 'Chindia.' Why China and India Are Not-So-Friendly Neighbours," *MacLeans*, 23

September 2010.; on other regions, see Klare, *Rising Powers, Shrinking Planet: The New Geopolitics of Energy.*

95. Appadurai (ed.) *The Social Life of Things: Commodities in Cultural Perspective*; E. Swyngedouw, "Modernity and Hybridity: Nature, Regeneracionismo, and the Production of the Spanish Waterscape, 1890–1930," *Annals of the Association of American Geographers* 89, no. 3 (1999); Zimmermann, *World Resources and Industries; a Functional Appraisal of the Availability of Agricultural and Industrial Materials.*

96. Habibollah Atarodi, *Great Powers, Oil and the Kurds in Mosul: Southern Kurdistan/Northern Iraq, 1910–1925* (Lanham, MD: University Press of America, 2003).

97. Turner, "Political Ecology and the Moral Dimensions of 'Resource Conflicts:' The Case of Farmer-Herder Conflicts in the Sahel."

98. Dalby, *Environmental Security*; Dalby, *Security and Environmental Change.*

3. OIL

1. Oil's strategic importance for military forces is barely a century old. It was only in the 1910s that navies started to be converted from coal to oil, and the first military uses of cars and tanks were frequently failures due to mechanical breakdowns and poor roads. Sonia Shah, *Crude: The History of Oil* (New York: Seven Stories, 2004).

2. Daniel Yergin, *The Prize: The Epic Quest for Oil, Money and Power* (New York: Free Press, 1993).

3. Maritime bottlenecks include, in ranking order of importance, Hormuz, Malacca, Bab el-Mandab, Bosphorus, Suez, and Panama: Jean-Paul Rodrigue, "Straits, Passages and Chokepoints. A Maritime Geostrategy of Petroleum Distribution," *Cahiers de Géographie du Québec* 48, no. 135 (2004).

4. The number of wars declined from fifty-two in 1992 to twenty-nine in 2003, and until 2006 had stabilised at thirty-two: Harbom and Wallensteen, "Armed Conflict, 1989–2006."

5. Michael L. Ross, "Blood Barrels," *Foreign Affairs* (2008).

6. RFI, "Kadhafi Opponents and Loyalists Battle for Oil Sites," *Radio France Internationale*, 4 March 2011.

7. Death tolls vary according to sources as well as types and circumstances between combatant deaths, battle deaths including civilians, and war deaths including victims of hunger and diseases. Estimates for Iran-Iraq are 664,500 for battle deaths and a range from 0.6 to 1.2 million for war deaths; for Biafra, 75,000 for battle deaths and a range of 0.5 to 2 million for war deaths; for Southern Sudan, 55,600 for battle deaths and a range of 1 to 2 million for war deaths; see Bethany Ann Lacina and Nils Petter Gleditsch, "Monitoring Trends in Global Combat: A New Dataset of Battle Deaths," *European Jour-*

nal of Population 21, no. 2–3 (2005); see also http://users.erols.com/ mwhite28/warstat2.htm, accessed 19 June 2009.

8. For an example of such Chinese scholarship, see Shuqin Gao, "The Factor "Natural Resources" in the Transformation of Global Geopolitics and Geo-Economy," *Resources Science* 31, no. 2 (2009).

9. Lang and Wang, "Russian Energy Geopolitic Strategy and the Prospects of Sino-Russia Energy Cooperation"; Li-mao Wang and Hongqiang Li, "Cooperation and Competition of Oil and Gas Resources Between China and its Neighboring Countries and its Impacts on Geopolitics," *Resources Science* 31, no. 10 (2009).

10. Shiv Kumar Verma, "Energy Geopolitics and Iran-Pakistan-India Gas Pipeline," *Energy Policy* 35, no. 6 (2007).

11. Ze-min Jiang, "Reflections on Energy Issues in China," *Journal of Shanghai Jiaotong University* 13, no. 3 (2008).

12. E.S. Downs, "The Fact and Fiction of Sino-African Energy Relations," *China Security* 3, no. 3 (2007); J.G. Frynas and M. Paulo, "A New Scramble for African Oil? Historical, Political, and Business Perspectives," *African Affairs* 106, no. 423 (2007).

13. Such as Western oil companies' resistance to a country-by-country disclosure of tax payments by resource extraction companies listed on US stock markets, required by the US Dodd-Frank Wall Street Reform and Consumer Protection Act (Pub.L. 111–203, H.R. 4173, section 1504), even if the two largest Chinese oil companies were listed in New York, and their support for the Extractive Industries Transparency Initiative. See Theodore H. Moran, "Promoting Universal Transparency in Extractive Industries: How and Why?" (Washington, DC: Center for Global Development, 2011).

14. Technically, Western and Chinese companies still work on mostly different types of projects, with Western companies focusing on more technologically complex projects, such as deep-water fields, while Chinese companies have initially focused on "politically sensitive" projects. Moreover, whereas companies compete fiercely for the operatorship of oil projects, they frequently collaborate to raise capital and address political risks. A likely example is that of Chad, where Chinese companies will probably come to rely on the US company-led consortium (which itself includes a Malaysian company, Petronas) to export excess oil from its fields in Bongor, and possibly Lake Chad. The US-led consortium could welcome such reliance as its own oil fields around Doba are already (and prematurely) declining.

15. Suzana Sawyer, "Fictions of Sovereignly: Of Prosthetic Petro-Capitalism, Neoliberal States, and Phantom-Like Citizens in Ecuador," *Journal of Latin American Anthropology* 6, no. 1 (2006).

16. Anna-Karin Hurtig and Miguel San Sebastián, "Geographical Differences in Cancer Incidence in the Amazon Basin of Ecuador in Relation to Resi-

dence Near Oil Fields," *International Journal of Epidemiology* 31 (2002). Opposite views are expressed and available on Texaco's web site, see for example an article co-written by a "Risk Management Resources" contractor and made available on http://www.texaco.com/sitelets/ecuador/docs/2007_oem_article.pdf.

17. S. Sawyer, *Crude Chronicles: Indigenous Politics, Multinational Oil, and Neoliberalism in Ecuador* (Durham, NC: Duke University Press, 2004).

18. I acknowledge the use of databases from the following studies: Ross, "A Closer Look at Oil, Diamonds, and Civil War" for an explanation of the oil rents per capita used throughout this article. For oil location, see P. Lujala, J.K. Rød and N. Thieme, "Fighting Over Oil: Introducing a New Dataset," *Conflict Management and Peace Science* 24, no. 3 (2007). For conflict location, see Halvard Buhaug and Scott Gates, "The Geography of Civil War," *Journal of Peace Research* 39, no. 4 (2002). "Oil rent" is used as shorthand for "fuel rents" that include all hydrocarbons, see Ross above.

19. The overlapping of oil field regions and the 9/11 terrorist attacks in the US is an example (see Figure 3.1). The attacks did not directly relate to oil exploitation in the US. However, links were widely drawn between US oil "imperialism" in Saudi Arabia and the attacks, and they echoed some of the rationale provided by Al Qaeda (N.J. Jhaveri, "Petroimperialism: US Oil Interests and the Iraq War," *Antipode* 36, no. 1 [2004]) while the intervention in Iraq falsely associated with 9/11 by the US and British governments was instrumented to access Iraqi oil fields, see Greg Muttit, *Fuel on Fire: Oil and Politics in Occupied Iraq* (London: Bodley Head, 2011).

20. This selection is based on a review of the literature, but does not claim to be exhaustive. For example, did the separatist conflict in Northern Ireland relate to oil? Most likely not, and it is therefore excluded. But links with oil and Scottish nationalism, active oil exploration in Northern Ireland, IRA support from oil-producing Libya, and the United Kingdom's oil producer status cannot be entirely ruled out without detailed field work and archival research: Milton J. Esman, "Scottish Nationalism, North Sea Oil, and the British Response" in Milton J. Esman (ed.) *Ethnic Conflict in the Western World* (Ithaca, NY: Cornell University Press, 1977); A.E. Griffith, "The Search for Petroleum in Northern Ireland," *Geological Society* 12, no. 213–22 (1983); J. Soule, "Problems in Applying Counterterrorism to Prevent Terrorism: Two Decades of Violence in Northern Ireland Reconsidered," *Studies in Conflict and Terrorism* 12, no. 1 (1989).

21. Conflicts in the Niger Delta are only accounted for in one year, 2004, with the Niger Delta People's Volunteer Force (NDPVF) insurrection. Three further conflicts are identified but unaccounted for: two "non-state conflicts"—in 2004 between the NDPVF and the Niger Delta Vigilantes (NDV)

over oil bunkering and state elections, and in 2003 between Ijaw and Itsekiri groups over "Host Community Status" for compensation from oil firms—and one "one-sided violence" conflict: the government's Mobile Police killing of eighty villagers, some of them protesting at a Shell flow station in Umuechem, Rivers State, in 1990: UCDP, *Uppsala Conflict Data Program, UCDP Database: www.Ucdp.Uu.Se/Database, Uppsala University* (2008), accessed 18 June 2009.

22. Indra de Soysa and Eric Neumayer, "Resource Wealth and the Risk of Civil War Onset: Results from a New Dataset of Natural Resource Rents, 1970–1999," *Conflict Management and Peace Science* 24 (2007); Michael L. Ross, *The Curse of Oil Wealth* (forthcoming).

23. Lujala, Rød and Thieme, "Fighting over Oil: Introducing a New Dataset"; Lujala, "Deadly Combat over Natural Resources: Gems, Petroleum, Drugs, and the Severity of Armed Civil Conflict."

24. The periods considered by these studies vary, from 1946–2006 for the longest—Matthias Basedau and Jann Lay, "Resource Curse or Rentier State? The Ambiguous Effects of Oil Wealth and Oil Dependence on Violent Conflict," *Journal of Peace Research* (2009).—to 1985–99 for the shortest: Fjelde, "Buying Peace? Oil Wealth, Corruption and Civil War, 1985—99." See also K.M. Morrison, "Oil, Non-Tax Revenue, and the Redistributional Foundations of Regime Stability," *International Organization* 63 (2009); Ross, *The Curse of Oil Wealth*.

25. Fearon, "Primary Commodities Exports and Civil War"; Ross, "A Closer Look at Oil, Diamonds, and Civil War."

26. Basedau and Lay, "Resource Curse or Rentier State? The Ambiguous Effects of Oil Wealth and Oil Dependence on Violent Conflict"; Christa N. Brunnschweiler and Erwin H. Bulte, "Natural Resources and Violent Conflict: Resource Abundance, Dependence and the Onset of Civil Wars," in *CER-ETH-Center of Economic Research at ETH Zurich, Working Paper No. 08/78* (2008) argue that the apparent link between oil dependence and war is the result of the increasing effect of war on oil dependence.

27. Lujala, "The Spoils of Nature: Armed Civil Conflict and Rebel Access to Natural Resources."

28. Lujala, Rød, and Thieme, "Fighting over Oil: Introducing a New Dataset."

29. Schollaert and Demuynck 2008; Dube and Vargas 2007.

30. Miguel, Satyanath and Sergenti, "Economic Shocks and Civil Conflict: An Instrumental Variables Approach"; Benjamin Smith, *Hard Times in the Lands of Plenty. Oil Politics in Iran and Indonesia* (Ithaca, NY: Cornell University Press, 2007).

31. Ross, "A Closer Look at Oil, Diamonds, and Civil War."

32. John James Quinn and Ryan T. Conway, "The Mineral Resource Curse in Africa: What Role Does Majority State Ownership Play?" (paper presented

at the Center for the Study of African Economies (CSAE) conference 2008, Oxford, 16–18 March2008); E. Weinthal and P.J. Luong, "Combating the Resource Curse: An Alternative Solution to Managing Mineral Wealth," *Perspectives on Politics* 4, no. 1 (2006).

33. According to a survey of "terrorist" and rebel attacks on the petroleum sector between 1968 and 2001, leftist and separatist groups accounted each for a third of attacks and apparent motives were opposition to current political regime and to foreign companies' involvement in oil, followed by economic motives. Ashild Kjok and Brynjar Lia, "Terrorism and Oil—an Explosive Mixture? A Survey of Terrorist and Rebel Attacks on Petroleum Infrastructure 1968–1999," in *FFI/Rapport-2001/04031* (Kjeller: Norwegian Defence Research Establishment, 2001).

34. A.H. Gelb, *Oil Windfalls: Blessing or Curse?* (Oxford University Press, 1988); Ross, *The Curse of Oil Wealth*.

35. Ross, *The Curse of Oil Wealth*. The effects of oil abundance are more open to debate, and oil wealth—at least in terms of endowment—may not negatively affect economic growth: C.N. Brunnschweiler, "Cursing the Blessings? Natural Resource Abundance, Institutions, and Economic Growth," *World Development* 36, no. 3 (2008). Resource abundance can influence economic performance positively or negatively through different channels; for a recent review see P. Stevens and E. Dietsche, "Resource Curse: An Analysis of Causes, Experiences and Possible Ways Forward," *Energy Policy* 36, no. 1 (2008).

36. The claim that states are "weak" when they nationalise or repudiate contracts is a matter of perspective. One may also assert that they are politically "strong" in the face of foreign investors and governments. Success in renegotiating disadvantageous fiscal terms over resource contracts is a classic example. Yet political strength and bureaucratic weakness can result in a dangerous overstretch.

37. Humphreys, "Natural Resources, Conflict, and Conflict Resolution: Uncovering the Mechanisms."

38. Lujala, "The Spoils of Nature: Armed Civil Conflict and Rebel Access to Natural Resources"; Ross, "A Closer Look at Oil, Diamonds, and Civil War."

39. O. Manzano and R. Rigobon, "Resource Curse or Debt Overhang?" *Natural Resources, Neither Curse Nor Destiny* (2006).

40. The effects of state weakness on the oil project cycle would depend in part on the financial schedule, through such variables as signature bonuses, share of cost oil, price capping, oil prices, and depletion rates.

41. See for example Miguel, Satyanath and Sergenti, "Economic Shocks and Civil Conflict: An Instrumental Variables Approach."

42. Thomas Demuynck and Arne Schollaert, "International Commodity Prices and the Persistence of Civil Conflict," Working Papers of the Faculty of

Economics and Business Administration, Ghent University, Belgium, 2008. Oeindrila Dube and Juan F. Vargas, "Commodity Price Shocks and Civil Conflict: Evidence from Colombia" (Cambridge, MA: Harvard Kennedy School, 2008).

43. Ross, *The Curse of Oil Wealth.*
44. Ross, "A Closer Look at Oil, Diamonds, and Civil War."
45. Smith, *Hard Times in the Lands of Plenty: Oil Politics in Iran and Indonesia.*
46. Ricardo Soares de Oliviera, *Oil and Politics in the Gulf of Guinea* (London: Hurst, 2007).
47. Gedicks, *The New Resource Wars: Native and Environmental Struggles Against Multinational Corporations*; Klare, *Rising Powers, Shrinking Planet: The New Geopolitics of Energy*; Ross, *The Curse of Oil Wealth*; M.J. Watts, "Righteous Oil?: Human Rights, the Oil Complex and Corporate Social Responsibility," *Annual Review of Environment and Resources* 30 (2005); C. Williams, "Environmental Victimization and Violence," *Aggression and Violent Behavior* 1, no. 3 (1996).
48. The presence of a military base of a permanent member of the UN Security Council decreases the risk of war for oil countries: Basedau and Lay, "Resource Curse or Rentier State? The Ambiguous Effects of Oil Wealth and Oil Dependence on Violent Conflict."
49. Luong and Weinthal, "Rethinking the Resource Curse: Ownership Structure, Institutional Capacity, and Domestic Constraints."
50. Some national companies may have worse records due to more limited capacity and external pressure; see the case of Ecuador with regard to environmental impact. Maria Sophia Steyn, "Oil Politics in Ecuador and Nigeria: A Perspective from Environmental History of the Struggles between Ethnic Minority Groups, Multinational Oil Companies and National Governments" (University of the Free State, 2003).
51. Many extractive companies also prefer to employ personnel not originating from the local area, even if local people are qualified, to better control labor risks such as strikes, community relations, and "criminal" activities.
52. Okechukwu Ibeanu, "Oiling the Friction: Environmental Conflict Management in the Niger Delta, Nigeria," *Environmental Change & Human Security Project Report* Issue 6, Summer 2000 (2000); Sawyer, *Crude Chronicles: Indigenous Politics, Multinational Oil, and Neoliberalism in Ecuador*; Williams, "Environmental Victimization and Violence."
53. The periods considered by these studies vary, from 1946–2006 for the longest—Basedau and Lay, "Resource Curse or Rentier State? The Ambiguous Effects of Oil Wealth and Oil Dependence on Violent Conflict"—to 1985–1999 for the shortest: Fjelde, "Buying Peace? Oil Wealth, Corruption and Civil War, 1985—99"; see also Morrison, "Oil, Non-Tax Revenue, and the

Redistributional Foundations of Regime Stability"; Ross, *The Curse of Oil Wealth.*

54. For example, Deputy Defence Secretary Paul Wolfowitz stressed to Congress: "There's a lot of money to pay for this [reconstruction] ...on a rough recollection, the oil revenues of [Iraq] ... could bring between US$50 and US$100 billion over the course of the next two or three years...We're dealing with a country that can really finance its own reconstruction, and relatively soon." House Committee on Appropriations Hearing on a Supplemental War Regulation, 27 March 2003.

55. Le Billon, "The Political Ecology of War: Natural Resources and Armed Conflicts."

56. The Italian company was eager to hasten the departure of the French to access Algerian oil. See Aissaoui, *Algeria: The Political Economy of Oil and Gas.* On the politics and corruption related to the Algerian oil sector, see Hocine Malti, *Histoire Secrète du Pétrole Algérien* (Paris: La Découverte, 2010).

57. Patrice Yengo, *La Guerre Civile du Congo-Brazzaville* (Paris: Karthala, 2006).

58. P. Englebert and J. Ron, "Primary Commodities and War: Congo-Brazzaville's Ambivalent Resource Curse," *Comparative Politics* 37, no. 1 (2004), and interview with former President Lissouba, London, 2001. Elf's bank, FIBA, facilitated Lissouba's payments for arms until the fall of his government. Antoine Glaser, Stephen Smith and Maria Mallagardis, "Un Rôle d'Intermédiaire dans le Conflit Congolais. Quand le Président Lissouba avait Besoin d'Armes Contre les Rebelles de Sassou N'guesso, il s'Adressait à la Fiba," *Libération*, 4 February 1998.

59. J.G. Frynas, "The Oil Boom in Equatorial Guinea," *African Affairs* 103, no. 413 (2004); A. Roberts, *The Wonga Coup: Guns, Thugs and a Ruthless Determination to Create Mayhem in an Oil-Rich Corner of Africa* (New York: PublicAffairs, 2006); Geoffrey Wood, "Business and Politics in a Criminal State: The Case of Equatorial Guinea," *African Affairs* 103, no. 413 (2004).

60. Corrupt practices were facilitated by Riggs Bank in Washington: Global Witness, "Undue Diligence: How Banks Do Business with Corrupt Regimes" (London: Global Witness, 2009). The American bank managed 60 accounts for senior Equatoguinean government members totaling between US$400 and 600 millions, created personal accounts and offshore shell companies for Obiang and his family members, accepted US$13 million in cash, and allowed transfers between private and public purpose accounts as well as cash deposits for transfer to offshore secret accounts. The Riggs, accounts manager also diverted money from Equatorial Guinea funds for his personal benefit, while the US regulator in charge "failed" to take action and was later hired by Riggs.

61. "Profile: Ely Calil: Smelly, the Missing Essence in a Coup Plot," *Sunday Times*, 5 December 2004, http://www.timesonline.co.uk/tol/comment/

article399180.ece, accessed 29 June 2009. Govan, Fiona, "Ely Calil: I Didn't Mastermind Equatorial Guinea Plot," *Daily Telegraph*, 7 July 2008, http://www.telegraph.co.uk/news/worldnews/2265114/Ely-Calil-I-didnt-mastermind-Equatorial-Guinea-plot.html, accessed 29 June 2009. In the *Telegraph* interview, Calil acknowledges that Mann was to provide protection for Moto's return in Equatorial Guinea, but denies his intention to support a coup. He suggests that the plan was to go overland from Gabon to the mainland part of Equatorial Guinea and gather supporters from Moto's home areas. Such a plan would probably have been more likely to end in a full-scale civil war than a coup.

62. Kjok and Lia, "Terrorism and Oil—an Explosive Mixture? A Survey of Terrorist and Rebel Attacks on Petroleum Infrastructure 1968–1999," based on ITERATE database. The number of attacks is likely to have sharply increased in the following decade, with 469 attacks in Iraq alone between 12 June 2003 and 27 March 2008: Iraq Pipeline Watch, IAGS and OGI-TM, www.iags.org/iraqpipelinewatch, accessed 15 June 2009. Owing to liabilities, and to benefit from "force majeure" contractual clauses dispensing a company from penalties, some accidents have allegedly been blamed on sabotage.

63. For a discussion of the broader legal context, see David Arce Rojas, "Petroleum and the Humanitarian Law," *International Law: Revista Colombiana de Derecho Internacional*, no. 3 (2004).

64. Interview with the president of an oil distributors federation, Bogotá, May 2009.

65. Human Rights Watch, "The Warri Crisis: Fueling Violence" (New York: Human Rights Watch, 2003). The term "bunkering" refers to the refueling of vessels at sea, but is used in Nigeria to refer to all forms of oil theft. Kombo Mason Braide, *The Political Economy of Illegal Bunkering in Nigeria* (Niger Delta Congress, 2003, http://www.nigerdeltacongress.com/particles/political_economy_of_illegal_bun.htm, accessed 29 June 2009. The term and its association with illegal armed groups are also instrumented by some government officials to explain away economic performances, through its extension into sabotage and other reasons undermining production: Hanson Okoh, "Nigeria Loses US$60 Billion Oil Revenue to Bunkering," *Ground Report*, 15 July 2008.

66. For a review of technical aspects, see Zhendi Wang and Scott A. Stout, *Oil Spills Environmental Forensics* (New York: Academic Press, 2007).

67. N. Alahmad, "The Politics of Oil and State Survival in Iraq (1991–2003): Beyond the Rentier Thesis," *Constellations* 14, no. 4 (2007); T. Dunning and L. Wirpsa, "Oil and the Political Economy of Conflict in Colombia and Beyond: A Linkages Approach," *Geopolitics* 9, no. 1 (2004); A. Ikelegbe, "The

Economy of Conflict in the Oil Rich Niger Delta Region of Nigeria," *Nordic Journal of African Studies* 14, no. 2 (2005); J. Pearce, "Policy Failure and Petroleum Predation: The Economics of Civil War Debate Viewed 'from the War-Zone,'" *Government and Opposition* 40, no. 2 (2005); N. Richani, "Multinational Corporations, Rentier Capitalism, and the War System in Colombia," *Latin American Politics and Society* 47, no. 3 (2005); Ross, "Oil, Drugs, and Diamonds: How Do Natural Resources Vary in Their Impact on Civil War? "

68. See Le Billon and Cervantes, "Oil Prices, Scarcity and Geographies of War."

69. The development of onshore oil fields was delayed by ongoing conflicts, but the little onshore infrastructure that existed was not massively affected, even when UNITA controlled oil infrastructures in Soyo province for two months in early 1993. Attacks on offices and vehicles occurred when UNITA withdrew before a government army assault, and a diesel tank and electricity generator were destroyed. Yet the rebel movement did not carry out its threat of destruction of the Kwanda port and offshore supply base through which about 40 percent of Angolan crude transited, mostly because it sought to avoid upsetting the US oil company and US government, its former key external source of support: CTC, "Angola Situation Report," (1993).

70. J.G. Frynas and K. Mellahi, "Political Risks as Firm-Specific (Dis) Advantages: Evidence on Transnational Oil Firms in Nigeria," *Thunderbird International Business Review* 45, no. 5 (2003).

71. Massimo Guidolin and Eliana La Ferrara, "Diamonds Are Forever, Wars Are Not—Is Conflict Bad for Private Firms?" *American Economic Review* 97, no. 5 (2007).

72. Oil dependence represented about of 50 percent of GDP, 90 percent of export earnings, and more than 80 percent of fiscal revenues in the 2000s.

73. The first two booms resulted from the 1973 Yom Kippur and 1980 Iran-Iraq wars; the third boom between 2003 and 2008 was more progressive and resulted in part from fast rising demand and supply tightened notably by particularly low investments during the previous decade and a combination of political crises in Venezuela, Iraq, Nigeria, and Iran.

74. Whereas the top 2 percent in the population earned the same total income as the bottom 17 percent in 1970, by 2000 it was equivalent to the bottom 55 percent of the population: see Xavier Sala-i-Martin and Arvind Subramanian, "Addressing the Natural Resource Curse: An Illustration from Nigeria," WP/03/139, (Washington, DC: International Monetary Fund, 2003).

75. World Bank Indicators and 2009 Country Brief.

76. Watts, "Antinomies of Community: Some Thoughts on Geography, Resources and Empire." Oil was not the only factor; see Abu Bakar Bah, *Breakdown*

and *Reconstitution: Democracy, the Nation-State, and Ethnicity in Nigeria* (Lanham, MD: Lexington Books, 2005).

77. Bah, *Breakdown and Reconstitution: Democracy, the Nation-State, and Ethnicity in Nigeria.*

78. Ibid.; Jedrzej George Frynas, *Oil in Nigeria: Conflict and Litigation Between Oil Companies and Village Communities* (Hamburg: LIT Verlag, 2000).

79. Tekena Tamuno, "Separatist Agitations in Nigeria since 1914," *Journal of Modern African Studies* 8, no. 4 (1970).

80. Augustine Ikelegbe, "Beyond the Threshold of Civil Struggle: Youth Militancy and the Militarization of the Resource Conflicts in the Niger Delta Region of Nigeria," *African Study Monographs* 27, no. 3 (2006); U. Ukiwo, "From "Pirates" To "Militants": A Historical Perspective on Anti-State and Anti-Oil Company Mobilization among the Ijaw of Warri, Western Niger Delta," *African Affairs* 106, no. 425 (2007).

81. Sofiri Joab-Peterside, "On the Militarization of Nigeria's Niger Delta: The Genesis of Ethnic Militia in Rivers States, Nigeria," in *Niger Delta Economies of Violence Working Paper No. 21* (Berkeley: 2007).

82. Released from prison after a counter-coup, Boro fought (and died in suspicious circumstances) on the federal government side in the Biafra war. Jibrin Ibrahim, "Political Transition, Ethnoregionalism, and the 'Power Shift' Debate in Nigeria," *Issue: A Journal of Opinion* 27, no. 1 (1999).

83. The creation of new states was announced on 27 May 1967, and the independence of the Republic of Biafra on 30 May 1967.

84. Augustine Ikelegbe, "Civil Society, Oil and Conflict in the Niger Delta Region of Nigeria: Ramifications of Civil Society for Regional Resource Struggle," *Journal of Modern African Studies* 39, no. 3 (2001); Ukiwo, "From "Pirates" To "Militants": A Historical Perspective on Anti-State and Anti-Oil Company Mobilization among the Ijaw of Warri, Western Niger Delta."

85. For example, the 1978 Land Use Act shifted land ownership from communities to state governors, dispossessing communities from a right of refusal over, or annual land rents, from oil projects, and resulted in low compensation. Frynas, *Oil in Nigeria: Conflict and Litigation Between Oil Companies and Village Communities.*

86. A formal model points at the importance of Nigerian governments' failed coercive policy of relocating the population of the Niger Delta through repression rather than improving local living conditions through environmental mitigation. As a result of conflicts with Delta migrants in other regions, much of the population of the Delta is trapped in a violent and polluted setting, with few livelihood options other than oil "bunkering." See Jean-Paul Azam, "Betting on Displacement: Oil and Strategic Violence in Nigeria," Paper presented at the International Studies Association 50th annual convention, New York, 2009.

87. Joab-Peterside, "On the Militarization of Nigeria's Niger Delta: The Genesis of Ethnic Militia in Rivers States, Nigeria." For a version of the incident from Shell's perspective, see Alan Detheridge and Noble Pepple, "A Response to Frynas," *Third World Quarterly* 19, no. 3 (1998).

88. On the construction of Ogoni identity and its effects on the oil conflict see Ade Isumonah, "The Making of the Ogoni Ethnic Group," *Africa* 74, no. 3, May (2004). On civil society movements in the late 1990s, see Ikelegbe, "Civil Society, Oil and Conflict in the Niger Delta Region of Nigeria: Ramifications of Civil Society for Regional Resource Struggle."

89. Ogoni Bill of Rights, October 1990, http://www.waado.org/nigerian_scholars/archive/docum/ogoni.html, accessed 2 July 2009.

90. Ibeanu, "Oiling the Friction: Environmental Conflict Management in the Niger Delta, Nigeria"; Claude E. Welch, "The Ogoni and Self-Determination: Increasing Violence in Nigeria," *Journal of Modern African Studies* 33, no. 4 (1995). Large-scale violence took the form of the sacking of Ogoni villages by members of the Andoni, Okrika and Ndoki groups allegedly enticed or assisted by government security forces in 1993 and 1994. Concessions were made by state authorities and oil companies, including greater direct revenue allocation (from 1.5 to 3 percent in 1992, and to 13 percent in 1999), the creation of Bayelsa State in 1996 following Ijaw ethnic group demands, and greater community development funding. The federal government and oil companies, in particular Shell, also spend millions of dollars on public relations. Jedrzej George Frynas, "Corporate and State Responses to Anti-Oil Protests in the Niger Delta," *African Affairs* 100, no. 398 (2001).

91. Ken Saro-Wiwa was accused by MOSOP dissidents of having already radicalised the movement and creating a private army through the National Youth Council of Ogoni People Ibeanu, "Oiling the Friction: Environmental Conflict Management in the Niger Delta, Nigeria."

92. Take, for example, the following quote: "In my community, we have a memorandum of understanding (MOU) with the [oil companies] to develop some projects. After a year, nothing was done. The youths decided to hold their management hostage. We went to their company, seized ten of their staff including expatriates. We brought them to the community. After a while, the [oil companies] agreed to go by the MOU. Today, there are some improvements. It is only when the people spring to action [that oil companies are] usually accomplishing their MOU." Cited in Ikelegbe, "Beyond the Threshold of Civil Struggle: Youth Militancy and the Militarization of the Resource Conflicts in the Niger Delta Region of Nigeria."

93. Ibeanu, "Oiling the Friction: Environmental Conflict Management in the Niger Delta, Nigeria."

94. Ikelegbe, "Beyond the Threshold of Civil Struggle: Youth Militancy and the Militarization of the Resource Conflicts in the Niger Delta Region of

Nigeria." One recent survey of youth in Delta and Rivers States suggests that at the individual level higher income, marriage, and immobile assets (e.g., house and farmland) reduce the probability of declaring a willingness to fight, while access to basic amenities, education, and employment as well as belonging to an ethnic majority group increase it: Aderoju Oyefusi, "Oil and the Probability of Rebel Participation among Youths in the Niger Delta of Nigeria," *Journal of Peace Research* 45, no. 4 (2008). At the community level, declared willingness to fight also increases with the number of oil wells in the area and remoteness from the state capital, while better infrastructure decreases it. The presence of government organisation and personal grievances appears less statistically significant.

95. Ikelegbe, "Civil Society, Oil and Conflict in the Niger Delta Region of Nigeria: Ramifications of Civil Society for Regional Resource Struggle." Oil areas did not have the monopoly on youth groups as agents of violence.

96. These "youth" and "militant" groups are often interrelated. For example, from the Ijaw Youth Council (IYC), created in 1998, came the Niger Delta Volunteer Force (NDVF) associated with Rivers State Governor Peter Odily (an Igbo minority member in this Ijaw majority state), and competing Niger Delta Vigilantes (NDV) aligned with the Ijaw Chief Edwin Clark, both groups fighting for the control of bunkering routes and (increasingly less) on behalf of their political patrons.

97. "Bunkering" refers to the refueling of vessels at sea, but is used in Nigeria to refer to all forms of oil theft. Braide, *The Political Economy of Illegal Bunkering in Nigeria*; Joab-Peterside, "On the Militarization of Nigeria's Niger Delta: The Genesis of Ethnic Militia in Rivers States, Nigeria."

98. Human Rights Watch, "The Warri Crisis: Fueling Violence"; M. Watts, "Petro-Insurgency or Criminal Syndicate? Conflict & Violence in the Niger Delta," *Review of African Political Economy* 34, no. 114 (2007).

99. Okoh, "Nigeria Loses US$60 Billion Oil Revenue to Bunkering."

100. Ikelegbe, "Beyond the Threshold of Civil Struggle: Youth Militancy and the Militarization of the Resource Conflicts in the Niger Delta Region of Nigeria."

101. Ibid. The risk of further escalation depends partly on the capacity of militias to counter this and partly on the level of abuses committed by government forces upon local communities and the resultant impact on motivation and recruitment for militias.

102. Floating Production, Storage and Offloading (FPSO) vessels combine production platform and floating oil terminal, thus reducing onshore activities. They have been increasingly used for remote and deep-water oil production. "Observing the Offshore "Bonga" Attack," 27 June 2008, http://www.informationdissemination.net/2008/06/observing-offshore-bonga-attack.html accessed 30 June 2009.

103. "To expunge offshore production from the derivation calculation is to expel Akwa Ibom and Ondo states from the club of oil producers. Their membership of NNDC, including their stout representation at the board of NNDC, would have to be annulled. In the face of such an action, can Mobil continue to operate its offshore fields? Will their Qua Iboe Terminal continue to function? Will the Itsekiris and Ijaws of Delta State allow Chevron to operate their offshore fields from Escravos? How will you tell the restive Ijaws and Ilajes of Ondo State that their modest oil-producing privileges have been severed and still expect Chevron, Conoco, Consolidated Oil, and Cavendish to continue their Western offshore operations? And in the face of all this, how will Obasanjo's campaign train be welcomed in these states come 2003?" Austin Avuru, "The Trouble with Onshore/Offshore Dichotomy" (Niger Delta Congress, undated).

104. Ibid.

105. Such as that of MEND on 19 June 2008 on the Bonga field FPSO located 120 km offshore, which resulted in a three-week shutdown of this 225,000 barrel per day field, cutting about 10 percent of Nigeria's oil production. The MEND commander later declared that this proved its group had the capacity to attack anywhere in the Niger Delta, see Emma Amaize, Kingsley Omonubi and Uduma Kalu, "Nigeria: attack on Bonga—MEND reveals how its men carried out raid," *Vanguard* 28 June 2008.

106. Klare, *Blood and Oil: The Dangers and Consequences of America's Growing Dependency on Imported Petroleum.*

107. I.A. Boal, *Afflicted Powers: Capital and Spectacle in a New Age of War* (London: Verso, 2005); J. Nitzan and S. Bichler, "Bringing Capital Accumulation Back In: The Weapondollar-Petrodollar Coalition-Military Contractors, Oil Companies and Middle East 'Energy Conflicts,'" *Review of International Political Economy* 2, no. 3 (1995).

108. Collier, "Doing Well out of War: An Economic Perspective."

109. Bridge, "Resource Triumphalism: Postindustrial Narratives of Primary Commodity Production": Christopher Cramer, *Civil War Is Not a Stupid Thing. Accounting for Violence in Developing Countries* (London: Hurst, 2006).

110. James D. Sidaway, "What Is in a Gulf? From the 'Arc of Crisis' to the Gulf War," in Simon Dalby and Gearoid O'Tuathail (eds) *Rethinking Geopolitics* (London: Routledge, 1998).

111. Watts, "Righteous Oil?: Human Rights, the Oil Complex and Corporate Social Responsibility."

112. Kobrin, "Diffusion as an Explanation of Oil Nationalization (or the Domino Effect Rides Again)."

113. Watts, "Antinomies of Community: Some Thoughts on Geography, Resources and Empire."

114. Two such examples were the cell phone call of a Niger Delta militant on 27 September 2004 that send crude price over US$50 per barrel, and the historical price peak of US$147.27 per barrel reached on 11 July 2008 a day after Iran tested medium-range missiles: see CNN, "Sizing Up Iran's Oil Threat," 10 July 2008; *Economist*, "Pumping up the Oil Price," 1 October 2004.

4. DIAMONDS

1. Paul Collier and Anke Hoeffler, "On Economic Causes of Civil War," *Oxford Economic Papers* 50 (1998); Global Witness, "Branching Out: Zimbabwe's Resource Colonialism in the Democratic Republic of Congo" (London: Global Witness, 2002); Keen, "The Economic Functions of Violence in Civil Wars"; Mac Ginty, "Looting in the Context of Violent Conflict: A Conceptualisation and Typology"; United Nations, "Report of the Panel of Experts on the Illegal Exploitation of Natural Resources and Other Forms of Wealth of the Democratic Republic of Congo" (New York: United Nations, 2001).

2. See for example Jordana Timerman, "The New Blood Diamonds," *Foreign Policy* (2010). For an in-depth journalistic treatment of diamonds, see Greg Campbell, *Blood Diamonds: Tracing the Deadly Path of the World's Most Precious Stones* (Boulder, CO: Westview Press, 2002); Robert Neil Cooper, "Conflict Goods: The Challenges for Peacekeeping and Conflict Prevention," *International Peacekeeping* 8, no. 3 (2001); Le Billon, "Fatal Transactions: Conflict Diamonds and the (Anti) Terrorist Consumer." On the case of tanzanite, which was purported to be financing al Qaeda according to the *Wall Street Journal*, see Richard A. Schroeder, "Tanzanite as Conflict Gem: Certifying a Secure Commodity Chain in Tanzania," *Geoforum* 41, no. 1 (2010).

3. B. Crossette, "U.N. Chief Faults Reluctance of U.S. To Help in Africa," *New York Times*, 13 May 2000.

4. Interview notes, Angola, July 2001; see also De Boeck, "Garimpeiro Worlds: Digging, Dying and "Hunting" for Diamonds in Angola"; PAC and Global Witness, "Rich Man, Poor Man. Development, Diamonds and Poverty: The Potential for Change in the Artisanal Diamond Fields of Africa" (Ottawa and London: Partnership Africa Canada and Global Witness, 2004).

5. Bridge, "Resource Triumphalism: Postindustrial Narratives of Primary Commodity Production."

6. Ian Bannon and Paul Collier, *Natural Resources and Violent Conflict: Options and Actions* (Washington, DC: World Bank, 2003); Berdal, *Greed and Grievance: Economic Agendas in Civil Wars*; Global Witness, "A Rough Trade. The Role of Companies and Governments in the Angolan Conflict" (London: 1998); Le Billon, "Fatal Transactions: Conflict Diamonds and the (Anti)

Terrorist Consumer"; François Misser and Olivier Vallée, *Les Gemmocraties: L'économie Politique du Diamant Africain* (Paris: Desclée de Brouwer, 1997); Reno, *Corruption and State Politics in Sierra Leone*; Ian Smillie, Lasana Gberie and Ralph Hazleton, "The Heart of the Matter: Sierra Leone, Diamonds and Human Security" (Ottawa: Partnership Africa Canada, 2000).

7. Castree, "Commodity Fetishism, Geographical Imaginations and Imaginative Geographies"; Hartwick, "Geographies of Consumption: A Commodity-Chain Approach"; Neumann, "Moral and Discursive Geographies in the War for Biodiversity in Africa"; M. Watts, "Resource Curse? Governmentality, Oil and Power in the Niger Delta, Nigeria," *Geopolitics* 9, no. 1 (2004).

8. John Barnett (2005); T.J. Bassett, "The Political Ecology of Peasant-Herder Conflicts in the Northern Ivory Coast," *Annals of the Association of American Geographers* 78, no. 3 (1988); Raymond L. Bryant and M.K. Goodman, "Consuming Narratives: The Political Ecology of "Alternative" Consumption," *Transactions of the Institute of British Geographers* 29, no. 3 (2004); Castree, "Commodity Fetishism, Geographical Imaginations and Imaginative Geographies"; Hartwick, "Geographies of Consumption: A Commodity-Chain Approach"; Leslie and Reimer, "Spatializing Commodity Chains"; Neumann, "Moral and Discursive Geographies in the War for Biodiversity in Africa."

9. Related fieldwork included visits of up to five weeks in Angola (1998, 2001), the DRC (2001), Ghana (2003), Sierra Leone (2001, 2006), and South Africa (2001). Interviews were also conducted with industry representatives, public officials, and members of non-governmental organizations (NGOs) in Belgium, Canada, England and France between 1999 and 2006. The research also included participant observation in four policy meetings related to the Kimberley Process Certification Scheme, the international diamond certification scheme set up to prevent the laundering of "conflict diamonds" by the industry.

10. Blomley, "Law, Property, and the Geography of Violence: The Frontier, the Survey, and the Grid"; Cole Harris, "How Did Colonialism Dispossess? Comments from an Edge of Empire," *Annals of the Association of American Geographers* 94, no. 1 (2004); G. Hart, "Denaturalizing Dispossession: Critical Ethnography in the Age of Resurgent Imperialism," *Antipode* 38, no. 5 (2006); David Harvey, *The New Imperialism* (Oxford University Press, 2003); McIlwaine, "Geography and Development: Violence and Crime as Development Issues"; Nancy Lee Peluso and Emily Harwell, "Territory, Custom, and the Cultural Politics of Ethnic War in West Kalimantan, Indonesia," in Nancy Lee Peluso and Michael Watts (eds) *Violent Environments* (Ithaca, NY: Cornell University Press, 2001); Turner, "Political Ecology and the Moral Dimensions of "Resource Conflicts": The Case of Farmer-Herder Conflicts in the Sahel."

11. K. Bakker and G. Bridge, "Material Worlds? Resource Geographies and the Matter of Nature," *Progress in Human Geography* 30, no. 1 (2006); Bridge, "Resource Triumphalism: Postindustrial Narratives of Primary Commodity Production"; Stephen G. Bunker, *Underdeveloping the Amazon: Extraction, Unequal Exchange and the Failure of the Modern State* (Urbana, IL: University of Illinois Press, 1985); Le Billon, "The Political Ecology of War: Natural Resources and Armed Conflicts."

12. These include six of the eight most diamond-dependent countries in the world, all of which are in Sub-Saharan Africa, with Angola, Sierra Leone and the DRC (former Zaire) being the countries most reported as affected by recent diamond wars.

13. Studies of diamond-related conflicts have until recently largely concentrated on the labor, capital, and racial dimensions of the diamond sector (Crush 1994; Zack-Williams 1995), with a focus on late eighteenth century Brazil (Bernstein 1988; Pinto Vallejos 1985) and late nineteenth century struggles over diamond mining in South Africa (Turrell 1981, 1987), the diamond mining and trading activities of De Beers (Newbury 1989; Carstens 2001), and the control of "strategic" industrial diamonds during the Second World War and the Cold War: Peter Carstens, *In the Company of Diamonds: De Beers, Kleinzee, and the Control of a Town* (Athens: Ohio University Press, 2001); R. Dumett, "Africa's Strategic Minerals During the Second World War," *Journal of African History* 26 (1985); C. Newbury, *The Diamond Ring: Business, Politics, and Precious Stones in South Africa, 1867–1947* (Oxford: Clarendon Press, 1989); R. Turrell, "The 1875 Black Flag Revolt on the Kimberley Diamond Fields," *Journal of Southern African Studies* 7, no. 2 (1981); R.V. Turrell, *Capital and Labour on the Kimberley Diamond Fields 1871–1890* (Cambridge University Press, 1987); A.B. Zack-Williams, *Tributors, Supporters and Merchant Capital: Mining and Underdevelopment in Sierra Leone* (Aldershot: Avebury, 1995).

14. Ross, "A Closer Look at Oil, Diamonds, and Civil War."

15. Buhaug and Lujala, "Accounting for Scale: Measuring Geography in Quantitative Studies of Civil War"; Lujala, Gleditsch, and Gilmore, "A Diamond Curse?: Civil War and a Lootable Resource."

16. Source: GDP is constant at US$2,000 from 1960 to 2004, from the World Development Indicators (2005). A multivariate analysis (beyond the scope of this study) would be necessary to assess a specific "diamond influence" on GDP, as well as on inequality and fiscal revenues.

17. The economist Ola Olsson found a negative relationship between economic growth and three diamond indicators (i.e., diamond production as share of GDP as a proxy for dependence, as well as diamond volume and value per square kilometer as proxies for abundance) in the 1990s, see O. Olsson,

"Conflict Diamonds," *Journal of Development Economics* 82, no. 2 (2007). However, this relationship could be spurious, since all diamond exporters with negative economic growth defining this trend were affected by political instability likely to affect both GDP growth and diamond dependence.

18. F. Ng and A. Yeats, "What Can Africa Expect of Its Traditional Exports?" in *Africa Region Working Papers Series No. 26* (Washington, DC: World Bank, 2002).

19. S.J. Khoury, *The Valuation and Investment Merits of Diamonds* (Greenwood, CT: Quorum Books, 1990). Diamond prices fluctuated sharply during the early 1980s and again during 2008–09. De Beers, which cannot react to fluctuations through stock management as it controls only about 40 percent of the rough diamonds market compared with about 70 percent until the late 1990s, shut down its diamond mines for several months in 2008–09, as did many other companies. See Samir Gupta *et al.*, "The Impact of External Forces on Cartel Network Dynamics: Direct Research in the Diamond Industry," *Industrial Marketing Management* 39 (2010).

20. So central that Misser and Vallée, *Les Gemmocraties: L'économie Politique du Diamant Africain*, call them "gemmocracies."

21. Ibid.; Reno, *Corruption and State Politics in Sierra Leone*.

22. Governmentality refers to Foucault's notion of *gouvernementalité*. It is applied here to describe the set of institutions, procedures, analyses and tactics that exercise power over (and derive power from) a resource and populations (dis) associated with it. Forms of governmentality, it is argued here, respond to the socially contextualised materiality and spatiality of resources.

23. Olsson, "Conflict Diamonds"; O. Olsson, "Diamonds Are a Rebel's Best Friend," *The World Economy* 29, no. 8 (2006).

24. Ross, "The Political Economy of the Resource Curse."

25. See Bakker and Bridge, "Material Worlds? Resource Geographies and the Matter of Nature."

26. Defined by Reno, *Corruption and State Politics in Sierra Leone*, in his seminal study of corruption in Sierra Leone.

27. Whilst ADM can be legalized by issuing diamond mining and trading licenses, it is hard to tax directly, largely because high taxes lead to illegal mining and smuggling and it is difficult to control a large number of small operations: Thomas Hentschel, Felix Hruschka, and Michael Priester, "Global Report on Artisanal & Small-Scale Mining" (London: International Institute for Environment and Development, 2002).

28. Victor A.B. Davies, "Diamonds, Poverty and War in Sierra Leone," in G.M. Hilson (ed.) *Small Scale Mining, Rural Subsistence and Poverty in West Africa* (Rugby: Intermediate Technology Publications, 2006); K. Sinding, "The Dynamics of Artisanal and Small-Scale Mining Reform," *Natural Resources Forum* 29 (2005).

29. Artisanal mining is often a seasonal and complementary activity within a household, being most commonly associated with farming and petty trading, see Estelle Levin, "From Poverty and War to Prosperity and Peace? Sustainable Livelihoods and Innovation in Governance of Artisanal Diamond Mining in Kono District, Sierra Leone" (University of British Columbia, 2005). There are also many links between artisanal mining and rural development, see Roy Maconachie and Tony Binns, "'Farming Miners' or 'Mining Farmers'?: Diamond Mining and Rural Development in Post-Conflict Sierra Leone," *Journal of Rural Studies* 23, no. 3 (2007).

30. T. Killick, "The Benefits of Foreign Direct Investment and its Alternatives: An Empirical Exploration," *The Journal of Development Studies* 9, no. 2 (1973).

31. M. Heemskerk, "Do International Commodity Prices Drive Natural Resource Booms? An Empirical Analysis of Small-Scale Gold Mining in Suriname," *Ecological Economics* 39 (2001).

32. PAC and Global Witness, "Rich Man, Poor Man. Development, Diamonds and Poverty: The Potential for Change in the Artisanal Diamond Fields of Africa"; Zack-Williams, *Tributors, Supporters and Merchant Capital: Mining and Underdevelopment in Sierra Leone.*

33. De Boeck, "Garimpeiro Worlds: Digging, Dying and 'Hunting' for Diamonds in Angola"; Richards, "To Fight or to Farm? Agrarian Dimensions of the Mano River Conflicts (Liberia and Sierra Leone)."

34. In the case of Sierra Leone, see Levin, "From Poverty and War to Prosperity and Peace? Sustainable Livelihoods and Innovation in Governance of Artisanal Diamond Mining in Kono District, Sierra Leone."

35. Lujala, Gleditsch, and Gilmore, "A Diamond Curse?: Civil War and a Lootable Resource."

36. Daron Acemoglu, Simon Johnson and James Robinson, "An African Success Story: Botswana," in Dani Rodrik (ed.) *In Search of Prosperity: Analytical Narrative on Economic Growth* (Princeton University Press, 2003); Olsson, "Diamonds Are a Rebel's Best Friend"; Reno, *Corruption and State Politics in Sierra Leone.*; on the case of oil, see Luong and Weinthal, "Rethinking the Resource Curse: Ownership Structure, Institutional Capacity, and Domestic Constraints."

37. Thad Dunning, "Resource Dependence, Economic Performance, and Political Stability," *Journal of Conflict Resolution* 49, no. 4 (2005); Olsson, "Conflict Diamonds."

38. Reno, *Corruption and State Politics in Sierra Leone*; Paul Richards, *Fighting for the Rain Forest: War, Youth & Resources in Sierra Leone, African Issues* (London: International African Institute, 1996); Snyder and Bhavnani, "Diamonds, Blood, and Taxes: A Revenue-Centered Framework for Explaining Political Order."

39. E.H. Bulte, R. Damania and R.T. Deacon, "Resource Intensity, Institutions, and Development," *World Development* 33, no. 7 (2005); J. Isham *et al.*, "The Varieties of Resource Experience: Natural Resource Export Structures and the Political Economy of Economic Growth," *The World Bank Economic Review* 19, no. 2 (2005).

40. Snyder and Bhavnani, "Diamonds, Blood, and Taxes: A Revenue-Centered Framework for Explaining Political Order"; see also Lujala, Gleditsch, and Gilmore, "A Diamond Curse?: Civil War and a Lootable Resource." The terms "point" and "diffuse" refer to both Euclidian spaces of resource location, and socially constructed spaces within which political economies and techniques of exploitation are concentrating or diffusing access to resources and their revenues. Thus not only is the physical location of resources important, but also the materiality and modes of production, regulation, and consumption shaping their broader spatiality. See Le Billon, "The Political Ecology of War: Natural Resources and Armed Conflicts."

41. For example, a dataset of worldwide diamond deposit locations (see Figure 1A, B) enables a spatially disaggregated assessment of the effects of diamond deposits and exploitation on the likelihood of civil war during the 1945 to 2002 period, see Lujala, Gleditsch and Gilmore, "A Diamond Curse?: Civil War and a Lootable Resource."

42. Ibid.

43. Le Billon, "Diamond Wars? Conflict Diamonds and Geographies of Resource Wars." This pattern is largely confirmed by examining the characteristics of these countries in the year preceding the start of hostilities (see USGS *Minerals Yearbooks* for 1974, 1988, 1990, 1996). Exceptions are Liberia, with lower diamond abundance; Namibia, with industrial exploitation; and Angola, whose diamond sector was still largely dominated by industrial exploitation until the early 1980s.

44. Dunning, "Resource Dependence, Economic Performance, and Political Stability"; P.K. Hall, "The Diamond Fields of Sierra Leone" (Freetown: Geological Survey of Sierra Leone, 1968); Reno, *Corruption and State Politics in Sierra Leone*.

45. The initial contract was unfavourable to Botswana and was renegotiated by the government: interview with former Botswana President Festus Mogae, February 2009.

46. Maria and Moortaza Jiwanji Sarraf, "Beating the Resource Curse—the Case of Botswana," (Washington, DC: Environmental Economics Series, World Bank Environmental Department, 2001).

47. R. Love, "Drought, Dutch Disease and Controlled Transition in Botswana Agriculture," *Journal of Southern African Studies* 20, no. 1 (1994).

48. Dunning, "Resource Dependence, Economic Performance, and Political Stability."

49. K. Good, "Resource Dependency and Its Consequences: The Costs of Botswana's Shining Gems," *Journal of Contemporary African Studies* 23, no. 1 (2005); Ian Taylor and Gladys Mokhawa, "Not Forever: Botswana, Conflict Diamonds and the Bushmen," *African Affairs* 102 (2003); UNDP, "Human Development Report" (New York: United Nations Development Programme, 2006).

50. David Keen, *Conflict and Collusion in Sierra Leone* (Oxford: James Currey, 2005); Reno, *Corruption and State Politics in Sierra Leone*; M. Silberfein, "The Geopolitics of Conflict and Diamonds in Sierra Leone," *Geopolitics* 9, no. 1 (2004).

51. Fred M. Hayward, "The Development of a Radical Political Organization in the Bush: A Case Study of Sierra Leone," *Canadian Journal of African Studies* 6, no. 1 (1972).

52. Reno, *Corruption and State Politics in Sierra Leone*; Richards, "To Fight or to Farm?: Agrarian Dimensions of the Mano River Conflicts (Liberia and Sierra Leone)."

53. Hayward, "The Development of a Radical Political Organization in the Bush: A Case Study of Sierra Leone"; Reno, *Corruption and State Politics in Sierra Leone*.

54. H.L. van der Laan, *The Sierra Leone Diamonds: An Economic Study Covering the Years 1952–1961* (Oxford University Press, 1965).

55. J.R. Cartwright, *Political Leadership in Sierra Leone* (Toronto University Press, 1978).

56. Reno, *Corruption and State Politics in Sierra Leone*.

57. This largely consisted in restarting industrial diamond mining with the help of dubious foreign investors and approval of international creditors anxious to replenish depleted state coffers, and using the military to crackdown on illegal artisanal mining. The crackdown contributed to mobilisation against Momoh's regime.

58. PAC, "Diamond Industry Annual Review: Sierra Leone 2004" (Ottawa: Partnership Africa Canada, 2004); J. Williams *et al.*, "Sierra Leone Diamond Policy Study" (AMCO-Robertson Mineral Services Ltd, 2002); Zack-William, *Tributors, Supporters and Merchant Capital: Mining and Underdevelopment in Sierra Leone*.

59. The RUF was supported by the Liberian warlord Charles Taylor, as well as Burkina Faso and Libya. Lansana Gberie, *A Dirty War in West Africa. The Revolutionary United Front and the Destruction of Sierra Leone* (London: Hurst, 2005).

60. Keen, *Conflict and Collusion in Sierra Leone*; J.B. Riddell, "Internal and External Forces Acting Upon Disparities in Sierra Leone," *Journal of Modern African Studies* 23, no. 3 (1985).

61. S. Bredeloup, "Les Territoires de L'Identité. Le Territoire, Lien ou Frontière?" in S. Bredeloup *et al.*, *Territoires du Diamant et Migrants du Fleuve Sénégal (Diamond Territories and Migrants from the Senegal River)* (Paris: L'Harmattan, 1999); Hugues Leclercq, "Le rôle économique du diamant dans le conflit congolais," in, Laurent Monnier, Bogumil Jewsiewicki and Gauthier de Villers (eds) *Chasse au Diamant au Congo/Zaïre* (Paris: Editions L'Harmattan, 2001); Newbury, *The Diamond Ring: Business, Politics, and Precious Stones in South Africa, 1867–1947.*

62. Diamond prices depend on four major characteristics: colour, clarity, cut, and carat (weight). Interview with diamond mine director and former diamond reforms consultant Jan Katelaar, Kono, December 2006.

63. B. Harden, "Africa's Diamond Wars," *New York Times*, 6 April 2000.

64. Louis Goreux, "Conflict Diamonds" (Washington, DC: African Region Working Paper Series, World Bank, 2001); PAC and Global Witness, "Rich Man, Poor Man. Development, Diamonds and Poverty: The Potential for Change in the Artisanal Diamond Fields of Africa."

65. Ross, "How Do Natural Resources Influence Civil War? Evidence from Thirteen Cases."

66. Leclercq, "Le Rôle Économique du Diamant dans le Conflit Congolais."

67. Olivier Vallée and François Misser, *Les Gemmocraties: L'économie Politique du Diamant Africain* (Paris: Desclée de Brouwer, 1997).

68. James Scott, *Domination and the Arts of Resistance: Hidden Transcripts* (New Haven, CT: Yale University Press, 1990).

69. Hayward, "The Development of a Radical Political Organization in the Bush: A Case Study of Sierra Leone."

70. Keen, *Conflict and Collusion in Sierra Leone*; Reno, *Corruption and State Politics in Sierra Leone.*

71. William Reno, "Political Networks in a Failing State. The Roots and Future of Violent Conflict in Sierra Leone," *Internationale Politik und Gesellschaft* 2 (2003).

72. Ross, "What Do We Know About Natural Resources and Civil Wars?"

73. Marcus Power, "Patrimonialism & Petro-Diamond Capitalism: Peace, Geopolitics & the Economics of War in Angola," *Review of African Political Economy* 28, no. 90 (2001).

74. Macartan Humphreys and Jeremy Weinstein, "What the Fighters Say: A Survey of Ex-Combatants in Sierra Leone, June-August 2003" (Freetown: PRIDE, 2004); Jimmy D. Kandeh, "Ransoming the State: Elite Origins of Subaltern Terror in Sierra Leone," *Review of African Political Economy* 26, no. 81 (1999); Paul Richards, "The Political Economy of Internal Conflict in Sierra Leone" (The Hague: Netherlands Institute of International Relations, 2003).

75. RUF, "Footpaths to Democracy: Towards a New Sierra Leone" (1995).

76. Richards, "To Fight or to Farm? Agrarian Dimensions of the Mano River Conflicts (Liberia and Sierra Leone)."

77. Léonce and Kisangani Emizet Ndikumana, "The Economics of Civil War: The Case of the Democratic Republic of Congo" (Amherst, MA: Department of Economics, University of Massachusetts and Department of Political Science, Kansas State University, 2002); J.D. Sidaway, "Sovereign Excesses? Portraying Postcolonial Sovereigntyscapes" *Political Geography* 22, no. 2 (2003).

78. Lanning and Mueller, *Africa Undermined: Mining Companies and the Under-development of Africa.*

79. Ross, "Oil, Drugs, and Diamonds: How Do Natural Resources Vary in Their Impact on Civil War?"

80. This process is still at work in "post-conflict" Angola, where a population of nearly one million in the diamond-rich Lunda Norte and Lunda Sul faces land seizures, travel and livelihood restrictions, arbitrary searches, repression, and public services neglect: Shawn Blore, "Angola 2007," in *Diamond Industry Annual Review* (Ottawa: Partnership Africa Canada, 2007); R. Marques and R. Falcao de Campos, "Lundas, the Stones of Death: Angola's Deadly Diamonds" (New York: Open Society Institute, 2005); Raphael Marques, "Operation Kissonde: The Diamonds of Humiliation and Misery" (Luanda: Open Society Institute, 2006).

81. Production of "conflict diamonds" peaked at about US$800 million in 1997; estimates based on industry sources, USGS *Minerals Yearbook* reports, Global Witness, "A Rough Trade: The Role of Companies and Governments in the Angolan Conflict"; United Nations, "Report of the Monitoring Mechanism on Sanctions against Unita" (New York: United Nations Secretariat, 2002), United Nations, "Report of the Panel of Experts on the Illegal Exploitation of Natural Resources and Other Forms of Wealth of the Democratic Republic of Congo"; United Nations, "Report of the Panel of Experts on Violations of Security Council Sanctions against Unita" (New York: United Nations Secretariat, 2000).

82. Clionadh Raleigh and Håvard Hegre, "Introducing Acled: An Armed Conflict Location and Event Dataset" (paper presented at the conference on "Disaggregating the Study of Civil War and Transnational Violence," University of California Institute of Global Conflict and Cooperation, San Diego, CA, 7–8 March 2005).

83. J. Bellows and E. Miguel, "War and Institutions: New Evidence from Sierra Leone," *American Economic Review* 96, no. 2 (2006); Humphreys and Weinstein, "What the Fighters Say: A Survey of Ex-Combatants in Sierra Leone, June-August 2003."

84. Keen, *Conflict and Collusion in Sierra Leone.*

85. This was the case for tens of thousands of Congolese in Angola and for thousands of people in Sierra Leone during the last couple of years of the conflict. For a detailed account of a Congolese woman involved in the UNITA diamond trafficking, see Filip De Boeck, "Des Chiens qui Brisent Leur Laisse: Mondialisation et Inversion des Catégories de Genre dans le Contexte du Trafic de Diamant Entre L'Angola et la République Démocratique du Congo," in Laurent Monnier, Bogumil Jewsiewicki and Gauthier de Villers (eds) *Chasse au Diamant Au Congo/Zaïre* (Paris: Editions L'Harmattan, 2001).

86. Interviews with Congolese diamond buyers, Malange province, Angola, 2001; "Violations of Security Council Sanctions Against UNITA," S/2000/203, p. 27; De Boeck, "Garimpeiro Worlds: Digging, Dying and "Hunting" for Diamonds in Angola."

87. Françoise Chipaux, "Des Mines d'Émeraudes Pour Financer la Résistance du Commandant Massoud," *Le Monde*, 17 July 1999.

88. On coltan, see Michael Nest, *Coltan* (Cambridge: Polity Press, 2011).

89. Interview notes, Angola, July 2001, and De Boeck, "Garimpeiro Worlds: Digging, Dying and "Hunting" for Diamonds in Angola."

90. Interview with Kennedy Hamutenya, Namibian Ministry of Mines and Energy official, April 2002.

91. Bredeloup, "Les Territoires de L'Identité: Le Territoire, Lien ou Frontière?"

92. Misser and Vallée, *Les Gemmocraties: L'économie Politique du Diamant Africain.*

93. About 80 percent of the world's rough diamonds pass through Antwerp: Global Witness, "Conflict Diamonds: Possibilities for the Identification, Certification and Control of Diamonds" (London: 2000). Data is collected on the basis of "country of provenance" (not "origin") and was obtained for the period 1987 to 2000, after which information on a per-country basis is not publicly available. The sharp decline in "trafficked" diamonds from 1996 mostly resulted from a reduction in the flow of Angolan (and mostly UNITA-controlled) diamonds through the DRC, although a sharp rise in the value per carat of "trafficked diamonds" compared with "producer diamonds" also suggested a shift to a smaller volume of higher quality diamonds.

94. De Boeck, "Garimpeiro Worlds: Digging, Dying and 'Hunting' for Diamonds in Angola"; United Nations, "Report of the Monitoring Mechanism on Sanctions against Unita"; United Nations, "Report of the Panel of Experts on Violations of Security Council Sanctions against Unita."

95. Interview notes, Angola, July 2001.

96. On the case of Angola, see Marcus Power, "Patrimonialism & Petro-Diamond Capitalism: Peace, Geopolitics & the Economics of War in Angola."

97. United Nations, "Report of the Panel of Experts Appointed Pursuant to

Security Council Resolution 1306 (2000), Paragraph 19, in Relation to Sierra Leone" (New York: United Nations, 2000).

98. Interview notes, Sierra Leone, April 2001.

99. Keen, *Conflict and Collusion in Sierra Leone.*

100. D. Farah, *Blood from Stones: The Secret Financial Network of Terror* (New York: Broadway Books, 2004); Global Witness, "For a Few Dollars More: How Al Qaeda Moved into the Diamond Trade" (London: Global Witness Limited, 2003).

101. TRC, "Final Report" (Freetown: Truth and Reconciliation Commission of Sierra Leone, 2004).

102. Le Billon, "Fatal Transactions: Conflict Diamonds and the (Anti) Terrorist Consumer."

103. C.J. Arnson and W.I. Zartmann (eds) *Rethinking the Economics of War: The Intersection of Need, Creed, and Greed* (Baltimore: Johns Hopkins University Press, 2005); Le Billon, *Fuelling War: Natural Resources and Armed Conflicts*; Ross, "How Do Natural Resources Influence Civil War? Evidence from Thirteen Cases." Recruitment of diamond miners also presented an "opportunity" for rebel groups, particularly for the RUF which initially recruited miners along the Liberian border and among 15,000 "illegal diggers" evicted through "Clean State Operation" in 1990 aimed at improving the operating conditions of multinationals (promoted by the IMF as a solution to the fiscal crisis faced by the government of Sierra Leone): C. Fithen, "Diamonds and War in Sierra Leone: Cultural Strategies for Commercial Adaptation to Endemic Low-Intensity Conflicts" (University College London, 1999); Paul Richards, "Are 'Forest Wars' in Africa Resource Conflicts? The Case of Sierra Leone," in Nancy Lee Peluso and Michael Watts (eds) *Violent Environments* (Ithaca, NY: Cornell University Press, 2001). Forced recruitment of miners continued in the mid-1990s (see for example, Henry, D., "Diamonds Are Not a Boy's Best Friend: What Happened When Alhadji Met the Rebels," in D. Cordell, ed., *The Human Tradition in Modern Africa* (Lanham, Md: Rowman Littlefield, 2011)). By the end of the war, however, only about 5 percent of combatants were miners when recruited, and 90 percent of combatants had been forcibly recruited: Humphreys and Weinstein, "What the Fighters Say: A Survey of Ex-Combatants in Sierra Leone, June-August 2003." UNITA mostly recruited in Ovimbundu areas with little mining activity, and diamond diggers were mostly Congolese with no military role. Finally, in the DRC, diamond diggers were taxed by armed groups but rarely recruited as soldiers.

104. Humphreys, "Natural Resources, Conflict, and Conflict Resolution: Uncovering the Mechanisms"; Philippe Le Billon, "Angola's Political Economy of War: The Role of Oil and Diamonds, 1975–2000," *African Affairs* 100,

no. 398 (2001); United Nations, "Report of the Panel of Experts Appointed Pursuant to Security Council Resolution 1306 (2000), Paragraph 19, in Relation to Sierra Leone"; Jeremy Weinstein, "Resources and the Information Problem in Rebel Recruitment," *Journal of Conflict Resolution* 49, no. 4 (2005).

105. Interview with diamond buyer, Angola, July 2001; Keen, *Conflict and Collusion in Sierra Leone.*

106. De Boeck, "Garimpeiro Worlds: Digging, Dying and 'Hunting' for Diamonds in Angola."

107. Philippe Le Billon and Eric Nicholls, "Ending 'Resource Wars': Revenue Sharing, Economic Sanction or Military Intervention?" *International Peacekeeping* 14, no. 5 (2007).

108. L. Bernstein, "Opting Out of the Legal System: Extralegal Contractual Relations in the Diamond Industry," *Journal of Legal Studies* 21, no. 1 (1992).

109. Misser and Vallée, *Les Gemmocraties: L'Économie Politique du Diamant Africain.*

110. Interview with HRD official, Antwerp, 1998.

111. Misser and Vallée, *Les Gemmocraties: L'Économie Politique du Diamant Africain.*

112. Global Witness, "A Rough Trade. The Role of Companies and Governments in the Angolan Conflict"; Le Billon, "Fatal Transactions: Conflict Diamonds and the (Anti) Terrorist Consumer"; Smillie, "The Heart of the Matter: Sierra Leone, Diamonds and Human Security."

113. United Nations, "Report of the Panel of Experts Appointed Pursuant to Security Council Resolution 1306 (2000), Paragraph 19, in Relation to Sierra Leone."

114. More radical organisations, however, advocated a total boycott of diamonds, arguing that the industry as a whole was tainted by human rights, environmental and consumer abuses, including the funding of small arms trafficking; child soldiers; slave labor in the cutting and polishing industry; the violation of indigenous land rights (especially those of the San in Botswana); environmental impacts; miners' exposure to HIV/AIDS; little resale value; overpricing; and constructed desire: see L. Stanton, J. Heintz and N. Folbre (eds) *Ten Reasons Why You Should Never Accept a Diamond Ring from Anyone, Ultimate Field Guide to the U.S. Economy* (New York: New Press, 2000).

115. The Republic of Congo, for example, was excluded in 2004.

116. PAC and Global Witness, "Rich Man, Poor Man. Development, Diamonds and Poverty: The Potential for Change in the Artisanal Diamond Fields of Africa."

117. DDI, "Diamond Development Initiative Begins: New Approach to Africa's Diamond Problems" (London: Diamond Development Initiative, 2005).

118. Levin, "From Poverty and War to Prosperity and Peace? Sustainable Live-lihoods and Innovation in Governance of Artisanal Diamond Mining in Kono District, Sierra Leone ".

119. Interview with US official, Freetown, December 2006.

120. Interview notes Sierra Leone, 2006.

121. Le Billon, *Fuelling War: Natural Resources and Armed Conflicts;*, I.J. Tamm, "Dangerous Appetites: Human Rights Activism and Conflict Commodi-ties," *Human Rights Quarterly* 26 (2004).

122. David Shearer, *Private Armies and Military Intervention, Adelphi Paper 316* (Oxford University Press, 1998).

123. C. Dietrich, "Power Struggle in the Diamond Fields," in J. Cilliers and C. Dietrich (eds) *Angola's War Economy*, (Pretoria: Institute for Security Stud-ies, 2000); Keen, *Conflict and Collusion in Sierra Leone*; Richards, "Are 'For-est Wars' in Africa Resource Conflicts? The Case of Sierra Leone."

124. M. Hart, *Diamond: A Journey to the Heart of an Obsession* (New York: Walker, 2001).

125. Le Billon, "Fatal Transactions: Conflict Diamonds and the (Anti) Terror-ist Consumer."

126. Goreux, "Conflict Diamonds"; Snyder and Bhavnani, "Diamonds, Blood, and Taxes: A Revenue-Centered Framework for Explaining Political Order."

127. Richards, "Are 'Forest Wars' in Africa Resource Conflicts? The Case of Sierra Leone."

128. Justin Pearce, "War, Peace and Diamonds in Angola: Popular Perceptions of the Diamond Industry in the Lundas," *Africa Watch* 13, no. 2 (2004).

129. T. Heaps, "The Heart of Darkness," *Corporate Knights* 2006; Human Rights Watch, "The Curse of Gold" (New York: Human Rights Watch, 2005); Marques and Falcao de Campos, "Lundas, the Stones of Death: Angola's Deadly Diamonds."

130. On the case of Sierra Leone, see Keen, *Conflict and Collusion in Sierra Leone*.

131. Le Billon, *Fuelling War: Natural Resources and Armed Conflicts*.

5. TIMBER

1. Mostly the Forces Nationales de Libération (FNL), with bases during the early 2000s in the nearby Kibira National Park: *Burundi: Security Situation* (ISS, 2005), http://www.iss.co.za/Af/profiles/Burundi/SecInfo.html.

2. Raymond L. Bryant, *The Political Ecology of Forestry in Burma, 1824–1994* (London: Hurst, 1997), http://www.khrg.org/khrg2008/khrg08b6.html.

3. Average tropical hardwood value is about US$200 per cubic meter, but some wood species or particularly large trees can fetch up to US$4,000: James

Jarvie *et al.*, "Conflict Timber: Dimensions of the Problem in Asia and Africa. Volume II Asian Cases" (Burlington, VE: ARD, undated).

4. Susanna Hecht and Alexander Cockburn, *The Fate of the Forest: Developers, Destroyers, and Defenders of the Amazon* (New York: Verso, 1989); Peluso, *Rich Forests, Poor People: Resource Control and Resistance in Java*; Jessica Wenban-Smith, "Forests of Fear: The Abuse of Human Rights in Forest Conflicts" (Moreton-in-Marsh: FERN, 2001).

5. Cited in "UN Study: Many Forest Areas Breeding Grounds for Conflict" http://www.cifor.cgiar.org/Publications/Corporate/NewsOnline/NewsOnline38/conflict.htm. For recent analysis, see Emily Harwell, Douglas Farah and Art Blundell, "Forests, Fragility and Conflict: Overview and Case Studies," Program on Forests, June 2011, Washington DC: World Bank. See also J.R. McNeill, "Woods and Warfare in World History," *Environmental History* 9, no. 3 (2004).

6. Cited in "UN Study: Many Forest Areas Breeding Grounds for Conflict" http://www.cifor.cgiar.org/Publications/Corporate/NewsOnline/NewsOnline38/conflict.htm

7. Based on national level data, see Collier, Hoeffler and Soderbom, "On the Duration of Civil War"; Paul Collier and Anke Hoeffler, "Greed and Grievance in Civil War," *Oxford Economic Papers* 56, no. 4 (2004). Their use of a lower death threshold for armed conflicts, yields a lower conflict onset risk and shorter conflict duration in forested countries, but only at a 0.1 level of significance. See also Rustad *et al.*, "Foliage and Fighting: Forest Resources and the Onset, Duration, and Location of Civil War."; Christopher Haid, Emily Meierding and Steven Wilkinson, "Environmental Scarcity and Conflict: Is There a Connection?" (Center for International Studies, University of Chicago, 2008). On a disaggregated sub-national level, see H. Buhaug and J.K. Rød, "Local Determinants of African Civil Wars, 1970–2001," *Political Geography* 25, no. 3 (2006), although Buhaug and Lujala, "Accounting for Scale: Measuring Geography in Quantitative Studies of Civil War," finds conflict duration and forest cover negatively related. The most thorough study tests three forest variables (10 percent crown cover for "forest resources," 40 percent crown cover for "forest terrain," and forest products export share for "forest dependence"). Its most significant, yet not robust results relate to conflict duration for post-Cold War insurgencies, which tend to last longer if they are located in forests near the coast (but not near international borders) or near oil and diamonds deposits: Rustad *et al.*, "Foliage and Fighting: Forest Resources and the Onset, Duration, and Location of Civil War."

8. Buhaug and Lujala, "Accounting for Scale: Measuring Geography in Quantitative Studies of Civil War."

9. At least once the case of Burma—a low-income country with major teak

exports and high levels of conflicts—is withdrawn: Rustad *et al.*, "Foliage and Fighting: Forest Resources and the Onset, Duration, and Location of Civil War."

10. Ole Magnus Theisen, "Blood and Soil? Resource Scarcity and Internal Armed Conflict Revisited," *Journal of Peace Research* 45, no. 6 (2008); Wenche and Tanja Ellingsen Hauge, "Beyond Environmental Scarcity: Causal Pathways to Conflict," *Journal of Peace Research* 35, no. 3 (1998) found a positive relationship, while Daniel C. Esty *et al.*, "State Failure Task Force Report: Phase II Findings" (State Failure Task Force, 1998) did not find one but did identify a possible indirect association through lower life quality. See http://globalpolicy.gmu.edu/pitf/ accessed on 31 May 2011.

11. In contrast, for lack of mountains and forests to retreat to, Dutch resistance to the Spanish was concentrated in cities, as initially was the resistance of Jewish populations against the Romans: see Atieno E.S. Odhiambo and John Lonsdale (eds) *Mau Mau and Nationhood* (Oxford: James Currey, 2003).

12. C. Seignebos, "Des Fortifications Végétales dans la Zone Soudano-Sahélienne (Tchad Et Nord Cameroun)," *Cahiers de Sciences Humaines* 17, no. 3, 4 (1980).

13. Duffy, "Peace Parks: The Paradox of Globalisation."

14. Joshua Marks, "Border in Name Only: Arms Trafficking and Armed Groups at the DRC-Sudan Border" (Geneva: Small Arms Survey, Graduate Institute of International Studies, 2007).

15. *Newsweek*, "America Deeply Involved in Kony War for Years," 22 May 2009.

16. US Army, *Field Manual 34–130: Intelligence Preparation of the Battlefield* (Washington, DC: Department of the Army, 1994). Mao Tse-tung stressed the importance of terrain in guerrilla warfare, but did not specifically refer to forests: Mao Tse-tung, *On Guerrilla Warfare* (Champaign: University of Illinois Press, 2000).

17. Ernesto "Che" Guevara, *Guerrilla Warfare* (Rowman and Littlefield, 1997 (1960)).

18. Jérôme Tubiana, *Chroniques du Darfour* (Grenoble, France: Glénat, 2010).

19. Geraint Hughes and Christian Tripodi, "Anatomy of a Surrogate: Historical Precedents and Implications for Contemporary Counter-Insurgency and Counter-Terrorism," *Small Wars and Insurgencies* 20, no. 1 (2009); Patrick K. Muana, "The Kamajoi Militia: Civil War, Internal Displacement and the Politics of Counter-Insurgency," *Africa Development* 22, no. 3/4 (1997).

20. Walter Laqueur, *Guerrilla Warfare. A Historical and Critical Study* (Transaction Books, 1997).

21. Interview with Department of Forestry official, Phnom Penh, 1993; David Chandler, *A History of Cambodia* (Boulder, CO: Westview Press, 2007).

22. Christon I. Archer *et al.*, *World History of Warfare* (Reno: University of Nevada Press, 2008).

23. Wilbur J. Scott, *The Politics of Readjustment: Vietnam Veterans since the War* (New York: Aldine De Gruyter, 1993).

24. Jeanne Mager Stellman *et al.*, "The Extent and Patterns of Usage of Agent Orange and Other Herbicides in Vietnam," *Nature* 422 (2003); see also Arthur H. Westing (ed.) *Herbicides in War: The Long-Term Ecological and Human Consequences* (London: Taylor and Francis, 1984).

25. Scott, *The Politics of Readjustment: Vietnam Veterans since the War.*

26. W.S. Hanson, "The Organisation of Roman Military Timber-Supply," *Britannia* 9 (1978), pp. 293–306. Fuelwood and charcoal were also crucial sources of energy to melt and transform metals for weapons. Lacking petroleum during the Second World War, Germany tried to switch to wood-based chemical fuels: FAO: "State of the World Forests" (Rome: UN Food and Agricultural Organisation, 2005).

27. McNeill, "Woods and Warfare in World History"; Joshua A. West, "Forests and National Security: British and American Forestry Policy in the Wake of World War One," *Environmental History* 8, no. 2 (2003).

28. Oak became a strategic raw material because it was the only species providing the strength and durability required for artillery-equipped warships: Per Eliasson and Sven G. Nilsson, "'You Should Hate Young Oaks and Young Noblemen': The Environmental History of Oaks in Eighteenth- and Nineteenth-Century Sweden," *Environmental History* 7, no. 4 (2002); William Bryant Logan, *Oak: The Frame of Civilization* (New York: W.W. Norton & Company, 2005).

29. Albion, *Forests and Sea Power: The Timber Problem of the Royal Navy, 1652–1862*; P.W. Bamford, *Forests and French Sea Power, 1660–1789* (University of Toronto Press, 1956).

30. Nam Rodger, *The Wooden World. An Anatomy of the Georgian Navy* (London: Collins, 1986).

31. In many respects the standardisation of (harmful) policies was also, after the Second World War, a result of the work of international organisations, especially the United Nations Food and Agricultural Organisation (FAO), see Peter Vandergeest and Nancy Lee Peluso, "Empires of Forestry: Professional Forestry and State Power in Southeast Asia, Part 2," *Environment and History* 12 (2006).

32. Bryant, *The Political Ecology of Forestry in Burma, 1824–1994*; Oliver B. Pollak, "The Origins of the Second Anglo-Burmese War (1852–53)," *Modern Asian Studies* 12, no. 3 (1978); Craig S. Revels, "Concessions, Conflict and the Rebirth of the Honduran Mahogany Trade," *Journal of Latin American Geography* 2, no. 1 (2003).

33. In 2007, the Colombian Minister of Defence accused the FARC of "ecocide" for having cleared 40,000 hectares of forests to grow coca, see EFE, "Colom-

bia, Victima Del Calentamiento," *El Universal*, 22 April 2007, while the Colombia police put the consolidated figure of deforestation by illegal groups between 1985 and 2010 at 2 million hectares—about 4 square meters of rainforest per gram of cocaine, César Morales Colon, "Guerrillas, Drug Traffickers Impacting Environment," *Infosurhoy.com*, 25 August 2010. For a discussion, see German Andres Quimbayo Ruiz, "Crops for Illicit Use and Ecocide" (Transnational Institute, 2008).

34. There is no statistical relationship between forest cover and institutional quality, except negative ones at the regional level for Latin America and Asia: Ruben de Koning *et al.*, "Forest-Related Conflict. Impact, Links, and Measures to Mitigate" (Washington, DC: Rights and Resources Initiative, 2008). This could be a reverse relationship, as forest cover indicates weak institutions unable to attract the kind of investment necessary to deforest large forested areas. Furthermore, timber export dependence, rather than forest cover, is the variable of concern here.

35. Duncan Brack and Gavin Hayman, "Intergovernmental Actions on Illegal Logging" (London: Royal Institute of International Affairs, 2001); Luca Tacconi (ed.) *Illegal Logging: Law Enforcement, Livelihoods and the Timber Trade* (London: Earthscan, 2007).

36. Increases in volume were initially decoupled from price increases, with demand increasing in the late 1990s without major impact on prices before 2003. Roughly 80 percent of wood products (including for paper) come from Europe and North America, with only US$1.2 billion from "Least Developed Countries," see FAOStat ForeStat database, http://faostat.fao.org.

37. Timber products can experience major volatility, often as a result of trade disputes, as in the case of the US-Canada softwood lumber dispute. See Daowei Zhang and Changyou Sun, "US-Canada Softwood Lumber Trade Disputes and Lumber Price Volatility," *Forest Products Journal* 51, no. 4 (2001).

38. Wood and paper products ranked last among these four categories for low and mid-income countries, see Gordon Hanson, "Export Dependence in Developing Countries" (UC San Diego and NBER, 2010).

39. On Indonesia, Malaysia (Sabah and Sarawak) and the Philippines. See Ross, *Timber Booms and Institutional Breakdown in Southeast Asia*. On the importance of logging in Burmese politics. See Bryant, *The Political Ecology of Forestry in Burma, 1824–1994*. On connections between logging interests in international aid for the case of Japan in Southeast Asia, see Peter Dauvergne, *Shadows in the Forest: Japan and the Politics of Timber in Southeast Asia* (Cambridge, MA: MIT Press, 1997).

40. Ross, *Timber Booms and Institutional Breakdown in Southeast Asia*.

41. Bayart, Ellis and Hibou, *The Criminalization of the State in Africa*; Bernard Conte, "Cote d'Ivoire: Clientélisme, Ajustement et Conflit," in *DT/101/2004*

(Bordeaux: CED/IFReDE-GRES, Université Montesquieu, 2004); R. Hardin, "Concessionary Politics in the Western Congo Basin: History and Culture in Forest Use," in J. Ribot and D. Stemper (eds) *Environmental Governance in Africa, Working Paper 6* (Washington, DC: WRI, 2002).

42. Patrick Johnston, "Timber Boom, State Busts: The Political Economy of Liberian Timber," *Review of African Political Economy* 31, no. 101 (2004); Reno, *Warlord Politics and African States*.

43. For the case of Sierra Leone, see Fenda Akiwumi, "Conflict Timber, Conflict Diamonds: Parallels in the Political Ecology of Nineteenth and Twentieth Century Resource Exploitation in Sierra Leone," in Kwadwo Konadu-Agyemang and Kwamina Panford (eds) *Africa's Development in the Twenty-First Century* (Aldershot: Ashgate Publishing, 2006); on the case of Burma, see Bryant, *The Political Ecology of Forestry in Burma, 1824–1994*.

44. In Southeast Asian cases, these peripheral populations sought to remain stateless after fleeing dangers such as forced labor, war and epidemics. See James C. Scott, *The Art of Not Being Governed* (New Haven, CT: Yale University Press, 2009). In the West African cases the hinterland population was in part marginalised by freed slaves constituting the new elites. On Liberia see Ellis *The Mask of Anarchy. The Destruction of Liberia and the Religious Dimension of an African Civil War*. On Sierra Leone see Jimmy D. Kandeh, "Politicization of Ethnic Identities in Sierra Leone," *African Studies Review* 35, no. 1 (1992).

45. James Scott, "'Zomia': Site of the Last Great Enclosure Movement of (Relatively) State-Less Peoples in Mountainous Southeast Asia" (University of Toronto, 2008). See also Willem van Schendel, "Geographies of Knowing, Geographies of Ignorance: Jumping Scale in Southeast Asia," *Environment and Planning D: Society and Space* 20 (2002).

46. Ian Baird, "Various Forms of Colonialism: The Social and Spatial Re-Organisation of the Brao in Southern Laos and Northeastern Cambodia" (Vancouver: University of British Columbia, 2008); Sara Colm, "The Highland Minorities and the Khmer Rouge in Northeastern Cambodia 1968–1979" (Phnom Penh: Document Center of Cambodia, 1996).

47. Michael K. Steinberg *et al.*, "Mapping Massacres: GIs and State Terror in Guatemala," *Geoforum* 37, no. 1 (2006).

48. Mingteh Chang, *Forest Hydrology* (CRC Press, 2006).

49. Dieudonne Alemagi, Anne-Sophie Samjee and Andrew Davis, "Comparison of Economic Growth and Governance between High Forest and Low Forest Countries. Background paper to "Seeing People Through the Trees" project. (Washington, DC: Rights and Resources Initiative, 2007).

50. For example, through sustained-yield management applied to logging activities.

51. Thomas Beckley, John Parkins and Richard Stedman, "Indicators of Forest-Dependent Community Sustainability: The Evolution of Research," *The Forestry Chronicle* 78, no. 5 (2002).

52. Edward Palmer Thompson, *Whigs and Hunters: The Origin of the Black Act* (London: Allen Lane, 1975).

53. Richard Grove, *Ecology, Climate, and Empire: Colonialism and Global Environmental History, 1400–1940* (Cambridge: White Horse Press, 1997).

54. Peluso, *Rich Forests, Poor People: Resource Control and Resistance in Java.*

55. Jugal Bhurtel and Saleem H. Ali, "The Green Roots of Red Rebellion: Environmental Degradation and the Rise of the Maoist Movement in Nepal," in Mahendra Lawoti and Anup Pahari (eds) *The Maoist Insurgency in Nepal: Dynamics and Growth in the Twenty-First Century* (New York: Routledge, 2009); Ramachandra Guha, *The Unquiet Woods: Ecological Change and Resistance in the Himalaya* (Berkeley, CA: University of California Press, 1990).

56. Hecht and Cockburn, *The Fate of the Forest: Developers, Destroyers, and Defenders of the Amazon.*

57. Neil Harvey, *The Chiapas Rebellion. The Struggle for Land and Democracy* (Durham, NC: Duke University Press, 1998); Philip N. Howard, "The History of Ecological Marginalization in Chiapas," *Environmental History* 3, no. 3 (1998).

58. Neumann, "Moral and Discursive Geographies in the War for Biodiversity in Africa."

59. Marco Armiero and Nancy Lee Peluso, "Insurgent Natures and Nations: Unpacking Socio-Environmental Histories of Forest Conflicts" (Paris: Ecole des Hautes Etudes de Sciences Sociales, 2008).

60. These processes are not always coercively imposed, however. Shrouded in ideologies of development, or simply driven by the realities of arduous living conditions and promises of a better and safer life, there are also voluntary moves. Yet populations can face new dangers. For example, isolation in forest areas can prevent the spread of communicable diseases, but also reduce immunity build-up. Relocation by remote forest communities, or even contact with outsiders, can thus result in loss of life.

61. Dawn Chatty and Marcus Colchester, *Conservation and Mobile Indigenous Peoples* (Oxford: Berghahn Books, 2002).

62. Armierro and Peluso, "Insurgent Natures and Nations: Unpacking Socio-Environmental Histories of Forest Conflicts."

63. de Koning *et al.*, "Forest-Related Conflict. Impact, Links, and Measures to Mitigate."

64. Gerry van Klinken, "Blood, Timber, and the State in West Kalimantan, Indonesia," *Asia Pacific Viewpoint* 49, no. 1 (2008).

65. Peluso and Harwell, "Territory, Custom, and the Cultural Politics of Ethnic War in West Kalimantan, Indonesia." Suharto's "New Order" regime was facing growing dissent and starting to collapse even prior to the 1997 Asian Crisis that precipitated its fall.

66. M.D. Vitug, *The Politics of Logging: Power From the Forest* (Manila: Philippine Center for Investigative Journalism, 1993).

67. Animesh Roul, "Gems, Timber and Jiziya: Pakistan's Taliban Harness Resources to Fund Jihad," *Terrorism Monitor* 7, no. 11 (2009). For a broader account of Taliban funding, see Arabinda Acharya, Syed Adnan Ali Shah Bukhari and Sadia Sulaiman, "Making Money in the Mayhem: Funding Taliban Insurrection in the Tribal Areas of Pakistan," *Studies in Conflict & Terrorism* 32, no. 2 (2009); Barnett Rubin, "The Political Economy of War and Peace in Afghanistan," *World Development* 28, no. 10 (2000).

68. Marites Danguilan Vitug, "The Politics of Logging in the Philippines," in Philip Hirsch and Carol Warren (eds) *The Politics of Environment in Southeast Asia: Resources and Resistance* (London: Routledge, 1998).

69. Armierro and Peluso, "Insurgent Natures and Nations: Unpacking Socio-Environmental Histories of Forest Conflicts."

70. Vitug, "The Politics of Logging in the Philippines."

71. Jake Sherman, "Burma: Lessons from the Cease-Fires," in Karen Ballentine and Jake Sherman (eds) *The Political Economy of Armed Conflict: Beyond Greed and Grievance* (Boulder: Lynne Rienner, 2003).

72. Other cases include: the Philippines, see Vitug, *The Politics of Logging: Power from the Forest*; Nicaragua, see David Kaimovitz and Angelica Fauné, "Contras and Comandantes: Armed Movements and Forest Conservation in Nicaragua's Bosawas Biosphere Reserve," in Steven V. Price (ed.) *War and Tropical Forests: Conservation in Areas of Armed Conflict* (New York: Routledge, 2003); Chiapas, see Harvey, *The Chiapas Rebellion. The Struggle for Land and Democracy*.

73. For an historical perspective see Judith A. Bennett, *Pacific Forest: A History of Resource Control and Contest in the Solomon Islands, c. 1800–1997* (Cambridge: White Horse Press, 2000); for more recent analyses on the political dimensions, see Tarcisius Tara Kabutaulaka, "Rumble in the Jungle: Land, Culture and (Un)Sustainable Logging in Solomon Islands," in Antony Hooper (ed.) *Culture and Sustainable Development in the Pacific* (2008).

74. On corporate environmental and tax evasion, see Peter Dauvergne, "Corporate Power in the Forest of Solomon Islands," *Pacific Affairs* 71, no. 4 (1998).

75. Jim Sandoms, "Logging in the Solomon Islands—the Lost Legacy," *ETFRN News* 43–45 (2005).

76. Many of the conflicts derive from the mishandling of the challenges posed by its political geography, which combines a high number of ethnic minor-

ity groups located at the periphery of a majority group; extensive borders with five countries; rich resources; and favourable terrain. See Peter John Perry, "Military Rule in Burma: A Geographical Analysis," *Crime, Law and Social Change* 19, no. 1 (1993); Martin Smith, *Burma: Insurgency and the Politics of Ethnicity* (London: Zed Books, 1999); Shelby Tucker, *Burma: The Curse of Independence* (Pluto Press, 2001).

77. For example, the Karen National Liberation Army (KNLA, or previously Karen National Defence Organization).

78. See van Schendel, "Geographies of Knowing, Geographies of Ignorance: Jumping Scale in Southeast Asia."

79. Other resources include opium and, more recently, methamphetamines—see Bertil Lintner, *Burma in Revolt: Opium and Insurgency since 1948* (Seattle: University of Washington Press, 2000)—and jade and gems: see Lintner, *Burma in Revolt: Opium and Insurgency since 1948*; as well as the taxation of border trade and local populations.

80. Bryant, *The Political Ecology of Forestry in Burma, 1824–1994*. The country still holds about 70 percent of natural teak forests and supplies about 80 percent of world trade.

81. Jake Brunner, Kirk Talbott and Chantal Elkin, "Logging Burma's Frontier Forests: Resources and the Regime" (Washington, DC: World Resource Institute, 1998). Burma (or Myanmar) has since been ruled by a military regime under the various names of the Burma Socialist Programme Party (BSPP), after 1988 the State Law and Order Restoration Council (SLORC), and since 1997 the State Peace and Development Council (SPDC).

82. Ken MacLean, "Capitalizing on Conflict: How Logging and Mining Contribute to Environmental Destruction" (Earth Rights International with Karen Environmental & Social Action Network, 2003); Sherman, "Burma: Lessons from the Cease-Fires"; Snyder, "Does Lootable Wealth Breed Disorder? A Political Economy of Extraction Framework."

83. Burma experienced two logging booms: along the Thai border between 1989 and 1993, and along the Chinese border (Kachin State) between 1999 and 2006. However, statistical data, such as that of the FAO, remains unreliable.

84. Thailand was conveniently located, with a border close to a rebel controlled and access to be the international market. It also had a large logging and processing overcapacity because of the domestic logging ban: Brunner, Talbott and Elkin, "Logging Burma's Frontier Forests: Resources and the Regime." Timber revenues represented about 40 percent of official foreign currency earnings.

85. Marc Innes-Brown and Mark Valencia, "Thailand's Resource Diplomacy in Indochina and Myanmar," *Contemporary Southeast Asia* 14, no. 4.

86. Raymond L. Bryant, "Kawthoolei and Teak: Karen Forest Management on the Thai Burmese Border," *Watershed* 3, no. 1 (1997).

87. Vicky Bamforth, Steven Lanjouw and Graham Mortimer, "Conflict and Displacement in Karenni: The Need for Considered Responses" (Burma Ethnic Research Group, 2000).

88. As with the KNLA/KNU's loss of its main permanent bases in Manerplaw and Kawmoora. The military campaign, ongoing since independence, was further motivated by the laying of a gas pipeline, while these defeats owed much to a split within the KNU by a defecting Buddhist Karen group. See "Manerplaw, Forteresse de la Résistance Birmane est Tombée," http://www.voltairenet.org/article6867.html, accessed 20 July 2009.

89. Global Witness, *A Conflict of Interests: The Uncertain Future of Burma's Forests* (London: Global Witness, 2003). For example, the Kachin Independence Organisation (KIO), which lost a main source of funds (jade mining) to government forces in 1994, then accepted a cease-fire agreement and turned to logging for financing.

90. Ibid.

91. Cited in Zao Noam, "Burma: Ceasefire, Logging and Mining Concessions in Kachin State," *World Rainforest Movement's Bulletin* no. 94 (May 2005).

92. Global Witness, *A Choice for China, Ending the Destruction of Burma's Northern Frontier Forests* (London: Global Witness, 2005); "China blocks timber imports from Burma," Global Witness, 30 May 2006, http://www.globalwitness.org/media_library_detail.php/439/en/china_blocks_timber_imports_from_burma, accessed 20 July 2009.

93. Both treaties proposed by the French to the Cambodian King included a request for access to timber. A first proposal in 1856 requested (hoped-for) teak for shipbuilding. The second, agreed in 1863, offered the King the protection of France "in exchange for timber concessions and mineral exploration rights" Chandler, *A History of Cambodia*.

94. See www.globalwitness.org.

95. Most of the logging activities served the domestic construction market, Vietnamese troops and companies exploited forests inside Cambodia to export them back home, while small Cambodian companies officially organised as "cooperatives" or foreign joint ventures did a little export.

96. Thayer, "Rubies are Rouge: Khmer War Effort Financed by Gem Finds."

97. FAO, "State of the World's Forests" (Rome: UN Food and Agriculture Organization, 1997).

98. Timber represented by far the main source of income, which also included gem mining and the trade in stone carvings from ancient temples, latex, gravel, rice, corn, fish, scrap metal, and non-timber forest products such as sandalwood oil: Le Billon, "Power Is Consuming the Forest."

99. Ibid.

100. Examples of disciplinary actions included killing of the commander of a Khmer Rouge unit in Kampot province, who was accused by the rebel

movement's leadership of being too cozy with the provincial governor and the murder of a logging crew. The Khmer Rouge movement itself split in part over the distribution of revenue, the "hardliners" in the Anlong Veng area having less access to timber and gem revenues and alleging corruption within part of the leadership in the richer Pailin area. Interviews with Khmer Rouge defectors, Cambodia, 1999 and 2001.

101. Global Witness, "Country for Sale" (London: Global Witness, 2008).

102. See Ellis, *The Mask of Anarchy: The Destruction of Liberia and the Religious Dimension of an African Civil War.*

103. Robert Taylor was managing director of the Forestry Development Authority.

104. Global Witness, "Logging Off: How the Liberian Timber Industry Fuels Liberia's Humanitarian Disasters and Threatens Sierra Leone" (London: Global Witness, 2002).

105. Liberia Truth and Reconciliation Commission, "Final Report of the Commission (Volume 2)" (Monrovia: 2008).

106. Global Witness, "The Logs of War: The Timber Trade and Armed Conflict."

107. Liberia Truth and Reconciliation Commission, "Final Report of the Commission (Volume 2)."

108. S/RES/1343 (2001) on all rough diamonds, and establishment of an expert panel; S/RES/1408 (2002) establishment by government of Liberia of transparent and internationally verifiable audit regimes on use of timber industry revenues; S/RES/1478 (2003) on all timber exports.

109. Africa Research Bulletin, "Liberia: What About Timber?," 1 April 2001.

110. Arthur G. Blundell, "Conflict Timber and Liberia's War," *ETFRN News* 43–44 (2005).

111. Ian G. Baird and Bruce Shoemaker, "Unsettling Experiences: Internal Resettlement and International Aid Agencies in Laos," *Development and Change* 38, no. 5 (2007); Peluso and Harwell, "Territory, Custom, and the Cultural Politics of Ethnic War in West Kalimantan, Indonesia."

112. Cited in http://www.cifor.cgiar.org/Publications/Corporate/NewsOnline/NewsOnline38/conflict.htm

113. Bill Weinberg, "Conservation as Counter Insurgency in the Chiapas Rainforest?" *ETFRN News* 43–44 (2005).

6. SPOILING WAR

1. K. Ballentine and H. Nitzschke, *Profiting from Peace: Managing the Resource Dimensions of Civil War* (Boulder, CO: Lynne Rienner, 2004); Bannon and Collier, *Natural Resources and Violent Conflict: Options and Actions.*

2. Ross, "A Closer Look at Oil, Diamonds, and Civil War."

3. David Cortright and George A. Lopez, *Sanctions and the Search for Security: Challenges to UN Action* (Boulder, CO: Lynne Rienner, 2002).
4. In both Angola and Sierra Leone, the government maintained control over diamonds by concentrating decision-making in entities that it controlled: the parastatal diamond company ENDIAMA in Angola and the Ministry of Mines and Minerals in Sierra Leone.
5. For a review of wealth-sharing arrangements, see Helga Malmin Binningsbo and Siri A. Rustad, "Resource Conflicts, Wealth Sharing and Post-conflict Peace" (Norwegian University of Science and Technology and International Peace Research Institute, 2009); Nicholas Haysom and Sean Kane, "Negotiating Natural Resources for Peace: Ownership, Control and Wealth-Sharing" (Geneva: Centre for Humanitarian Dialogue, 2009); A. Wennmann, "Economic Provisions in Peace Agreements and Sustainable Peacebuilding," *Négociations* 1, no. 11 (2009).
6. Neil Cooper, "State Collapse as Business: The Role of Conflict Trade and the Emerging Control Agenda," *Development & Change* 33, no. 5 (2002); Neil R. Cooper, "Chimeric Governance and the Extension of Resource Regulation," *Conflict, Security and Development* 6, no. 3 (2006); Le Billon, "The Political Ecology of War: Natural Resources and Armed Conflicts"; Mandy Turner, "Taming Mammon: Corporate Social Responsibility and the Global Regulation of Conflict Trade," *Conflict, Security and Development* 6, no. 3 (2006).
7. Siri Camilla Aas Rustad, Helga Malmin Binningsbo and Philippe Le Billon, "Do Resource-Related Peacebuilding Initiatives Build Peace?" (paper presented at the Annual conference of the International Studies Association, New York, 2009).
8. The study uses a cross-sectional time series regression, see Jenny R. Kehl, "Oil, Water, Blood and Diamonds: International Intervention in Resource Disputes," *International Negotiation* 15 (2010).
9. Neither do codes of conduct and the trials of leaders and businesses, although in this latter case there may not be enough cases to statistically test this hypothesis.
10. M.W. Doyle and N. Sambanis, "International Peacebuilding: A Theoretical and Quantitative Analysis," *American Political Science Review* 94, no. 4 (2000); James Fearon, "Why Do Some Civil Wars Last So Much Longer Than Others?" (Washington, DC: World Bank, 2002); Lujala, "The Spoils of Nature: Armed Civil Conflict and Rebel Access to Natural Resources"; Ross, "How Do Natural Resources Influence Civil War? Evidence from Thirteen Cases"; Stephen J. Stedman, "Implementing Peace Agreements in Civil Wars: Lessons and Recommendations for Policymakers," in *IPA*

Policy Paper Series on Peace Implementation (New York: International Peace Academy, 2001).

11. Humphreys, "Natural Resources, Conflict, and Conflict Resolution: Uncovering the Mechanisms." Paul Collier and Anke Hoeffler, "Resource Rents, Governance and Conflict," *Journal of Conflict Resolution* 49, no. 4 (2005).

12. Humphreys, "Natural Resources, Conflict, and Conflict Resolution: Uncovering the Mechanisms."

13. Weinstein, "Resources and the Information Problem in Rebel Recruitment."

14. The growing use of private contractors by foreign governments in security tasks is blurring this distinction, as illustrated in the case of Iraq under the Coalition Provisional Authority occupation.

15. This varies across time and countries, see Sarah Percy, *Mercenaries: The History of a Norm in International Relations* (Oxford University Press, 2007). South Africa, for example, put in place specific legislation to prohibit mercenarism, see Hin-Yan Liu, "Leashing the Corporate Dogs of War: The Legal Implications of the Modern Private Military Company," *Journal of Conflict and Security Law* 15, no. 1 (2010).

16. Shearer, *Private Armies and Military Intervention.*

17. I differentiate, in this regard, PMCs from illegal arms brokers generally assisting rebel movements.

18. Anthony Regan, "Causes and Course of the Bougainville Conflict," *Journal of Pacific History* 33, no. 3 (1998).

10. Enrique Bernales Ballesteros, "Report on the Question of the Use of Mercenaries as a Means of Violating Human Rights and Impeding the Exercise of the Right of Peoples to Self-Determination" (New York: United Nations General Assembly, 1997).

20. Englebert and Ron, "Primary Commodities and War: Congo-Brazzaville's Ambivalent Resource Curse."

21. The military arm of the Economic Community of West African States (ECOWAS).

22. Dunning and Wirpsa, "Oil and the Political Economy of Conflict in Colombia and Beyond: A Linkages Approach."

23. Jonathan Goodhand, "Corrupting or Consolidating the Peace? The Drugs Economy and Post-Conflict Peacebuilding in Afghanistan," *International Peacekeeping* 15, no. 3 (2008).

24. UN Security Council Resolution 1856, adopted on 22 December 2008, requested MONUC to "coordinate operations with the FARDC integrated brigades deployed in the eastern part of the Democratic Republic of the Congo and support operations led by and jointly planned with these brigades in accordance with international humanitarian, human rights and refugee law with a view to: … preventing the provision of support to illegal armed

groups, including support derived from illicit economic activities; … Use its monitoring and inspection capacities to curtail the provision of support to illegal armed groups derived from illicit trade in natural resources."

25. UN Security Council Resolution 1857, adopted on 22 December 2008, applied to "individuals or entities supporting the illegal armed groups in the eastern part of the Democratic Republic of the Congo through illicit trade of natural resources." The list included only Congolese, Rwandan and Ugandan companies; see www.un.org/sc/committees/1533/pdf/1533_list.pdf.

26. Personal communication, Johan Pelemnan, chief of Joint Mission Analysis Cell, Office of the Special Representative of the UN Secretary General, August 2009.

27. Global Witness, "Bisie Killings Show Minerals at Heart of Congo Conflict" (London: Global Witness, 2009).

28. Global Witness, "'Faced with a Gun, What Can You Do?' War and the Militarisation of Mining in Eastern Congo" (London: Global Witness, 2009).

29. See www.ipisresearch.be/mapping.php.

30. Lieutenant Colonel Jean-Paul Dietrich, cited in "Congo-Kinshasa: Charcoal Profits Fuel War in East," IRIN, 28 July 2009.

31. Global Witness, "Bisie Killings Show Minerals at Heart of Congo Conflict."

32. Jeroen Raeymaekers and Tim Cuvelier, "Supporting the War Economy in the DRC: European Companies and the Coltan Trade" (Antwerp: International Peace Information Service (IPIS), 2002).

33. MONUSCO official, personal communication with the author, 2009.

34. United Nations, "Final Report of the UN Expert Panel Pursuant Resolution 1533," in S/2008/733 (2008).

35. Raf Custers, "Le Plan Starec du Gouvernement Congolais: Une Analyse Préliminaire" (Antwerp: IPIS, 2009).

36. Le Billon, *Fuelling War: Natural Resources and Armed Conflicts.*

37. Gregory Mthembu-Salter, "An Assessment of Sanctions against Burundi" (London: Action Aid, 1999).

38. UN Security Council resolution S/RES/1295 (2000), para. 27.

39. Charles Recknagel, "Oil Smuggling Produces High Profits," *RFE/EL* (2000).

40. David Cortright and George A. Lopez, *The Sanctions Decade: Assessing UN Strategies in the 1990s* (Boulder, CO: Lynne Rienner, 2000).

41. Andrew Mack and Asif Khan, "The Efficacy of UN Sanctions," *Security Dialogue* 31, no. 3 (2000).

42. Steven L. Myers, "UN Concludes, Fining Shell, That Tanker Carried Iraq Oil," *New York Times*, 26 April 2000.

43. Cortright and Lopez, *Sanctions and the Search for Security: Challenges to UN Action*; Philippe Le Billon, "Getting It Done: Instruments of Enforcement,"

in Ian Bannon and Paul Collier (eds) *Natural Resources and Violent Conflict: Options and Actions* (Washington, DC: World Bank, 2003).

44. Cortright and Lopez, *Sanctions and the Search for Security: Challenges to UN Action.*

45. Interview with Ambassador Mahmoud Kassem, chair of the DRC expert panel, New York, December 2001.

46. Interview with Ian Smillie, Ottawa, March 2002.

47. See the reports of the Independent Inquiry Committee into the United Nations Oil-for-Food Programme, http://www.iic-offp.org/documents.htm.

48. See Dunning and Wirpsa, "Oil and the Political Economy of Conflict in Colombia and Beyond: A Linkages Approach"; Pearce, "Policy Failure and Petroleum Predation: The Economics of Civil War Debate Viewed 'from the War-Zone'"; Richani, "Multinational Corporations, Rentier Capitalism, and the War System in Colombia." Interviews with oil industry officials, Bogotá, April 2009.

49. In 2008, the UN Security Council did request all states to take "the necessary measures to prevent … the financing" of military activities by all non-governmental entities and individuals operating in the territory of the DRC (UN Security Council Resolution 1807, dated 31 March 2008). By May 2010, the UN Security listed four individuals or commercial entities Council as subjected to travel ban and asset freeze.

50. IRIN-CEA, "DRC: Sabena/Swissair Declares Embargo on Transport of Coltan," 16–22 June 2001.

51. Global Witness, "Afrimex (UK) Democratic Republic of Congo. Complaint to the UK National Contact Point under the Specific Instance Procedure of the OECD Guidelines for Multinational Enterprises" (2007).

52. Aloys Tegera, "The Coltan Phenomena" (Goma: POLE Institute, 2002). At the time of writing, the UN Mission in the DRC had set up several pilot mineral trading centers in North and South Kivu, and a regional Conflict Mineral Certification Scheme was being set up through the International Conference on the Great Lakes Region (ICGLR) with assistance from a Canadian NGO, see Shawn Blore and Ian Smillie, "Taming the Resource Curse: Implementing the ICGLR Certification Mechanism for Conflict-prone Minerals" (Ottawa: Partnership Africa Canada, 2011).

53. Chevron's move was also supported by a US government opposing neighbouring "communist" Ethiopia.

54. J. Rone, *Sudan, Oil, and Human Rights* (Washington, DC: Human Rights Watch, 2003).

55. L.A. Patey, "State Rules: Oil Companies and Armed Conflict in Sudan," *Third World Quarterly* 28, no. 5 (2007).

56. J. Young, "Sudan: Liberation Movements, Regional Armies, Ethnic Militias

& Peace," *Review of African Political Economy* 30, no. 97 (2003). Some oil companies presented oil development as "an incentive for peace insofar as oil activities could not be pursued in a war context": C. Batruch, "Oil and Conflict: Lundin Petroleum's Experience in Sudan," in A.J.K. Bailes and I. Frommelt (eds) *Business and Security: Public-Private Sector Relationships in a New Security Environment* (Oxford University Press, 2004). The supposed "peace" was marked by brutal population displacements and aerial bombing, see Rone, *Sudan, Oil, and Human Rights*.

57. Interview with Taban Deng Gai, former Governor of Unity Province, 2001.

58. Oil development continued, however, in part because of the prospect of rising prices, lower exposure to reputational risk for Western juniors and Asian parastatal oil companies, and China's push for access to oil reserves. In contrast, major Western companies holding concessions refrained from reinvesting despite offers of military support by the Government of Sudan. Interview with European oil major company manager, June 2006.

59. For a critique of the agreement as an exclusive deal between the two main contending Northern and Southern political parties, see J. Young, "Sudan: A Flawed Peace Process Leading to a Flawed Peace," *Review of African Political Economy* 32, no. 103 (2005); for concerns about the impact of oil, especially on future local conflicts, see Patey, "Crude Days Ahead? Oil and the Resource Curse in Sudan."

60. Thomas I. Palley, "Oil and the Case of Iraq," *Challenge* 47 (2004).

61. Human Rights Watch, "The Curse of Gold" (New York: Human Rights Watch, 2005); Lutundula Commission Report (http://www.freewebs.com/congo-kinshasa/).

62. Philippe Le Billon, "Buying Peace or Fuelling War: The Role of Corruption in Armed Conflicts," *Journal of International Development* 15, no. 4 (2003).

63. Paul Collier, Anke Hoeffler and Mans Soderbom, "On the Duration of Civil War" (Washington, DC: Development Research Group, World Bank and Centre for the Study of African Economies, University of Oxford, 2001); Roy Licklider, "The Consequences of Negotiated Settlements in Civil Wars, 1945–1993," *American Political Science Review* 89, no. 3 (1995); P M. Regan and A. Aydin, "Diplomacy and Other Forms of Intervention in Civil Wars," *Journal of Conflict Resolution* 50, no. 5 (2005).

64. These results are tentative since they derive from somewhat subjective and non-standardised measures. Furthermore, in part because of the small number of cases, I do not control for the influence of one initiative on the implementation effectiveness of the other. Arguably, military intervention can be more effective following sanctions that have weakened a party. Such military intervention, in turn, can affect the likelihood of a successful sharing agreement. I note that in fourteen cases only one instrument was used; in eight

cases two were used; in four cases three instruments were used (Angola-UNITA, Cambodia, Liberia, and Sierra Leone).

65. On the potential importance of the specific characteristics and modes of production of different types of resources on the likelihood, type or duration of armed conflicts, see Le Billon, "The Political Ecology of War: Natural Resources and Armed Conflicts"; Ross, "Oil, Drugs, and Diamonds: How Do Natural Resources Vary in Their Impact on Civil War?"; Snyder, "Does Lootable Wealth Breed Disorder? A Political Economy of Extraction Framework."

66. It should be noted, however, that many "non-lootable" resources are nevertheless "obstructable," see Ross, "Oil, Drugs, and Diamonds: How Do Natural Resources Vary in Their Impact on Civil War?" For a discussion of the case of a water dam, see Fako Johnson Likoti, "The 1998 Military Intervention in Lesotho: SADC Peace Mission or Resource War?," *International Peacekeeping* 14, no. 2 (2007).

67. The low traceability of resources can also facilitate trading and the collaboration of business intermediaries with rebel groups. Difficulties in identification of the origin of diamonds, for example, delayed the effective application of sanctions and required significant reforms in rough diamond trading, particularly through the Kimberley Certification Process Scheme.

68. Letter dated 18 July 2006 from the Chairman of the UN Security Council Committee established pursuant to resolution 1533 (2004) concerning the DRC addressed to the President of the UN Security Council, S/2006/525, accessed at http://daccessdds.un.org/doc/UNDOC/GEN/N06/391/16/PDF/N0639116.pdf?OpenElement.

69. Duncan Brack and Gavin Hayman, "Building Markets for Conflict-Free Goods," in Oli Brown, *et al.* (eds) *Trade, Aid and Security: An Agenda for Peace and Development* (London: Earthscan, 2007).

70. Adapted from Ibid.

71. Although sanctions move a commodity from a legal to an illegal category, for the purpose of analysis I maintain the pre-sanctions legal status of the commodity. This allows us to measure the effect of the sanctions on commodities with pre-existing systems of trade controls (i.e. against illegal commodities), from systems specifically established against legal commodities under sanctions. Since the Kimberley Process Certification Scheme was established in 2003, conflict diamonds are in effect illegal commodities. I have nevertheless maintained conflict diamonds, even after 2003, in the same "legal" category for this analysis.

72. Vanda Felbab-Brown, "Afghanistan: When Counternarcotics Undermines Counterterrorism," *Washington Quarterly* 28, no. 4 (2005).

73. Le Billon, "The Political Ecology of War: Natural Resources and Armed

Conflicts"; Lujala, "The Spoils of Nature: Armed Civil Conflict and Rebel Access to Natural Resources."

74. Collier and Hoeffler, "Greed and Grievance in Civil War."

75. I follow here a broad categorisation of conflicts in terms of territorial (i.e. secessionist) or governmental incompatibilities (i.e. non-secessionist civil wars), using the UCDP/PRIO Armed Conflicts Dataset: Uppsala Conflict Data Project and Peace Research Institute, Oslo, accessed at http://new.prio. no/CSCW-Datasets/Data-on-Armed-Conflict/UppsalaPRIO-Armed-Conflicts-Dataset/

76. Ross, "Oil, Drugs, and Diamonds: How Do Natural Resources Vary in Their Impact on Civil War?"

77. There appears not to be any particular trend resulting from the specific number or sequencing of initiatives, with the exception that a series of initiatives starting with military intervention, rather than sanctions, is on average more likely to be associated with a rapid settlement of conflict. Yet further research is required.

78. Humphreys, "Natural Resources, Conflict, and Conflict Resolution: Uncovering the Mechanisms"; Ross, "A Closer Look at Oil, Diamonds, and Civil War."

79. Jean and Rufin (eds) *Economie des Guerres Civiles*.

80. In the absence of a multivariate analysis that controls for these other factors, the findings of this study should be treated as hypotheses for further investigation, rather than definitive statements about the causal link between conflict resolution mechanisms and outcomes. A more precise analysis would result from a standardisation of the assessment of instrument effectiveness (e.g. standard questionnaires sent to conflict specialists) and a measure of the potential impact of instruments on conflict duration for all wars since 1946 (e.g. using the PRIO/Uppsala conflict dataset).

81. Dylan Balch-Lindsay and Andrew J. Enterline, "Killing Time: The World Politics of Civil War Duration, 1820–1992," *International Studies Quarterly* 44, no. 4 (2000).

82. Ian Smillie, "What Lessons from the Kimberley Process Certification Scheme?" in K. Ballentine and H. Nitzschke (eds) *Profiting From Peace: Managing the Resource Dimensions of Civil War* (Boulder, CO: Lynne Rienner, 2004).

7. RESOURCES FOR PEACE

1. Halvard Buhaug, Scott Gates and Päivi Lujala, "Introduction to Special Issue on "Disaggregating Civil War," *Journal of Conflict Resolution*, Vol. 53, No. 4 2009, pp. 487–95. Rustad and Binningsbo, "Rapid Recurrence: Natural Resources, Armed Conflicts and Peace."

2. For example, recent progress in remote sensing (e.g. satellite imagery) or better advice on tax avoidance mechanisms can grant an advantage to companies.

3. Hostilities and "high risk" may be considered an advantage for some companies. For example, the stock market responded negatively to the end of hostilities in Angola, probably considering that diamond companies would face higher competition and stronger government bargaining power, see Guidolin and La Ferrara, "Diamonds Are Forever, Wars Are Not—Is Conflict Bad for Private Firms?"

4. Risk insurance to resource projects may erode accountability and fiscally hurt citizens in both exporting and importing countries. Many financial institutions and credit agencies have sought to prevent such outcomes through principles of conduct and selection criteria. See, for example, the World Bank Group's Extractive Industries Review, and the voluntary Equator Principles for the banking sector (http://www.equator-principles.com/) that build on the International Financial Corporation guidelines but remain voluntary and do not address major incentives such as bank staff bonuses linked with approved project financing. For discussion, see Andreas Missbach, "The Equator Principles: Drawing the Line for Socially Responsible Banks? An Interim Review from an NGO Perspective," *Development* 47, no. 3 (2004). For a critique of the role of export credit agencies, see FOE, "Extractive Sector Projects Financed by Export Credit Agencies: The Need for Foreign Investment Contract and Revenue Reform" (Friends of the Earth and Pacific Environment 2005).

5. See, for example, Patey, "State Rules: Oil Companies and Armed Conflict in Sudan."

6. For discussion, see M. Humphreys, J. Sachs and J.E. Stiglitz, *Escaping the Resource Curse* (New York: Columbia University Press, 2007).

7. Adapted from Global Witness, "Lessons Unlearned: How the UN and Member States Must Do More to End Resource-Fuelled Conflict" (London: Global Witness, 2010). A detailed list of policy options is available from Siri A. Rustad, Paivi Lujala and Philippe Le Billon, "Building or Spoiling the Peace? Management of High Value Natural Resources in Post-Conflict Countries" in Paivi Lujala and Siri A. Rustad (eds) *High-Value Natural Resources and Post-Conflict Peacebuilding* (London: EarthScan, 2011).

8. Interest among resource companies will depend on a host of factors, including political risks, such as security and reputational risks, as well as commercial considerations, including reserve characteristics, resource prices, exploration and development costs, financing opportunities, competing resource projects and the broad economic conjuncture. For a discussion, see John Bray, "Attracting Reputable Companies to Risky Environments: Petroleum and Mining Companies," in Ian Bannon and Paul Collier (eds) *Natural Resources*

and Armed Conflicts: Options and Actions (Washington, DC: World Bank, 2003).

9. In 1992, internal armed conflict was only ranked twentieth among the investment criteria considered by international mining companies for exploration and mining; see James M. Otto, "Position of the Peruvian Taxation System as Compared to Mining Taxation Systems in Other Nations," 2002. Paper prepared for the Peruvian Ministry of Economy and Finance, http://www.mef.gob.pe/contenidos/pol_econ/documentos/perufinalreport_280504Otto.pdf accessed on 31 May 2011; Jane Nelson, "The Business of Peace. The Private Sector as Partner in Conflict Prevention and Resolution" (London: International Alert, Council on Economic Priorities, and the Prince of Wales Business Leaders Forum, 2000).

10. See M. Drohan, *Making a Killing: How and Why Corporations Use Armed Force to Do Business* (Toronto: Random House, 2003); Damian Lilly and Philippe Le Billon, "Regulating Business in Zones of Conflict: A Synthesis of Strategies" (London: Overseas Development Institute, 2002).

11. Interviews with UNAMSIL officers, April 2001.

12. This principle is recognised in article 55 of the 1907 Hague Regulation (occupying state as "administrators and usufructuary"), and was upheld by a 1976 US Department of Justice Memorandum, in the case of oil exploitation by Israel in the Sinai (reprinted 16 ILM 753, 1977). This principle can be applied to domestic transitional governments through local legislation, peace agreement, or UN Security Council resolution.

13. See for example, Le Billon, "Getting It Done: Instruments of Enforcement"; Philippe Le Billon, "Getting it Done," in Ian Bannon and Paul Collier (eds) *Natural Resources and Armed Conflicts: Actions and Options* (Washington, DC: World Bank, 2005), pp. 215–86.

14. See Philippe Le Billon, "Contract Renegotiation and Asset Recovery in Post-Conflict Settings," in Paivi Lujala and Siri A. Rustad (eds) *High-Value Natural Resources and Post-Conflict Peacebuilding* (London: EarthScan, 2011).

15. For a presentation of challenges and options, see the joint Office on Drugs and Crime (UNODC) and World Bank "Stolen Assets Recovery" (StAR) initiative (http://siteresources.worldbank.org/NEWS/Resources/Star-rep-full.pdf).

16. The concept of "odious contract" is also applied to "odious debt" contracted by past governments against the interests of the people, without their consent, and with the full awareness of the creditor. For discussion, see Patricia Alvarez-Plata and Tilman Bruck, "Postwar Debts: Time for a New Approach," in James K. Boyce and Madalene O'Donnell (eds) *Peace and the Public Purse: Economic Policies for Postwar Statebuilding* (Boulder: Lynne Rienner, 2007); Ashfaq Khalfan, Jeff King and Bryan Thomas, "Advancing the Odious Debt

Doctrine" (Montreal: Centre for International Sustainable Development Law, 2003).

17. See Jonathan M. Winer and Trifin J. Roule, "Follow the Money: The Finance of Illicit Resource Extraction," in Ian Bannon and Paul Collier (eds) *Natural Resources and Armed Conflicts: Actions and Options* (Washington, DC: World Bank, 2003). Emily Harwell and Philippe Le Billon, "Natural Connections: Linking Transitional Justice and Development through a Focus on Natural Resources," in Pablo de Grieff and Roger Dutie (eds) *Transitional Justice and Development* (New York: International Center on Transitional Justice, 2009).

18. Human Rights Watch, "The Curse of Gold"; Lutundula Commission Report, December 2005 (http://www.freewebs.com/congo-kinshasa/).

19. J. Clayton, "Mining groups face Congo shake-up after review," *The Times*, 8 November 2007. http://business.timesonline.co.uk/tol/business/industry_sectors/industrials/article2827329.ece accessed on 31 May 2011.

20. Tax Justice Network, "Breaking the Curse: How Transparent Taxation and Fair Taxes can turn Africa's Mineral Wealth into Development," 2009.

21. Carter Center, "The Mining Review in the Democratic Republic of the Congo: Missed Opportunities, Failed Expectations, Hopes for the Future" (Atlanta: Carter Center, 2009); LP, "Congo-Kinshasa: contrats miniers; L'heure de vérité a sonné," *Le Potentiel*, 27 October 2009. Some mining companies and foreign governments also unsuccessfully lobbied the World Bank and IMF to stop Congolese debt cancellation to resist contract renegotiation, while the IMF exercised its lending leverage to have a mining contract with China revised: Global Witness, "China and Congo: Friends in Need" (London: 2011); Macho Philipovich, "Why is Canada blocking Congo debt forgiveness," *The Dominion*, 11 August 2010.

22. Global Witness, "Heavy Mittal? A State within a State. The Inequitable Mineral Development Agreement between the Government of Liberia and Mittal Steel Holdings NV" (London: Global Witness, 2006); R. Kaul and A. Heuly, "Getting a Better Deal from the Extractive Sector. Concession Negotiation in Liberia, 2006–2008" (New York: Revenue Watch Institute, 2009).

23. Global Witness, "Update on the Renegotiation of the Mineral Development Agreement between Mittal Steel and the Government of Liberia" (London: Global Witness, 2007).

24. Bridge, "Mapping the Bonanza: Geographies of Mining Investment in an Era of Neoliberal Reform"; Otto, "Global Changes in Mining Laws, Agreements and Tax Systems."

25. In Azerbaijan, for example, oil and gas fields with weak future prospects were operated by the state oil company (SOCAR), whereas "new fields are

developed and managed under the leadership of international partners" and their income is shared between government and companies according to a pre-determined production sharing agreements, see IMF, "Azerbaijan Republic—Selected Issues and Statistical Appendix," in *IMF Country Report No. 03/130* (Washington, DC: International Monetary Fund, 2004). Such a model was also promoted under a controversial draft oil law for Iraq. For a critique, see Greg Muttit, "Crude Designs—the Rip-Off of Iraq's Oil Wealth" (London: Platform, 2005).

26. The main stated argument was that the windfall tax was based on revenue, and not profits, thus not accounting for production costs: Nicholas Bariyo, "Zambia Opposition: 2008 Mining Tax Regime Triggering Job Losses," *Dow Jones Newswire*, 3 September 2010; John Lungu, "The Politics of Reforming Zambia Mining Tax Regime" (Johannesburg: Southern Africa Resource Watch, 2009); TZ, "Mines agree to pay tax arrears, says Finance Minister," *Times of Zambia*, 26 November 2010.

27. In Sub Saharan Africa, this norm stood at 3.5 percent for gold royalty rate even if many companies were exempted from profits tax, thus leaving local authorities with a pitiful share of gross revenue; see for example Saji Thomas, "Mining Taxation: An Application to Mali," in *WP/10/126* (Washington, DC: International Monetary Fund, 2010).

28. Weinthal and Luong, "Combating the Resource Curse: An Alternative Solution to Managing Mineral Wealth."

29. This table builds on the case of mining in Sierra Leone. See Killick, "The Benefits of Foreign Direct Investment and Its Alternatives: An Empirical Exploration." Some domestic-artisanal profits are repatriated by exporters with transnational ties (e.g. diasporas, or domestic elites with family members abroad). See also D.F. Stewart, "Large-Scale or Small Scale Mining: Meeting the Needs of Developing Countries," *Natural Resources Forum* 13, no. 1 (1989). Repatriated profits in domestic artisanal correspond to "capital flight," especially from diaspora and dual-nationality exporters (such as Sierra Leonean Lebanese).

30. More indirectly, resource revenue can also affect land markets and land use.

31. Frances Stewart, Graham Brown and Alex Cobham, "Promoting Group Justice: Fiscal Policies in Post-Conflict Countries," in *Policy Paper on Public Finance in Post-Conflict Environments* (New York and Amherst, MA: Center on International Cooperation, and Political Economy Research Institute, 2007).

32. For a general overview of stolen-asset recovery, see Mark Pieth (ed.) *Recovering Stolen Assets* (New York: Peter Lang, 2008). On the role of banks in laundering stolen assets, see Global Witness, "Undue Diligence: How Banks Do Business with Corrupt Regimes." On the role of transitional justice

mechanisms and the possibility of using recovered assets for war reparations, see Ruben Carranza, "Plunder and Pain: Should Transitional Justice Engage with Corruption and Economic Crimes?" *International Journal of Transitional Justice* 2 (2008); Harwell and Le Billon, "Natural Connections: Linking Transitional Justice and Development through a Focus on Natural Resources."

33. Although some funds may be recovered through the repatriation of assets, others may appear irretrievable because of contractual provisions inherited from previous governments. International aid can temporarily mask these losses, but they will become more apparent when foreign aid declines and countries are most in need of sustained revenue.

34. Harwell and Le Billon, "Natural Connections: Linking Transitional Justice and Development through a Focus on Natural Resources."

35. On conflict financing and prosecution, see Winer and Roule, "Follow the Money: The Finance of Illicit Resource Extraction."

36. Jack Smith, Mark Pieth and Guillermo Jorge, "The Recovery of Stolen Assets: A Fundamental Principle of the UN Convention against Corruption," in *U4 Brief* (Anti-Corruption Resource Centre and International Centre for Asset Recovery, 2007).

37. UNSG, "Report of the Secretary-General on Enhancing Mediation and Its Support Activities" (New York: United Nations, 2009).

38. Accessible through http://www.sierra-leone.org/TRCDocuments.html

39. See www.bernlieb.com/news/iraq-oil-food-lawsuit/index.html.

40. See Chapter V of the convention, www.unodc.org/documents/treaties/UNCAC/Publications/Convention/08–50026_E.pdf. For an analysis of the challenges facing UNCAC, see Smith, Pieth, and Jorge, "The Recovery of Stolen Assets: A Fundamental Principle of the UN Convention against Corruption."

41. For more information on the joint effort, see www.worldbank.org/StAR.

42. World Bank and UNODC StAR Progress Report, Washington, DC: World Bank. July 2009, http://siteresources.worldbank.org/EXTSARI/Resources/ProgressReport2009.pdf?resourceurlname=ProgressReport2009.pdf

43. The Group of Seven (G-7) established the Financial Action Task Force (FATF) in 1989 to address money laundering. More recently, it has begun to address terrorism financing (see www.fatf-gafi.org/). The International Centre for Asset Recovery is based at the Basel Institute of Governance (see www.baselgovernance.org/big/) and provides various resources, including assistance and training for asset recovery (see www.assetrecovery.org).

44. On the case of EU implementation of UN Security Council asset freezing, see Jorge Godinho, "When Worlds Collide: Enforcing United Nations Security Council Asset Freezes in the EU Legal Order," *European Law Journal* 16, no. 1 (2009).

45. UNITA's leader Jonas Savimbi, for example, was in possession of a large amount of diamonds when he was killed by Angolan army troops in 2002, while UNITA assets had been frozen by decision of the UN Security Council.

46. See Jostein F. Tellnes, "The Unexpected Deal: Why the Government of Sudan and the SPLM/A Reached an Agreement on Oil Issues through the IGAD Peace Talks 2002–04" (Centre for the Study of Civil War, PRIO, 2005).

47. Béatrice Labonne, "The Mining Industry and the Community: Joining Forces for Sustainable Social Development," *Natural Resources Forum* 23, no. 4 (1999).

48. Philippe Le Billon and Estelle Levin, "Building Peace with Conflict Diamonds? Merging Security and Development in Sierra Leone's Diamond Sector," *Development and Change* (2009); Leo C. Zulu and Sigismond A. Wilson, "Minerals for Whose Development? Rhetoric and Reality on Mineral-Led Poverty Reduction in Post-Conflict Sierra Leone" (Department of Geography, Michigan State University, 2011).

49. Young, "Sudan: A Flawed Peace Process Leading to a Flawed Peace."

50. Yash Ghai, "Decentralization and the Accommodation of Ethnic Diversity," in C. Young (ed.) *Ethnic Diversity and Public Policy. A Comparative Inquiry* (Basingstoke: Palgrave, 1998); Watts, "Antinomies of Community: Some Thoughts on Geography, Resources and Empire."

51. The clause of the 2005 Iraqi constitution guaranteeing a distribution of "oil and gas revenues in a fair manner in proportion to the population distribution in all parts of the country" only applies to currently developed fields. Revenue from undeveloped fields was left under the control of regional authorities.

52. Patrick O'Mahony, "Assessing the Merits of Decentralization as a Conflict Mitigation Strategy" (Development Alternatives Inc., 2007); Arild Schou and Marit Haug, "Decentralisation in Conflict and Post-Conflict Situations," in *Working Paper 2005: 139* (Blindern: Norwegian Institute for Urban and Regional Research, 2005).

53. The Alaska Permanent Fund Dividend established in 1976 is one of the oldest schemes specifically aimed at direct disbursement (see http://www.apfc.org/; Scott Goldsmith, "The Alaska Permanent Fund Dividend: An Experiment in Wealth Distribution" (paper presented at the Ninth Congress of Basic Income European Network, Geneva, 12–14 September 2002). See also Xavier Sala-i-Martin and Arvind Subramanian, "Addressing the Natural Resource Curse: An Illustration from Nigeria," in *NBER Working Paper 9804* (Cambridge, MA: 2003). http://www.nber.org/papers/w9804 accessed on 31 May 2011; Todd Moss, "Oil-to-Cash: Fighting the Resource Curse

through Cash Transfers," in *CGD Working Paper 237* (Washington, DC: Center for Global Development, 2011). Several Latin American countries have instituted conditional cash transfers, which helped to reduce extreme poverty and improve educational outcomes, see Fábio Veras Soares, Rafael Perez Ribas and Rafael Guerreiro Osório, "Evaluating the Impact of Brazil's Bolsa Família: Cash Transfer Programs in Comparative Perspective," *Latin American Research Review* 45, no. 2 (2010).

54. Paul Harvey, "Cash-Based Responses in Emergencies," in *HPG Report 24* (London: Overseas Development Institute, 2007).

55. Palley, "Oil and the Case of Iraq."

56. Robert E. Hinson, "Banking the Poor: The Role of Mobiles," *Journal of Financial Services Marketing* 15, no. 4 (2011); Katharine Vincent and Tracy Cull, "Cell Phones, Electronic Delivery Systems and Social Cash Transfers: Recent Evidence and Experiences from Africa," *International Social Security Review* 64, no. 1 (2011).

57. For example, direct disbursement was made in the 1950s by the government of Alberta, in Canada just prior to an election. See Robert Bacon and Silvana Tordo, "Experiences with Oil Funds: Institutional and Financial Aspects" (Washington, DC: Energy Sector Management Assistance Program, World Bank, 2006).

58. See M.E. Sandbu, "Natural Wealth Accounts: A Proposal for Alleviating the Natural Resource Curse," *World Development* 34, no. 7 (2006). Income levels may be difficult to determine and enforce. A possible option is to have individuals self-identify as poor, middle or rich, with their tax rates varying accordingly. Self-identification could be posted on a public notice board at the post office (or wherever dividend payments are disbursed), letting social pressure/status concerns act as an enforcement mechanism for truthful self-identification (James Boyce, personal communication, October 2007).

59. See Auty (ed.) *Resource Abundance and Economic Development*. In principle, reinvesting revenue into other sectors could assist diversification, but in practice, many countries fail to efficiently manage this process owing to misdirected resource revenue allocation (e.g. through so-called "white elephant" projects, protection of uncompetitive "infant industry," or corruption), constraints on labor skills, and trade barriers. There are also incentives not to diversify the economy in order to curtail the risk of political competition coming from independent sectors. Further, diversification is harder now that much of the manufacturing sector has already been "captured" by the first and second generations of Newly Industrialized Countries, most recently China. For discussion of the latter constraint, see Ian Coxhead, "A New Resource Curse? Impacts of China's Boom on Comparative Advantage and Resource Dependence in Southeast Asia," *World Development* 35, no. 7

(2007); Raphael Kaplinsky, Dorotha McCormick, and Mike Morris, "The Impact of China on Sub-Saharan Africa" (London: China Office, Department for International Development, 2006)); Mauricio Mesquita Moreira, "Fear of China: Is There a Future for Manufacturing in Latin America?," *World Development* 35, no. 3 (2007).

60. Leite and Weidmann, "Does Mother Nature Corrupt? Natural Resources, Corruption, and Economic Growth."

61. Philippe Le Billon, "Corrupting Peace? Corruption, Peacebuilding and Reconstruction," *International Peacekeeping* 15, no. 3 (2008).

62. For information, see http://www.publishwhatyoupay.org/english/; and http://www.eitransparency.org/.

63. A few governments were in effect expelled from the initiative, including that of Equatorial Guinea, which demonstrated the application of minimal validation criteria, but also the limits of such a voluntary approach, while others exited the process, such as the Angolan government, which was a prime initial target of the scheme and the Publish What You Pay campaign.

64. Susan Ariel Aaronson, "Limited Partnership: Business, Government, Civil Society, and the Public in the Extractive Industries Transparency Initiative (EITI)," *Public Administration and Development* 31, no. 1 (2011); Liliane C. Mouan, "Exploring the Potential Benefits of Asian Participation in the Extractive Industries Transparency Initiative: The Case of China," *Business Strategy and the Environment* 19, no. 6 (2010).

65. I. Kolstad, Arne Wilg and A. Williams, "Mission Improbable: Does Petroleum-Related Aid Address the Resource Curse?" *Energy Policy* 37, no. 3 (2008); Audun Solli, "From Good Governance to Development? A Critical Perspective on the Case of Norway's Oil for Development," *Forum for Development Studies* 38, no. 1 (2011).

66. IAG, "Chad-Cameroon Petroleum Development and Pipeline Project. Assessment Report" (Montreal: International Advisory Group, 2009); Scott Pegg, "Chronicle of a Death Foretold: The Collapse of the Chad-Cameroon Pipeline Project," *African Affairs* 108, no. 431 (2009).

67. Multilateral schemes to lessen commodity price shocks, such as the IMF's Compensatory and Contingency Financing Facility and the EU's Flex mechanisms, are limited in scope and hard to access.

68. These strategies were exacerbated by low prices of many commodities from the mid-1980s to the late 1990s and the race for market share, see Christopher L. Gilbert, "International Commodity Agreements: An Obituary Notice," *World Development* 24, no. 1 (1996).

69. John Baffes and Tassos Haniotis, "Placing the 2006/08 Commodity Price Boom into Perspective," in *World Bank Policy Research Working Paper No. 5371* (Washington, DC: World Bank, 2010); Jennifer Clapp and Eric Helleiner,

"Troubled Futures? The Global Food Crisis and the Politics of Agricultural Derivatives Regulation" *Review of International Political Economy* (2010).

70. For discussion, see Richard M. Auty and Raymond F. Mikesell, *Sustainable Development in Mineral Economies* (Oxford: Clarendon Press, 1998); Ugo Fasano, "Review of the Experience with Oil Stabilization and Savings Funds in Selected Countries," in *Working Paper WP/00/112* (Washington, DC: International Monetary Fund, 2000); Humphreys, Sachs and Stiglitz, *Escaping the Resource Curse.*

71. While the Chad Cameroon Project was hailed as a "new model" for oil development in poor countries, and benefited from unprecedented attention and efforts, the project failed to ensure that strong institutions were in place before oil revenue started flowing, and the Chadian government faced bankruptcy in the face of armed opposition. See Ian Gary and Nikki Reisch, "Chad's Oil: Miracle or Mirage? Following the Money in Africa's Newest Petro-State" (Catholic Relief Service and Bank Information Center, 2005).

72. Boyce, James K. Investing in *Peace: Aid and Conditionality After Civil Wars. Adelphi Paper* 351. (New York: Oxford University Press, 2002)

73. Le Billon, "Contract Renegotiation and Asset Recovery in Post-Conflict Settings."

74. Philippe Le Billon and Estelle Levin, "Building Peace with Conflict Diamonds? Merging Security and Development in Sierra Leone's Diamond Sector," *Development and Change* (2009).

75. Cumbersome regulatory measures and "crackdowns" on so-called illegal logging or mining are common in post-conflict countries and can represent a barrier to local livelihoods recovery and bias favouring revenue concentration by large corporations. See N. Cooper, "Picking out the Pieces of the Liberal Peaces: Representations of Conflict Economies and the Implications for Policy," *Security Dialogue* 36, no. 4 (2005); H. Nitzschke and K. Studdard, "The Legacies of War Economies: Challenges and Options for Peacemaking and Peacebuilding," *International Peacekeeping* 12, no. 2 (2005).

76. See, for example, Business Principles for Sudan during the Interim Period (www.ecosonline.org). In this case, the forum was a consortium of European civil society organisations that spelled out the principles, activities, normative framework, and benchmarks for oil companies to play a positive role in Sudan.

77. See Paul Collier, *The Bottom Billion: Why the Poorest Countries Are Failing and What Can Be Done About It* (Oxford University Press, 2007), and www.naturalresourcecharter.org.

78. The joint task force could draw upon the experience of the Kimberley process, the World Bank extractive industries review, the Mining, Minerals and Sustainable Development project, the Canadian Government roundtable on extractive industries, the Natural Resource Charter, and civil society

initiatives such as the Publish What You Pay campaign or CIDSE and OXFAM programmes on extractive sectors and poverty.

79. Global Witness, "The Sinews of War: Eliminating the Trade in Conflict Resources" (London: Global Witness, 2007); Le Billon, "Getting It Done: Instruments of Enforcement."

CONCLUSION

1. See Bridge, "Resource Triumphalism: Postindustrial Narratives of Primary Commodity Production."

2. Downward cycles are likely in the future, possibly due to an even more severe and prolonged global economic crisis or for example a pandemic. Not all resource sectors will react in the same way, some experiencing sharper downturns due to overproduction, while other sectors facing greater supply constraints will fare better.

3. Botswana is rightly praised for its macroeconomic performances and its universal access to core public services, yet faces criticism for high inequalities and limited democracy, see Kenneth Good, *Diamonds, Dispossession and Democracy in Botswana* (Woodbridge, Suffolk: James Currey, 2009).

4. On the case of Mozambique, see Mark F. Chingono, *The State, Violence and Development: The Political Economy of War in Mozambique 1975–1992* (Aldershot: Avebury, 1996).

5. Cramer, *Civil War Is Not a Stupid Thing: Accounting for Violence in Developing Countries.*

6. Soares de Oliviera, *Oil and Politics in the Gulf of Guinea.*

7. Paul Collier, *The Plundered Planet. How to Reconcile Prosperity with Nature* (London: Penguin, 2010); Humphreys, Sachs and Stiglitz, *Escaping the Resource Curse.* See also the recent wave of protests in the Middle East and North Africa, where social protests challenged the long established status quo of "political stability."

8. For example, see on diamonds Leo C. Zulu and Sigismond A. Wilson, "Sociospatial Geographies of Civil War in Sierra Leone and the New Global Diamond Order: Is the Kimberley Process the Panacea?" *Environment and Planning C: Government and Policy* 27, no. 6 (2009). On fair trade and organic products, Daniel and Philip H. Howard Jaffee, "Corporate Cooptation of Organic and Fair Trade Standards," *Agriculture and Human Values* 27, no. 4 (2009); Kate Macdonald and Shelley Marshall (eds) *Fair Trade, Corporate Accountability and Beyond* (Farnham: Ashgate, 2010).

9. Email from Simon Springer dated 8 January 2010.

10. Corin de Freitas, personal communication, March 2011.

11. Peter Foster, "Kill the Avatar Bill!" *Financial Post*, 9 March 2010.

12. See also the recent films *Syriana* and *Blood Diamonds*.

13. The mining-related conflict in Bougainville and oil-related conflicts in the Niger Delta are given as examples, but these are mostly about the redefinition of resource control, with environmental rights forming only a subset.

14. James Risen, "US Identifies Vast Mineral Riches in Afghanistan," *New York Times*, 13 June 2010.

15. The "abundant mineral resources" of Afghanistan were recognised in prior USGS reports, see Chin S. Kuo, "The Mineral Industry of Afghanistan" (US Geological Survey, 2008).

16. My suggested answers are: yes; only to a limited extent; probably not; yes and many more sacrifices were made by the Afghan population.

BIBLIOGRAPHY

Aaronson, Susan Ariel. "Limited Partnership: Business, Government, Civil Society, and the Public in the Extractive Industries Transparency Initiative (EITI)." *Public Administration and Development* 31, no. 1 (2011): 50–63.

Acemoglu, Daron, Simon Johnson and James Robinson. "An African Success Story: Botswana." In Dani Rodrik (ed.) *In Search of Prosperity: Analytical Narrative on Economic Growth*. Princeton University Press, 2003.

Acemoglu, Daron, Simon Johnson and James A. Robinson. "The Colonial Origins of Comparative Development: An Empirical Investigation." *American Economic Review* 91, no. 5 (2001): 1369–401.

Acemoglu, Daron and James A. Robinson. *Economic Origins of Dictatorship and Democracy*. Cambridge University Press, 2006.

Acharya, Arabinda, Syed Adnan Ali Shah Bukhari and Sadia Sulaiman. "Making Money in the Mayhem: Funding Taliban Insurrection in the Tribal Areas of Pakistan." *Studies in Conflict & Terrorism* 32, no. 2 (2009): 95–108.

Aissaoui, A. *Algeria: The Political Economy of Oil and Gas*. Oxford University Press, 2001.

Akiwumi, Fenda. "Conflict Timber, Conflict Diamonds: Parallels in the Political Ecology of Nineteenth and Twentieth Century Resource Exploitation in Sierra Leone." In Kwadwo Konadu-Agyemang and Kwamina Panford (eds) *Africa's Development in the Twenty-First Century*, 109–25. Aldershot: Ashgate Publishing, 2006.

Alahmad, N. "The Politics of Oil and State Survival in Iraq (1991–2003): Beyond the Rentier Thesis." *Constellations* 14, no. 4 (2007): 586–612.

Alam, Undala Z. "Questioning the Water Wars Rationale: A Case Study of the Indus Waters Treaty." *Geographical Journal* 168, no. 4 (2002): 341–53.

Albion, Robert Greenhalgh. *Forests and Sea Power: The Timber Problem of the Royal Navy, 1652–1862, Harvard Economic Studies Vol. XXIX*. Hamden, CN: Archon Books, 1926.

Alemagi, Dieudonne, Anne-Sophie Samjee and Andrew Davis. "Comparison of Economic Growth and Governance between High Forest and Low Forest

Countries. Background paper to "Seeing People through the Trees" project. Washington, DC: Rights and Resources Initiative. Washington, DC: Rights and Resources Initiative, 2007.

Ali, S.H. *Peace Parks: Conservation and Conflict Resolution.* Cambridge, MA: MIT Press, 2007.

Allan, J.A. "Hydro-Peace in the Middle East: Why No Water Wars? A Case Study of the Jordan River Basin." *SAIS Review* 22, no. 2 (2002): 255–72.

Alston, Julian, Richard Gray and Daniel A. Sumner. "The Wheat War of 1994." *Canadian Journal of Agricultural Economics* 42, no. 3 (2005): 231–51.

Alvarez-Plata, Patricia and Tilman Bruck. "Postwar Debts: Time for a New Approach." In James K. Boyce and Madalene O'Donnell (eds) *Peace and the Public Purse: Economic Policies for Postwar Statebuilding*, Boulder: Lynne Rienner, 2007.

Amaize, E., K. Omonubi and U. Kalu. "Nigeria: Attack on Bonga—MEND Reveals How its Men Carried Out Raid." *Vanguard*, 28 June 2008. http://allafrica.com/stories/200806280011.html accessed on 31 May 2011.

Anderson, E.W. and L.D. Anderson. *Strategic Minerals: Resource Geopolitics and Global Geo-Economics.* Chichester: John Wiley & Sons, 1997.

Angell, N. *Raw Materials, Population Pressure and War.* Boston, MA: World Peace Foundation, 1936.

Appadurai, A. (ed.). *The Social Life of Things: Commodities in Cultural Perspective.* Cambridge University Press, 1988.

Arad, R.W. and U. B. Arad (eds). *Sharing Global Resources.* New York: McGraw-Hill, 1979.

Arbatov, Alexander A. "Oil as a Factor in Strategic Policy and Action: Past and Present." In A.H. Westing (ed.) *Global Resources and International Conflict: Environmental Factors in Strategic Policy and Action.* Oxford University Press, 1986.

Archer, Christon I., John R. Ferris, Holger H. Herwig and Timothy H.E. Travers. *World History of Warfare.* Reno: University of Nevada Press, 2008.

Armierro, Marco and Nancy Lee Peluso. "Insurgent Natures and Nations: Unpacking Socio-Environmental Histories of Forest Conflicts." Paris: Ecole des Hautes Etudes de Sciences Sociales, 2008.

Armitage, David and Michael J. Braddick (eds). *The British Atlantic World.* Basingstoke: Palgrave Macmillan, 2002.

Arnson, C.J. and W.I. Zartmann (eds) *Rethinking the Economics of War: The Intersection of Need, Creed, and Greed.* Baltimore: Johns Hopkins University Press, 2005.

Aron, Raymond. *War and Peace: A Theory of International Relations.* London: Doubleday, 1962.

Arriola, Leonardo R. "Patronage and Political Stability in Africa." *Comparative Political Studies* 42, no. 10 (2009): 1339–62.

Atarodi, Habibollah. *Great Powers, Oil and the Kurds in Mosul: Southern Kurdistan/Northern Iraq, 1910–1925*. Lanham, MD: University Press of America, 2003.

Autesserre, Séverine. *The Trouble with the Congo: Local Violence and the Failure of International Peacebuilding*. Cambridge University Press, 2010.

Auty, Richard. "Natural Resources and Civil Strife: A Two-Stage Process." *Geopolitics* 9, no. 1 (2004): 29–49.

Auty, Richard (ed.) *Resource Abundance and Economic Development, Wider Studies in Development Economics*. New York: Oxford University Press, 2001.

Auty, Richard M. and Raymond F. Mikesell. *Sustainable Development in Mineral Economies*. Oxford: Clarendon Press, 1998.

Avuru, Austin. "The Trouble with Onshore/Offshore Dichotomy." Niger Delta Congress, undated.

Ayres, C.E. *The Theory of Economic Progress*. Chapel Hill, NC: The University of North Carolina Press, 1943.

Azam, Jean-Paul. "Betting on Displacement: Oil and Strategic Violence in Nigeria." Paper presented at International Studies Association Fiftieth annual convention, New York, 2009.

Azama, Maj. Rodney. "The Huks and the New People's Army: Comparing Two Postwar Filipino Insurgencies." Quantico, VA: Marine Corps Command and Staff College, 1985.

Bacon, Robert and Silvana Tordo. "Experiences with Oil Funds: Institutional and Financial Aspects." Washington, DC: Energy Sector Management Assistance Program, World Bank, 2006.

Baechler, G. and K.R. Spillman. *Environmental Degradation as a Cause of War*. Zurich: Ruegger, 1996.

Baffes, John and Tassos Haniotis. "Placing the 2006/08 Commodity Price Boom into Perspective." In *World Bank Policy Research Working Paper No. 5371*. Washington, DC: World Bank, 2010.

Bah, Abu Bakar. *Breakdown and Reconstitution. Democracy, the Nation-State, and Ethnicity in Nigeria*. Lanham, MD: Lexington Books, 2005.

Baird, Ian. "Various Forms of Colonialism: The Social and Spatial Re-Organisation of the Brao in Southern Laos and Northeastern Cambodia." Vancouver: University of British Columbia, 2008.

Baird, Ian G. and Bruce Shoemaker. "Unsettling Experiences: Internal Resettlement and International Aid Agencies in Laos." *Development and Change* 38, no. 5 (2007): 865–88.

Bakker, K. and G. Bridge. "Material Worlds? Resource Geographies and the Matter of Nature." *Progress in Human Geography* 30, no. 1 (2006): 5–27.

Balch-Lindsay, Dylan and Andrew J. Enterline. "Killing Time: The World Politics of Civil War Duration, 1820–1992." *International Studies Quarterly* 44, no. 4 (2000): 615–42.

Ballentine, K. and H. Nitzschke. *Profiting from Peace: Managing the Resource Dimensions of Civil War*. Boulder, CO: Lynne Rienner, 2004.

Ballesteros, Enrique Bernales. "Report on the Question of the Use of Mercenaries as a Means of Violating Human Rights and Impeding the Exercise of the Right of Peoples to Self-Determination." New York: United Nations General Assembly, 1997.

Bamford, P.W. *Forests and French Sea Power, 1660–1789*. University of Toronto Press, 1956.

Bamforth, Vicky, Steven Lanjouw and Graham Mortimer. "Conflict and Displacement in Karenni: The Need for Considered Responses." Burma Ethnic Research Group, 2000.

Bannon, Ian and Paul Collier. *Natural Resources and Violent Conflict: Options and Actions*. Washington, DC: World Bank, 2003.

Barbieri, Katherine. *The Liberal Illusion: Does Trade Promote Peace?* Ann Arbor: University of Michigan Press, 2005.

Bariyo, Nicholas. "Zambia Opposition: 2008 Mining Tax Regime Triggering Job Losses." *Dow Jones Newswire*, 3 September 2010.

Barnett, John. "Shopping for Gucci on Canal Street: Reflections on Status Consumption, Intellectual Property and the Incentive Thesis." American Law and Economics Association Annual Meetings Paper 28, 2005. http://law.bepress.com/alea/15th/bazaar/art28 accessed on 31 May 2011

———. *The Meaning of Environmental Security: Ecological Politics and Policy in the New Security Era*. London: Zed Books, 2001.

Basedau, Matthias and Jann Lay. "Resource Curse or Rentier State? The Ambiguous Effects of Oil Wealth and Oil Dependence on Violent Conflict." *Journal of Peace Research* (2009).

Bassett, T.J. "The Political Ecology of Peasant-Herder Conflicts in the Northern Ivory Coast." *Annals of the Association of American Geographers* 78, no. 3 (1988): 453–72.

Batruch, C. "Oil and Conflict: Lundin Petroleum's Experience in Sudan." In A.J.K. Bailes and I. Frommelt (eds) *Business and Security: Public–Private Sector Relationships in a New Security Environment*, 148–60, Oxford University Press, 2004.

Baudrillard, J. *Le Système des Objets*. Paris: Gallimard, 1968.

Bayart, J.F., Stephen Ellis and Béatrice Hibou. *The Criminalization of the State in Africa*. Oxford: Currey, 1999.

Bazenguissa-Ganga, Rémy. "Les Milices Politiques dans les Affrontements." *Afrique Contemporaine* 186 (1998): 52.

Beckley, Thomas, John Parkins and Richard Stedman. "Indicators of Forest-Dependent Community Sustainability: The Evolution of Research." *The Forestry Chronicle* 78, no. 5 (2002): 626–36.

Bellows, J. and E. Miguel. "War and Institutions: New Evidence from Sierra Leone." *American Economic Review* 96, no. 2 (2006): 394–9.

316

Bennett, Judith A. *Pacific Forest: A History of Resource Control and Contest in the Solomon Islands, c. 1800–1997*. Cambridge: White Horse Press, 2000.

Berdal, Mats and David Malone (eds) *Greed and Grievance: Economic Agendas in Civil Wars*. Boulder, CO: Lynne Rienner Publishers, 2000.

Bergsten, C.F. "The Threat from the Third World." *Foreign Policy* 11 (1973): 102–24.

Bernstein, L. "Opting out of the Legal System: Extralegal Contractual Relations in the Diamond Industry." *Journal of Legal Studies* 21, no. 1 (1992): 115–57.

Bhurtel, Jugal and Saleem H. Ali. "The Green Roots of Red Rebellion: Environmental Degradation and the Rise of the Maoist Movement in Nepal." In Mahendra Lawoti and Anup Pahari (eds) *The Maoist Insurgency in Nepal: Dynamics and Growth in the Twenty-First Century*. New York: Routledge, 2009.

Binningsbo, Helga Malmin and Siri A. Rustad. "Resource Conflicts, Wealth Sharing and Postconflict Peace." Norwegian University of Science and Technology and International Peace Research Institute, 2009.

Blattman, Christopher and Edward Miguel. "Civil War." *Journal of Economic Literature* 48, no. 1 (2010): 3–57.

Blomley, Nicholas. "Law, Property, and the Geography of Violence: The Frontier, the Survey, and the Grid." *Annals of the Association of American Geographers* 93, no. 1 (2003): 121–41.

Blore, Shawn. "Angola 2007." In *Diamond Industry Annual Review*. Ottawa: Partnership Africa Canada, 2007.

Bloxam, Elizabeth. "Miners and Mistresses: Middle Kingdom Mining on the Margins." *Journal of Social Archaeology* 6, no. 2 (2006): 277–303.

Blundell, Arthur G. "Conflict Timber and Liberia's War." *ETFRN News* 43–44 (2005): 32–5.

Boal, I.A. *Afflicted Powers: Capital and Spectacle in a New Age of War*. London: Verso, 2005.

Boge, Volker. "Mining, Environmental Degradation and War: The Bougainville Case." In Mohamed Suliman (ed.) *Ecology, Politics and Violent Conflicts*, 211–27. London: Zed Books, 1999.

Boschini, Anne D., Jan Pettersson and Jesper Roine. "Resource Curse or Not: A Question of Appropriability." *Scandinavian Journal of Economics* 109, no. 3 (2007): 593–617.

Bowman, I. *The New World: Problems in Political Geography*. New York: World Book Company, 1921.

Boyce, James K. *Investing in Peace: Aid and Conditionality After Civil Wars*. *Adelphi Paper* 351 (New York: Oxford University Press, 2002).

Brack, Duncan and Gavin Hayman. "Building Markets for Conflict-Free Goods." In Oli Brown, Mark Halle, Sonia Pena Moreno and Sebastian Winkler (eds) *Trade, Aid and Security: An Agenda for Peace and Development*, 92–125. London: Earthscan, 2007.

————. "Intergovernmental Actions on Illegal Logging." London: Royal Institute of International Affairs, 2001.

Bradley, Robert L. "Resourceship: An Austrian Theory of Mineral Resources." *Review of Austrian Economy* 20 (2007): 63–90.

Braide, Kombo Mason. 2003. The Political Economy of Illegal Bunkering in Nigeria. In, Niger Delta Congress, http://www.nigerdeltacongress.com/particles/political_economy_of_illegal_bun.htm, accessed 29 June 2009.

Brautigam, Deborah. *The Dragon's Gift: The Real Story of China in Africa*. Oxford University Press, 2009.

Bray, John. "Attracting Reputable Companies to Risky Environments: Petroleum and Mining Companies." In Ian Bannon and Paul Collier (eds) *Natural Resources and Armed Conflicts: Options and Actions*, 287–352. Washington, DC: World Bank, 2003.

Bredahl, Maury, Andrew Schmitz and Jimmye S. Hillman. "Rent Seeking in International Trade: The Great Tomato War." *American Journal of Agricultural Economics* 69, no. 1 (1987): 1–10.

Bredeloup, S. "Les Territoires de L'Identité: Le Territoire, Lien ou Frontière?" In S. Bredeloup, J. Bonnemaison, L. Cambrezy and L. Quinty-Bourgeois (eds) *Territoires du Diamant et Migrants du Fleuve Sénégal (Diamond Territories and Migrants from the Senegal River)*, 283–96. Paris: L'Harmattan, 1999.

Bridge, G. and P. McManus. "Sticks and Stones: Environmental Narratives and Discursive Regulation in the Forestry and Mining Sectors." *Antipode* 32, no. 1 (2000): 10–47.

Bridge, Gavin. "Exploiting: Power, Colonialism and Resource Economies." In Ian Douglas, Richard Huggett and Chris Perkins (eds) *Companion Encyclopedia of Geography*, London: Routledge, 2006.

————. "Mapping the Bonanza: Geographies of Mining Investment in an Era of Neoliberal Reform." *Professional Geographer* 56, no. 3 (2004): 406–21.

————. "Resource Triumphalism: Postindustrial Narratives of Primary Commodity Production." *Environment and Planning A* 33, no. 12 (2001): 2149–73.

Broad, W.J. "Resource Wars: The Lure of South Africa." *Science* 210, no. 4474 (1980): 1099–100.

Brown, L. *Redefining National Security*. Washington, DC: World Watch Institute, 1977.

Browne, Malcolm W. "Ice cap shows ancient mines polluted the globe." *New York Times*, 9 December 1997. http://www.nytimes.com/1997/12/09/science/ice-cap-shows-ancient-mines-polluted-the-globe.html accessed on 31 May 2011.

Brunner, Jake, Kirk Talbott and Chantal Elkin. "Logging Burma's Frontier Forests: Resources and the Regime." Washington, DC: World Resource Institute, 1998.

Brunnschweiler, C.N. "Cursing the Blessings? Natural Resource Abundance, Institutions, and Economic Growth." *World Development* 36, no. 3 (2008): 399–419.

Brunnschweiler, Christa N. and Erwin H. Bulte. "Natural Resources and Violent Conflict: Resource Abundance, Dependence and the Onset of Civil Wars." In *CER-ETH-Center of Economic Research at ETH Zurich, Working Paper No. 08/78* (2008).

Brunnschweiler, C.N. and E.H. Bulte. "The Resource Curse Revisited and Revised: A Tale of Paradoxes and Red Herrings." *Journal of Environmental Economics and Management* 55, no. 3 (2008): 248–64.

Bryant, Raymond L. "Kawthoolei and Teak: Karen Forest Management on the Thai Burmese Border." *Watershed* 3, no. 1 (1997).

———. *The Political Ecology of Forestry in Burma, 1824–1994*. London: Hurst, 1997.

Bryant, Raymond L. and M.K. Goodman. "Consuming Narratives: The Political Ecology of 'Alternative' Consumption." *Transactions of the Institute of British Geographers* 29, no. 3 (2004): 344–66.

Buchanan, James M., Robert D. Tollison and Gordon Tullock (eds) *Toward a Theory of the Rent-Seeking Society*. College Station: Texas A&M University, 1980.

Buhaug, H. and P. Lujala. "Accounting for Scale: Measuring Geography in Quantitative Studies of Civil War." *Political Geography* 24, no. 4 (2005): 399–418.

Buhaug, H. and J.K. Rød. "Local Determinants of African Civil Wars, 1970–2001." *Political Geography* 25, no. 3 (2006): 315–35.

Buhaug, Halvard. "Geography, Rebel Capability, and the Duration of Civil Conflict." *Journal of Conflict Resolution* 53, no. 4 (2009): 544–69.

Buhaug, Halvard and Scott Gates. "The Geography of Civil War." *Journal of Peace Research* 39, no. 4 (2002): 417–33.

Bulloch, John and Adel Darwish. *Water Wars: Coming Conflicts in the Middle East*. London: Gollancz, 1993.

Bulte, E.H., R. Damania and R.T. Deacon. "Resource Intensity, Institutions, and Development." *World Development* 33, no. 7 (2005): 1029–44.

Bunker, Stephen G. *Underdeveloping the Amazon: Extraction, Unequal Exchange and the Failure of the Modern State*. Urbana, IL: University of Illinois Press, 1985.

Burtsev, Mikhail S. and Andrey Korotayev. "An Evolutionary Agent-Based Model of Pre-State Warfare Patterns: Cross-Cultural Tests." Moscow, undated.

Burundi: Security Situation. 2005. In, ISS, http://www.iss.co.za/Af/profiles/Burundi/SecInfo.html.

Campbell, Greg. *Blood Diamonds: Tracing the Deadly Path of the World's Most Precious Stones*. Boulder, CO: Westview Press, 2002.

Carranza, Ruben. "Plunder and Pain: Should Transitional Justice Engage with Corruption and Economic Crimes?" *International Journal of Transitional Justice* 2 (2008): 310–30.

Carstens, Peter. *In the Company of Diamonds: De Beers, Kleinzee, and the Control of a Town*. Athens: Ohio University Press, 2001.

Carter Center. "The Mining Review in the Democratic Republic of the Congo: Missed Opportunities, Failed Expectations, Hopes for the Future." Atlanta: Carter Center, 2009.

Cartwright, J.R. *Political Leadership in Sierra Leone*. Toronto University Press, 1978.

Cashdan, Elizabeth. "Territoriality among Human Foragers: Ecological Models and an Application to Four Bushman Groups." *Current Anthropology* 24, no. 1 (1983): 47–66.

Castree, N. "Commodity Fetishism, Geographical Imaginations and Imaginative Geographies." *Environment and Planning A* 33, no. 9 (2001): 1519–25.

Champion, Craige Brian. *Roman Imperialism: Readings and Sources*: Wiley-Blackwell, 2004.

Chandler, David. *A History of Cambodia*. Boulder, CO: Westview Press, 2007.

Chang, Mingteh. *Forest Hydrology*: CRC Press, 2006.

Chatty, Dawn and Marcus Colchester. *Conservation and Mobile Indigenous Peoples*. Oxford: Berghahn Books, 2002.

Chingono, Mark F. *The State, Violence and Development: The Political Economy of War in Mozambique 1975–1992*. Aldershot: Avebury, 1996.

Chipaux, Françoise. "Des Mines d'Émeraudes Pour Financer la Résistance du Commandant Massoud." *Le Monde*, 17 July 1999.

Chivers, C.J. "Russia plants underwater flag at North Pole." *New York Times*, 2 August 2007.

Chossudovsky, Michel. "'Operation Libya' and the Battle for Oil: Redrawing the Map of Africa." 2011. In Centre for Research on Globalization, http://www.globalresearch.ca/index.php?context=va&aid=23605, accessed 18 March 2011.

Chouvy, Pierre-Arnaud. *Opium: Uncovering the Politics of the Poppy*. Cambridge, MA: Harvard University Press, 2010.

Clapp, Jennifer and Eric Helleiner. "Troubled Futures? The Global Food Crisis and the Politics of Agricultural Derivatives Crisis and the Politics of Agricultural Derivatives Regulation." *Review of International Political Economy* (2010): 1–27.

Clarence-Smith, W.G. *The Third Portuguese Empire, 1825–1975: A Study in Economic Imperialism*. Manchester University Press, 1985.

Claxton, Karl. *Bougainville 1988–98: Five Searches for Security in the North Solomons Province of Papua New Guinea, No. 130*. Canberra: Strategic and Defence Studies Centre, Australian National University, 1998.

Clayton, J. "Mining groups face Congo shake-up after review." *The Times*, 8

November 2007. http://business.timesonline.co.uk/tol/business/industry_sectors/industrials/article2827329.ece accessed on 31 May 2011.

CNN. "Sizing up Iran's oil threat." 10 July 2008.

Cohen, David. "Earth Audit." *New Scientist* 194, no. 2605 (2007): 34–41.

Cohen, S.B. *Geography and Politics in a World Divided.* New York: Random House, 1973.

Collier, P., A. Hoeffler and M. Soderbom. "On the Duration of Civil War." *Journal of Peace Research* 41, no. 3 (2004): 253–73.

Collier, Paul. "Doing Well out of War: An Economic Perspective." In Mats Berdal and David M. Malone (eds) *Greed and Grievance: Economic Agendas in Civil Wars*, 91–111. Boulder, CO: Lynne Rienner, 2000.

———. *The Bottom Billion. Why the Poorest Countries are Failing and What can be Done about it.* Oxford University Press, 2007.

———. *The Plundered Planet. How to Reconcile Prosperity with Nature* London: Penguin, 2010.

Collier, Paul, Anke Hoeffler and Mans Soderbom. "On the Duration of Civil War." 1–32. Washington, DC: Development Research Group, World Bank and Centre for the Study of African Economies, University of Oxford, 2001.

Collier, Paul and Anke Hoeffler. "Greed and Grievance in Civil War." *Oxford Economic Papers* 56, no. 4 (2004): 563–95.

———. "On Economic Causes of Civil War." *Oxford Economic Papers* 50 (1998): 563–73.

———. "Resource Rents, Governance and Conflict." *Journal of Conflict Resolution* 49, no. 4 (2005): 451–82.

———. "The Political Economy of Secession." In Hurst Hannun and Eileen Babbitt (eds) *Negotiating Self-Determination*, 37–59. Lanham, MD: Lexington Books, 2006.

Colm, Sara. "The Highland Minorities and the Khmer Rouge in Northeastern Cambodia 1968–1979." Phnom Penh: Document Center of Cambodia, 1996.

Conca, K. and G.D. Dabelko. *Environmental Peacemaking.* Baltimore: Johns Hopkins University Press, 2002.

Connell, Christopher. "Q&A with Patrick Alley, Co-Founder of Global Witness, Winner of the 2007 Commitment to Development Ideas in Action Award." Center for Global Development, 2007.

Conte, Bernard. "Côte d'Ivoire: Clientélisme, Ajustement et Conflit." In *DT/101/2004.* Bordeaux: CED/IFReDE-GRES, Université Montesquieu, 2004.

Cook, I. and P. Crang. "The World on a Plate: Culinary Culture, Displacement, and Geographical Knowledges." *Journal of Material Culture* 1 (1996): 131–53.

Cooper, N. "Picking Out the Pieces of the Liberal Peaces: Representations of Conflict Economies and the Implications for Policy." *Security Dialogue* 36, no. 4 (2005): 463–78.

————. "State Collapse as Business: The Role of Conflict Trade and the Emerging Control Agenda." *Development & Change* 33, no. 5 (2002): 935–55.

————. "Chimeric Governance and the Extension of Resource Regulation." *Conflict, Security and Development* 6, no. 3 (2006): 315–35.

————. "Conflict Goods: The Challenges for Peacekeeping and Conflict Prevention." *International Peacekeeping* 8, no. 3 (2001): 21–38.

Cornell, Svante. "Narcotics and Armed Conflict: Interaction and Implications." *Studies in Conflict and Terrorism* 30, no. 3 (2007): 207–27.

Cortright, David and George A. Lopez. *Sanctions and the Search for Security: Challenges to UN Action.* Boulder, CO: Lynne Rienner, 2002.

————. *The Sanctions Decade: Assessing UN Strategies in the 1990s.* Boulder, CO: Lynne Rienner, 2000.

Coxhead, Ian. "A New Resource Curse? Impacts of China's Boom on Comparative Advantage and Resource Dependence in Southeast Asia." *World Development* 35, no. 7 (2007): 1099–119.

Cramer, Christopher. "Homo Economicus Goes to War: Methodological Individualism, Rational Choice and the Political Economy of War." *World Development* 30, no. 11 (2002): 1845–64.

————. *Civil War Is Not a Stupid Thing: Accounting for Violence in Developing Countries.* London: Hurst, 2006.

Crossette, B. "U.N. Chief Faults Reluctance of U.S. To Help in Africa." *New York Times*, 13 May 2000.

CTC. "Angola Situation Report." 1993.

Custers, Raf. "Le Plan Starec du Gouvernement Congolais: Une Analyse Préliminaire." Antwerp: IPIS, 2009.

Cuvelier, Jeroen and Tim Raeymaekers. "Supporting the War Economy in the DRC: European Companies and the Coltan Trade." 1–29. Antwerp, Belgium: International Peace Information Service (IPIS), 2002.

Dal Lago, Enrico and Constantina Katsari. *Slave Systems.* Cambridge University Press, 2008.

Dalby, S. *Environmental Security.* Minneapolis, MN: University of Minnesota Press, 2002.

Dalby, Simon. *Security and Environmental Change.* Cambridge: Polity Press, 2009.

Dañguilan-Vitug, Marites. *Power from the Forest: The Politics of Logging.* Manila: Philippine Center for Investigative Journalism, 1993.

Dauvergne, Peter. "Corporate Power in the Forest of Solomon Islands." *Pacific Affairs* 71, no. 4 (1998): 524–46.

————. *Shadows in the Forest: Japan and the Politics of Timber in Southeast Asia.* Cambridge, MA: MIT Press, 1997.

Davies, Victor A.B. "Diamonds, Poverty and War in Sierra Leone." In G.M. Hilson (ed.) *Small Scale Mining, Rural Subsistence and Poverty in West Africa*, 165–80. Rugby: Intermediate Technology Publications, 2006.

DDI. "Diamond Development Initiative Begins: New Approach to Africa's Diamond Problems." London: Diamond Development Initiative, 2005.

De Boeck, F. "Domesticating Diamonds and Dollars: Identity, Expenditure and Sharing in Southwestern Zaire (1984–1997)." *Development and Change* 29, no. 4 (1998): 777–810.

De Boeck, Filip. "Des Chiens qui Brisent leur Laisse: Mondialisation et Inversion des Catégories de Genre dans le Contexte du Trafic de Diamant Entre L'Angola et la République Démocratique du Congo." In Laurent Monnier, Bogumil Jewsiewicki and Gauthier de Villers (eds) *Chasse au Diamant au Congo/Zaïre*, Paris: Editions L'Harmattan, 2001.

———. "Garimpeiro Worlds: Digging, Dying and 'Hunting' for Diamonds in Angola." *Review of African Political Economy* 28, no. 90 (2001): 549–62.

De Gregori, Thomas R. "Resources Are Not; They Become: An Institutional Theory." In Marc R. Tool (ed.) *Evolutionary Economics: Foundations of Institutional Thought*, 291–314. Armonk, NY: M.E. Sharpe, 1987.

de Jong, Will (ed.) *Extreme Conflict and Tropical Forests*. New York: Springer, 2007.

de Koning, Ruben, Doris Capistrano, Yurdi Yasmi and Paolo Cerutti. "Forest-Related Conflict. Impact, Links, and Measures to Mitigate." Washington, DC: Rights and Resources Initiative, 2008.

de Soysa, Indra. "Ecoviolence: Shrinking Pie, or Honey Pot?" *Global Environmental Politics* 2, no. 4 (2002): 1–27.

de Soysa, Indra and Eric Neumayer. "Resource Wealth and the Risk of Civil War Onset: Results from a New Dataset of Natural Resource Rents, 1970–1999." *Conflict Management and Peace Science* 24 (2007): 201–18.

De Villiers, Marq. *Water Wars: Is the World Running Out of Water?* London: Phoenix Press, 1999.

Demuynck, Thomas and Arne Schollaert. "International Commodity Prices and the Persistence of Civil Conflict." Working Papers of the Faculty of Economics and Business Administration, Ghent University, Belgium, 2008.

Detheridge, Alan and Noble Pepple. "A Response to Frynas." *Third World Quarterly* 19, no. 3 (1998): 479–86.

Dietrich, C. "Power Struggle in the Diamond Fields." In J. Cilliers and C. Dietrich (eds) *Angola's War Economy*, Pretoria: Institute for Security Studies, 2000.

Dodds, K. "Licensed to Stereotype: Popular Geopolitics, James Bond and the Spectre of Balkanism." *Geopolitics* 8, no. 2 (2003): 125–56.

Downs, E.S. "The Fact and Fiction of Sino-African Energy Relations." *China Security* 3, no. 3 (2007).

Doyle, M.W. and N. Sambanis. "International Peacebuilding: A Theoretical and Quantitative Analysis." *American Political Science Review* 94, no. 4 (2000): 779–801.

Drohan, M. *Making a Killing: How and Why Corporations Use Armed Force to Do Business*. Toronto: Random House, 2003.

Dube, Oeindrila and Juan F. Vargas. "Commodity Price Shocks and Civil Conflict: Evidence from Colombia." Cambridge, MA: Harvard Kennedy School, 2008.

Dubois, B. "The Timor Gap Treaty: Where to Now?" In *Briefing Paper (Community Aid Abroad, Australia) no. 25*: Oxfam Australia, 2000.

Duffield, M. *Global Governance and the New Wars: The Merging of Development and Security*. London: Zed Books, 2001.

Duffy, R. "Peace Parks: The Paradox of Globalisation." *Geopolitics* 6, no. 2 (2001): 1–26.

Dumett, R. "Africa's Strategic Minerals During the Second World War." *Journal of African History* 26 (1985): 381–408.

Dunning, T. and L. Wirpsa. "Oil and the Political Economy of Conflict in Colombia and Beyond: A Linkages Approach." *Geopolitics* 9, no. 1 (2004): 81–108.

Dunning, Thad. "Resource Dependence, Economic Performance, and Political Stability." *Journal of Conflict Resolution* 49, no. 4 (2005): 451–82.

Dyson-Hudson, Rada and Eric Alden Smith. "Human Territoriality: An Ecological Reassessment." *American Anthropologist* 80, no. 1 (1978): 21–41.

Eckel, Edwin Clarence. *Coal, Iron and War: A Study in Industrialism, Past, and Future*. New York: Henri Holt, 1920.

Economist. "Pumping up the Oil Price." 1 October 2004.

Edmondson, J.C. "Mining in the Later Roman Empire and Beyond: Continuity or Disruption?" *Journal of Roman Studies* 79 (1989): 84–102.

EFE. "Colombia, Victima del Calentamiento." *El Universal*, 22 April 2007.

Eliasson, Per and Sven G. Nilsson. "'You Should Hate Young Oaks and Young Noblemen': The Environmental History of Oaks in Eighteenth- and Nineteenth-Century Sweden." *Environmental History* 7, no. 4 (2002): 659–77.

Ellis, Stephen. *The Mask of Anarchy: The Destruction of Liberia and the Religious Dimension of an African Civil War*. London: Hurst, 1999.

Ember, Carol R. and Melvin Ember. "Resource Unpredictability, Mistrust, and War: A Cross-Cultural Study." *Journal of Conflict Resolution* 36, no. 2 (1992): 242–62.

Engdahl, William F. *A Century of War: Anglo-American Oil Politics and the New World Order*. London: Pluto, 2004.

Englebert, P. and J. Ron. "Primary Commodities and War: Congo-Brazzaville's Ambivalent Resource Curse." *Comparative Politics* 37, no. 1 (2004): 61–81.

Esman, Milton J. "Scottish Nationalism, North Sea Oil, and the British Response." In Milton J. Esman (ed.) *Ethnic Conflict in the Western World*, Ithaca, NY: Cornell University Press, 1977.

Esty, Daniel C. *et al*. "State Failure Task Force Report: Phase II Findings." State Failure Task Force, 1998. http://globalpolicy.gmu.edu/pitf/ accessed on 31 May 2011.

European Commission. "Critical Raw Materials for the EU." Raw Materials Supply Group, 2010. http://ec.europa.eu/enterprise/sectors/metals-minerals/files/fiches_raw_materials_supply_group_en.pdf accessed on 31 May 2011.

Evelyn, J. *Navigation and Commerce, Their Original and Progress*. London: B. Tooke, 1674.

Falk, R.A. *This Endangered Planet: Prospects and Proposals for Human Survival.* New York: Random House, 1971.

FAO. "State of the World Forests." Rome: UN Food and Agricultural Organisation, 1997.

———. "State of the World's Forests." Rome: UN Food and Agriculture Organization, 2005.

Farah, D. *Blood from Stones: The Secret Financial Network of Terror.* New York: Broadway Books, 2004.

Faris, Stephan. "The Real Roots of Darfur." *The Atlantic Monthly*, April 2007.

Fasano, Ugo. "Review of the Experience with Oil Stabilization and Savings Funds in Selected Countries." In *Working Paper WP/00/112.* Washington, DC: International Monetary Fund, 2000.

Fearon, J.D. "Primary Commodities Exports and Civil War." *Journal of Conflict Resolution* 49, no. 4 (2005): 483–507.

———. "Why Do Some Civil Wars Last So Much Longer Than Others?" 1–43. Washington, DC: World Bank, 2002.

———. "Why Do Some Civil Wars Last So Much Longer Than Others?" *Journal of Peace Research* 41, no. 3 (2004): 275–302.

Fearon, James and David Laitin. "Ethnicity, Insurgency and Civil War." *American Political Science Review* 97, no. 1 (2003): 75–90.

Felbab-Brown, Vanda. "Afghanistan: When Counternarcotics Undermines Counterterrorism." *Washington Quarterly* 28, no. 4 (2005): 55–72.

Ferguson, R. Brian. "Explaining War." In Jonathan Haas (ed.) *The Anthropology of War.* Cambridge University Press, 1990.

———. "Introduction: Studying War." In R. Brian Ferguson (ed.) *Warfare, Culture, and Environment.* Orlando, FL: Academic Press, 1984.

Field, Julie S. "Environmental and Climatic Considerations: A Hypothesis for Conflict and the Emergence of Social Complexity in Fijian Prehistory." *Journal of Anthropological Archaeology* 23, no. 1 (2004): 79–99.

———. "Land Tenure, Competition and Ecology in Fijian Prehistory." *Antiquity* 79 (2005): 586–600.

Filiu, J.P., *The Arab Revolution: Ten Lessons from the Democratic Uprising* (London: Hurst Books, 2011).

Findlay, Ronald, and Kevin H. O'Rourke. *Power and Plenty: Trade, War, and the World Economy in the Second Millenium.* Princeton University Press, 2007.

Fithen, C. "Diamonds and War in Sierra Leone: Cultural Strategies for Commercial Adaptation to Endemic Low-Intensity Conflicts." University College London, 1999.

Fjelde, Hanne. "Buying Peace? Oil Wealth, Corruption and Civil War, 1985—99." *Journal of Peace Research* 46, no. 2 (2009): 199–218.

Fjelde, Hanne and Indra de Soysa. "Coercion, Co-Optation, or Cooperation? State Capacity and the Risk of Civil War, 1961—2004." *Conflict Management and Peace Science* 26, no. 1 (2009): 5–25.

FOE. "Extractive Sector Projects Financed by Export Credit Agencies: The Need for Foreign Investment Contract and Revenue Reform." Friends of the Earth and Pacific Environment, 2005.

Foster, Peter. "Kill the Avatar Bill!" *Financial Post,* 9 March 2010.

Freidberg, S. "The Ethical Complex of Corporate Food Power." *Environment and Planning D: Society and Space* 22, no. 4 (2004): 513–31.

Frynas, J.G. "The Oil Boom in Equatorial Guinea." *African Affairs* 103, no. 413 (2004): 527–46.

Frynas, J.G. and K. Mellahi. "Political Risks as Firm-Specific (Dis) Advantages: Evidence on Transnational Oil Firms in Nigeria." *Thunderbird International Business Review* 45, no. 5 (2003): 541–65.

Frynas, J.G. and M. Paulo. "A New Scramble for African Oil? Historical, Political, and Business Perspectives." *African Affairs* 106, no. 423 (2007): 229–51.

Frynas, Jedrzej George. "Corporate and State Responses to Anti-Oil Protests in the Niger Delta." *African Affairs* 100, no. 398 (2001): 27–54.

———. *Oil in Nigeria: Conflict and Litigation between Oil Companies and Village Communities.* Hamburg: LIT Verlag, 2000.

Galtung, J. "Cultural Violence." *Journal of Peace Research* 27, no. 3 (1990): 291–305.

———. "Violence, Peace and Peace Research." *Journal of Peace Research* 6 (1969): 167–91.

Gao, Shuqin. "The Factor "Natural Resources" in the Transformation of Global Geopolitics and Geo-Economy." *Resources Science* 31, no. 2 (2009): 343–51.

Gary, Ian and Nikki Reisch. "Chad's Oil: Miracle or Mirage? Following the Money in Africa' s Newest Petro-State." Catholic Relief Service and Bank Information Center, 2005.

Gat, Azar. *War in Human Civilization.* Oxford University Press, 2006.

Gberie, Lansana. *A Dirty War in West Africa. The Revolutionary United Front and the Destruction of Sierra Leone.* London: Hurst, 2005.

Gedicks, A. *The New Resource Wars: Native and Environmental Struggles Against Multinational Corporations.* Cambridge, MA: South End Press, 1993.

Gelb, A.H. *Oil Windfalls: Blessing or Curse?* Oxford University Press, 1988.

Ghai, Yash. "Decentralization and the Accommodation of Ethnic Diversity." In C. Young (ed.) *Ethnic Diversity and Public Policy. A Comparative Inquiry.* Basingstoke: Palgrave, 1998.

Gibbs, David N. *The Political Economy of Third World Intervention: Mines, Money, and US Policy in the Congo Crisis.* University of Chicago Press, 1991.

Gilbert, Christopher L. "International Commodity Agreements: An Obituary Notice." *World Development* 24, no. 1 (1996): 1–19.

Gilman, Robert. "Structural Violence." *In Context* 4, no. Autumn (1983): 8.

Glaser, Antoine, Stephen Smith and Maria Mallagardis. "Un Rôle d'Intermédiaire dans le Conflit Congolais. Quand le Président Lissouba avait Besoin d'Armes Contre les Rebelles de Sassou N'Guesso, il s'Adressait à la Fiba." *Libération,* 4 February 1998.

Gleditsch, N.P., K. Furlong, H. Hegre, B. Lacina and T. Owen. "Conflicts Over Shared Rivers: Resource Scarcity or Fuzzy Boundaries?" *Political Geography* 25, no. 4 (2006): 361–82.

Gleditsch, N.P. "Armed Conflict and the Environment: A Critique of the Literature." *Journal of Peace Research* 35, no. 3 (1998): 381–401.

Global Witness. *A Choice for China: Ending the Destruction of Burma's Northern Frontier Forests.* London: Global Witness, 2005.

———. *A Conflict of Interests: The Uncertain Future of Burma's Forests.* London: Global Witness, 2003.

———. "A Rough Trade. The Role of Companies and Governments in the Angolan Conflict." London, 1998.

———. "Afrimex (UK) Democratic Republic of Congo. Complaint to the UK National Contact Point under the Specific Instance Procedure of the OECD Guidelines for Multinational Enterprises." 2007.

———. "Bisie Killings Show Minerals at Heart of Congo Conflict." London: Global Witness, 2009.

———. "Branching Out: Zimbabwe's Resource Colonialism in the Democratic Republic of Congo." 1–16. London, UK: Global Witness, 2002.

———. "China and Congo: Friends in Need." London, 2011.

———. "Conflict Diamonds: Possibilities for the Identification, Certification and Control of Diamonds." London, 2000.

———. "Country for Sale." London: Global Witness, 2008.

———. "'Faced with a Gun, What Can You Do?': War and the Militarisation of Mining in Eastern Congo." London: Global Witness, 2009.

———. "For a Few Dollars More: How Al Qaeda Moved into the Diamond Trade." 1–96. London, UK: Global Witness Limited, 2003.

———. "Forests, Famine and War: The Key to Cambodia's Future." London: Global Witness, 1995.

———. "Heavy Mittal? A State within a State: The Inequitable Mineral Development Agreement between the Government of Liberia and Mittal Steel Holdings NV." London: Global Witness, 2006.

———. "Lessons Unlearned: How the UN and Member States Must Do More to End Resource-Fuelled Conflict." London: Global Witness, 2010.

———. "Logging Off: How the Liberian Timber Industry Fuels Liberia's Humanitarian Disasters and Threatens Sierra Leone." London: Global Witness, 2002.

———. "Taylor Made: The Pivotal Role of Liberia's Forests and Flag of Convenience in Regional Conflict." London: Global Witness, 2001.

———. "The Logs of War: The Timber Trade and Armed Conflict." 1–66. Oslo, Norway: Programme for International Co-operation and Conflict Resolution, Fafo Institute for Applied Social Sciences, 2002.

———. "The Sinews of War: Eliminating the Trade in Conflict Resources." London: Global Witness, 2007.

———. "Undue Diligence: How Banks Do Business with Corrupt Regimes." London: Global Witness, 2009.

———. "Update on the Renegotiation of the Mineral Development Agreement Between Mittal Steel and the Government of Liberia." London: Global Witness, 2007.

Godinho, Jorge. "When Worlds Collide: Enforcing United Nations Security Council Asset Freezes in the EU Legal Order." *European Law Journal* 16, no. 1 (2009): 67–93.

Goldsmith, Scott. "The Alaska Permanent Fund Dividend: An Experiment in Wealth Distribution." Paper presented at the Ninth Congress of Basic Income European Network, Geneva, 12–14 September 2002.

Good, K. "Resource Dependency and Its Consequences: The Costs of Botswana's Shining Gems." *Journal of Contemporary African Studies* 23, no. 1 (2005): 27–50.

———*Diamonds, Dispossession and Democracy in Botswana*. Woodbridge, Suffolk: James Currey, 2009.

Goodhand, Jonathan. "Corrupting or Consolidating the Peace?: The Drugs Economy and Post-Conflict Peacebuilding in Afghanistan." *International Peacekeeping* 15, no. 3 (2008): 405–23.

———. "Frontiers and Wars: The Opium Economy in Afghanistan." *Journal of Agrarian Change* 5, no. 2 (2005): 191–216.

Goodman, Peter S. "Booming China Devouring Raw Materials." *Washington Post*, 21 May 2004.

Goreux, Louis. "Conflict Diamonds." 1–34. Washington, DC: African Region Working Paper Series, World Bank, 2001.

Griffith, A.E. "The Search for Petroleum in Northern Ireland." *Geological Society* 12, no. 213–222 (1983).

Grove, Richard. *Ecology, Climate, and Empire: Colonialism and Global Environmental History, 1400–1940*. Cambridge: White Horse Press, 1997.

Guevara, Ernesto "Che." *Guerrilla Warfare*. Rowman and Littlefield, 1997 (1960).

Guha, Ramachandra. *The Unquiet Woods: Ecological Change and Resistance in the Himalaya*. Berkeley, CA: University of California Press, 1990.

Guidolin, Massimo, and Eliana La Ferrara. "Diamonds Are Forever, Wars Are Not—Is Conflict Bad for Private Firms?" *American Economic Review* 97, no. 5 (2007): 1978–93.

Gunn, Mary M. "Aggression and Alliance: The Impact of Resource Distribution on Exchange Strategies Chosen by Prehispanic Philippine Chiefs." *Indo-Pacific Prehistory Association Bulletin* 14 (1996): 242–9.

Gupta, Samir, Michael Polonsky, Arch Woodside and Cynthia M. Webster. "The Impact of External Forces on Cartel Network Dynamics: Direct Research in the Diamond Industry." *Industrial Marketing Management* 39 (2010): 202–10.

Haas, Jonathan. *The Evolution of the Prehistoric State*. New York: Columbia University Press, 1982.

———. "Warfare and the Evolution of Culture." In Gary M. Feinman and T. Douglas Price (eds) *Archeology at the Millenium: A Sourcebook*, 329–50. New York: Springer, 2007.

Haas, Jonathan (ed.) *The Anthropology of War*. Cambridge University Press, 1990.

Haid, Christopher, Emily Meierding and Steven Wilkinson. "Environmental Scarcity and Conflict: Is There a Connection?" Center for International Studies, University of Chicago, 2008.

Hall, P.K. "The Diamond Fields of Sierra Leone." Freetown: Geological Survey of Sierra Leone, 1968.

Hamblin, William James. *Warfare in the Ancient Near East to 1600 BC: Holy Warriors at the Dawn of History*. London: Routledge, 2006.

Hanson, Gordon. "Export Dependence in Developing Countries." University of California, San Diego and NBER, 2010.

Hanson, W.S. "The Organisation of Roman Military Timber-Supply." *Britannia* 9 (1978): 293–306.

Harbom, L. and P. Wallensteen. "Armed Conflict, 1989 2006." *Journal of Peace Research* 44, no. 5 (2007): 623–34.

Harbom, Lotta, Erik Melander and Peter Wallensteen. "Dyadic Dimensions of Armed Conflicts, 1946–2008." *Journal of Peace Research* 46, no. 4 (2009): 577–87.

Harden, B. "Africa's diamond wars." *New York Times*, 6 April 2000.

Hardin, R. "Concessionary Politics in the Western Congo Basin: History and Culture in Forest Use." In J. Ribot and Stemper D. (eds) *Environmental Governance in Africa*, Washington, DC: WRI, 2002.

Harris, Cole. "How Did Colonialism Dispossess? Comments From an Edge of Empire." *Annals of the Association of American Geographers* 94, no. 1 (2004): 165–82.

Hart, G. "Denaturalizing Dispossession: Critical Ethnography in the Age of Resurgent Imperialism." *Antipode* 38, no. 5 (2006): 977–1004.

Hart, M. *Diamond: A Journey to the Heart of an Obsession*. New York: Walker, 2001.

Hartwick, E. "Geographies of Consumption: A Commodity-Chain Approach." *Environment and Planning D: Society and Space* 16 (1998): 423–37.

Harvey, David. *The Limits to Capital*. University of Chicago Press, 1982.

———. *The New Imperialism*. Oxford University Press, 2003.

Harvey, Neil. *The Chiapas Rebellion: The Struggle for Land and Democracy*. Durham, NC: Duke University Press, 1998.

Harvey, Paul. "Cash-Based Responses in Emergencies." In *HPG Report 24*. London: Overseas Development Institute, 2007.

Harwell, Emily and Philippe Le Billon. "Natural Connections: Linking Transitional Justice and Development through a Focus on Natural Resources." In Pablo de Grieff and Roger Dutie (eds) *Transitional Justice and Development*, 282–330. New York: International Center on Transitional Justice, 2009.

Hauge, Wenche and Tanja Ellingsen. "Beyond Environmental Scarcity: Causal Pathways to Conflict." *Journal of Peace Research* 35, no. 3 (1998): 299–317.

Haushofer, K. *Geopolitik Der Pan-Ideen*. Berlin: Zentral-Verlag, 1931.

Haysom, Nicholas and Sean Kane. "Negotiating Natural Resources for Peace: Ownership, Control and Wealth-Sharing." Geneva: Centre for Humanitarian Dialogue, 2009.

Hayter, Roger. "'The War in the Woods': Post-Fordist Restructuring, Globalization, and the Contested Remapping of British Columbia's Forest Economy." *Annals of the Association of American Geographers* 93, no. 3 (2003): 706–29.

Hayward, Fred M. "The Development of a Radical Political Organization in the Bush: A Case Study of Sierra Leone." *Canadian Journal of African Studies* 6, no. 1 (1972): 1–28.

Hayward, Joel. "Too Little, Too Late: An Analysis of Hitler's Failure in August 1942 to Damage Soviet Oil Production." *Journal of Military History* 64 (2000): 769–94.

Heaps, T. "The Heart of Darkness." *Corporate Knights* 2006, 19–22.

Hecht, Susanna and Alexander Cockburn. *The Fate of the Forest: Developers, Destroyers, and Defenders of the Amazon*. New York: Verso, 1989.

Heemskerk, M. "Do International Commodity Prices Drive Natural Resource Booms? An Empirical Analysis of Small-Scale Gold Mining in Suriname." *Ecological Economics* 39 (2001): 295–308.

Heinberg, Richard. *Peak Everything: Waking up to the Century of Declines*. Gabriola Island: New Society Publishers, 2007.

Hendrix, Cullen. "Leviathan in the Tropics: Geography, Bargaining, and State Extractive Capacity." University of North Texas, 2007.

Henry, D. "Diamonds Are Not a Boy's Best Friend: What Happened When Alhadji Met the Rebels." In D. Cordell (ed.) *The Human Tradition in Modern Africa*. Lanham, Md: Rowman Littlefield, 2011.

Hentschel, Thomas, Felix Hruschka and Michael Priester. "Global Report on Artisanal & Small-Scale Mining." London: International Institute for Environment and Development, 2002.

Hinson, Robert E. "Banking the Poor: The Role of Mobiles." *Journal of Financial Services Marketing* 15, no. 4 (2011): 320–33.

Hodges, Tony. *Western Sahara: The Roots of a Desert War*. Westport, CT: Lawrence Hill, 1983.

Homer-Dixon, Thomas F. *Environment, Scarcity and Violence*. Princeton University Press, 1999.

Hook, Leslie. "China reins in Rare Earth Exports." *Financial Times*, 19 October 2010.

Horton, L. *Peasants in Arms: War and Peace in the Mountains of Nicaragua, 1979–1994*. Athens, Ohio: Ohio University Press, 1998.

Howard, Philip N. "The History of Ecological Marginalization in Chiapas." *Environmental History* 3, no. 3 (1998): 357–77.

HRW. "The Curse of Gold." New York: Human Rights Watch, 2005.

Hughes, Geraint and Christian Tripodi. "Anatomy of a Surrogate: Historical Precedents and Implications for Contemporary Counter-Insurgency and Counter-Terrorism." *Small Wars and Insurgencies* 20, no. 1 (2009): 1–35.

Human Rights Watch. "The Curse of Gold." New York: Human Rights Watch, 2005.

———. "The Warri Crisis: Fueling Violence." New York: Human Rights Watch, 2003.

Humphreys, M. "Natural Resources, Conflict, and Conflict Resolution: Uncovering the Mechanisms." *Journal of Conflict Resolution* 49, no. 4 (2005): 508–37.

Humphreys, M., J. Sachs and J.E. Stiglitz. *Escaping the Resource Curse.* New York: Columbia University Press, 2007.

Humphreys, Macartan and Jeremy Weinstein. "What the Fighters Say: A Survey of Ex-Combatants in Sierra Leone, June-August 2003." Freetown: PRIDE, 2004.

Hunt, Peter. "The Slaves and the Generals of Arginusae." *American Journal of Philology* 122, no. 3 (2001): 359–80.

Huntington, Samuel P. *Political Order in Changing Societies.* New Haven: Yale University Press, 1968.

Hurtig, Anna-Karin and Miguel San Sebastián. "Geographical Differences in Cancer Incidence in the Amazon Basin of Ecuador in Relation to Residence near Oil Fields." *International Journal of Epidemiology* 31 (2002): 1021–27.

Hutchinson, S.E. *Nuer Dilemmas: Coping with Money, War, and the State.* Berkeley, CA: University of California Press, 1996.

IAG. "Chad-Cameroon Petroleum Development and Pipeline Project. Assessment Report." Montreal: International Advisory Group, 2009.

Ibeanu, Okechukwu. "Oiling the Friction: Environmental Conflict Management in the Niger Delta, Nigeria." *Environmental Change & Human Security Project Report* Issue 6, Summer 2000: 19–32.

Ibrahim, Jibrin. "Political Transition, Ethnoregionalism, and the 'Power Shift' Debate in Nigeria." *Issue: A Journal of Opinion* 27, no. 1 (1999): 12–16.

IEA. "World Energy Outlook." Paris: International Energy Agency, 2010.

Ikelegbe, A. "The Economy of Conflict in the Oil Rich Niger Delta Region of Nigeria." *Nordic Journal of African Studies* 14, no. 2 (2005): 208–34.

Ikelegbe, Augustine. "Beyond the Threshold of Civil Struggle: Youth Militancy and the Militarization of the Resource Conflicts in the Niger Delta Region of Nigeria." *African Study Monographs* 27, no. 3 (2006): 87–122.

———. "Civil Society, Oil and Conflict in the Niger Delta Region of Nigeria: Ramifications of Civil Society for Regional Resource Struggle." *Journal of Modern African Studies* 39, no. 3 (2001): 437–69.

IMF. "Azerbaijan Republic—Selected Issues and Statistical Appendix." In *IMF Country Report No. 03/130.* Washington, DC: International Monetary Fund, 2004.

Innes-Brown, Marc and Mark Valencia. "Thailand's Resource Diplomacy in Indochina and Myanmar." *Contemporary Southeast Asia* 14, no. 4: 332–51.

IRIN-CEA. "DRC: Sabena/Swissair Declares Embargo on Transport of Coltan." 16–22 June 2001.

Isham, J., M. Woolcock, L. Pritchett and G. Busby. "The Varieties of Resource Experience: Natural Resource Export Structures and the Political Economy of Economic Growth." *The World Bank Economic Review* 19, no. 2 (2005): 141–74.

ISS. Burundi: Security Situation (updated February 2005). Pretoria: Institute for Security Studies, 2005. http://www.iss.co.za/Af/profiles/Burundi/SecInfo.html accessed on 31 May 2011.

Isumonah, Ade. "The Making of the Ogoni Ethnic Group." *Africa* 74, no. 3, May 2004: 433–53.

Jaffee, Daniel and Philip H. Howard. "Corporate Cooptation of Organic and Fair Trade Standards." *Agriculture and Human Values* 27, no. 4 (2009): 387–99.

Jarvie, James, Ramzy Kanaan, Michael Malley, Trifin Roule and Jamie Thomson. "Conflict Timber: Dimensions of the Problem in Asia and Africa. Volume II Asian Cases." Burlington, VE: ARD, undated.

Jean, François and Jean-Christophe Rufin (eds) *Economie des Guerres Civiles.* Paris: Hachette, 1996.

Jhaveri, N.J. "Petroimperialism: US Oil Interests and the Iraq War." *Antipode* 36, no. 1 (2004): 2–11.

Jiang,, Ze-min. "Reflections on Energy Issues in China." *Journal of Shanghai Jiaotong University* 13, no. 3 (2008): 257–74.

MONUSCO official, personal communication with the author, 2009.

Joab-Peterside, Sofiri. "On the Militarization of Nigeria's Niger Delta: The Genesis of Ethnic Militia in Rivers States, Nigeria." In *Niger Delta Economies of Violence Working Paper No. 21.* Berkeley, 2007.

Johnson Likoti, Fako. "The 1998 Military Intervention in Lesotho: SADC Peace Mission or Resource War?" *International Peacekeeping* 14, no. 2 (2007): 251–63.

Johnston, Patrick. "Timber Boom, State Busts: The Political Economy of Liberian Timber." *Review of African Political Economy* 31, no. 101 (2004): 441–56.

Josling, Timothy Edward and Thomas Geoffrey Taylor (eds) *Banana Wars: The Anatomy of a Trade Dispute.* Wallingford: CABI, 2003.

Kabutaulaka, Tarcisius Tara. "Rumble in the Jungle: Land, Culture and (Un)Sustainable Logging in Solomon Islands." In Antony Hooper (ed.) *Culture and Sustainable Development in the Pacific,* 2008.

Kaimovitz, David and Angelica Fauné. "Contras and Comandantes: Armed Movements and Forest Conservation in Nicaragua's Bosawas Biosphere

Reserve." In Steven V. Price (ed.) *War and Tropical Forests: Conservation in Areas of Armed Conflict*, New York: Routledge, 2003.

Kalyvas, Stathis N. *The Logic of Violence in Civil War*. Cambridge University Press, 2006.

Kandeh, Jimmy D. "Politicization of Ethnic Identities in Sierra Leone." *African Studies Review* 35, no. 1 (1992): 81–99.

———. "Ransoming the State: Elite Origins of Subaltern Terror in Sierra Leone." *Review of African Political Economy* 26, no. 81 (1999): 349–66.

Kaplinsky, Raphael, Dorotha McCormick and Mike Morris. "The Impact of China on Sub-Saharan Africa." London: China Office, Department for International Development, 2006.

Karl, Terry L. *The Paradox of Plenty. Oil Booms and Petro-States*. Berkeley: University of California Press, 1997.

Kaul, R. and A. Heuly. "Getting a Better Deal from the Extractive Sector. Concession Negotiation in Liberia, 2006–2008." New York: Revenue Watch Institute, 2009.

Keen, David. *Conflict and Collusion in Sierra Leone*. Oxford: James Currey, 2005.

———. "The Economic Functions of Violence in Civil Wars." 1–88. London: International Institute of Strategic Studies (IISS), 1998.

Kehl, Jenny R. "Oil, Water, Blood and Diamonds: International Intervention in Resource Disputes." *International Negotiation* 15 (2010): 391–412.

Kelly, Raymond C. *Warless Societies and the Origin of War*. Ann Arbor: University of Michigan Press, 2000.

Khalfan, Ashfaq, Jeff King and Bryan Thomas. "Advancing the Odious Debt Doctrine." Montreal: Centre for International Sustainable Development Law, 2003.

Khoury, S.J. *The Valuation and Investment Merits of Diamonds*. Greenwood, CT: Quorum Books, 1990.

Killick, T. "The Benefits of Foreign Direct Investment and Its Alternatives: An Empirical Exploration." *Journal of Development Studies* 9, no. 2 (1973): 301.16.

Kjok, Ashild and Brynjar Lia. "Terrorism and Oil—an Explosive Mixture? A Survey of Terrorist and Rebel Attacks on Petroleum Infrastructure 1968–1999." In *FFI/Rapport-2001/04031*. Kjeller: Norwegian Defence Research Establishment, 2001.

Klare, M.T. *Blood and Oil: The Dangers and Consequences of America's Growing Dependency on Imported Petroleum*. New York: Metropolitan Books, 2004.

———. "Resource Wars: On the Navy's Case for Unlimited Expansion." *Harper's Magazine* 262 (1981): 20–23.

———. *Resource Wars: The New Landscape of Global Conflict*. First ed. New York: Metropolitan Books, 2001.

———. *Rising Powers, Shrinking Planet: The New Geopolitics of Energy*. New York: Metropolitan Books, 2008.

————. "The New Geography of Conflict." *Foreign Affairs* 80, no. 3 (2001): 49–62.

Kobrin, S.J. "Diffusion as an Explanation of Oil Nationalization (or the Domino Effect Rides Again)." *Journal of Conflict Resolution* 29, no. 1 (1985): 3–32.

Kolstad, I., Arne Wilg and A. Williams. "Mission Improbable: Does Petroleum-Related Aid Address the Resource Curse?" *Energy Policy* 37, no. 3 (2008): 954–65.

Korf, B. and H. Fünfgeld. "War and the Commons: Assessing the Changing Politics of Violence, Access and Entitlements in Sri Lanka." *Geoforum* 37, no. 3 (2006): 391–403.

Krasner, S.D. *Defending the National Interest: Raw Materials Investments and US Foreign Policy*. Princeton University Press, 1978.

Kunstler, J.H. *The Long Emergency: Surviving the End of Oil, Climate Change, and Other Converging Catastrophes of the Twenty-First Century*. New York: Grove Press, 2006.

Kuo, Chin S. "The Mineral Industry of Afghanistan." US Geological Survey, 2008.

Labonne, Béatrice. "The Mining Industry and the Community: Joining Forces for Sustainable Social Development." *Natural Resources Forum* 23, no. 4 (1999): 315–22.

Labrousse, Alain. "Colombie-Pérou: Violence Politique et Logique Criminelle." In François Jean and Jean-Christophe (eds) *Economie des Guerres Civiles*. Rufin. Paris: Hachette, 1996.

Lacina, Bethany Ann and Nils Petter Gleditsch. "Monitoring Trends in Global Combat: A New Dataset of Battle Deaths." *European Journal of Population* 21, no. 2–3 (2005): 145–65.

Land, Bryan. "Capturing a Fair Share of Fiscal Benefits in the Extractive Industry." *Transnational Corporations* 18, no. 1 (2009): 157–73.

Lang, Yi-huan and Li-mao Wang. "Russian Energy Geopolitic Strategy and the Prospects of Sino-Russia Energy Cooperation." *Resources Science* 29, no. 5 (2007): 201–06.

Lanning, G. and M. Mueller. *Africa Undermined: Mining Companies and the Underdevelopment of Africa*. London: Penguin, 1979.

Laqueur, Walter. *Guerrilla Warfare. A Historical and Critical Study*. Transaction Books, 1997.

Le Billon, Philippe. "Angola's Political Economy of War: The Role of Oil and Diamonds, 1975–2000." *African Affairs* 100, no. 398 (2001): 55–81.

————. "Buying Peace or Fuelling War: The Role of Corruption in Armed Conflicts." *Journal of International Development* 15, no. 4 (2003): 413–26.

————. "Contract Renegotiation and Asset Recovery in Post-Conflict Settings." In Paivi Lujala and Siri A. Rustad (eds) *High-Value Natural Resources and Post-Conflict Peacebuilding*. London: EarthScan, 2011.

————. "Corrupting Peace? Corruption, Peacebuilding and Reconstruction." *International Peacekeeping* 15, no. 3 (2008): 344–61.

———. "Diamond Wars? Conflict Diamonds and Geographies of Resource Wars." *Annals of the Association of American Geographers* 98, no. 2 (2008): 345–72.

———. "Fatal Transactions: Conflict Diamonds and the (Anti) Terrorist Consumer." *Antipode* 38, no. 4 (2006): 778–801.

———. "Fueling War or Buying Peace: The Role of Corruption in Conflicts." *Journal of International Development* 15, no. 4 (2003): 413–26.

———. *Fuelling War: Natural Resources and Armed Conflicts, Adelphi Paper No. 373.* London: Routledge, 2005.

———. "Geographies of War: Perspectives on 'Resource Wars.'" *Compass* 1, no. 2 (2007): 163–82.

———. "Getting It Done: Instruments of Enforcement." In Ian Bannon and Paul Collier (eds) *Natural Resources and Violent Conflict: Options and Actions*, 1–72. Washington, DC: World Bank, 2003.

———. "Power Is Consuming the Forest." Unpublished DPhil thesis, Oxford University, 1999.

———. "The Political Ecology of Transition in Cambodia 1989–1999: War, Peace and Forest Exploitation." *Development & Change* 31, no. 4 (2000): 784–805.

———. "The Political Ecology of War: Natural Resources and Armed Conflicts." *Political Geography* 20, no. 5 (2001): 561–84.

———. "The Political Economy of War: An Annotated Bibliography." 1–41. London: Humanitarian Policy Group (HPG), Overseas Development Institute, 2000.

Le Billon, Philippe and Alejandro Cervantes. "Oil Prices, Scarcity and Geographies of War." *Annals of the Association of American Geographers* 99, no. 5 (2009): 836–44.

Le Billon, Philippe and Fouad El Khatib. "From Free Oil to 'Freedom Oil': Terrorism, War and US Geopolitics in the Persian Gulf." *Geopolitics* 9, no. 1 (2004): 109–37.

Le Billon, Philippe and Estelle Levin. "Building Peace with Conflict Diamonds? Merging Security and Development in Sierra Leone's Diamond Sector." *Development and Change* (2009).

Le Billon, Philippe and Eric Nicholls. "Ending 'Resource Wars': Revenue Sharing, Economic Sanction or Military Intervention?" *International Peacekeeping* 14, no. 5 (2007): 613–32.

Leclercq, Hugues. "Le Rôle Économique du Diamant dans le Conflit Congolais." In Laurent Monnier, Bogumil Jewsiewicki and Gauthier de Villers (eds), *Chasse au Diamant au Congo/Zaïre*, 47–78. Paris: Editions L'Harmattan, 2001.

Lee, Pak K. "China's Quest for Oil Security: Oil (Wars) in the Pipeline?" *Pacific Review* 18, no. 2 (2005): 265–301.

Leite, Carlos and Jens Weidmann. "Does Mother Nature Corrupt? Natural Resources, Corruption, and Economic Growth." In George T. Abed and

Sanjeev Gupta (eds) *Governance, Corruption, and Economic Performance*, 159–96. Washington, DC: International Monetary Fund, 2002.

Leith, C.K. *World Minerals and World Politics: A Factual Study of Minerals in Their Political and International Relations*. New York: Whittlesey House, 1931.

Leng, Yuen Choy. "Japanese Rubber and Iron Investments in Malaya, 1900–1941." *Journal of Southeast Asian Studies* 5, no. 1 (1974): 18–36.

Leslie, D. and S. Reimer. "Spatializing Commodity Chains." *Progress in Human Geography* 23, no. 3 (1999): 401.

Lesser, I.O. *Resources and Strategy: Vital Materials in International Conflict, 1600-Present Day*. New York: St. Martin's Press, 1989.

Levin, Estelle. "From Poverty and War to Prosperity and Peace? Sustainable Livelihoods and Innovation in Governance of Artisanal Diamond Mining in Kono District, Sierra Leone," University of British Columbia, 2005.

Liberia Truth and Reconciliation Commission. *Final Report of the Commission Volume II*. Monrovia, 2008.

Licklider, Roy. "The Consequences of Negotiated Settlements in Civil Wars, 1945–1993." *American Political Science Review* 89, no. 3 (1995): 681–90.

Lilly, Damian and Philippe Le Billon. "Regulating Business in Zones of Conflict: A Synthesis of Strategies." London: Overseas Development Institute, 2002.

Linnér, Bjorn Ola. *The Return of Malthus: Environmentalism and Post-War Population-Resource Crises*. Cambridge: White Horse Press, 2004.

Lintner, Bertil. *Burma in Revolt: Opium and Insurgency since 1948*. Seattle: University of Washington Press, 2000.

Lipschutz, R.D. *When Nations Clash: Raw Materials, Ideology, and Foreign Policy*. New York: Ballinger Pub. Co., 1989.

Liu, Hin-Yan. "Leashing the Corporate Dogs of War: The Legal Implications of the Modern Private Military Company." *Journal of Conflict and Security Law* 15, no. 1 (2010): 141–68.

Logan, William Bryant. *Oak: The Frame of Civilization*. New York: W.W. Norton & Company, 2005.

Lopez, Robert Sabatino. *The Commercial Revolution of the Middle Ages, 950–1350*. Cambridge University Press, 1976.

Love, R. "Drought, Dutch Disease and Controlled Transition in Botswana Agriculture." *Journal of Southern African Studies* 20, no. 1 (1994): 71–83.

LP. "Congo-Kinshasa: Contrats Miniers; L'Heure de Vérité a Sonné." *Le Potentiel*, 27 October 2009.

Lujala, P., N.P. Gleditsch and E. Gilmore. "A Diamond Curse?: Civil War and a Lootable Resource." *Journal of Conflict Resolution* 49, no. 4 (2005): 538–62.

Lujala, P., J.K. Rød and N. Thieme. "Fighting over Oil: Introducing a New Dataset." *Conflict Management and Peace Science* 24, no. 3 (2007): 239–56.

Lujala, Paivi. "Deadly Combat over Natural Resources: Gems, Petroleum, Drugs, and the Severity of Armed Civil Conflict." *Journal of Conflict Resolution* 53, no. 1 (2008): 50–71.

————. "The Spoils of Nature: Armed Civil Conflict and Rebel Access to Natural Resources." *Journal of Peace Research* 47, no. 1 (2010): 15–28.

Lungu, John. "The Politics of Reforming Zambia Mining Tax Regime." Johannesburg: Southern Africa Resource Watch, 2009.

Luong, P.J. and E. Weinthal. "Rethinking the Resource Curse: Ownership Structure, Institutional Capacity, and Domestic Constraints." *Annual Review of Political Science* 9 (2006): 241–63.

Luxemburg, Rosa. *The Accumulation of Capital*, 1913.

Mac Ginty, Roger. "Looting in the Context of Violent Conflict: A Conceptualisation and Typology." *Third World Quarterly* 25, no. 5 (2004): 857–70.

Macdonald, Kate and Shelley Marshall (eds) *Fair Trade, Corporate Accountability and Beyond*. Farnham: Ashgate, 2010.

Macdonald, Nancy. "So Much for 'Chindia.' Why China and India Are Not-So-Friendy Neighbours." *MacLeans*, 23 September 2010.

Mack, Andrew and Asif Khan. "The Efficacy of UN Sanctions." *Security Dialogue* 31, no. 3 (2000): 279–92.

MacLean, Ken. "Capitalizing on Conflict: How Logging and Mining Contribute to Environmental Destruction." Earth Rights International with Karen Environmental & Social Action Network, 2003.

Maconachie, Roy and Tony Binns. "'Farming Miners' or 'Mining Farmers'?: Diamond Mining and Rural Development in Post-Conflict Sierra Leone." *Journal of Rural Studies* 23, no. 3 (2007): 367–80.

Mahan, A.T. *The Influence of Sea Power Upon History, 1660–1783*. London: Low and Marston, 1890.

Malthus, Thomas. *An Essay on the Principle of Population*. St Paul's Church-Yard: Johnson, 1798.

Malti, Hocine. *Histoire Secrète du Pétrole Algérien*. Paris: La Découverte, 2010.

Mansfield, Edward D. *Power, Trade and War*. Princeton University Press, 1995.

Manzano, O. and R. Rigobon. "Resource Curse or Debt Overhang?" *Natural Resources, Neither Curse Nor Destiny* (2006).

Mao Tse-Tung. *On Guerrilla Warfare*. Champaign, IL: University of Illinois Press, 2000.

Marchal, Roland and Christine Messiant. "De L'Avidité des Rebelles: L'Analyse Économique de la Guerre Civile Selon Paul Collier." *Critique Internationale* 16 (2002): 58–69.

Marino, Lori. "Convergence of Complex Cognitive Abilities in Cetaceans and Primates." *Brain, Behaviour and Evolution* 59 (2002): 21–32.

Marks, Joshua. "Border in Name Only: Arms Trafficking and Armed Groups at the DRC-Sudan Border." Geneva: Small Arms Survey, Graduate Institute of International Studies, 2007.

Marques, R. and R. Falcao de Campos. "Lundas, the Stones of Death: Angola's Deadly Diamonds." New York: Open Society Institute, 2005.

Marques, Raphael. "Operation Kissonde: The Diamonds of Humiliation and Misery." Luanda: Open Society Institute, 2006.

Marshall, Jonathan. *To Have and Have Not: Southeast Asian Raw Materials and the Origins of the Pacific War.* Berkeley: University of California Press, 1995.

Marx, Karl. *Capital: The Process of Production of Capital,* 1867 [1887].

Maull, Hanns. *Oil and Influence: The Oil Weapon Examined, Adelphi Paper 117.* London: Routledge, 1975.

McGhie, Stuart. "Private Military Companies: Soldiers, Inc." *Janes Defence Weekly* (2002).

McIlwaine, C. "Geography and Development: Violence and Crime as Development Issues." *Progress in Human Geography* 23, no. 3 (1999): 453–63.

McNeill, J.R. "Woods and Warfare in World History." *Environmental History* 9, no. 3 (2004).

McQuaig, Linda. *It's the Crude, Dude: Greed, Gas, War, and the American Way.* Thomas Dunne, 2006.

Meadows, Donella H., Dennis L. Meadows, Jorgen Randers and William W. Behrens III. *The Limits to Growth.* New York: Universe Book, 1972.

Mehlum, H., K. Moene and R. Torvik. "Institutions and the Resource Curse." *Economic Journal* 116, no. 508 (2006): 1–20.

Mesquita Moreira, Mauricio. "Fear of China: Is There a Future for Manufacturing in Latin America?" *World Development* 35, no. 3 (2007): 355–76.

Miguel, E., S. Satyanath and E. Sergenti. "Economic Shocks and Civil Conflict: An Instrumental Variables Approach." *Journal of Political Economy* 112, no. 4 (2004): 725–53.

Military Advisory Board. "Powering America's Defense: Energy and the Risks to National Security." Centre for Navy Analyses, 2009.

Mirza, Nasrullah. *Water, War and India–Pakistan Relations.* London: Routledge, 2011.

Missbach, Andreas. "The Equator Principles: Drawing the Line for Socially Responsible Banks? An Interim Review from an NGO Perspective." *Development* 47, no. 3 (2004): 78–84.

Misser, François and Olivier Vallée. *Les Gemmocraties: L'Économie Politique du Diamant Africain.* Paris: Desclée de Brouwer, 1997.

Montgomery, Michael. "Indian Steel Producers Aggressively Seek Raw Materials." *Manganese Investment News,* 11 January 2011.

Moore, Mick. "Revenues, State Formation, and the Quality of Governance in Developing Countries." *International Political Science Review* 25, no. 3 (2004): 297–319.

Morales Colon, César. "Guerrillas, Drug Traffickers Impacting Environment." *Infosurhoy.com,* 25 August 2010.

Moran, Theodore H. "Promoting Universal Transparency in Extractive Industries: How and Why?" Washington, DC: Center for Global Development, 2011.

Morrison, K.M. "Oil, Non-Tax Revenue, and the Redistributional Foundations of Regime Stability." *International Organization* 63 (2009): 107–38.

Moss, Todd. "Oil-to-Cash: Fighting the Resource Curse through Cash Transfers." In *CGD Working Paper 237*. Washington, DC: Center for Global Development, 2011.

Mouan, Liliane C. "Exploring the Potential Benefits of Asian Participation in the Extractive Industries Transparency Initiative: The Case of China." *Business Strategy and the Environment* 19, no. 6 (2010): 367–76.

Mthembu-Salter, Gregory. "An Assessment of Sanctions against Burundi." London: Action Aid, 1999.

Muana, Patrick K. "The Kamajoi Militia: Civil War, Internal Displacement and the Politics of Counter-Insurgency." *Africa Development* 22, no. 3/4 (1997): 77–100.

Muttit, Greg. "Crude Designs—the Rip-Off of Iraq's Oil Wealth." London: Platform, 2005.

Muttit, Greg, *Fuel on Fire: Oil and Politics in Occupied Iraq.* London: Bodley Head, 2011.

Myers, Norman. *Ultimate Security: The Environmental Basis of Political Stability.* New York: Norton, 1993.

Myers, Steven L. "UN Concludes, Fining Shell, That Tanker Carried Iraq Oil." *New York Times*, 26 April 2000.

Nakou, G. "The Cutting Edge: A New Look at Early Aegean Metallurgy." *Journal of Mediterranean Archeology* 8, no. 2 (1995): 1–32.

Nazaruddin, Sjamsuddin. "Issues and Politics of Regionalism in Indonesia: Evaluating the Acehnese Experience." In Lim Joo-Jock and S. Vani (eds) *Armed Separatism in Southeast Asia*. Singapore: Institute of Southeast Asian Studies, 1984.

Ndikumana, Léonce and Kisangani Emizet. "The Economics of Civil War: The Case of the Democratic Republic of Congo." 1–53. Amherst, MA: Department of Economics, University of Massachusetts and Department of Political Science, Kansas State University, 2002.

Nearing, Scott. *Oil and the Germs of War*. Ridgewood, NJ: Nellie Seeds Nearing, 1923.

Nelson, Jane. "The Business of Peace. The Private Sector as Partner in Conflict Prevention and Resolution." London: International Alert, Council on Economic Priorities, and the Prince of Wales Business Leaders Forum, 2000.

Nest, Michael. *Coltan*. Cambridge: Polity Press, 2011.

Neumann, R.P. "Moral and Discursive Geographies in the War for Biodiversity in Africa." *Political Geography* 23, no. 7 (2004): 813–37.

Neumayer, E. "Does the 'Resource Curse' Hold for Growth in Genuine Income as Well?" *World Development* 32, no. 10 (2004): 1627–40.

Newbury, C. *The Diamond Ring: Business, Politics, and Precious Stones in South Africa, 1867–1947*. Oxford: Clarendon Press, 1989.

BIBLIOGRAPHY

Newsweek. "America Deeply Involved in Kony War for Years." 22 May 2009.

Ng, F. and A. Yeats. "What Can Africa Expect of Its Traditional Exports?" In *Africa Region Working Papers Series No. 26*. Washington, DC: World Bank, 2002.

Nitzan, J. and S. Bichler. "Bringing Capital Accumulation Back In: The Weapondollar-Petrodollar Coalition-Military Contractors, Oil Companies and Middle East 'Energy Conflicts.'" *Review of International Political Economy 2*, no. 3 (1995): 446–515.

Nitzschke, H. and K. Studdard. "The Legacies of War Economies: Challenges and Options for Peacemaking and Peacebuilding." *International Peacekeeping* 12, no. 2 (2005): 222–39.

Noam, Zao. "Burma: Ceasefire, Logging and Mining Concessions in Kachin State." *World Rainforest Movement's Bulletin* 94, no. May 2005 (2005).

O'Lear, S. and P. Diehl. "Not Drawn to Scale: Research on Resource and Environmental Conflict." *Geopolitics* 12, no. 1 (2007): 166–82.

O'Mahony, Patrick. "Assessing the Merits of Decentralization as a Conflict Mitigation Strategy." Development Alternatives Inc., 2007.

Obst, E. "Wir Forden Unsere Kolonien Zurück!" *Zeitschrift für Geopolitik* 3 (1926): 151–60.

Odhiambo, Atieno E.S. and John Lonsdale (eds) *Mau Mau and Nationhood*. Oxford: James Currey, 2003.

Okoh, Hanson. "Nigeria Loses US$60 Billion Oil Revenue to Bunkering." *Ground Report*, 15 July 2008.

Olsson, O. "Conflict Diamonds." *Journal of Development Economics* 82, no. 2 (2007): 267–86.

———. "Diamonds Are a Rebel's Best Friend." *The World Economy* 29, no. 8 (2006): 1133–50.

OTA. "An Assessment of Alternative Economic Stockpiling Policies." Washington, DC: Office of Technology Assessment, 1975.

Otterbein, Keith F. *How War Began*: Texas A&M University Press, 2004.

Otto, J. *Mining Royalties: A Global Study of Their Impact on Investors, Government, and Civil Society*. Washington, DC: World Bank Publications, 2006.

Otto, James M. "Global Changes in Mining Laws, Agreements and Tax Systems." *Resources Policy* 24, no. 2 (1998): 79–86.

———"Position of the Peruvian Taxation System as Compared to Mining Taxation Systems in Other Nations." 2002. Paper prepared for the Peruvian Ministry of Economy and Finance. http://www.mef.gob.pe/contenidos/pol_econ/documentos/perufinalreport_280504Otto.pdf accessed on 31 May 2011.

Oyefusi, Aderoju. "Oil and the Probability of Rebel Participation among Youths in the Niger Delta of Nigeria." *Journal of Peace Research* 45, no. 4 (2008): 539–55.

PAC. "Diamond Industry Annual Review. Sierra Leone 2004." Ottawa: Partnership Africa Canada, 2004.

PAC and Global Witness. "Rich Man, Poor Man: Development, Diamonds and Poverty: The Potential for Change in the Artisanal Diamond Fields of Africa." Ottawa and London: Partnership Africa Canada and Global Witness, 2004.

Pakenham, Thomas. *The Boer War*. London: Weidenfeld and Nicolson, 1979.

Palley, Thomas I. "Oil and the Case of Iraq." *Challenge* 47 (2004): 94–112.

Paterson, Matthew. *Automobile Politics: Ecology and Cultural Political Economy*. Cambridge University Press, 2007.

Patey, L.A. "State Rules: Oil Companies and Armed Conflict in Sudan." *Third World Quarterly* 28, no. 5 (2007): 997–1016.

Patey, Luke A. "Crude Days Ahead? Oil and the Resource Curse in Sudan." *African Affairs* 109, no. 437 (2010): 617–36.

Pearce, J. "Policy Failure and Petroleum Predation: The Economics of Civil War Debate Viewed 'from the War-Zone.'" *Government and Opposition* 40, no. 2 (2005): 152–80.

Pearce, Jenny. "From Civil War to 'Civil Society': Has the End of the Cold War Brought Peace to Central America?" *International Affairs* 74, no. 3 (1998): 587–615.

Pearce, Justin. "War, Peace and Diamonds in Angola: Popular Perceptions of the Diamond Industry in the Lundas." *Africa Watch* 13, no. 2 (2004): 51–64.

Pegg, Scott. "Chronicle of a Death Foretold: The Collapse of the Chad-Cameroon Pipeline Project." *African Affairs* 108, no. 431 (2009): 1–10.

Peimani, H. "Turks threaten: 10,000 fighters in Kirkuk." *Asia Times*, 21 December 2002.

Pelletiere, Stephen. *Iraq and the International Oil System: Why America Went to War in the Gulf*. Westport, CT: Praeger, 2001.

Peluso, N.L. *Rich Forests, Poor People: Resource Control and Resistance in Java*: University of California Press, 1992.

Peluso, N.L. and M. Watts. *Violent Environments*. Ithaca, NY: Cornell University Press, 2001.

Peluso, Nancy Lee and Emily Harwell. "Territory, Custom, and the Cultural Politics of Ethnic War in West Kalimantan, Indonesia." In Nancy Lee Peluso and Michael Watts (eds) *Violent Environments*. Ithaca, NY: Cornell University Press, 2001.

Percy, Sarah. *Mercenaries: The History of a Norm in International Relations*. Oxford University Press, 2007.

Perreault, T. "From the Guerra Del Agua to the Guerra Del Gas: Resource Governance, Popular Protest and Social Justice in Bolivia." *Antipode* 38, no. 1 (2006): 150–72.

Perry, Peter John. "Military Rule in Burma: A Geographical Analysis." *Crime, Law and Social Change* 19, no. 1 (1993): 17–32.

Peters, Krijn and Paul Richards. "'Why We Fight': Voices of Youth Combatants." *Africa* 68, no. 2 (1998): 183–210.

Philipovich, Macho. "Why is Canada Blocking Congo Debt Forgiveness." *The Dominion*, 11 August 2010.

Phillips, William D. *Slavery from Roman Times to the Early Transatlantic Trade*. Manchester University Press, 1985.

Pierson, David. "Libyan strife exposes China's risks in global quest for oil." *Los Angeles Times*, 9 March 2011.

Pieth, Mark (ed.). *Recovering Stolen Assets*. New York: Peter Lang, 2008.

Pollak, Oliver B. "The Origins of the Second Anglo-Burmese War (1852–53)." *Modern Asian Studies* 12, no. 3 (1978): 483–502.

Polomka, P. *Bougainville: Perspectives on a Crisis*. Canberra: Strategic and Defence Studies Centre, Research School of Pacific Studies, Australian National University, 1990.

Posner, E. "The new race for the Arctic." *Wall Street Journal*, 3 August 2007. http://online.wsj.com/article/SB118610915886687045.html?mod=google-news_wsj accessed on 31 May 2011.

Potter, David Stone. *A Companion to the Roman Empire*: Wiley-Blackwell, 2006.

Pourtier, Roland. "1997: Les Raisons d'une Guerre 'Incivile.'" *Afrique Contemporaine* 186 (1998): 7–32.

Power, Marcus. "Patrimonialism & Petro-Diamond Capitalism: Peace, Geopolitics & the Economics of War in Angola." *Review of African Political Economy* 28, no. 90 (2001): 489–502.

Queiroga, F.M.V.R. *War and Castros. New Approaches to Northwestern Portuguese Iron Age*. Oxford: British Archaeological Reports, 2003.

Quimbayo Ruiz, German Andres. "Crops for Illicit Use and Ecocide." Transnational Institute, 2008.

Quinn, John James and Ryan T. Conway. "The Mineral Resource Curse in Africa: What Role Does Majority State Ownership Play?" Paper presented at the Center for the Study of African Economies (CSAE) Conference 2008, Oxford, 16–18 March 2008.

Radetzki, Marian. *A Handbook of Primary Commodities in the Global Economy*. Cambridge University Press, 2008.

Radtke, Katrin. "From Gifts to Taxes: The Mobilisation of Tamil and Eritrean Diaspora in Intrastate Warfare." In *Working Papers Micropolitics No. 2*. Berlin: Humboldt University, 2005.

Raleigh, Clionadh and Håvard Hegre. "Introducing Acled: An Armed Conflict Location and Event Dataset." Paper presented at the conference on "Disaggregating the Study of Civil War and Transnational Violence," University of California Institute of Global Conflict and Cooperation, San Diego, CA, 7–8 March 2005.

Raleigh, Clionadh and Henrik Urdal. "Climate Change, Environmental Degradation and Armed Conflict." *Political Geography* 26, no. 6 (2007): 674–94.

Randerson, James. "UK's Ex-Science Chief Predicts Century of 'Resource' Wars." *The Guardian*, 13 February 2009.

Recknagel, Charles. "Oil Smuggling Produces High Profits." *RFE/EL* (2000).

Regan, Anthony. "Causes and Course of the Bougainville Conflict." *Journal of Pacific History* 33, no. 3 (1998): 269–85.

Regan, P.M. and A. Aydin. "Diplomacy and Other Forms of Intervention in Civil Wars." *Journal of Conflict Resolution* 50, no. 5 (2005): 736–56.

Reno, W. *Warlord Politics and African States*. Boulder, CO: Lynne Rienner Publishers, 1999.

———. *Corruption and State Politics in Sierra Leone*. Cambridge University Press, 1995.

———. "Political Networks in a Failing State. The Roots and Future of Violent Conflict in Sierra Leone." *Internationale Politik und Gesellschaft* 2 (2003).

"Resources for Freedom." In *Communication from the President of the United States, Transmitting the Report of the President's Materials Policy Commission*. Washington, DC: US Government Printing Office, 1952.

Revels, Craig S. "Concessions, Conflict and the Rebirth of the Honduran Mahogany Trade." *Journal of Latin American Geography* 2, no. 1 (2003): 1–17.

RFI. "Kadhafi opponents and loyalists battle for oil sites." *Radio France Internationale*, 4 March 2011.

Ribot, J.C. and N.L. Peluso. "A Theory of Access." *Rural Sociology* 68, no. 2 (2003): 153–81.

Rich, John and Graham Shipley. *War and Society in the Greek World*. London: Routledge, 1993.

Richani, N. "Multinational Corporations, Rentier Capitalism, and the War System in Colombia." *Latin American Politics and Society* 47, no. 3 (2005): 113–44.

Richani, Nazih. *Systems of Violence: The Political Economy of War and Peace in Colombia*. New York: SUNY, 2002.

Richards, Paul. "Are 'Forest Wars' in Africa Resource Conflicts? The Case of Sierra Leone." In Nancy Lee Peluso and Michael Watts (eds) *Violent Environments*, Ithaca, NY: Cornell University Press, 2001.

———. *Fighting for the Rain Forest: War, Youth & Resources in Sierra Leone*, *African Issues*. London: International African Institute, 1996.

———. "The Political Economy of Internal Conflict in Sierra Leone." The Hague: Netherlands Institute of International Relations, 2003.

———. "To Fight or to Farm? Agrarian Dimensions of the Mano River Conflicts (Liberia and Sierra Leone)." *African Affairs* 104, no. 417 (2005): 571–90.

Riddell, J.B. "Internal and External Forces Acting Upon Disparities in Sierra Leone." *Journal of Modern African Studies* 23, no. 3 (1985): 389–406.

Risen, James. "US Identifies Vast Mineral Riches in Afghanistan." *New York Times*, 13 June 2010.

Roberts, A. *The Wonga Coup: Guns, Thugs and a Ruthless Determination to Create Mayhem in an Oil-Rich Corner of Africa*. New York: Public Affairs, 2006.

Roberts, Rebecca and Jacque Emel. "Uneven Development and the Tragedy of the Commons: Competing Images for Nature-Society Analysis." *Economic Geography* 68, no. 3 (1992): 249–71.

Robinson, J.A., R. Torvik and T. Verdier. "Political Foundations of the Resource Curse." *Journal of Development Economics* 79, no. 2 (2006): 447–68.

Rodger, Nam. *The Wooden World. An Anatomy of the Georgian Navy.* London: Collins, 1986.

Rodrigue, Jean-Paul. "Straits, Passages and Chokepoints. A Maritime Geostrategy of Petroleum Distribution." *Cahiers de Géographie du Québec* 48, no. 135 (2004): 357–74.

Rojas, David Arce. "Petroleum and the Humanitarian Law." *International Law: Revista Colombiana de Derecho Internacional*, no. 3 (2004): 275–92.

Ron, James. "Paradigm in Distress? Primary Commodities and Civil War." *Journal of Conflict Resolution* 49, no. 4 (2005): 443–50.

Rone, J. *Sudan, Oil, and Human Rights.* Washington, DC: Human Rights Watch, 2003.

Rose-Ackerman, Susan. *Corruption and Government: Causes, Consequences and Reform.* Cambridge University Press, 1999.

Rosenthal, Jacob. "Georg Gondos, an Heb Jewish Combatant on the Middle-Eastern Front." *Qatedrah le-tôldôt Eres Yîsra'el el we-yîššûbah* 117 (2005): 127–38.

Ross, M.L. "How Do Natural Resources Influence Civil War? Evidence from Thirteen Cases." *International Organization* 58, no. 01 (2004): 35–67.

———. "What Do We Know About Natural Resources and Civil Wars?" *Journal of Peace Research* 41 (2004): 337–56.

———. "A Closer Look at Oil, Diamonds, and Civil War." *Annual Review of Political Science* 9 (2006): 265–300.

———. "Blood Barrels." *Foreign Affairs* (2008).

———. "Extractive Sectors and the Poor." 1–28. Boston, MA: Oxfam America, 2001.

———. "Oil, Drugs, and Diamonds: How Do Natural Resources Vary in Their Impact on Civil War?" In Karen and Jake Sherman Ballentine (eds) *Beyond Greed and Grievance: The Political Economy of Armed Conflict*, 47–67. Boulder, CO: Lynne Rienner Publishers, 2003.

———. *The Curse of Oil Wealth*, now titled *The Oil Curse: How Petroleum Wealth Shapes the Development of Nations.* Princeton, NJ: Princeton University Press, 2012.

———. "The Political Economy of the Resource Curse." *World Politics* 51, no. 2 (1999): 297–322.

———. *Timber Booms and Institutional Breakdown in Southeast Asia.* 1st edition New York: Cambridge University Press, 2001.

Rosser, A. "The Political Economy of the Resource Curse: A Literature Survey." Brighton, UK: University of Sussex IDS, 2006.

Roul, Animesh. "Gems, Timber and Jiziya: Pakistan's Taliban Harness Resources to Fund Jihad." *Terrorism Monitor* 7, no. 11 (2009): 9–11.

Rubin, Barnett. "The Political Economy of War and Peace in Afghanistan." *World Development* 28, no. 10 (2000): 1789–803.

RUF. "Footpaths to Democracy: Towards a New Sierra Leone." 1995.

Russett, B. "Security and the Resources Scramble: Will 1984 Be Like 1914?" *International Affairs* 58, no. 1 (1981): 42–58.

Rustad, Siri A., and Helga M. Binningsbo. "Rapid Recurrence: Natural Resources, Armed Conflicts and Peace." In *PRIO*. Olso, 2011.

Rustad, Siri A., Paivi Lujala and Philippe Le Billon. "Building or Spoiling the Peace? Management of High Value Natural Resources in Post-Conflict Countries." In Paivi Lujala and Siri A. Rustad (eds) *High-Value Natural Resources and Post-Conflict Peacebuilding*, London: EarthScan, 2011.

Rustad, Siri Camilla Aas, Jan Ketil Rød, Wenche Larsen and Nils Petter Gleditsch. "Foliage and Fighting: Forest Resources and the Onset, Duration, and Location of Civil War." *Political Geography* 27, no. 7 (2008): 761–82.

Rustad, Siri Camilla Aas, Helga Malmin Binningsbo and Philippe Le Billon. "Do Resource-Related Peacebuilding Initiatives Build Peace?" Paper presented at the Annual Conference of the International Studies Association, New York 2009.

Sachs, Jeffrey and Andrew Warner. "The Curse of Natural Resources." *European Economic Review* 45, no. 4–6 (2001): 827–38.

Sagan, Scott D. "The Origins of the Pacific War." *Journal of Interdisciplinary History* 18, no. 4 (1988): 893–922.

Sala-i-Martin, Xavier and Arvind Subramanian. "Addressing the Natural Resource Curse: An Illustration from Nigeria." *NBER Working Paper 9804*. Cambridge, MA, 2003. http://www.nber.org/papers/w9804 accessed on 31 May 2011.

Sandbu, M.E. "Natural Wealth Accounts: A Proposal for Alleviating the Natural Resource Curse." *World Development* 34, no. 7 (2006): 1153–70.

Sandoms, Jim. "Logging in the Solomon Islands—the Lost Legacy." *ETFRN News* 43–45 (2005): 93–7.

Sarraf, Maria and Moortaza Jiwanji. "Beating the Resource Curse—the Case of Botswana." 1–34. Washington, DC: Environmental Economics Series, World Bank Environmental Department, 2001.

Sawyer, S. *Crude Chronicles: Indigenous Politics, Multinational Oil, and Neoliberalism in Ecuador*. Durham, NC: Duke University Press, 2004.

Sawyer, Suzana. "Fictions of Sovereignty: Of Prosthetic Petro-Capitalism, Neoliberal States, and Phantom-Like Citizens in Ecuador." *Journal of Latin American Anthropology* 6, no. 1 (2006): 156–97.

Schou, Arild and Marit Haug. "Decentralisation in Conflict and Post-Conflict Situations." In *Working Paper 2005: 139*. Blindern: Norwegian Institute for Urban and Regional Research, 2005.

Schroeder, Richard A. "Tanzanite as Conflict Gem: Certifying a Secure Commodity Chain in Tanzania." *Geoforum* 41, no. 1 (2010): 56–65.

Scott, James. *Domination and the Arts of Resistance: Hidden Transcripts*. New Haven, CT: Yale University Press, 1990.

———. "'Zomia': Site of the Last Great Enclosure Movement of (Relatively) State-Less Peoples in Mountainous Southeast Asia." University of Toronto, 2008.

———. *The Art of Not Being Governed.* New Haven, CT: Yale University Press, 2009.

Scott, Wilbur J. *The Politics of Readjustment: Vietnam Veterans since the War.* New York: Aldine De Gruyter, 1993.

Seignebos, C. "Des Fortifications Végétales dans la Zone Soudano-Sahélienne (Tchad et Nord Cameroun)." *Cahiers de Sciences Humaines* 17, no. 3,4 (1980): 191–222.

Shah, Sonia. *Crude: the History of Oil.* New York: Seven Stories, 2004.

Shearer, David. *Private Armies and Military Intervention, Adelphi Paper 316.* Oxford University Press, 1998.

Sherman, Jake. "Burma: Lessons from the Cease-Fires." In Karen Ballentine and Jake Sherman (eds) *The Political Economy of Armed Conflict: Beyond Greed and Grievance*, 225–55. Boulder: Lynne Rienner, 2003.

Sidaway, J.D. "Sovereign Excesses?: Portraying Postcolonial Sovereigntyscapes." *Political Geography* 22, no. 2 (2003): 157–78.

Sidaway, James D. "What Is in a Gulf? From the 'Arc of Crisis' to the Gulf War." In Simon Dalby and Gearoid O'Tuathail (eds) *Rethinking Geopolitics*, 224–39. London: Routledge, 1998.

Silberfein, M. "The Geopolitics of Conflict and Diamonds in Sierra Leone." *Geopolitics* 9, no. 1 (2004): 213–41.

Simmons, C.S. "The Political Economy of Land Conflict in the Eastern Brazilian Amazon." *Annals of the Association of American Geographers* 94, no. 1 (2004): 183–206.

Sinding, K. "The Dynamics of Artisanal and Small-Scale Mining Reform." *Natural Resources Forum* 29 (2005): 243–52.

Smillie, Ian. "What Lessons from the Kimberley Process Certification Scheme?" In K. Ballentine and H. Nitzschke (eds) *Profiting from Peace: Managing the Resource Dimensions of Civil War*, 47–67. Boulder, CO: Lynne Rienner, 2004.

Smillie, Ian, Lansana Gberie and Ralph Hazleton. "The Heart of the Matter: Sierra Leone, Diamonds and Human Security." 1–93. Ottawa: Partnership Africa Canada, 2000.

Smith, Benjamin. *Hard Times in the Lands of Plenty: Oil Politics in Iran and Indonesia.* Ithaca, NY: Cornell University, 2007.

Smith, Jack, Mark Pieth and Guillermo Jorge. "The Recovery of Stolen Assets: A Fundamental Principle of the UN Convention against Corruption." In *U4 Brief* Anti-Corruption Resource Centre and International Centre for Asset Recovery, 2007.

Smith, M.D. "The Empire Filters Back: Consumption, Production, and the Politics of Starbucks Coffee." *Urban Geography* 17, no. 6 (1996): 502–25.

Smith, Martin. *Burma: Insurgency and the Politics of Ethnicity.* London: Zed Books, 1999.

Smith, Neil. *Uneven Development: Nature, Capital, and the Production of Space.* Oxford: Basil Blackwell, 1984.

Smith, Raymond L. "The Impact of Metals on Society." *Journal of the Minerals, Metals and Materials Society* 50 (1998).

Snyder, R. and R. Bhavnani. "Diamonds, Blood, and Taxes: A Revenue-Centered Framework for Explaining Political Order." *Journal of Conflict Resolution* 49, no. 4 (2005): 563.

Snyder, Richard. "Does Lootable Wealth Breed Disorder? A Political Economy of Extraction Framework." *Comparative Political Studies* 39, no. 8 (2006): 943–68.

Soares de Oliviera, Ricardo. *Oil and Politics in the Gulf of Guinea.* London: Hurst, 2007.

Solli, Audun. "From Good Governance to Development? A Critical Perspective on the Case of Norway's Oil for Development." *Forum for Development Studies* 38, no. 1 (2011): 65–85.

Solvit, Samuel. *RDC: Rêve ou Illusion: Conflits et Ressources Naturelles en République Démocratique du Congo.* Paris: L'Harmattan, 2009.

Soule, J. "Problems in Applying Counterterrorism to Prevent Terrorism: Two Decades of Violence in Northern Ireland Reconsidered." *Studies in Conflict and Terrorism* 12, no. 1 (1989): 31–46.

Spence, M.W. "The Social Context of Production and Exchange." In J.E. Ericson and T.K. Earle (eds) *Contexts for Prehistoric Exchange*, 173–97. London: Academic Press, 1982.

Sprout, H. and M. Sprout. "Environmental Factors in the Study of International Politics." *Journal of Conflict Resolution* 1, no. 4 (1957): 309–28.

Staley, E. *Raw Materials in Peace and War.* New York: Council on Foreign Relations, 1937.

Stanton, L., J. Heintz and N. Folbre (eds). *Ten Reasons Why You Should Never Accept a Diamond Ring From Anyone.* Edited by Center for Popular Economics, *Ultimate Field Guide to the U.S. Economy.* New York: New Press, 2000.

Starr, Joyce R. "Water Wars." *Foreign Policy* 82 (1991): 17–36.

Stedman, Stephen J. "Implementing Peace Agreements in Civil Wars: Lessons and Recommendations for Policymakers." In *IPA Policy Paper Series on Peace Implementation.* New York: International Peace Academy, 2001.

Steinberg, Michael K., Carrie Height, Rosemary Mosher and Mathew Bampton. "Mapping Massacres: GIs and State Terror in Guatemala." *Geoforum* 37, no. 1 (2006): 62–8.

Stellman, Jeanne Mager, Steven D. Stellman, Richard Christian, Tracy Weber and Carrie Tomasallo. "The Extent and Patterns of Usage of Agent Orange and Other Herbicides in Vietnam." *Nature* 422 (2003): 681–7.

Stevens, P. and E. Dietsche. "Resource Curse: An Analysis of Causes, Experiences and Possible Ways Forward." *Energy Policy* 36, no. 1 (2008): 56–65.

Stewart, D.F. "Large-Scale or Small Scale Mining: Meeting the Needs of Developing Countries." *Natural Resources Forum* 13, no. 1 (1989): 44–52.

Stewart, Frances, Graham Brown and Alex Cobham. "Promoting Group Justice: Fiscal Policies in Post-Conflict Countries." In *Policy Paper on Public Finance in Post-Conflict Environments*. New York and Amherst, MA: Center on International Cooperation, and Political Economy Research Institute, 2007.

Steyn, Maria Sophia. "Oil Politics in Ecuador and Nigeria: A Perspective from Environmental History of the Struggles between Ethnic Minority Groups, Multinational Oil Companies and National Governments." University of the Free State, 2003.

Strayer, Robert W. *Why Did the Soviet Union Collapse?: Understanding Historical Change*. New York: M.E. Sharpe, 1998.

Striffler, Steve, and Mark Moberg (eds). *Banana Wars: Power, Production, and History in the Americas*. Durham, NC: Duke University Press, 2003.

Swyngedouw, E. "Modernity and Hybridity: Nature, Regeneracionismo, and the Production of the Spanish Waterscape, 1890–1930." *Annals of the Association of American Geographers* 89, no. 3 (1999): 443–65.

Tacconi, Luca (ed.) *Illegal Logging: Law Enforcement, Livelihoods and the Timber Trade*. London: Earthscan, 2007.

Talbot, J.M. "Information, Finance and the New International Inequality: The Case of Coffee." *Journal of World-Systems Research*, VIII, 2, Spring 2002 (2002): 214–50.

Tamm, I.J. "Dangerous Appetites: Human Rights Activism and Conflict Commodities." *Human Rights Quarterly* 26 (2004): 687–704.

Tamuno, Tekena. "Separatist Agitations in Nigeria since 1914." *Journal of Modern African Studies* 8, no. 4 (1970): 563–84.

Tarrow, Sydney. "Inside Insurgencies: Politics and Violence in an Age of Civil War." *Perspectives on Politics* 5, no. 3 (2007): 587–600.

Taylor, Ian. "China's Oil Diplomacy in Africa." *International Affairs* 82, no. 5 (2006): 937–59.

Taylor, Ian and Gladys Mokhawa. "Not Forever: Botswana, Conflict Diamonds and the Bushmen." *African Affairs* 102 (2003): 261–83.

Tegera, Aloys. "The Coltan Phenomena." Goma: POLE Institute, 2002.

Tellnes, Jostein F. "The Unexpected Deal: Why the Government of Sudan and the SPLM/A Reached an Agreement on Oil Issues through the IGAD Peace Talks 2002–04." Centre for the Study of Civil War, PRIO, 2005.

Thayer, Nate. "Rubies Are Rouge: Khmer War Effort Financed by Gem Finds." *Far Eastern Economic Review*, 7 February 1991.

Theisen, Ole Magnus. "Blood and Soil? Resource Scarcity and Internal Armed Conflict Revisited." *Journal of Peace Research* 45, no. 6 (2008): 801–18.

Thomas, Saji. "Mining Taxation: An Application to Mali." In *WP/10/126*. Washington, DC: International Monetary Fund, 2010.

Thompson, Edward Palmer. *Whigs and Hunters: The Origin of the Black Act*. London: Allen Lane, 1975.

Thoumi, Francisco E. *Illegal Drugs, Economy and Society in the Andes*. Baltimore: Johns Hopkins University Press, 2003.

Tilly, Charles. "War Making and State Making as Organized Crime." In Peter Evans, Dietrich Rueschemeyer and Theda Skocpol (eds) *Bringing the State Back In*. Cambridge University Press, 1985.

Timberlake, L. and J. Tinker. "Environment and Conflict." In *Earthscan Briefing Document*. London: International Institute for Environment and Development, 1984.

Timerman, Jordana. "The New Blood Diamonds." *Foreign Policy* (2010).

TRC. "Final Report." Freetown: Truth and Reconciliation Commission of Sierra Leone, 2004.

Tubiana, Jérôme. *Chroniques du Darfour*. Grenoble, France: Glénat, 2010.

Tucker, Shelby. *Burma: The Curse of Independence*: Pluto Press, 2001.

Turner, Mandy. "Taming Mammon: Corporate Social Responsibility and the Global Regulation of Conflict Trade." *Conflict, Security and Development* 6, no. 3 (2006): 365–87.

Turner, Matthew D. "Political Ecology and the Moral Dimensions of "Resource Conflicts": The Case of Farmer-Herder Conflicts in the Sahel." *Political Geography* 23, no. 7 (2004): 863–89.

Turrell, R. "The 1875 Black Flag Revolt on the Kimberley Diamond Fields." *Journal of Southern African Studies* 7, no. 2 (1981): 194–235.

Turrell, R.V. *Capital and Labour on the Kimberley Diamond Fields 1871–1890*. Cambridge University Press, 1987.

TZ. "Mines agree to pay tax arrears, says Finance Minister." *Times of Zambia*, 26 November 2010.

UCDP. 2008. Uppsala Conflict Data Program. UCDP Database: www.Ucdp. Uu.Se/Database, Uppsala University, accessed 18 June 2009.

Ukiwo, U. "From "Pirates" To "Militants": A Historical Perspective on Anti-State and Anti-Oil Company Mobilization among the Ijaw of Warri, Western Niger Delta." *African Affairs* 106, no. 425 (2007): 587–610.

Ullman, Richard H. "Redefining Security." *International Security* 8, no. 1 (1983): 129–53.

UN Secretary General. "Climate Change and its Possible Security Implications." New York: United Nations, 2009.

UNDP. *Human Development Report*. New York: United Nations Development Programme, 2009.

———. "Human Development Report." New York: United Nations Development Programme, 2006.

United Nations. "Final Report of the UN Expert Panel Pursuant Resolution 1533." In *S/2008/733*, 2008.

———. "Report of the Monitoring Mechanism on Sanctions against Unita." New York: United Nations Secretariat, 2002.

———. "Report of the Panel of Experts Appointed Pursuant to Security

Council Resolution 1306 (2000), Paragraph 19, in Relation to Sierra Leone." New York: United Nations, 2000.

———. "Report of the Panel of Experts on the Illegal Exploitation of Natural Resources and Other Forms of Wealth of the Democratic Republic of Congo." New York: United Nations, 2001.

———. "Report of the Panel of Experts on Violations of Security Council Sanctions against Unita." New York: United Nations Secretariat, 2000.

UNSG. "Report of the Secretary-General on Enhancing Mediation and Its Support Activities." New York: United Nations, 2009.

Urry, John. "The 'system' of Automobility." *Theory, Culture and Society* 21, no. 4/5 (2004): 25–39.

US Army. *Field Manual 34–130: Intelligence Preparation of the Battlefield.* Washington, DC: Department of the Army, 1994.

US Department of Energy. "Critical Materials Strategy." 2010.

Vallée, Olivier and François Misser. *Les Gemmocraties: L'économie Politique du Diamant Africain.* Paris: Desclée de Brouwer, 1997.

van der Laan, H.L. *The Sierra Leone Diamonds: An Economic Study Covering the Years 1952–1961.* Oxford University Press, 1965.

van Klinken, Gerry. "Blood, Timber, and the State in West Kalimantan, Indonesia." *Asia Pacific Viewpoint* 49, no. 1 (2008): 35–47.

van Schendel, Willem. "Geographies of Knowing, Geographies of Ignorance: Jumping Scale in Southeast Asia." *Environment and Planning D: Society and Space* 20 (2002): 647–68.

van Schendel, W. and I. Abraham (eds) *Illicit Flows and Criminal Things: States, Borders, and the Other Side of Globalization.* Bloomington, IN: Indiana University Press., 2005.

Vandergeest, Peter and Nancy Lee Peluso. "Empires of Forestry: Professional Forestry and State Power in Southeast Asia, Part 2." *Environment and History* 12 (2006): 359–93.

———. "Territorialization and State Power in Thailand." *Theory and Society* 24, no. 3 (1995): 385–426.

Veras Soares, Fábio, Rafael Perez Ribas and Rafael Guerreiro Osório. "Evaluating the Impact of Brazil's Bolsa Família: Cash Transfer Programs in Comparative Perspective." *Latin American Research Review* 45, no. 2 (2010): 173–90.

Verma, Shiv Kumar. "Energy Geopolitics and Iran-Pakistan-India Gas Pipeline." *Energy Policy* 35, no. 6 (2007): 3280–301.

Verwimp, Philip. "The Political Economy of Coffee, Dictatorship, and Genocide." *European Journal of Political Economy* 19, no. 2 (2002): 161–81.

Vincent, Katharine and Tracy Cull. "Cell Phones, Electronic Delivery Systems and Social Cash Transfers: Recent Evidence and Experiences from Africa." *International Social Security Review* 64, no. 1 (2011): 37–51.

Vitug, M.D. *The Politics of Logging: Power from the Forest.* Manila: Philippine Center for Investigative Journalism, 1993.

Vitug, Marites Danguilan. "The Politics of Logging in the Philippines." In Philip Hirsch and Carol Warren (eds) *The Politics of Environment in Southeast Asia: Resources and Resistance*, 122–36. London: Routledge, 1998.

Wang, Li-mao and Hongqiang Li. "Cooperation and Competition of Oil and Gas Resources between China and Its Neighboring Countries and Its Impacts on Geopolitics," *Resources Science* 31, no. 10 (2009): 1633–9.

Wang, Zhendi and Scott A. Stout. *Oil Spills Environmental Forensics*. New York: Academic Press, 2007.

Watts, David P. and John C. Mitani. "Boundary Patrols and Intergroup Encounters in Wild Chimpanzees." *Behaviour* 138 (2001): 299–327.

Watts, M. "Petro-Insurgency or Criminal Syndicate? Conflict & Violence in the Niger Delta." *Review of African Political Economy* 34, no. 114 (2007): 637–60.

———. "Resource Curse? Governmentality, Oil and Power in the Niger Delta, Nigeria." *Geopolitics* 9, no. 1 (2004): 50–80.

———. "Righteous Oil?: Human Rights, the Oil Complex and Corporate Social Responsibility." *Annual Review of Environment and Resources* 30 (2005): 373–407.

———. "Antinomies of Community: Some Thoughts on Geography, Resources and Empire." *Transactions of the Institute of British Geographers* 29, no. 2 (2004): 195–216.

Weinberg, Bill. "Conservation as Counter Insurgency in the Chiapas Rainforest?" *ETFRN News* 43–44 (2005): 72–4.

Weinstein, Jeremy. "Resources and the Information Problem in Rebel Recruitment." *Journal of Conflict Resolution* 49, no. 4 (2005): 598–624.

Weinstein, Jeremy M. *Inside Rebellion: The Politics of Insurgent Violence*. Cambridge University Press, 2007.

Weinthal, E. and P.J. Luong. "Combating the Resource Curse: An Alternative Solution to Managing Mineral Wealth." *Perspectives on Politics* 4, no. 01 (2006): 35–53.

Welch, Claude E. "The Ogoni and Self-Determination: Increasing Violence in Nigeria." *Journal of Modern African Studies* 33, no. 4 (1995): 635–50.

Wenban-Smith, Jessica. "Forests of Fear. The Abuse of Human Rights in Forest Conflicts." Moreton-in-Marsh: FERN, 2001.

Wennmann, A. "Economic Provisions in Peace Agreements and Sustainable Peacebuilding." *Négociations* 1, no. 11 (2009): 43–61.

West, Joshua A. "Forests and National Security: British and American Forestry Policy in the Wake of World War One." *Environmental History* 8, no. 2 (2003).

Westing, A.H. (ed.). *Global Resources and International Conflict: Environmental Factors in Strategic Policy and Action*. Oxford University Press, 1986.

Westing, Arthur H. (ed.). *Herbicides in War: The Long-Term Ecological and Human Consequences*. London: Taylor and Francis, 1984.

Williams, C. "Environmental Victimization and Violence." *Aggression and Violent Behavior* 1, no. 3 (1996): 191–204.

...ams, J., D. Sutherland, K. Cartwright and M. Byrnes. "Sierra Leone Diamond Policy Study." AMCO-Robertson Mineral Services Ltd, 2002.

Williams, M. "Dark Ages and Dark Areas: Global Deforestation in the Deep Past." *Journal of Historical Geography* 26, no. 1 (2000): 28–46.

Wilson, Michael L., William R. Wallauer and Anne E. Pusey. "New Cases of Intergroup Violence among Chimpanzees in Gombe National Park, Tanzania." *International Journal of Primatology* 25, no. 3 (2004): 523–49.

Winer, Jonathan M. and Trifin J. Roule. "Follow the Money: The Finance of Illicit Resource Extraction." In Ian Bannon and Paul Collier (eds) *Natural Resources and Armed Conflicts: Actions and Options*, 161–214. Washington, DC: World Bank, 2003.

Wolf, A.T., K. Stahl and M.F. Macomber. "Conflict and Cooperation within International River Basins: The Importance of Institutional Capacity." *Water Resources Update* 125 (2003): 31–40.

———. "Conflict and Cooperation along International Waterways." *Water Policy* 1, no. 2 (1998): 251–65.

Wolf, Eric R. *Peasant Wars of the Twentieth Century*. Oklahoma: University of Oklahoma Press, 1999.

Wood, Elisabeth Jean. *Insurgent Collective Action and Civil War in El Salvador*. Cambridge University Press, 2003.

Wood, Geoffrey. "Business and Politics in a Criminal State: The Case of Equatorial Guinea." *African Affairs* 103, no. 413 (2004): 547–67.

Wood, R.M. "Rebel Capability and Strategic Violence against Civilians." *Journal of Peace Research* 47, no. 5, September 2010.

Wright, Quincy. *A Study of War*. University of Chicago Press, 1983.

Wursig, B. "Occurrence and Group Organization of Atlantic Bottlenose Porpoises (Tursiops Truncatus) in an Argentine Bay." *Biological Bulletin* 154, no. 348–359 (1978).

Xu, Ming, and Tianzhu Zhang. "Material Flows and Economic Growth in Developing China." *Journal of Industrial Ecology* 11, no. 1 (2008): 121–40.

Yengo, Patrice. *La Guerre Civile du Congo-Brazzaville*. Paris: Karthala, 2006.

Yergin, Daniel. *The Prize: The Epic Quest for Oil, Money and Power*. New York: Free Press, 1993.

Young, J. "Sudan: A Flawed Peace Process Leading to a Flawed Peace." *Review of African Political Economy* 32, no. 103 (2005): 99–113.

———. "Sudan: Liberation Movements, Regional Armies, Ethnic Militias & Peace." *Review of African Political Economy* 30, no. 97 (2003): 423–34.

Zack-Williams, A.B. *Tributors, Supporters and Merchant Capital: Mining and Underdevelopment in Sierra Leone*. Aldershot: Avebury, 1995.

Zhang, Daowei and Changyou Sun. "US-Canada Softwood Lumber Trade Disputes and Lumber Price Volatility." *Forest Products Journal* 51, no. 4 (2001): 21–7.

Zimmermann, E.W. *World Resources and Industries: A Functional Appraisal of the*

Availability of Agricultural and Industrial Materials. New York: Harper & Brothers, 1951.

Zulu, Leo C. and Sigismond A. Wilson. "Minerals for Whose Development? Rhetoric and Reality on Mineral-Led Poverty Reduction in Post-Conflict Sierra Leone." Department of Geography, Michigan State University, 2011.

———. "Sociospatial Geographies of Civil War in Sierra Leone and the New Global Diamond Order: Is the Kimberley Process the Panacea?" *Environment and Planning C: Government and Policy* 27, no. 6 (2009): 1107–30.

Zweig, David and B. Jianhai. "China's Global Hunt for Energy." *Foreign Affairs* 84, no. 5 (2005): 25–38.

INDEX